W9-ABR-581

United States–Latin American Relations, 1800–1850

Basil Langel [illegible] [illegible]
a good [illegible] [illegible]
Most sincerely Christopher Penn
[illegible]

United States–
Latin American
Relations,
1800–1850

The Formative Generations

Edited by

T. Ray Shurbutt

The University of Alabama Press
Tuscaloosa and London

Library of Congress Cataloging-in-Publication Data

United States–Latin American relations, 1800–1850 : the formative
generations / edited by T. Ray Shurbutt.
    p.   cm.
    Includes bibliographical references.
    ISBN 0-8173-0482-7 (alk. paper)
    1. Latin America—Foreign relations—United States. 2. United
States—Foreign relations—Latin America. 3. United States—Foreign
relations—1801–1815. 4. United States—Foreign
relations—1815–1861. I. Shurbutt, Thomas Ray.
F1418.U685 1991   89–38363
327.7308—dc20   CIP

British Library Cataloguing-in-Publication Data available

Earlier versions of two chapters appeared as journal articles and are used here with
permission: "Diplomatic Dullard: The Career of Thomas Sumter, Jr., and Diplomatic
Relations of the United States with the Portuguese Court in Brazil, 1809–1821" by Phil
Brian Johnson, West Georgia College *Studies in the Social Sciences* 17 (1978); and "Private
Matters: The Origins and Nature of United States–Peruvian Relations, 1820–1850" by
Lawrence A. Clayton, *The Americas* 42:4 (April 1986).

In honor of

Alfred Barnaby Thomas

and in memory of

Richard K. Murdoch

"*Dare* you enter that labyrinth of history? I confess to you, I would not undertake to get and give a distinct view of events in South America, since 1805, under many thousands. It must be a task of Hercules. I am glad, however, if it is to be done, that Hercules has it in hand."

When in 1823, Jared Sparks, editor of the *North American Review*, requested documents from the State Department concerning the independence struggles in Latin America, this quote was part of the reply he received. During their teaching careers, A. B. Thomas and Dick Murdoch labored toward completing this Herculean task.

For Sylvia and Rae

Contents

Preface

An analysis of any era in the history of U.S.–Latin American diplomacy is fraught with difficulties; this is especially true for one attempting to deal with its formative generations. The adolescent United States had begun sending envoys and agents—official and unofficial—to various areas of Latin America in the 1790s, increasing their number during the independence period (1810–1823), and with the pronouncement of the Monroe Doctrine, Washington had adopted a statement of formal policy. Yet upon close examination, it becomes apparent that, beyond this policy statement, there were few consistencies in U.S.–Latin American relations.

Each newly independent nation had its own unique set of political, economic, and cultural problems and aspirations for the future, and each therefore established its own agenda of priorities in promoting relations with Washington. The overwhelming majority of U.S. diplomats posted to Latin America possessed little knowledge or understanding of the history, traditions, and people of the countries to which they were assigned. Indeed, most were mere political appointees who embarked upon their missions with little or no experience in statesmanship and who soon found themselves in strange locales and encumbered with tasks quite different from those they had naively envisioned. Couple this unfortunate scenario with the fact that Washington, at best, offered sketchy instructions and limited, irregular communications, and it is not surprising that many of these envoys were quickly disappointed with their positions. For many agents, their unhappiness and frustrations measurably detracted from their effectiveness.

Each chapter of this work represents the views of a recognized scholar who has conducted specialized research in a particular nation's relations with the United States. Authors were given leeway to emphasize the aspects that they felt were most significant in interpreting this era's diplomacy. The chapter on Mexico, owing to its subject's obvious complexities and importance in U.S. history, was allocated the extra length of what one might call a "double chapter." Each chapter is meant to stand alone yet is interconnected with the others by the general thesis of the volume.

It is our hope that this work will contribute to the general study of U.S.–Latin American relations and will focus renewed attention upon the formative era from 1800 to 1850.

We are especially grateful for the assistance of Julius F. Ariail, director of libraries at Georgia Southern University, for preparing the index.

T. Ray Shurbutt

1

Origins of United States– Latin American Relations

Wesley P. Newton

During the era when Brazil, the French colony of Saint Dominique, and most of the Spanish possessions in the New World were casting off the yoke of colonial status, the relatively young United States was endeavoring to define itself culturally, economically, constitutionally, geographically, and diplomatically. As Latin America began to emerge from the crucible of revolution and international power politics, it was affected by and in varying degrees affected the United States with regard to these various aspects of the latter's search for identity. In fact, Latin America, even during the era of its wars for independence, began to undertake a similar search.

In the western hemisphere, a great deal of misinformation existed to cloud Latin Americans' view of Anglo-Americans and vice versa. José de Onís, who studied the cultures of both, summed up the causalities: "Generations of European wars [and] political, religious, and ideological differences had fixed in the minds of the Spanish Americans and those of the Anglo-Saxon colonists a consciousness of rivalry. Distrust had been deliberately fomented between them by the governments of the mother countries."[1] Images of Drake and Morgan lingered in the southern psyche; *La leyenda negra* was embedded in the mythology of the northerners. The Brazilians had less cause to be hostile, given the traditional political and economic ties between England and Portugal, but seemingly less impetus to acquire knowledge of the people to the north, with the absence of printing presses and universities until after 1808. However, educated Brazilians read extensively from imported books, and their level of knowledge was not far below that of their Spanish American counterparts.[2]

This is not to say that the picture was one of total bias and lack of accurate information on the part of the Luso-Hispanic and Anglo-

President James Monroe (The National Portrait Gallery, Smithsonian Institution)

Saxon worlds. Almost from the beginning of European colonization in the New World, there existed a "white legend, so to speak," wrote Harry Bernstein, a leading scholar on inter-American cultural relations, "impelled by science and knowledge toward a rational and intelligent curiosity about" Latin America, and "its European origins were soon renewed and advanced in the United States." This curiosity had been stimulated in England and other intrigued European nations by the translated letters and chronicles of such figures as Hernán Cortés and Peter Martyr. Their influence is reflected in such classics as Sir Thomas More's *Utopia*, whose setting is an island somewhere in the New World. In Spain, curiosity about the Anglo-Saxons seems to have been relatively slight. The great literary figures, Cervantes and Lope de Vega, wrote about the English, but they fixated on such adventurers as Drake and treated them in a romantic way. A rarity was a more realistic study of the English from the late sixteenth to the mid-seventeenth centuries and authored by a Spanish colonial figure.[3]

The peoples of Latin America and English-speaking America found their interest in one another quickened by that profound movement of the late seventeenth and eighteenth centuries—the Enlightenment. This essay will not elaborate on the nature of the Enlightenment in Spain, Portugal, England, France, or their colonial extensions except to examine some of its literary, scientific, and revolutionary influences on the last mentioned and the factors that led to a meaningful growth of cultural interaction in the Americas, with particular emphasis on U.S. understanding of Latin American culture. Arthur Whitaker, an authority on the Enlightenment in Latin America, saw that movement as not only creating "for the first time a basic kinship of ideas between the two Americas, but . . . also [giving] them for the first time a reciprocal interest in, and some knowledge about, each other's culture."[4]

Before the American Revolution, not much of substance was known in Spain's New World colonies about the British North American colonies that were to become the United States. None of the classic descriptive works about the latter, such as William Bradford's *History of Plymouth Plantation*, had been translated into Spanish, and few Spaniards had a reason or a desire to visit the English colonies. Only in the borderlands and the Caribbean had there been lengthened threads of relationship, and these were interwoven mainly in a pattern of hostilities, although the Caribbean trade relations, legal and illegal, formed a part of this pattern. Literate English colonists, on the other hand, had been exposed to translated versions of the works of the early Spanish explorers, conquerors, and chroniclers and to such classics of Spanish literature as *Don Quixote*. While some of these works, especially those of Bartolomé de las Casas, had fostered the image of the Black Legend, others had given insight into pre- and post-Columbian Indian cultures, geography, flora and fauna, and colonial societies.[5]

At the outset of the eighteenth century, a religious focus on Latin

America was directed by the Puritan theologian Cotton Mather, who was also noted for his Enlightenment-inspired interest in science. But religion, not science, caused Mather to learn Spanish so that he could proselytize for the Puritanization of the whole of the New World. He was joined in this effort by Samuel Sewell and other Boston Puritans. Sewell, in fact, hoped their efforts might inspire the Spanish colonies to separate from the mother country. These religious plans had little chance of succeeding, but their legacy was to add New England to the mainstream of Anglo-Saxon interest in Latin America.[6]

As the Age of Reason took firmer hold in the Western world, North American religious interest in Latin America yielded to the secular. Among the urban centers, Philadelphia became the focus of the latter. It was "the capital of Hispanic studies. . . . Its literary resources went far beyond travel literature into serious historical treaties which systematized the study of Spanish America," and intellectuals in North America and those in both Spain and the colonies began contacting one another to explore mutual interests in science and the humanities. Leading examples were Benjamin Franklin in the north, and Alejandro Ramírez, the Spanish colonial botanist and bureaucrat, in the south.[7]

In Philadelphia, Franklin was a founder in 1746 of the American Philosophical Society for the Promotion of Useful Knowledge, the first English colonial version of organizations, sometimes called societies and sometimes academies, that had already been formed in Europe and Latin America to advance the ideas of the Enlightenment. At least one earlier Latin American version had existed in Brazil in 1724–25, but the first society of this type to endure was the Sociedad Económica de Amigos del País in Cuba.[8] The interaction between these societies in Spain, Spanish America, and Anglo-America is illustrated by the fact that Alejandro Ramírez, fellow of the Spanish Academy of History, was elected by the American Philosophical Society as corresponding member for Spanish America, the first Latin American so chosen, and by the fact that Franklin was chosen by the Spanish Academy of History as its member in the United States.[9] Societies for the promotion of useful knowledge were but one aspect of the cultural and intellectual fermentation spreading from the Old World to the New, a transfer process to which governments lent goodwill and subsidization.

During the reign of such "enlightened despots" as Charles III of Spain, the colonial effects of the Enlightenment were manifested in various ways. The expedition of the Frenchman La Condamine to

Quito to measure the equatorial arc in South America was the first of several scientific expeditions allowed and aided by the Spanish monarchs in the spirit of rational inquiry. There were similar expeditions in Brazil, the most famous of which was led by Alexandre Rodrigues de Ferreira of Bahia to explore Amazonia. The Spanish crown, anxious to encourage foreigners as well as Spaniards to take part in scientific expeditions and missions, tolerated the religious practices of those who were Protestants. The fruits of all this royal encouragement and toleration can be seen in the work of such figures as José Celestino Mutís of Bogotá, who gained fame in the United States and in Europe for his botanical research and collections, and the German scientist Alexander von Humboldt, who traveled extensively in Latin America and became one of the best-known foreign commentators on the physical and cultural state of that area of the world. Also a traveler in the United States, Humboldt testified that Mexico City was as fine a center for scientific studies as existed in the New World,[10] and hence by his work he fostered the interchange of knowledge between Anglo-America and Latin America.

If the European-born Enlightenment was the mechanism for clearer knowledge and better understanding of one another by the two Americas, that movement also provoked a defensive posture shared by the two, a commonality that resulted from an effort by certain European writers in the last decades of the eighteenth century to "put down" the western hemisphere. In various works the Frenchmen Georges Buffon and Abbe Guillaume Raynal, the Britisher William Robertson, the Spaniard Juan Bautista Muñoz, and other historians and naturalists depicted the New World as distinctly inferior to the Old with respect to human society and its natural surroundings. Whitaker has called their effort "the anti-American thesis," and it was soon challenged in both Americas. Thomas Jefferson lighted the torch of reaction in his *Notes on Virginia* (1784–85). Latin Americans and Anglos took flame from each other's torches. Benjamin Smith Barton, a U.S. scientist who had a strong respect for Latin American scientific endeavors, had Father Juan Ignacio Molina's *Historia de Chile* (1776), which contained a rebuttal of the anti-American thesis, translated into English in 1808, while a leading Chilean intellectual, Manuel de Salas, cited Franklin as proof that the New World was at least equal to the Old.[11]

The interest of Latin American and U.S. intellectuals in one another's cultures, an interest stimulated by the Enlightenment, continued after the Enlightenment itself died in the violence of the

French Revolution, whose radical phase brought into question and even led to widespread rejection of the Enlightenment's thesis that truth and justice were to be arrived at by the application of human reason. Yet it was the advent of the revolutionary age, itself stimulated by the Enlightenment, and its resultant spasms in France, in the English colonies that became the United States, and ultimately in Latin America that broadened the two Americas' interest in one another. The interchange of Enlightenment-inspired ideas among a relative few in the United States, its colonial predecessors, and Latin America laid a basis for broader understanding, but it was not enough to effect a change in popular and long-held prejudices or an end to ignorance in both Americas. A shared revolutionary experience gave promise of such a change and such an end. After all, the chaos of revolution and the accomplishment of independence were bound to eliminate certain barriers that, in the colonial past, had hampered not only cultural ties but commercial intercourse as well.

Iberian mercantilism was one such barrier. The efforts of non-Iberian nations to breach this barrier were almost as old as Spain's and Portugal's presence in the western hemisphere. The Iberian nations had, of course, endeavored to prevent foreign encroachment upon their colonial preserves, with mixed results. Legal New World commerce with foreigners, as is also well known, was occasionally tolerated by the Iberian mother countries but only under special circumstances. The picture of commercial intercourse, both legal and illegal, was complicated by the exigencies of British, French, and Dutch fiscal policies, alliances, war and piracy, treaties, the slave trade, and the dichotomies of colonial and cosmopolitan interests.[12]

Out of this picture emerge the origins of U.S. economic interest in Latin America. One of the roots of this interest was whaling. Before the outbreak of the American Revolution, New England whalers had, in their quest for prey, broken their long voyages in southern waters by putting into South American harbors for supplies. While these visits can be seen as establishing a tentative basis for economic ties and for promoting understanding between alien cultures, the whalers were on occasion smugglers as well and instead promoted hostility through smuggling enterprises that ranged from Chile to Mexico. On two occasions after the American Revolution, U.S. whalers were expelled from the Falkland islands (Islas Malvinas) after attempting settlements.[13]

Another root of U.S. economic interest was privateering and an earlier variation that can be characterized as official piracy; taken together, both were incursions into Iberian trade for over two centuries, the French, British, and Dutch having been particularly adept at one or both of these kindred pursuits. The American Revolution saw the Spanish encourage privateering by permitting ships of the rebelling English colonists to put in at Spanish colonial ports, notably Buenos Aires and New Orleans, sometimes with their prizes at New Orleans. Spain, however, never became a direct ally of the struggling Continentals, for the government of Charles III feared the example to its own colonies of an alliance with another nation's rebelling colonies and desired to keep the latter away from the Mississippi River and the Gulf coast. Privateers of the Continental Congress, as well as similar ships fitted out by the Loyalists, therefore sometimes seized Spanish vessels in the Gulf-Caribbean.[14]

Privateering, whaling, and smuggling were therefore indexes of a persistent Anglo interest in Latin American commerce, and the *asiento* and ship-a-year features of the Treaty of Utrecht (1713) evidence that the Spanish had to bow now and then to political reality in their effort to maintain a rigid mercantilism. The American Revolution merely quickened a process that had long been evident, namely, the trade of Anglo settlers of North America and Jamaica with Spain's Caribbean colonies and continuous mainland territory, a trade whose paths whalers and privateers had charted even to faraway South America. It involved the logwood cutters of Central America and was sometimes channeled in and out of European ports. As noted, this trade was for the most part technically illegal under Iberian policies, yet it had continued to exist despite these policies and their *guardacostas*, the restrictions of British mercantilism, and conflicts of interest within national spheres, such as that between New Englanders and Jamaicans.[15]

The Bourbon application of extensive reform to Spanish mercantilism beginning in 1765 had various effects on Spain and its colonies, effects that in the long run were mainly detrimental to the latter.[16] Certain aspects of these reforms, however, had a positive effect on colonial trade relations with foreigners, permitting foreigners indirect trade with the Spanish colonies through Spain, although the Spanish crown dictated that this commerce had to be carried in Spanish ships. Foreign cosmopolitan and colonial merchants alike were quick to benefit from these reforms, and smugglers, of course, were quick to try to avoid the Spanish middlemen. Then the American Revolution came along to broaden the basis for inter-American trade itself. Spain's declaration of war on England in 1779, while falling short of a direct alliance with the English colonists in revolt, nonetheless intensified the relationship with those who were in revolt and those English colonists who were not. Privateering was one element of this intensification; another was the creation of a situation that acted to boost inter-American trade, for war with England and its powerful navy disrupted communications between Spain and its New World colonies, forcing the former to suspend prohibitions against direct trade between foreigners and these colonies. The effect of the suspension was most noticeable in Cuba, where there was a marked increase in the volume of imports, mainly from the United States,[17] in the form of food and other provisions but not merchandise. The obvious intent of the Spanish crown was to meet an emergency while not allowing the suspension to act as a precedent for peacetime. In 1781, the U.S. government dispatched Robert Smith to serve as consul in Havana. Smith was in the van of similar U.S. figures during the American Revolution, when Madrid was compelled to suspend its trade monopoly in certain respects. These consuls were most often expelled when the crisis that permitted their presence had diminished. The U.S. government, however, would then replace them with less formal "agents" for seamen and commerce.[18]

The door was thus cracked wider for trade between the United States and the Iberian possessions. Slaves borne in foreign ships, including U.S. ships, were legally discharged after 1789 in the ports of Cuba, Puerto Rico, Santo Domingo, New Grenada, Venezuela, the Platine region (Buenos Aires), and Chile (Valparaíso). During crisis periods when Spain was immersed in the respective conflicts growing out of the French Revolution and the Napoleonic tide, direct imperial trade was hampered, and Spanish colonial officials authorized their own ships to bring flour and other necessities directly from the United States. In Cuba, for example, rectilinear trade between that island and the United States at times exceeded trade between Cuba and Spain. Also during these crisis times, U.S. ships transshipped European manufacturers to such places as Chile, the Platine region, and Venezuela from Philadelphia and New York. In the other direction, Spanish colonial commodities—principally liquor, molasses and its by-products, coffee, indigo, salt, salt meat, and tallow—were fetched in U.S. bottoms to Philadelphia and other U.S. ports from colonies that ranged across the imperial New World: Caribbean islands, the Platine region, Florida, Louisiana, Mexico.

U.S. trade with colonial Brazil existed, but it was far less extensive than that with the Spanish colonies, for the English supplied most of the trade through Lisbon when, with the coming of the Portuguese court to Brazil, the colony's ports were thrown open to free trade. An early indication of Anglo interest in Luso-Brazilian trade, however, was the attraction of that trade to U.S. privateers during the American Revolution. Then, too, the United States had used the French colony of Saint Dominique as a source of trade and as a viaduct for communications with Spanish Caribbean and continental colonies until the first Latin American movement for independence broke out there as a result of the French Revolution and turned especially violent.[19] In short, inter-American commercial intercourse stemming from various origins became fairly brisk as a result of the opportunities presented by the revolutionary and Napoleonic eras.

Various factors would add dimensions to inter-American economic relations. The continental expansion of the United States and the beginning of U.S. regionalism had a natural impact upon commercial relations with Spanish Louisiana and Florida. The naval and maritime ramifications of the French Revolution and the Napoleonic Wars affected inter-American trade in several beneficial and not so beneficial ways: Javier Cuenca Esteban has demonstrated that during the era encompassed by the French Revolution and the Napoleonic rampage, U.S. trade with Spain's western hemispheric colonies and the Philippines "was regarded as a valuable source of badly needed specie to cover deficits with the Far East and elsewhere." Jacques A. Barbier and Allan J. Kuethe have noted a special twist to this situation: "It is ironic that, in the years of the most intensive Spanish admiration for Anglo-American material progress, this well-being should have been based partly on the United States profits from trade with its southern neighbors." Spanish Louisiana was opened to trade with the rebelling English colonies during the American Revolution, and although Spanish authorities closed it after the United States won independence, trade never fully ceased, flaring again in the 1790s and continuing in a mutually beneficial way until first the French and then the U.S. takeover of the territory. The port of La Guaira in Venezuela, among others, felt the impact of the U.S. trade that began in earnest with the opening of Spanish colonial ports to neutral shipping in 1797; this trade flourished until 1807, when Jefferson's embargo pinched it off. When the embargo ended in 1809 and U.S. ships returned, they found the British trading in La Guaira, an omen of vigorous British commercial penetration of Latin America.[20]

From 1803 to 1811, British naval vessels harassed U.S. maritime trade with Spanish colonies to please the Spanish and to disrupt inter-American trade to Great Britain's possible advantage, and, in addition, the British opened up several of their Caribbean-area ports (Kingston, Port of Spain) for trade with Spanish colonists to rival U.S. trade; the Spanish began to retighten their mercantilism in the decade before the movements for independence in Spanish America. Despite impediments, the trade continued, stimulated by the wars for independence but hampered now and again by such policies as the Jefferson embargo. For the Spanish colonies in the western hemisphere, "trade with the northern neighbor helped erode the mother country's monopoly and serve as a catalyst for the eventual breakdown of the empire." For the United States, the trade with the neighbors to the south was crucial.[21]

The Latin American movements for independence promised to stimulate inter-American cultural and economic relations and offered the United States an opportunity to influence the shaping of new governments. The greatest constitutional effect that the United States had on Latin America during the latter's independence era was probably as a role model of the first successful and apparently enduring federal republic. Once they had freed themselves from their monarchical bondsmen, most of the Latin American former colonists opted for republican forms of government (ultimately all did), and many of the new nations at one time or another experimented with federalism. In serving the function of role model, the United States was not alone; it shared the function with the republican governments of the French Revolution. The specific influences of the U.S. Constitution of 1789, its Bill of Rights, and the earlier constitutional models of the confederation period were not all pervasive. Again, the United States had to share with the French and also with the Spanish and the British. The Venezuelan constitution of 1811 bore marked resemblances to the U.S. Constitution of 1789, but the early and also abortive Constitution of Apatzingán of 1814 in Mexico was influenced less by the U.S. document of 1789 than by the French constitutions of 1791 and 1795 and the Spanish constitution of 1812.[22] Glen Dealy has persuasively argued that from the beginning, Spanish American constitutional norms, while resembling those of such countries as the United States and France, have generally had quite different underlying assumptions—assumptions that stemmed from the Spanish colonial experience and not the Enlightenment tradition from which came U.S. and French norms.[23]

What interest was there in the United States in influencing contemporary and future Latin American constitutions during Latin America's struggle for independence and the resulting course of politics?

There does not in fact seem to have been much interest in tutoring the Latin Americans in constitution making and implementation. In a seemingly rare episode, Stephen F. Austin, who was in Mexico at the time of its political reorganization following its brief flirtation with monarchy under Agustín Iturbide, drafted several documents to aid Mexican constitution framers in their work, at least one of which was a condensation of the principles of the U.S. Constitution.[24]

In the private sector and in government in the United States, there did exist a fairly widespread hope and even expectation that when the colonial peoples of Latin America wrestled free of European domination, they would adopt viable, preferably republican representative forms of government. Two leading examples of this optimism were the private citizen and publicist for the independence cause in Latin America, Henry M. Brackenridge, and the congressional champion of early U.S. recognition of independence, Henry Clay. Although Benjamin Franklin, in his zest for Enlightenment ideas, had earlier expressed a desire that the "Rights of Man" become so fixed worldwide that their advocates would feel at home everywhere, many in the United States a decade after his death believed that only in the western hemisphere were these rights flourishing, and they were doing so as a result of the independence movements.[25]

Whatever has been and will be said for and against the Bolton theory of a commonality of hemispheric experience, a commonality of independence experience certainly existed, and this gave people in the United States a solid reason to be interested in the outcome of the wars of independence in Latin America. But not all the North Americans had great expectations for the political future of the liberated Latin Americans. Both John Adams, in the dawn of the Latin American era of independence, and John Quincy Adams, a few years before the U.S. government began to recognize the newly independent southern nations, were pessimistic about the ability of Latin Americans to establish free societies and stable governments. Other important U.S. citizens shared this sentiment: John Randolph of Roanoke, for example, expressed before Congress in 1816 his belief that "the struggle of liberty in South America will turn out in the end something like the French liberty, a detestable despotism." Even the ardent publicist of the Latin American cause, Brackenridge, admitted that a number of his fellow citizens viewed their southern neighbors with contempt. The continuing influence of the Black Legend, Spanish royalist propaganda, and factionalism among the rebels combined to contribute to this outlook.[26]

Indeed, John Quincy Adams seems to have anticipated the Dealy thesis,[27] if expressed with the prejudice of those Anglo-Saxons who looked upon Hispanic culture as inferior: "[The Latin Americans] are not likely to promote the spirit either of freedom or order by their example. They have not the first elements of good or free government. Arbitrary power, military and ecclesiastical, is stamped upon their education, upon their habits, and upon all their institutions." The Dealy thesis does not support the idea that Latin American constitutions and governing techniques were devoid of a concern for order. It does, however, tend to go along with the rest of Adams's statement:

> In framing their bill of rights . . . [the Latin Americans] found no contradiction in almost uniformly establishing Catholicism as the state religion and prohibiting the free exercise of all other "cults"; abridging, if not abolishing freedom of speech and of the press; and in some cases even denying the right of peaceable assembly. . . . At the very core of the early constitutions was an attempt to achieve a uniformity of opinion, an attempt grounded in the belief that similar passions and interests were not only possible but desirable. . . . A key to understanding Spanish American government . . . is the recognition that there is nothing in the way of rights or privileges that may not be constitutionally abridged by passage of a law. . . . [A step further is] the constitutional provision whereby basic rights may be set aside altogether, usually by the chief executive . . . a clear indication of the possibility of our "reverse" theory of democracy, i.e., the process by which leaders exert control over ordinary citizens. When rights of speech, assembly, and press are curtailed, the right of political opposition is in effect being squashed.[28]

The Dealy thesis, in asserting the important role of clergymen in early constitution making, pointed to the colonial past: "[The clergy] . . . became perhaps the most politically minded body of men in the Spanish bureaucracy." In addition, "frequently those following a military career were also deeply involved in political matters." And thus, after the revolutionary transition from colony to country, it was sometimes the case that "the armed forces have been placed in the position of defending the constitutional order. . . . An armed force charged with insuring 'respect for the Constitution,' surely has some reason to intervene when it feels a threat to the constitution exists." But whereas Adams saw that traditions had molded Latin America to be unfit for democracy, the Dealy thesis holds that Spanish Americans deliberately embrace these traditions and did not and still do not "generally . . . aspire . . . to democratic goals."[29]

It was natural that some in the United States were skeptical about the ability of the independence-seeking Latin Americans to achieve what the North Americans considered viable republican institutions and democratic societies, even if their skepticism was based more on instinct than on the historical insight, and hindsight, of Dealy. But it is ironic that, whatever else could be said in John Quincy Adams's or in Dealy's time against any Latin American innate tendency for viable republicanism and representative democracy, the Latin Americans would in the nineteenth century divest themselves of that most complete antithesis of democracy, human slavery, and would do so for the most part peacefully, while it was accomplished in the United States as part of a bloody, wrenching process.

In spite of its regional differences, the institution of slavery was an example of a shared experience in the Americas. Yet another shared experience was geography, in its various ramifications, witnessed by the common reaction to slurs on the New World by intellectuals of the Old. In developing the concept of the "two axes of relationships" in the history of the western hemisphere, Harold Eugene Davis identifies the north-south axis as being "geographic in origin," whose "geographic bonds arise from the configuration of the continent, its common coast lines, its mountain chains, plains and table lands, and its international river systems." Davis goes on to state that the "historical and cultural ties of the north-south axis derive from the common American historical experiences, those of discovery, exploration, conquest, colonization, . . . Christianization of the natives, the achievement of national independence, and the movement for regional political unity in various forms."[30]

There was, however, another dimension to the geographic axis that began to emerge shortly after the independence of the United States, and this was the initial expansion of that nation. During the period discussed in this essay, expansion was basically at the expense of Spain and France, if one considers Napoleon's fast shuffle with the Louisiana Territory as a true loss to France; apart from Canada, much of the territory that the United States sought to encompass early on, in part successfully and in part not, must be considered as Latin American in that it belonged to Spain or France. Spanish Cuba came to play a special role in U.S. imperialism once U.S. concern for its status as a colony arose in 1808 to outstrip mere desire to trade with the island. Cuba and independent, if truncated, Mexico came to represent the northernmost geographic thrust of Latin America once the United States, by the mid-nineteenth century, established its southern and western boundaries through seizure or peaceful acquisition of territory from Spain, France, and Mexico.

Early expansion of the United States was in part an effort to redeem the boundaries established in the Treaty of Paris of 1783, when Great Britain formally recognized the independence of the United States. Spain, in fact, had been more interested in keeping the United States away from the Mississippi River and regaining the Florida territories than in aiding it to secure independence. Although there was aid in various forms, Governor Bernardo de Gálvez, Spanish governor of New Orleans, refused a request by Patrick Henry and Thomas Jefferson for unrestricted navigation of the Mississippi and free port status for U.S. traders at New Orleans. Once in the war, both to forestall an ambitious British plan to take, with the aid of Indians, Spanish territory along the Mississippi and to keep the rebel English colonists away from the river, the Spanish under Gálvez and Balthazar de Villiers took possession of much of the river region south and north of Natchez. Gálvez ensured Spanish repossession of the Floridas by conquering both Mobile and Pensacola. British efforts to take Saint Louis failed, but Spanish attempts to keep British traders out of the territory north of Saint Louis were also futile, and Spanish control of the upper Mississippi-Missouri region grew weaker.[31]

The treaty settlements of the American Revolution ensured instability where the southern and western boundaries of the United States were concerned. In the formal settlement with Great Britain, the new nation received recognition of the thirty-first parallel north as the southern boundary and the Mississippi's length for much of the western boundary. Navigation of the Mississippi was to be free and open to Great Britain and the United States. In the treaty with Spain, the British ceded the Floridas with no definition of its boundaries. Not a party to the British–United States treaty, Spain did not feel bound to recognize either the U.S. western or southern boundaries or the right of free navigation of the river.[32] The British in the north and the Spanish in the south were both determined to keep the fledgling nation from expanding, and both conspired "in sinister symmetry . . . [to] coop the United States up between the Allegheny Mountains and the sea," intriguing with Indians and westward-migrating settlers and setting up new outposts or refusing to evacuate old ones.

The United States might have remained indefinitely cooped up, weak as it was as a confederation, but two events, both in 1789, combined to end the Anglo-Spanish "blockade." One, the French Revolution, soon embroiled the British and Spanish in turbulent European warfare, in naval strategies, and in shifting alliances, with the Napoleonic juggernaut refocusing British and Spanish diplomacy and energy from their North American game. The second, the launching of a new constitutional arrangement in the United States, meant the establishment of a government that had the centralized authority to cope with tough diplomatic problems. President George Washington took advantage of Spanish and British involvement, sometimes as allies and sometimes as enemies, in crises that stemmed from the French Revolution to breach his country's confinement to the land between the Alleghenies and the sea. In the Jay Treaty with the British (1794) and the Pinckney Treaty with the Spanish (1795), the boundary definitions of 1783 were concretely reasserted. Although in the British negotiations the United States failed to obtain recognition of its definition of neutral rights at sea, this was in a sense compensated for with Spain when the United States obtained the prized rights of free navigation of the Mississippi and deposit at New Orleans.[33]

The Spanish had not always behaved in a manner tailored to prevent or calm U.S. resentment of their presence on a continent and eventually in a hemisphere that the United States increasingly wished to dominate. Not only had Spain prolonged unnecessarily the recognition of the new nation, but it delayed implementing the Pinckney Treaty for two years and illegally suspended the right of deposit for a time in 1802. The Spanish cession of Santo Domingo to France in 1795, while it represented something the United States would firmly oppose on future occasions, namely, the transfer of New World territory by one European nation to another, was not viewed with alarm, perhaps because Santo Domingo seemed fairly distant. But when Spain gave the Louisiana Territory to France in 1800, it appeared to be a replay of the old containment game.[34]

U.S. relations with France had gone downhill since the treaties of mutual support of 1778, in which the former pledged to aid in the defense of French possessions in the New World. The Jay Treaty with Great Britain marked the point of departure from good relations, and the decline was intensified by U.S. material support to Toussaint L'Ouverture in Saint Dominique[35] and climaxed by the "undeclared war" between the United States and France in 1798. So it was with dismay that the United States discovered that France had gained the vast if undefined amount of territory on its western flank, including New Orleans. Napoleon was indeed planning on establishing in the

Mississippi Valley a French colonial tract related to trade to an island and naval bastion, Saint Dominique. Once again, events in Europe came to the North Americans' rescue: faced with both a renewal of the death struggle with the British and the French failure to subdue the black and mulatto rebels of Saint Dominique, Napoleon decided to unload Louisiana, an act that more or less doubled the existing territory of the United States. Afterward, the United States could hardly be checked in its continental expansion, an expansion whose progress to the Pacific, while laying the geographic basis for great nationhood, defined much of the northern boundary of Latin America.[36]

To Jefferson and his successors through James Monroe, possession of the Floridas seemed a necessary complement to the Louisiana Territory. The United States tried to assert its opinion that West Florida was a part of the great purchase, a contention that the Spanish, of course, denied.[37] It was logical that the United States would desire the Floridas for the purposes of both further expansion and preventing them from falling into the hands of a stronger power than Spain, namely, France or Great Britain. The latter purpose also conditioned U.S. policy toward Spanish Cuba in the period discussed in this essay.

The important theme of the Floridas in U.S. diplomatic interaction with Spain soon became related to another important theme, the Latin American movements for independence—the third such spasm, following the Anglo-American and the French spasms, that represented continuations of earlier colonial rivalries while at the same time being shaped by the philosophies of the Enlightenment.[38] Intertwined in these kindred themes were continued cultural and trade relations between the United States and the Luso-Hispanic world and the beginnings of U.S. constitutional and political influences on evolving Latin American nations.

As stated, the United States had claimed West Florida to the Perdido River as part of the Louisiana Purchase, and the Spanish, having objected to the purchase itself, continued to deny that claim. After the Napoleonic occupation of Spain in 1808 and the resultant loosening of the Bourbon grip (which events set the Latin American movements for independence in motion, if slowly at first), Thomas Jefferson consulted with his cabinet about U.S. policy toward the increasingly fluid Spanish situation. The president and his cabinet formulated a policy statement, augmented by Jefferson several days later and meant initially to apply to Mexico and Cuba, in which the U.S. government was content to see these places remain under Spain if that nation overcame the Napoleonic occupation; if Mexico and Cuba were to declare independence, however, the United States, while it could not commit itself to make "common cause," would guide its actions both by "existing circumstances" and by a feeling of friendship based on mutual interests. Perhaps most significant, Jefferson and his secretaries warned that the United States would not be content to see these places become subordinate to France or England "either politically or commercially." Jefferson, in augmenting the initial statement, declared to the governor of Louisiana that the "object of both [the United States and the Iberian colonies who might win independence] must be to exclude all European influence from this hemisphere."[39] These statements by Jefferson and his cabinet foreshadowed both the cautious step the United States would take in terms of recognition of the rebelling Iberian colonies and the determination to keep especially the nearby ones out of the hands of nations stronger than Spain. And they seemed to acknowledge the golden chance the United States had for exclusive commercial relations with Latin America. The statements, however, did not address themselves to the near borderlands, the Floridas, whose populations were sparse and to a significant degree Anglo, due to the attraction of Spanish land grants.

While the Creoles of Mexico for the present and Cuba indefinitely chose in the main to stay loyal to the deposed Bourbon monarchy, the Anglo settlers of West Florida decided to cast off weak Spanish authority. Having been encouraged by Jefferson's administration to act when the time appeared ripe, the Anglo settlers felt the time had come late in 1810, and the resultant revolt was endorsed by James Madison, Jefferson's successor. Madison, by secret proclamation in October, annexed West Florida between the Mississippi and the Perdido but authorized occupation only as far east as the Pearl River, to avoid confrontations with Spanish troops in Mobile and Pensacola. This was followed by Madison's request to Congress for authority to take possession of any Spanish territory threatened with occupation by a stronger European power. Madison's request was initiated by strong British protest over U.S. backing of the West Florida revolt, a protest that was made on behalf of the non-Napoleonic Spanish government and that implied possible British occupation of the Floridas in the name of the impotent government. The congressional response was the "no-transfer" resolution of January 15, 1811, which provided for "temporary occupation" of the Spanish territory "adjoining the southern border of the United States . . . under certain contingencies." An enabling act authorized the chief executive to occupy East Florida if these "certain contingencies" arose. Most of West Florida was formally annexed in 1812, although the Spanish refused to accept the loss of any of the Floridas.[40]

Despite this aggressive action toward the Floridas, the U.S. government, first under Jefferson, then under Madison, failed to realize, in Arthur Whitaker's term, "the large policy of 1808." That policy envisioned a hemisphere in which the United States had more or less free play commercially as well as politically with respect to Latin America. Jefferson had declared in 1808 that the object of both the United States and Latin America was "to exclude all European influence from this hemisphere."[41]

This large policy was implemented under neither Jefferson nor Madison because of the intrusion of various countervailing factors: embargoes under both presidents, U.S. trade in foodstuffs with the Iberian Peninsula, a move under Madison to cooperate with France in the revolutionizing of Latin America, the advent of the War Hawks, and the War of 1812. Arthur Whitaker has analyzed all these factors, and only certain points need to be emphasized here. The Jeffersonian embargo came at a time when the Latin American independence movements were just commencing and, of course, limited commercial contacts when there was an opportunity for the broad expansion of these. At the same time, a campaign for trade relations with the decaying Spanish empire in the New World was launched by Great Britain, the most logical power to take advantage of the free trade policy inaugurated by the Portuguese crown when it took up residence in Brazil in 1808. As Whitaker stated, "The net result of Jefferson's course . . . was that, instead of forwarding his professed purpose of excluding European influence from Latin America, it tended to transfer control of Latin America from two of the weakest powers in Europe, Spain and Portugal, to the most formidable of them all, Great Britain."[42]

The second embargo was a prelude to the War of 1812 and cut back trade contacts with Latin America that had been revived and extended after 1808. Perhaps more damaging to U.S.–Latin American trade relations were the shipment of foodstuffs from the United States to the Iberian Peninsula for the use of civilians and the contending armies, mainly the British, as well as the use of the peninsula for indirect trade with the British and the French, trade otherwise forbidden by various U.S., French, and British prohibitions. This trade came from every part of the United States and was therefore not crimped by regional rivalry. By 1811, it was three times greater than that with Latin America, undercutting what might have been the realization of extensive commercial relations with Latin America to keep the United States abreast of the British.[43]

The flirtation of Madison's administration with Bonapartist France to make common cause in promoting independence in Latin America stemmed from various sources. Among these were Bonapartist agents in the United States who used that country as a place of communications with Latin America in France's effort to win Latin American acceptance of Joseph as their monarch and common recognition of Great Britain as their major rival in Latin America. Madison tolerated not only the presence of Bonapartist agents in the United States but also the presence of Luis de Onís, agent for the non-Napoleonic or "patriot" Spanish government, and agents for revolutionary factions in Spanish America. At the same time the U.S. government expanded its sparse net of agents in Latin America—consuls, agents on special missions, and agents for commerce and seamen. These agents soon discovered that Great Britain was gaining a favored commercial position in Latin America, aided by the Caribbean free port system and the strategic stationing of British warships. The British, however, were careful not to embrace openly the rebel cause in Spanish America. Long a protector of Portugal, Great Britain was forced to side with the non-Napoleonic government of Spain both because of their common cause against Napoleon and because of Spain's having allowed the British a trade foothold in its colonies. After the defeat of Napoleon and the restoration of the Bourbons in Spain, the British were then motivated by commercial, humane, and political reasons to move slowly toward recognition of Latin American independence,[44] a movement that was, however, to follow in the wake of U.S. recognition.

While the issue of freedom of the seas was probably the major cause that brought the United States into war with England in 1812, the pressure of the War Hawks or Expansionists of 1812 helped bring on the conflict. Southerners wanted the whole of the Floridas and westerners wanted Canada for similar reasons—security against Indian attacks, land hunger, and the urge to expand the frontiers because they were expandable. But one result of the war, as Samuel Flagg Bemis characterized it, was that "the early military disasters of the war blotted out the ambitious plans of the Expansionists of 1812. . . . Fortunate indeed was the United States to escape with its territory intact." Another result, as described by Arthur Whitaker, was that "one of the chief victims of the war of 1812 was the Latin American policy of the United States." As the strength of the British navy took its toll, commerce between the United States and Latin America lessened, and contacts in general shrunk. The British were thus able to consolidate their favorable position in the area to the south. While the United States, during the course of the war, was able to annex most of the rest of West Florida, Bourbon Spain was determined to keep what remained of the Floridas, from Pensacola eastward.[45]

When Napoleon was finally banished for good and peace was made between England and the United States, both these countries took somewhat divergent paths to reach the same end—recognition of the independence of the rebelling Spanish and Portuguese colonies. For the British, the most important thing was the founding of commercial beachheads, no matter who won the struggle in Latin America; at first, the British government, committed at Vienna to the principle of legitimacy, moved cautiously, even while popular sentiment in England swung increasingly toward the Latin American rebels and against the reactionary Bourbon regime. Depredations against its shipping by both sides were a factor in moving the British government toward recognition in order to stabilize the situation, although the British were willing to mediate between Spain and the rebels, so long as the beachheads were not disturbed.[46]

For its part, the United States, while delaying recognition, nonetheless repaired some of the damage wrought by embargoes and by focusing trade on the Iberian Peninsula when its government took certain diplomatic steps. First, it recognized in 1815 the belligerency of the insurgents and proclaimed neutrality, afterward accepting rebel ships in its ports and selling contraband to rebel agents on equal footing with agents from Spain itself; in practical effect the U.S. posture favored the rebels. The chief objectives of the U.S. government were to gain East Florida and to have Spain recognize Texas as part of the Louisiana Purchase; until these could be accomplished, the U.S. government was unwilling to recognize the independence of the Latin American insurgents.[47]

John Quincy Adams, secretary of state in James Monroe's cabinet, was the prime mover in securing part of these territorial objectives. Adams's negotiations with Onís, which led to the signing of the monumental Adams-Onís, or Transcontinental, Treaty of 1819 and its final ratification, are the subject of Philip C. Brooks's work and bear no lengthy repetition here. The Spanish, who were brought to signing the treaty in order to preserve U.S. neutrality and to prevent recognition, surrendered what remained of the Floridas in exchange for U.S. assumption of its citizens' claims against Spain of up to $5.5 million.

John Quincy Adams (The National Portrait Gallery, Smithsonian Institution)

The United States gave up its claim to Texas in return for a new boundary definition between U.S. and Spanish territory from the Atlantic to the Pacific, a boundary definition that, when put together with the boundary treaty of 1818 with Great Britain for the northern boundary of the Louisiana Territory and for equal rights beyond the

Rocky Mountains, undeniably laid the territorial basis for great nationhood and was accomplished peacefully in the main.[48]

Adams had accomplished his mighty diplomatic feat against considerable odds. Violations of U.S. neutrality laws, filibustering activities
in New Spain, intrigues and turmoil in and off East Florida involving
the likes of such figures as Gregor McGregor, Louis Aury, Xavier
Mina, and Andrew Jackson, and Spain's procrastination in hopes of
securing European aid to resecure all the Floridas and protect its other
territory all complicated the negotiations.[49]

One persistent difficulty Adams faced was the dogged effort of
Henry Clay, the former War Hawk, to have the United States recognize the independence of the rebelling Spanish American colonies.
Clay's effort reflected the anti-Spanish feeling of his western constitu-
ency, his own personal ambitions to create an issue that might enable
him to succeed Monroe as president, and the influence on him of the
large policy of 1808 that neither Jefferson nor Madison had been able
to carry out. The large policy became in Clay's hands, through his
rhetoric and maneuverings as Speaker of the House of Representatives, an "American System" in which the nations of the western
hemisphere would be bound together politically and economically to
the exclusion of Europe. Adams, both because of his doubts of the
viability of Hispanic institutions and because his desire to see his
Transcontinental Treaty through to ratification, opposed immediate
recognition. The Spanish delayed ratification and even attempted to
attach new conditions, including a U.S. promise not to recognize any
of the insurgent governments. Adams refused on the grounds that
such a promise would violate U.S. neutrality but hinted that his government would not be rash. A liberal revolution in Spain in 1820 (the
Riego revolt) and knowledge that the United States, if ratification were
not soon forthcoming, would soon take all the Floridas without promising to keep hands off Texas finally led to the mutual, final acceptance of the treaty in 1821.[50]

Despite some relatively minor obstacles in recognition, such as rebel privateering and in some instances piracy, which began to affect
even neutral shipping such as that of the United States, the way was
increasingly smoother. In 1819 Congress gave the president authority
to extend recognition when he felt it expedient. The danger of intervention by the powers of the concert of Europe subsided as rebel victories began to mount. No longer at odds with Clay over the issue,
Adams in a Fourth of July address in 1821 hinted his acceptance that
unilateral recognition was now possible. Monroe, now convinced that

Henry Clay (The National Portrait Gallery, Smithsonian Institution)

recognition was expedient if the goodwill of the obviously successful rebel governments was to be maintained, sought in March 1822 and obtained in May funds from Congress for establishing formal relations with Chile, Argentina, Peru, Colombia, and Mexico. The United States was the first non–Latin American state to recognize independence, and its example proved crucial.[51]

In the following year was laid that momentous and controversial cornerstone in U.S. policy toward Latin America, the Monroe Doctrine. It is perhaps time to revisit it historically, but this essay will not attempt to do so. Dexter Perkins has advanced the thesis that its origin was twofold: to check the Russian advance down the northwest coast of America and to deter any European effort to restore to Spain the colonies whose independence was now being acknowledged by others. Edward H. Tatum, Jr., has offered the idea that the doctrine was actually designed as a shield against English designs on Cuba and other parts of Latin America. Whitaker wrote that it was aimed primarily against France.[52]

While these diplomatic episodes were developing, resulting in independent nations with whom the United States was to have checkered relations in the next century and a half, the image of Latin America in the minds of North Americans was still not clear or free of prejudice in 1823. Anti-Spanish, or pro-independence, propagandists had vied with pro-Spanish propagandists in the years of diplomacy leading to recognition and the Monroe Doctrine. The most skillful of the former, Henry M. Brackenridge, tried to paint Latin Americans as diverse, liberty-loving, and inherently good peoples whose rich resources and population growth argued well for their future as peoples of independent nations. In contrast were the sentiments of Edward Everett, editor of the *North American Review*, who wrote in April 1821 an article attacking the American System proposed by Clay and suggesting that it was merely a cover for imperialism of the type practiced by Russia in Asia. Everett had serious misgivings about the political and social nature of the Latin Americans.[53] Given the contemporary conflict of opinion in the United States over its involvement in Central America and Panama, not to mention in the South American drug crisis, one wonders at the progress made in understanding Latin America in a century and a half.

2

United States–Central American Relations, 1824–1850

Charles L. Stansifer

To the founders of the Central American Confederation of 1824, the United States was an important model. The federal system created by the U.S. Constitution of 1789 served as an inspiration to Central American liberals. Similarly inspiring were the democratic processes and the bulwark of protection for individual liberties that were established in the first thirty years of the history of the United States. These achievements, imperfectly known but widely admired by Central America's political leadership, were the goals of the architects of the Central American constitution of 1824. These men realized, of course, that deep Spanish imperial roots and a distinct ethnic situation would determine compromises between goals and reality. They also perforce drew upon Spanish constitutional precedent, particularly the Spanish constitution of 1812, for the structure of government. Without being blinded by the success of the political system in the United States, Central American leaders in the first year of independence were favorably inclined toward its system of government and were confident of friendly relations with the United States.[1]

Impressions of Central America in the United States in the first half of the nineteenth century, as judged by infrequent statements of government spokesmen and reports in newspapers, were vague. In general there was a tendency to applaud the achievement of independence and to expect advantageous commercial intercourse in the future, but the absence of a genuine war for independence and the relative unimportance of Central America (compared to Mexico or Colombia or even distant Argentina) led to slight consideration of Central America in the United States in the first forty-five years of the nineteenth century. For instance, to cite a nonpolitical event, the eruption of Coseguina in Nicaragua in January 1835, at that time the

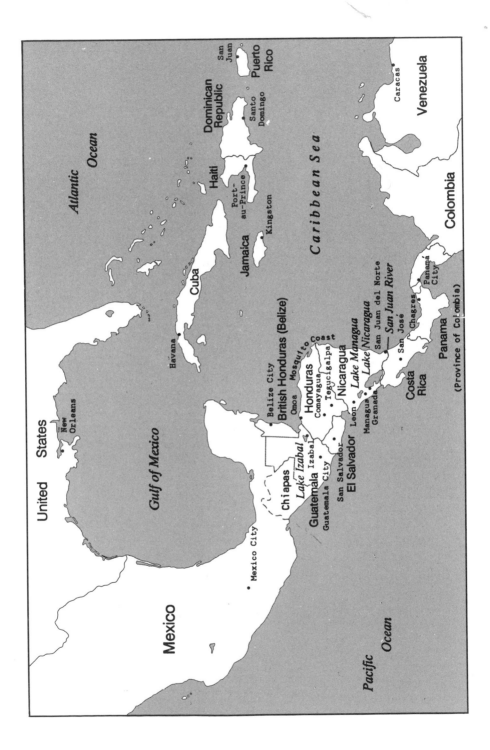

largest volcanic eruption in the world, passed virtually unnoticed in U.S. newspapers.

As the center of gravity in the United States moved south and west in the first half of the nineteenth century and as Central America took pains to separate itself from its European origins, the United States and Central America moved rapidly into the same orbit. This trend, discernible in the 1820s, accelerated rapidly in the 1840s, particularly from 1846 to 1850, until United States–Central American relations at midcentury were of the highest priority to both. Indeed, in the period 1824–50, it is doubtful that any region of the world moved more rapidly from obscurity to the focal point of U.S. diplomacy than Central America.

The reverse is also true, for Central American leaders came to realize in this twenty-five-year period that the destiny of the Central American isthmus was inexorably bound to the United States. For Central America, earlier vague but favorable impressions of the United States were replaced by visions of U.S. support against European representatives and then by a slow realization that the United States itself was a threat to Central American independence. The wave of adventurers and travelers bound for California by way of the isthmus at the close of the 1840s contributed to this realization.

Despite the dramatic shift from vague contact to crisis diplomacy in the short span of two and a half decades, and details of early United States–Central American relations have attracted little recent investigation by scholars in either region. Perhaps the sharpest focus on the subject is Joseph B. Lockey's article "Diplomatic Futility," which treats U.S. diplomats to Central America from 1825 to 1848 and which was written over fifty years ago.[2] No historian has yet explored in detail the ground that Lockey covered. Even in the thirty-year period before Lockey's article appeared, only one significant historical study, that of Mary Wilhelmine Williams, treated United States–Central American relations, and her focus, like that of a number of nineteenth-century studies, was on United States–British rivalry in the Central American isthmus, not on Central America.[3] United States–Central American relations from 1824 to 1850, those narrowly diplomatic as well as those broadly cultural and economic, still await detailed critical historical reexamination.

The Captaincy-General, or Kingdom, of Guatemala, consisting of the provinces of Chiapas, Guatemala, San Salvador, Honduras, Nicaragua, and Costa Rica, broke loose from Spain by a declaration of independence in 1821. The lateness of the declaration, compared to other parts of the Spanish empire, and Spanish weakness enabled the Central Americans to escape a war of liberation. But the former Kingdom of Guatemala did pass through a period of intense debate on allegiances and forms of government and even a brief attachment to the Iturbide empire of Mexico (1822–23). In 1823 independence from Mexico was achieved, and a constituent assembly, with elected representatives of five of the six provinces of the former Kingdom of Guatemala (Chiapas chose to remain with Mexico), began to draw up a constitution. It is this constituent assembly, having drawn up in 1824 the constitution creating the United Provinces of Central America, that first sought the opening of diplomatic relations with the United States.

Much criticism has been leveled at the writers of the constitution of 1824 for their failure to bring forth a document that assured unity and economic progress. Perhaps the problems were too great. In the first place, there was a serious population imbalance. Guatemala, the most populous of the five provinces, had approximately 660,000 inhabitants, or more than the combined populations of the other four. The Senate and House of Deputies were arranged so as to deny Guatemala a majority control of the assembly, but the fear of Guatemalan dominance remained an obstacle to the consolidation of the new government. In the second place, the first assembly faced an immediate financial crisis caused by the dismantling of the Spanish imperial financial structure before any agreement on its replacement had been reached. Other problems added to the new government's weakness. Due to the large unassimilated Indian population, especially in Guatemala, there was a lack of ethnic homogeneity. Differences of opinion on the role of the church, already important in the last years of the Spanish empire, broke out into the open upon independence and contributed to disunion. Residents in the smaller provinces tended to resent Guatemalan privileges and wealth, thus creating an atmosphere of rivalry and jealousy instead of the harmony needed to make the new government work.[4]

Central America's weaknesses made the confederation vulnerable to an informal British colonialism that replaced the formal Spanish colonialism. Even before Spain's withdrawal, Great Britain, particularly in the last two decades of the eighteenth century and the first twenty-five years of the nineteenth century, had begun to wield a multidimensional influence on Central America. As the proprietor of a settlement (not yet called a colony) on the isthmus, that of British Honduras (often called Belize), and as the ally and protector of the

Miskito Indians on the Atlantic coasts of Honduras and Nicaragua, Great Britain was already the filter for goods and ideas arriving in Central America from the Caribbean and the North Atlantic before independence.[5] Leaders in Central America, like those elsewhere in Latin America, looked to British and French political and economic ideas as tools of modernization. Now, upon Spain's defeat, British influence sharply increased. London loans to the new government and London financing for the purchase of manufactured goods from Europe tended to harden the dependency.

In 1825 the United States, despite its favorable image in Central America, was in no position to contest British–Central American rapprochement. Although a few U.S. citizens and government spokesmen looked to Latin America for opportunities of commercial exchange or territorial aggrandizement, in general the United States was commercially too weak to take advantage of the opening created by the demise of the Spanish empire in America and militarily too weak to contemplate seriously noncontiguous expansion. Not only were no voices raised in the United States to forestall the establishment of informal British dependency in Central America, but there is no evidence to suggest that any significant segment of U.S. public opinion was even aware of the infiltration.

It could not have been otherwise, considering the lack of information about Central America in the United States in the early nineteenth century. Before John L. Stephens and E. George Squier undertook to educate North Americans about Central America, there was not a single authoritative book about the isthmus written by a North American.[6] Travel literature was also scarce. Aside from Thomas Gage's somewhat fanciful account of Central America in his *Travels in the New World*, originally published in 1699, the English reader had only Henry Dunn's *Guatimala, or The Republic of Central America in 1827–1828* as a guide to the isthmus.[7] Dunn's account focuses sharply on Belize, Guatemala City, and the road in between. As the only substantial book source on the confederation before 1841, it must have been read assiduously by early North American diplomats assigned to Central America. Newspapers provided an uncertain alternative. Certainly the State Department of the United States was in no position to help its diplomats headed for Central America. When Thomas N. Mann, the first U.S. diplomat to be given an assignment in Central America, asked Secretary of State John Q. Adams in 1824 for information about his post, Adams replied that he had practically none to give, that Mann was being sent to Central America specifically to acquire information about the Central American government then in formation.[8]

To illustrate further the point of information scarcity, it should be added that authoritative information about Central America in the early part of the nineteenth century lagged behind that about other parts of the Spanish empire in America. Central America, lacking in minerals and lacking in agricultural lands, mines, and Indian labor on the scale of those in Mexico and Peru, had long been neglected by the Spanish crown. There had been no Spanish scientific expeditions like those that had visited the more attractive parts of the empire in the colonial period. Alexander von Humboldt's dramatic expedition to Venezuela, Peru, Mexico, and Cuba, which resulted in his classic account *Political Essay on the Kingdom of New Spain* (published in 1808), never touched Central American soil and had no counterpart in Central America. To diplomats and scientists alike, Central America was terra incognita in the early nineteenth century in Europe and the United States.

In the early nineteenth century, any North American citizen wanting to know Central America firsthand or any Central American wanting to know the United States firsthand faced formidable transportation obstacles. There were no regular overland routes or sea connections. Travelers to Central America from the United States made their way as best they could from ports such as New York, Norfolk, Pensacola, Key West, and New Orleans to the islands of Cuba or Jamaica and then waited for a vessel heading for one of the small, infrequently visited ports in British Honduras, Guatemala, or Honduras. Shipping to the Atlantic ports of Nicaragua and Costa Rica was even more erratic. Travelers to Guatemala were often forced to take shallow-draft vessels from British Honduras or Omoa, Honduras (now Puerto Cortés), to Izabal, Guatemala, on the Golfo Dulce. Not until the mid-1840s was there any regular ship service from any of the West Indies islands to the Central American mainland. Once on the Atlantic shore of Central America, travelers used *bongoes* (dugout canoes), mules, or footpaths to cross the mountains and swamps of the Atlantic and reach the highlands of the Pacific, where the capitals were located and where most Central Americans lived. Not until 1855 was it possible to cross the isthmus by rail and then only in Panama, where travelers faced uncertain prospects of finding sea passage from Panama City to the Central American ports to the north.[9]

In this atmosphere of vague awareness, theoretical admiration, and poor transportation services, it is not surprising that, at first, United

States–Central American relations preoccupied the leaders of neither region. Nevertheless, the confederation earnestly sought diplomatic recognition from the United States. Recognition was granted by the United States in May 1824, just as the Central American constituent assembly was completing its work. President James Monroe's reception of Antonio José Cañas as the confederation's minister to the United States opened the era of formal diplomatic relations between the two nations. The United States was the first major nation to recognize Central America as an independent state. An elementary commercial treaty, the principal object, after recognition, of Cañas's mission, was signed and ratified one year later.[10]

The overriding reason for the Central American confederation's desire for recognition was security against the possibility, seemingly remote in hindsight but all too real at the time, of a Spanish effort to recapture its American possessions. Having gained Spanish agreement to the Florida cession in the previous year, the United States was free to open up official lines of communication with the confederation, as well as with other newly independent Latin American states, in order to follow up commercial possibilities.

Once the issue of diplomatic recognition was resolved, Central America and the United States turned to a number of problem areas. Foremost of the problems that concerned the two nations from 1824 to 1850 was that of national security, which, given the threat of Spanish reconquest, caused the Central Americans some anxiety. To North Americans the problem was an indirect one. European colonization or recolonization anywhere in the western hemisphere, but particularly in the Caribbean region, posed a potential threat to the security of the United States and had already brought forth a response in the form of the Monroe Doctrine of 1823. Both Central America and the United States had an opportunity to deal with the European threat at the Panama Congress in 1827 called by Simón Bolívar. However, neither the United States nor Central America was represented, and the threat passed.[11] Another problem area, dimly perceived in the first decade after 1835 but attaining monumental dimensions later, was the British presence, which probably had more to do with the establishment of friendly relations between the United States and Central America than any other problem. The prospect of commercial intercourse, although primarily of long-range consideration, was an area of diplomatic discussions as the two regions sought to build a structure to foster interchange. Commerce depended on transportation, and, as leaders in both regions realized, transportation development depended on the building of an isthmian canal or other transportation facility. This was more a dream than an immediate prospect in 1824, but in twenty-five years it had become a problem of the highest priority. By the end of the 1824–50 period, the expansionism of the United States, although at first encouraged by Central Americans, had become a problem area, particularly at the end of the Mexican War in 1848. The outcome of the Mexican War disclosed the United States itself as a potential threat to Central American security.

Perhaps the most convenient way of getting across the difficulties facing the two nations in firmly establishing a harmonious relationship is to review the efforts of the United States to provide diplomatic representation in Central America in this period.[12]

Thomas Mann of North Carolina was the first to receive a diplomatic appointment, that of special agent, to Central America. Mann received his letter of appointment in April 1824, and, after struggling for two months with the depressing reality of the lack of a secure transportation system between the East Coast of the United States and Central America, he finally persuaded Secretary of State John Quincy Adams to arrange a sloop of war to take him to his destination. Unfortunately, Mann fell ill and died on board this vessel in July 1824.

The next U.S. diplomatic representative, also from North Carolina, was William Miller. Because U.S. recognition had been granted since Mann's death, Miller was designated chargé d'affaires rather than special agent. Miller reached Key West, Florida, on his way to his post but died there in September 1825, a victim of yellow fever.

In May 1826, the first representative of the United States government actually to serve in Central America arrived at his post having traveled by sloop of war from Norfolk to Havana and thence to the Atlantic coast of Guatemala to Izabal, then overland to Guatemala City by foot and on muleback. He was John Williams, a former Tennessee senator and political opponent of Andrew Jackson. Williams stayed only six months, long enough to sketch some of the first signs of instability of the confederation, before turning over the legation's papers to an acting consul and returning to the United States.

The next chargé d'affaires to Central America, William B. Rochester of Rochester, New York, was another who never reached his post. Commissioned in March 1827 while he was in Mexico, presumably on his way to attend the second meeting of the Panama Congress, which never materialized, Rochester returned to the United States and eventually took passage from Norfolk. A sloop of war brought him directly to Omoa, Honduras, where, had he waited, he might have encountered a vessel to the Golfo Dulce in Guatemala, but instead he took the next ship bound for the United States and never returned to Central American shores. In October 1828 he was dismissed with inexplicable commendations by Secretary of State Henry Clay. Rochester had collected his salary for more than a year and a half but had performed no service.

Nearly three years elapsed before the United States ventured another appointment. Secretary of State Edward Livingston, serving in the Andrew Jackson administration, restored the position in June 1831 by appointing William N. Jeffers of New Jersey as chargé d'affaires. Upon Jeffers's resignation a few months later and before he reached Central America, Livingston, who knew Spanish and was intensely interested in Latin America, appointed James Shannon of Kentucky. Shannon, accompanied by his wife, son, and niece, did indeed reach Guatemala (by way of Pensacola, Belize, and Omoa), but at Izabal, Guatemala, he and his niece contracted yellow fever and died Shannon was the third of the first six U.S. diplomatic agents to Central America to die en route to their posts. During the nine years since the United States had formally recognized the Central American Confederation, a United States diplomat had been in residence only six months.

The seventh appointee, Charles G. Dewitt of New York, received his appointment in January 1833. Dewitt suffered hardships, which he carefully detailed in his dispatches in his journey from Washington to Guatemala City, but he arrived safely in December 1833 and stayed for five long years. During these years of political crisis resulting in the disintegration of the Central American Confederation, Dewitt's dispatches revealed little understanding of what was going on around him in Guatemala, not to speak of the other four provinces, which he never visited. Dewitt was granted leave to visit his sick wife and returned to New York in 1839. He committed suicide soon after learning from Secretary of State John Forsyth of his reassignment to Guatemala. Despite instructions from the Department of State and the favorable attitude of the government of the United Provinces, Dewitt inexplicably had failed his principal assignment, the negotiation of an extension of the commercial treaty of 1825.

Secretary of State Forsyth in 1839 appointed a successor, William Leggett, editor of the *New York Evening Post*. Leggett, however, was seriously ill at the time he received his appointment and died soon thereafter.

John L. Stephens, the ninth diplomatic appointee to Central America, was a traveler of considerable accomplishments. Before receiving his commission as chargé d'affaires to Central America, he had journeyed extensively in the Middle East and eastern Europe and had written two popular books on his travels.[13] His appointment owed more to Stephens's desire to explore the ruins of the Maya civilization in Central America than to President Martin Van Buren's hope of establishing U.S. influence in Central America. The two aims were not incompatible; nevertheless, it seems clear that with regard to the Stephens appointment, Van Buren was more eager to marshal political credit for his patronage of scholarship than to insist on quality representation in Central America.

As it turned out, Stephens's trip in 1839–40 coincided with the demise of the confederation. Arriving in Guatemala City, Stephens found that there was no government to receive his diplomatic credentials. All the former provinces but Costa Rica had formally withdrawn from the confederation and were in the process of organizing themselves as separate nations; Costa Rica was soon to follow. Remnants of the confederation government had fled to El Salvador in an unsuccessful attempt to restore control. Stephens seized the opportunity. In an amazingly swift and successful fact-finding journey, with an emphasis on archaeology rather than contemporary affairs, Stephens visited all five former provinces and, on his return, passed through Chiapas and Yucatán in Mexico. Within a year he had completed and published his two-volume *Incidents of Travel in Central America, Chiapas, and Yucatan*, the quintessential travel account of Central America.[14]

Stephens did more than open the eyes of the scholarly world to the magnificence of the Maya civilization. He traveled along the San Juan River and Lake Nicaragua in Nicaragua and provided the best information then available in English about the Nicaraguan transit route. He also provided for the first time a comprehensive, reliable introduction to Central America. Later, as an entrepreneur, he headed the firm that in the mid-1850s constructed the railroad across the Isthmus of Panama. He died in Panama of yellow fever.

Stephens's successor was William S. Murphy, who became "special confidential agent" in Central America for the William Henry Harrison administration in July 1841. His special status was due to the uncertainties surrounding the confederation, and his primary responsibility was to gather information about the confederation, to evaluate the prospects for its revival, and to encourage union. This mission, which lasted only three months, was unsuccessful, for Murphy was excessively optimistic about the confederation, and the United States could do nothing to reverse the decline of unionist sentiment. Murphy did sense the importance of British encroachments on the isthmus and prepared the Department of State to eventually take a greater interest in Central America.

Nevertheless, it was not until the closing months of the Mexican War, in 1848, that another chargé d'affaires to Central America was appointed. Elijah Hise of Kentucky accepted the position in March 1848, and, after a series of misadventures that took him as far as Panama City and back to Cuba, he arrived in Guatemala in December 1848. He took up where Murphy left off in calling attention to the British threat and even negotiated with Nicaragua an unauthorized treaty challenging Great Britain, but like those of so many of his predecessors, his stay was too short to be effective. By the time he had arrived in Guatemala, presidential elections in the United States had resulted in a change from a Democratic to a Whig administration. The new administration of President Zachary Taylor, with John M. Clayton as secretary of state, recalled Hise and repudiated the negotiations that he had undertaken with Nicaragua.

The last U.S. diplomat to be appointed in the 1824–50 period was the most important. E. George Squier, who was appointed in April 1849 and who remained in Central America for one year after arriving in June 1849, was the first of the United States' diplomatic representatives to be assigned to residence in Nicaragua instead of Guatemala and the first to be accredited to all five Central American republics. Like Stephens, Squier, who was an amateur anthropologist, hoped to concentrate on archaeological research and to write a book on his travels. He did write a highly informative and successful travel book on Nicaragua, but his archaeological investigations he had to neglect, for he found himself in the midst of a controversial and dangerous diplomatic clash between the United States and Great Britain over their influence in Central America. As a diplomat in 1849–50 and as a publicist in the 1850s, Squier had much to do with the establishment of U.S. influence on the isthmus and the corresponding decline of the British position.[15]

During the periods when U.S. diplomats were absent, U.S. consuls, often with long residences and local connections, supplied basic information. Consuls in Omoa, Trujillo, León, and Guatemala City provided skeletal political information along with their commercially oriented reports.[16] Altogether, though, it must be concluded that

E. George Squier (Latin American Library, Tulane University)

throughout the 1824–50 period the State Department had to formulate policy on an extremely sketchy factual base.

Sporadic Central American diplomatic representation in the United States in the same period compares with the largely futile efforts of the United States to inform itself about events in Central America, let alone influence them. Central American policymakers operated from an equally flimsy information base. Antonio José Cañas was the first diplomatic representative of the Central American Confederation to serve in the United States. He was in Washington in 1825 long enough to be received as minister plenipotentiary and to negotiate and sign a commercial treaty, but he returned to Central America soon after. He did send information about canals, roads, and products in the United States to Central American officials.[17]

Ten years later, Juan Galindo, a Central American promoter-adventurer of Irish parentage, stopped in Washington on an official mission on his way to his diplomatic post as representative of the Republic of Guatemala in England. The purpose of his two-month visit in Washington was to persuade the United States government to support the Central American position in the boundary controversy between Guatemala and British Honduras. It was not successful.[18] However, like the Murphy mission of 1841, the Galindo mission did help to prepare the ground for eventual U.S. opposition to British influence on the isthmus.

After the breakup of the confederation, five individual Central American states contented themselves with occasional special representation until they agreed on Antonio José Irisarri as diplomatic agent in 1855. He stayed on in that position until the United States Civil War and was the dean of the Washington diplomatic corps when he died in 1868.[19] Such length of service was as unusual for Central American diplomats in the United States as for United States diplomats in Central America. The common practice of Central American governments throughout the nineteenth century was to eschew long-term diplomatic appointments, largely for financial reasons, and to rely on brief appointments for specific purposes.

The collapse of the Central American Confederation in 1838–40 was such a disappointment to unionists and seemed to contradict the best interests of all Central Americans to such a degree that some observers sought to blame outsiders for its demise. Central American writers cast blame on Great Britain first and the United States second. With respect to the British role, Robert Naylor and Mario Rodríguez, in two important publications, have effectively laid this ghost to rest.[20] The fact is that although Frederick Chatfield, British consul general in Central America at the time of the confederation's collapse, occasionally took positions well calculated to divide one Central American nation from another, the British government looked upon the issue of union or disunion as a matter of little concern. The Department of State of the United States, far from opposing union, consistently instructed its diplomatic representatives to support the confederation and, after its collapse, to support unification efforts. Although not always explicit, U.S. policy appears to have been based on a preoccupation with Mexico and a concept of a balance of powers in isthmian international relations. The highest priority of the United States was to keep pressure on Mexico, which could more readily be achieved by a unified Central America. A divided Central America, from Washington's perspective, might even present undesirable opportunities to Mexico for territorial aggrandizement.

One of the cornerstones of United States foreign policy in the western hemisphere in this period is, of course, the Monroe Doctrine. In general, in the nineteenth century the United States opposed European influence or colonization in the western hemisphere. The closer the European threat to the southern borders of the United States, the stronger Washington's opposition would be, at least theoretically. Therefore, any European threat to Central America would supposedly be taken seriously by the United States. Notwithstanding the declaration of Monroe, in the period from 1824 to 1850, except in the final two or three years Washington perceived no serious European threat in Central America. It is true that British activities in British Honduras, in the Bay Islands (off the Atlantic coast of Honduras),[21] and on the Miskito Shore in this period aroused anxiety among many Central American leaders, but in the United States there was little or no reaction to these events and little disposition to appeal to the Monroe Doctrine until after the Mexican War of 1846–48.

Although U.S. officials generally chose not to invoke the Monroe Doctrine in the period from 1824 to 1850, the issue of United States–British rivalry on the isthmus was real and deserves more detailed consideration. To the Central Americans it was not a theoretical issue; they had faced British encroachment, gunboat diplomacy, and assorted commercial bullying from the mid-1830s, and their response was to urge the United States to enter the scene as a counterpoise to Great Britain. Problems accumulated during the years of the confederation, intensified in the 1830s, and reached such a dangerous climax in 1849–50 that the fledgling Central American republics were shunted aside by the superpowers, Great Britain and the United States, which assigned their most skilled diplomats to work out an amicable solution with no representation from Central America and with little or no regard for Central American interests.

With British Honduras the British had a firm foothold on the isthmus. Although it did not formally become a colony in the British system until 1862, the "informal settlement" of British Honduras constituted a threat first to the territorial aspirations of the confederation and then to the Republic of Guatemala.[22] Belizeans, who earned their living mainly by cutting and exporting mahogany logs, paid little attention to eighteenth-century Anglo-Spanish agreements aimed at regulating and containing their activity.[23] Galindo's mission to Washington and London in 1835 failed to forestall log-cutting encroachments on Guatemalan soil and failed to interest the United States in Central America's plight. Galindo's efforts on this mission and elsewhere did help to arouse Central Americans to the realities of the British presence and to potential expansion.

Although involved politically primarily in the state government of Guatemala and a prime defender of Guatemalan interests, Galindo was also concerned about the little-hindered activities of British log cutters on the Miskito Shore of Honduras and Nicaragua, the restoration of the British protectorate of the Miskito Indians in the 1830s, and the return of British settlers in 1832 to the Bay Islands off the Atlantic coast of Honduras. Because of poor communications between the capital cities of Comayagua, Honduras, and León, Nicaragua, and the Atlantic coast and because of conflicting impressions of British intentions on the coast, Honduras and Nicaragua were slow to react to British activities.[24] Overwhelming British power and Central American dependency on British financial policy also discouraged a military reaction. Nonetheless, Honduras and Nicaragua regularly and futilely protested the British presence in the Bay Islands and on the Miskito Shore after the mid-1830s. Guatemala and Costa Rica, partly because of more commercial exchange, enjoyed better relations with Great Britain.[25] Although the United States occasionally expressed sympathy and mild support for the Central American cause against British imperialism, it took no action in the 1830s. Between the tenures of Murphy (1841) and Hise (1848), when the issue began to assume international importance, the United States had no diplomatic representation in Central America at all. The United States in the early and middle 1840s was obviously much more concerned with Mexico and with negotiations with Great Britain over the United States–Canadian boundary than with defending Central American interests against Great Britain.

To clarify further the imbalance of British versus North American influence on the isthmus, it is necessary to discuss British diplomatic representation and policy. Personifying British policy in Central America in the period under consideration was Frederick Chatfield. The imperious Chatfield was British consul and consul general from 1833 to 1849 and chargé d'affaires in Central America from 1849 to 1852. It was he who pressed the Central American republics for payment of the claims of private British citizens, who occasionally suggested that the countries pay their debts in territory rather than in money, who defended Belizean and Miskito expansion, and who boasted of his ability to call upon British gunboats to enforce his views. While it is clear from hindsight that Chatfield often overstepped the bounds of diplomatic propriety, twisted facts to support his interpretations in his reports to his superiors, and went beyond his instructions, these factors were not generally known by Central Americans at the time.[26]

British policy was, in fact, not necessarily expansive in Central America at this time. In London policymakers were concerned more with consolidation and protection of existing colonies and with avoiding being excluded from important transit routes than with the acquisition of additional territory. Confident of their international position, the British sought no commercial treaties and scorned formal diplomatic recognition of the five republics until 1848. In Central America British agents such as Chatfield and British citizens in British Honduras and the Miskito Shore occasionally took aggressive actions well calculated to draw London to the defense of their interests. Generally, these actions were then repudiated by the British Colonial Office and/or the Foreign Office.[27] This situation eventually brought the United States into the Central American arena as a defender of Central American interests.

The British occupation of the port of San Juan del Norte in 1848 illustrates the clash of British and Central American interests and United States involvement. San Juan del Norte, at the mouth of the San Juan River on the Atlantic coast of Nicaragua, was considered by engineers to be the most likely terminus of an isthmian canal. Since the United States had already apparently semiexcluded the British from the Panamanian transit route by signing the Bidlack Treaty with Colombia in 1846, the British feared exclusion from the Nicaragua route. The Bidlack Treaty, named after Benjamin A. Bidlack, United

States representative in Bogotá, granted passage across Panama for U.S. citizens in return for a guarantee of Colombian sovereignty over Panama. San Juan del Norte was located within the bounds of the Miskito kingdom, protected and manipulated by the British. Therefore, in the name of the Miskito kingdom, Great Britain sent a force of fifty marines to occupy the town. The Nicaraguan government protested to the British to no avail and appealed to the United States for support.

Before we take up the strong United States response to this appeal, it is necessary to trace the developing interest of the United States in isthmian transportation. Shortly after the enunciation of the Monroe Doctrine and as a clear result of the initiative of Henry Clay, the most outspoken U.S. defender of close ties with Latin America, the United States officially laid out a policy on isthmian transportation. Secretary of State Clay, in his instructions to the U.S. delegates to the Panama Congress of 1826, declared, "If the work should ever be executed . . . the benefits of it ought not to be exclusively appropriated to any one nation, but should be extended to all parts of the globe, upon the payment of a just compensation or reasonable tolls."[28] The proposition of exclusive United States control, which won many adherents in the late nineteenth century, could not have been seriously entertained in the period between 1824 and 1850 because of the lack of military strength and transportation connections. Capital was also lacking in the United States for such a gigantic undertaking outside its borders. Indeed, although Central American and North American officials occasionally voiced their support for the idea of a canal or other isthmian transportation facility, it did not become a prime item for diplomatic agendas until 1848.

A series of momentous events in the 1840s abruptly changed the situation. The Oregon migrations starting in 1842, the Oregon boundary settlement of 1846, the growing overland traffic to California of the mid-1840s, the Mexican War of 1846–48, the acquisition of California by the Treaty of Guadalupe Hidalgo with Mexico in 1848, and finally the discovery of gold in California in 1848 followed by the celebrated gold rush of 1849 drew Central America into the spreading orbit of the United States and forced the United States to deal with the issue of transportation across the Central American isthmus.

Secretary of State James Buchanan's instructions to Elijah P. Hise, written on June 3, 1848, provide an insight into the abrupt change of U.S. policy when contrasted to instructions written one year later. Buchanan said that the United States had not yet determined what to do about the British protectorate of the Miskito kingdom. There was no mention of any protest to the occupation of San Juan del Norte. Hise was simply to observe (as usual) and to negotiate commercial treaties with Guatemala and El Salvador.[29] These instructions, it should be remembered, came from the James K. Polk administration, which was known for its vocal defense of the doctrine of Monroe. Despite these instructions, Hise nevertheless sensed a need to do something to identify with the Central American cause and to resist British encroachment, and he negotiated a treaty with Nicaragua instead of Guatemala or El Salvador. The Hise Treaty guaranteed Nicaraguan sovereignty not only over the line of the proposed Nicaraguan canal but also over its entire territory. It did not matter. Hise had arrived in Guatemala after the elections of 1848, and the new Zachary Taylor administration, which took office in March 1849, recalled Hise and discarded the Hise Treaty.

In the presidential election campaign of 1848, Taylor had proposed a moderate international course so as not to antagonize Great Britain unduly. He had even criticized Polk for his reckless defense of the Monroe Doctrine. Once in office, however, Taylor and his secretary of state, John M. Clayton, chose as their diplomatic representative in Central America a strong proponent of the Monroe Doctrine, E. George Squier, and gave him instructions well calculated to precipitate a clash of United States–British interests on the isthmus.

Clayton's instructions to Squier were explicit. He was to go to Nicaragua rather than Guatemala. He was to assist the efforts of North American business agents who were in Nicaragua negotiating for a canal contract. And he was to negotiate a treaty with the government of Nicaragua to provide protection for the company that ended up with the contract. He was not to offer any territorial guarantees. At the same time he could assure the Nicaraguan authorities of U.S. sympathy and willingness to use its offices in frustrating the designs of the British on the Atlantic coast.[30] In short, Squier's purpose was to further a canal controlled by North American business interests, but he was not to antagonize Great Britain unduly.

Squier's arrival in Nicaragua in June 1849 signaled a new era in United States–Central American relations. Squier genuinely liked the Nicaraguans and openly sympathized with their cause against the British. The Nicaraguans saw Squier as their one hope for resisting British encroachment on their Atlantic shores and as a fit rival for the hated Chatfield. At public and private receptions in León, the capital, the Nicaraguans showered Squier with affection and laid before him their frustrations over British encroachments. In this atmosphere it was easy for Squier to carry out the first part of his instructions. Freely assisting the agents of the American Atlantic and Pacific Ship-Canal Company (the Cornelius Vanderbilt interest), Squier proudly announced the signing of a contract between the company and the Nicaraguan government on August 27, 1849.[31]

Six days later Squier signed the Squier-Zepeda Treaty. The Squier-Zepeda Treaty, which was never ratified by the United States Senate, offered the protection of both governments to the canal and the company that constructed the canal. U.S. protection was conceded only so long as the canal company was under the control of U.S. citizens. In return, the United States guaranteed Nicaraguan sovereignty over the line of the projected canal. Squier maintained that supplementary instructions from Clayton allowed Squier to go this far, but the fact is he, like Hise before him, had stretched his instructions to demonstrate solidarity with the Nicaraguan position.[32] Inasmuch as British marines at this time occupied San Juan del Norte in the name of the Miskito kingdom, an Anglo–North American confrontation appeared to be inevitable. The treaty was a vote for the repudiation of the Clay doctrine of an open canal and for the acceptance of the idea of an exclusive canal controlled by the United States.

The Taylor administration privately indicated to Squier its disapproval of the treaty he had negotiated, although it proved to be a powerful bargaining chip in negotiations with the British. But Squier was far from through. The Squier-Zepeda Treaty, he thought, took care of the Atlantic terminus of the proposed canal, San Juan del Norte, but the Pacific terminus remained. In 1849, before any detailed examination of the Nicaraguan canal route had taken place, Squier assumed, as did most authorities, that the projected canal would terminate on Nicaraguan territory in Fonseca Bay. Guarding the supposed outlet is a small volcanic island, a Honduran possession called Tigre. To forestall British action to gain control of Fonseca Bay, Squier hit upon the idea of a cession to the United States of the island of Tigre. In hasty negotiations arranged by Squier in León, Squier persuaded a Honduran government representative to sign a treaty, dated September 28, 1849, with an appended protocol, handing over Tigre to the United States. Chargé d'affaires Chatfield, however, was not so easily outmaneuvered. Fully aware of Squier's Honduran diplomatic negotiations, Chatfield ordered Captain James A. Paynter of the HMS *Gorgon* of the British South Pacific squadron to seize Tigre. The seizure of Tigre took place on October 16, 1849, before Squier's courier could plant the United States flag on the island.[33]

Neither Squier nor Chatfield had diplomatic instructions for these provocative actions. Animated by a spirit of exaggerated urgency and personal rivalry and by a feeling that protection of their countries' respective interests required bold expansion, they had placed the United States and Great Britain on the brink of war on the Central American isthmus. Both Squier and Chatfield arrogantly assumed that they knew what was best for Central America.

These were the circumstances that led to the negotiation of the Clayton-Bulwer Treaty of 1850. Clearly, neither the United States nor Great Britain wanted war over Central America, and neither fully approved of the actions of their overzealous diplomatic agents. Clayton repudiated the Honduras protocol providing for the cession of Tigre upon receiving it, and Admiral Phipps Hornby, knowing better than Chatfield did his government's determination not to acquire territory on the Pacific side of Central America, disavowed the action of Captain Paynter and restored Tigre to its owners.[34] Nevertheless, trivial reprimands to both agents from their superiors were an indication that both governments were not altogether opposed to tactical aggressiveness at the point of conflict. To hasten a settlement, London sent Sir Henry Lytton Bulwer to Washington in December 1849 with ample powers to begin what proved to be an intense four months negotiating session with Clayton. Signed on April 19, 1850, the Clayton-Bulwer Treaty was ratified by the United States one month later. Nicaragua's special diplomatic representative, Eduardo Carcache, was in Washington at the time of these negotiations, but he had little if any effect on the outcome. Carcache's mission was to procure senate ratification of the Squier-Zepeda Treaty.[35]

The Clayton-Bulwer Treaty is the most significant treaty in the history of the isthmian rivalry between the United States and Great Britain. Opting for partnership rather than risky competition, the two powers agreed to promote jointly a canal or other transportation facility on the isthmus of Central America. They agreed not to seek exclusive control of any such facility and not to erect fortifications in its vicinity. Finally, they agreed not to "occupy, or fortify, or colonize, or assume or exercise any dominion over . . . any part of Central America."[36] The war fever on both sides of the Atlantic cooled with the signing and quick ratification of this treaty.

In the decade following the signing of the Clayton-Bulwer Treaty, there was heated discussion of how these clauses affected the British settlement in Belize and the British protectorate of the Miskito kingdom. Discussion of "the Central American question," as it was called, involved the public as well as diplomats, Central Americans as well as North Americans and British. By the end of the decade it was clear that the Clayton-Bulwer Treaty had largely ended Central American fears of territorial aggrandizement at the hands of Great Britain and the United States. Central Americans needed to go to no great lengths in favor of the principle of noncolonization—that had been accepted by both major powers in 1850 and adhered to during the heated discussions afterward. The Clayton-Bulwer Treaty did not prevent Great Britain from consolidating its possession of British Honduras, which formally became a colony in 1862, nor did it prevent the North American filibuster William Walker from seriously threatening the independence of Nicaragua in the mid-1850s, but it did effectively curb the Central American territorial ambitions of the two powers. Most significantly, the Clayton-Bulwer Treaty laid the basis for a series of bilateral negotiations leading to British withdrawal from the Miskito Coast of Honduras and Nicaragua and to a boundary settlement with Guatemala in 1859.[37]

The events of 1849–50, terminating with the signing of the Clayton-Bulwer Treaty, marked the beginning of a new era for Central American–United States relations. It was the beginning of the end of British domination. It marked the end of "diplomatic futility" and the beginning of extraordinary United States involvement in Central American affairs. Led by Squier, who became a Central American publicist and promoter of business projects in Central America, the English-speaking public became much more aware of Central America in the 1850s. Squier alone published four books on Central America between 1851 and 1859.[38] The William Walker imbroglio in Nicaragua was the most immediate and threatening result of the new exposure, but in the long run the beginning of North American economic penetration in the 1850s and the consequently diminished British commercial presence had the most impact on Central American society.

Steps of Considerable Delicacy: Early Relations with Peru

Lawrence A. Clayton

"We are still almost in a state of seige from the operations of the armed bands who rob and plunder almost daily, on the great thoroughfare between this city [Lima] and its port-town, Callao, and, amongst others, some of our countrymen have been attacked and wounded," wrote Samuel Larned, United States charge d'affaires at Lima on November 16, 1835.[1] Lima and its environs were indeed in an uproar, made so by the revolt of the impetuous twenty-eight-year-old general, Felipe Santiago de Salaverry, against the government.[2] While Salaverry the usurper was prosecuting his campaign in the interior, bands of soldiers prowled about the capital area, and discipline and order were loosened by the quicksilver political situation. Furthermore, Salaverry's attitudes were antiforeign, and his campaign seemed to the American charge "worthy of the times of Attila or Genghis Kan." Little wonder that on December 10, 1835, a few marines were landed at Callao to protect American interests and property. Next month they packed up and reboarded their ship, only to return to Lima in August to continue their vigil. On December 2, 1836, less than a year after first setting ashore, the marines once more withdrew, and never again would the United States intervene militarily in Peruvian affairs.[3]

The episode occurred during a period that has formerly been perceived as a relatively quiet one in the formation of United States–Peruvian relations. In fact, nothing could be further from the truth. From the end of the Wars of Independence to midcentury, American diplomats and naval officers jockeyed actively and very often successfully for power and influence in Peruvian affairs. From 1825 to 1850, they held the confidence and trust of presidents and ministers, lobbied well on behalf of U.S. commercial interests in Peru, and helped to

promote a consistent and continuous presence in the face of a Peruvian political situation that can be accurately labeled as tumultuous.
The first American minister for Peru was not appointed until after
midcentury, but a series of able, interested, and knowledgeable
chargés d'affaires and consuls served continuously after the Wars of
Independence. They not only looked after the interests of the United
States but also promoted peace and amity in a near-volcanic situation
in South America as the newly emerged nations searched for a viable
international political order to replace the hegemony of Spain.

The consuls and diplomats were ably supported in Peruvian
matters by American captains and commodores commanding the
squadron stationed in South American waters since the Wars of Independence. The squadron, officially known as the United States Naval
Forces on Pacific Station, was established in 1818 to protect American
commerce in the eastern Pacific. Never numbering more than two or
three ships, it nonetheless represented the most forceful intentions of
the United States to preserve and extend its interests on the west
coast of Latin America.[4] These captains and commodores usually
maintained their independence of judgment and action, and while
this was a source of some frustration to American diplomats and consuls, who on occasion would have preferred the option of calling out a
frigate's guns for persuasion, it bestowed upon the naval commanders
a remarkable degree of latitude to act on behalf of their country as
they saw fit, answering only to the secretary of the navy.

William Tudor, Extraordinary Consul

The events of 1824 in Peru all seemed to have pointed to the climac-
tic Battle of Ayacucho. Fought on a breathtaking battlefield 11,600 feet
up in the Andes, the battle proved decisive in breaking Spanish
power in Peru. Indeed, after December 9, 1824, any serious Spanish
resistance to the independence of South America ceased to exist. The
Battle of Ayacucho lasted only one hour. Taken as prisoners were
the viceroy José de la Serna, 13 generals, 16 colonels, 68 lieutenant
colonels, 484 subalterns, and 3,200 privates.[5] The significance of
Ayacucho was as readily apparent to contemporaries as it is to historians observing through their prism of hindsight. William Tudor, U.S.
consul at Lima, reported optimistically to his secretary of state, John
Quincy Adams, that "this memorable battle secured in one day the
independence of Peru and terminated the Spanish empire in America;

and as this country [Peru] was the last of this continent in which Spain maintained a struggle, the world may now hope that the South American republics will be recognized by every civilized state, peace restored to the world, and the cause of freedom and national improvements obtain a lasting triumph."[6] These were noble and earnest sentiments. That they were expressed by the individual who did more than any other to form the earliest relations between an independent Peru and the United States invests them with some importance, for individuals rather than deliberate national policies molded United States–Peruvian relations in this highly fluid and formative period.

Tudor was the first U.S. consul accredited to Peru in 1824, but he was not the first American citizen to act officially on the western coast of South America. Captain David Porter had sailed the frigate *Essex* into the Pacific in 1813 to carry the War of 1812 to the British in that remote part of the world. His voyage was remarkably successful: he destroyed a great part of the English whaling fleet before he was trapped in Valparaíso harbor by two British men-of-war and was forced to strike his flag after a terrific battle.[7] Even before the war, Joel R. Poinsett had served for a time as consul general to Buenos Aires and Chile. He was succeeded by Judge John B. Prevost, who was sent as a special agent of the United States to Peru, Buenos Aires, and Chile between 1818 and 1826. Along with the captains and commodores commanding the U.S. naval forces stationed in the Pacific after 1818, the special agents and consuls of the United States were trying to deal with the extremely volatile situation of a people in revolution. As republicans who had freed themselves from a European monarchy, most Americans were sympathetic to the patriot cause. As a people who had recently fought Great Britain to defend the rights of neutrals, most were also deeply committed to defending these rights, whether violated by royalists or by patriots. Furthermore, during the course of the last five or six years of the South Americans' struggle to destroy Spanish dominions, it became difficult to distinguish between heroes and cads, between those deserving U.S. support and those at odds with American principles and commitments.

As early as 1821 Captain Charles G. Ridgely, commanding the American squadron, had offended Prevost by allegedly favoring royalists. Ridgely had humanely given temporary refuge to the former viceroy of Peru, Joaquín de la Pezuela, who had been overthrown by a coup of his officers and replaced by José de la Serna.[8] Pezuela stayed aboard the U.S. frigate *Constellation* for only a short while before being transferred to a merchantman en route to Spain, but it was long enough to prompt not only Prevost but also José de San Martín's patriot government to rebuke Ridgely for his act of bad faith.[9] To Ridgely, it was a simple act of political asylum. In fact, it was the first such act by an American warship on Pacific station and set a precedent that was to be observed during the next half century.[10]

Ridgely's successor, Commodore Charles Stewart, commanded the squadron from 1821 to 1824, and he caught the brunt of trying to maintain and protect United States neutrality in a near-impossible situation. Whatever Stewart did, he was bound to offend either the patriots or the royalists. Indeed, upon his return to the United States in 1826, Stewart was court-martialed for his behavior on station in the Pacific. What did the commodore do to deserve this most serious threat to his honor and his career?

Stewart was one of the most celebrated officers in the young naval service, and the trial, set in a steamy Washington in August, drew national attention. The most serious of four charges pressed against Stewart in the court-martial was "un-officer-like conduct." The specifications illuminated the real allegations being made against Stewart: favoritism to the royalist cause or, at the least, such rigid observation of the laws of neutrality that any passive assistance to the patriots' cause was precluded. He was accused of having transported specie for American merchants, of occasionally carrying civilian passengers, of interfering with patriot vessels in the observation of their duties (for example, in taking American merchant ships suspected of engaging in contraband trade), and of other acts generally considered partial to the royalists.[11] John B. Prevost was especially hostile to the commodore, but Prevost died in Peru in March 1825, more than a year before the court-martial convened. However, Prevost's testimony would not have swayed the court from not only exonerating Stewart but commending him for honorably discharging his duties.

Three members of the board—Ridgely, James Biddle, and John Downes—had all served as commanding officers on the Pacific naval station before Stewart's tour, and they knew full well the hazards of trying to maintain neutrality in an atmosphere charged with hostility. They all testified not only that Stewart's behavior had been consistent with U.S. interpretation of neutrality laws but also that they themselves had engaged in many of the same practices for which Stewart was being unjustly tried. Biddle was succinct in summarizing the dilemma of naval commanders during the Wars of Independence: "I believe it is impossible for any commanding officer to be in the Pacific without giving offence to the one side or the other. The royal party, knowing the general feelings of our countrymen, are jealous of them; the patriots, on the other hand, expecting too much, are dissatisfied."[12] Stewart was acquitted. Meanwhile, his brother-in-law, William Tudor, had landed in Peru and was rapidly getting a measure of the land and its people. Tudor, it turned out, was an extraordinary individual.

Tudor's credentials as an American patriot were impeccable. Son of a Congregationalist minister in Massachusetts, a graduate of Harvard in the 1790s, cosmopolitan and well traveled among the capitals of Europe, he was the quintessential Yankee. His father, William Tudor, Sr., had delivered in 1779 the annual denunciation of the Boston Massacre of 1770, and his son, too young to have been a revolutionary, was nonetheless ardent in his patriotism. After leaving Harvard, he acquired a reputation as a literary celebrity in the Boston area, and among his many tracts, pamphlets, and books was a biography of James Otis, whose ardent defense of colonial rights prefigured the Revolution.[13] Tudor helped to found the *North American Review*, was instrumental in preserving historical sites associated with the American Revolution, and was a keen observer of men and movements. Furthermore, he was willing to act with swiftness and perseverance at the highest levels to accomplish his objectives. When he arrived in Peru in March 1824, he would need all of his talents to see his way through the tangle of Peruvian politics.

Peru in 1824 was in the final stages of its independence movement, which culminated with the Battle of Ayacucho in December. Tudor's official position was awkward at the very onset. His commission as consul was to a Peruvian government absent from the capital, for the royalists at this juncture were once more in control of Callao and Lima.[14] Meanwhile, Simón Bolívar was traveling through other parts of Peru and preparing for a decisive campaign that led to the Battle of Junín on August 6, 1824. Fought silently by cavalry with only swords and lances high on the cold Plain of Junín (which had an altitude of twelve thousand feet), it was the first act of the grand campaign that ended with the triumph at Ayacucho. Tudor, however, was in Callao, where the royalist general José Ramón Rodil held the key forts. Prevost, ever faithful to the patriot cause, was with Bolívar's government in Trujillo and was urging Tudor to join him. What to do?

Tudor wisely stayed in Callao. Lima was the nerve center of Peru, and Callao was its port. Whatever transpired in the provinces would eventually be reflected in the capital, where all the principals would rendezvous to deal with the matter of power—its nature and its distribution. Tudor sensed this. Besides, his brother-in-law, Stewart, before being relieved as commander of the naval forces by Commodore Isaac Hull, had established cordial relations with Rodil and recommended Tudor to the Spanish general. The American consul, in spite of his republican propensities, became an admirer of the Spanish leaders and their behavior, if not their cause.

He was appalled by the possibilities of the war continuing. It was dragging Peru down, and he fervently hoped for a rapid conclusion. But who should win? He cited the Spanish as despotic bigots who, if they won, would perpetuate an awful system based on the Inquisition and a rigid commercial monopoly. Showing a nice touch for history, Tudor nonetheless admired Viceroy la Serna (who had succeeded the unlucky Pezuela) as a man "distinguished for his moderation, humanity and uprightness" and looked favorably on certain of his generals—José Canterac, Jerónimo Valdez, Juan Antonio Monet, and Rodil—as men in the prime of life who "recall the character of their countrymen in the 16th century."[15] What higher compliment than to be favorably compared with the great Spanish conquistadores? Indeed, some of Tudor's American contemporaries were already intrigued by or immersed in the heroic period of Spanish history. In the next few years Washington Irving would romanticize the Moorish occupation of Spain in his *Alhambra* and also produce one of the great literary biographies of Columbus. From Boston, William Hickling Prescott would delight the literary world with his almost lyrical histories of the Spanish conquests of the New World. Furthermore, the Spanish people had sacrificed their own treasure and blood for the patriot cause during the American Revolution. Their cause now, though royalist, Catholic, and monopolistic—all anathema to the republican Tudor—was yet not to be despised so easily. On the other hand, if Bolívar's forces triumphed, "the consequences will be a further exhaustion of the inhabitants by a protracted civil war."[16] Tudor's assessment was remarkably perceptive. Indeed, it was difficult being a neutral consul in a country torn by revolutionary passions. It was no easier doing business in Peru.

Tudor, as were all consuls in South America in this period, was there on his own business while secondarily tending to matters of state. He soon crossed paths with one of the earliest American firms on the west coast, A. Alsop y Compañía.[17] Alsop and Company was founded by Richard Alsop during the last days of the viceroyalty. Alsop inherited a fortune from his father, increased it by trading in the

West Indies, and then moved around the horn into the Pacific. Americans had been sailing into the Pacific since the late 1780s. Some were engaged in the fur trade between the northwest and China; others bought sandalwood in the Hawaiian islands; some searched for sealskins and oil; and after 1791, when the first seven American whalers rounded the horn, Yankee ships appeared in the South Seas with increasing frequency in search of leviathans. Some also began clandestine trade with Spain's west coast colonies, and among those who established themselves firmly were the Alsops of New England.[18] Unlike Tudor and his family, the Alsops were no friends of revolution. Their ties with the viceregal government in Lima developed cordially and were born of a mutual interest in trade and a common view of politics. The royalists in turn favored the ships of Alsop and Company.

Furthermore, Richard Alsop was one of the Americans who had opposed the American Revolution, and he had done so with wit and irony. He poked fun at Thomas Jefferson's pronouncements on the equality of man—was it truly so?—at Sam Adams's inability to manage his own wealth but freeness in advising the government on how to handle its revenues, and at the vain, ambitious John Hancock.[19] Clearly, the Alsop family was not cut from the same bolt of cloth as the Tudors. They may have clashed in New England; their descendants most certainly did in Peru.

Within a few months after arriving in Peru, Tudor discovered that a Trujillo newspaper, then in the control of Bolívar's patriot army, had accused Tudor of favoring the royalist cause in his business dealings.[20] It was a libel that incensed Tudor, especially since it not only compromised his status with the patriots but would probably be repeated in the United States.[21] A businessman was only as good as his reputation, and the feisty consul therefore set out to discover the author of the damaging accusation, which implied that he had received a vessel, the brig *Fredric*, for his servility to the Spaniards. When stonewalled by the patriot government, Tudor turned to the Liberator himself.[22] Bolívar also balked at revealing the source, and Tudor left in a high dudgeon.[23] A bit more sleuthing revealed that Alsop had been behind the scenes, but even a letter to his good friend Daniel Webster back home did not bring the Alsops to justice.

Alsop and Company continued to do business in Peru through the middle of the century, apparently unscathed by the indignant Tudor. After all, the Alsops had been in Peru for at least two decades, and Tudor was a mere newcomer. Furthermore, Peruvian merchants and politicians were notoriously fickle in their political loyalties during this period, and the Alsops had obviously shifted about nicely to accommodate themselves to the prevailing patriotic currents. It was not a case of political apostasy. It was a case of good business sense.

In spite of Bolívar's inadequate response to Tudor's request, the Yankee consul was irresistibly drawn to Bolívar. However, Tudor's admiration for Bolívar was to be short-lived. By 1825 Tudor began to sour on the Liberator, and all through 1826 Tudor's letters to Henry Clay, President John Quincy Adams's secretary of state, are freighted with compelling criticism of and disgust for Bolívar's style, his political creations, his seemingly massive egotism.

Bolívar in 1825 and 1826 ruled Peru dictatorially, having been declared president for life under a constitution created by himself. He traveled through the country for many months after Ayacucho, receiving the acclamations of his many supporters and partisans; he was virtually worshiped by those who believed in the immortal qualities of the Liberator. Arriving on the shores of Lake Titicaca, high up on the altiplano bordering Peru and Bolivia, the Liberator was met by a delegation of Indians headed by Chuqui-huanca, the chief of Azangaro, who offered the following encomium:

> It pleased God to form a great empire of savages and He created Manco Capac. The people sinned and He delivered them up to Pizarro. After three centuries of expiation He has taken compassion on their sufferings, and has sent you. You, then, are the fulfiller of the design of providence, and no former deeds appear equal to those which have been done by you. You have liberated five nations. In the great destiny to which they are called, they will raise your fame higher still. As the ages roll on, your glory will increase, as the shade lengthens when the sun goes down.[24]

Bolívar reveled in such flattery. Tudor despised him for it.

Tudor observed Bolívar as he evolved rapidly from liberator to tyrant. The changes in the Liberator dismayed the consul, as he admitted in an extraordinary note sent in May 1826 to Clay.

> It is not without the most painful feelings, that I have come to the conclusions in this letter. I have believed Gen. Bolivar, animated by the most pure and loftly ambition, and that notwithstanding some defects of private character, and personal traits and habits wholly dissimilar, that he had taken a model [George Washington] in view, of which we are so proud and the world so admiring. Nor am I ashamed of my

credulity; the fame within his reach was so glorious, that I could never believe any man would descend from that lofty eminence where posterity would have recognized him, to confound himself with the ignoble herd of ambitious, usurping, military chieftains.[25]

Tudor was very much a civil being, while Bolívar's military background made him appear insensitive to the principles Tudor cherished, especially the subordination of the military to civil authority. "The Liberator . . . has achieved such great things, has had such a sole direction of affairs, that the jarring movements of civil government are regarded by him too much in the light of military insubordination, and to be resisted in the same summary way."[26]

The flow of events that had transformed revolutionary France in the 1790s to imperial France under Napoleon was inevitably suggested by the transition Bolívar seemed to be undergoing. "This state of things gives occasion to the enemies of Bolivar to look wise and exult in the truth of their prophecies and that he would discover his ambition and designs of usurpation, etc. A Frenchman of liberal and intelligent character said to me, 'He will lose himself just as Napoleon did—' and this may perhaps serve to convey the best idea of the danger he is exposed to."[27]

Tudor was especially repelled by the "base, oriental flattery that he [Bolívar] has received from his dependents here."[28] Surrounded by devoted partisans, such as three young Englishmen who served as officers and aides, Bolívar lacked "characters of weight and dignity near him, who can sustain a contrary opinion."[29] Tudor thought that "there is a tone of excessive adulation and absolute deference in those of this country who approach him, that has nothing of a republican complexion."[30] Sycophancy. Excessive adulation. "Nothing of a republican complexion." In several instances, Tudor simply could not contain himself, and the reporter gained ascendancy over the diplomat.

> Were I to repeat to you some authentic anecdotes they would seem incredible. An idea may be formed from the single fact that on his [Bolívar's] birthday last week, when he completed his 43rd year, taking fire at a toast given at his own table, he declared himself a greater man than any which history has recorded, that not only the heroes of antiquity were inferiour to him in "liberal ideas," but Washington and Napoleon he had left in the rear.[31]

To elevate himself above the noble Washington was probably the nearest thing to blasphemy Bolívar could commit in the eyes of Tudor.

Tudor recognized Bolívar, egotist or not, as the genius that he was. Yet, in spite of Tudor's well-founded respect for Bolívar's genius, the American consul could not help but sadly bear witness to the turn Bolívar had taken from enlightened republican to tyrant. As Tudor said, "Military glory is his predominant passion, conquest and extensive empire his aim. . . . He will at last be only a brilliant, military usurper, to be cursed by the present generation: add another to the list of military madmen."[32]

Tudor was off in foreseeing the Bolivarian legacy. It runs strong and deep through five countries of South America, and the modern chorus gratefully acknowledges the man's genius. Tudor also misread Bolívar's militarism. The Liberator's political survival and success depended upon his military prowess, and in a land that had been ravaged by the forces of war, the military often was the only hand to stay the very forces of disorder and chaos that Tudor loathed.

Tudor's attention was by no means monopolized by the spectacular Bolivarian comet. He astutely observed all those about him who shared power, had once carried weight, or promised to in the future. Andrés Santa Cruz, a mestizo from Bolivia who later became president of both Bolivia and Peru, reminded Tudor that mixed-bloods were possessed of volatile, mercurial temperaments. He has "some mixture of Pocahontas blood, which mixtures are here called Cholos; is amiable and affable in his manners, but his conduct was wavering and uncertain in the progress of recent events: . . . cursed with an unfortunate mixture of qualities, [he] is timid, indecisive and ambitious."[33] Santa Cruz, in fact, became one of the United States' strongest supporters in the coming decade.

Antonio José Sucre, Bolívar's great lieutenant who led the patriot forces at Ayacucho, was a favorite of the consul, who described him as possessing ample talents and skills perhaps superior to those of Bolívar himself.

Tudor was more than an observer. He was very much an active participant in the political life flowing and ebbing around him, practicing the art of personal diplomacy with gusto and some skill.

In early 1826, General José de La Mar was recalled to Peru from Guayaquil by Bolívar to serve as president of Peru. La Mar originally demurred for reasons of health. Many thought it was a political disease. Tudor viewed La Mar, whom he described as "extremely beloved and respected," as perhaps the only individual capable of uniting public opinion in Peru.[34] La Mar had commanded the Peruvian division at the glorious Battle of Ayacucho, a fact that alone ensured him a large following among the Peruvian people, even though he was a native of Cuenca in Ecuador. Bolívar finally persuaded La Mar to come from Guayaquil, and Tudor worked on the general in an attempt to influence his decision on the presidency: "I had recently a long and frank conversation with him, in which being exempt from all suspicion of flattery, I spoke to him of the state of public opinion and the feeling of all parties towards him; and tho' perhaps not obliged to play the part of Curtius, yet his acceptance of the place, would prevent the opening of that gulph which it might be feared faction would create if he retired."[35]

But La Mar, even though he accepted the presidency forced on him by Bolívar, was determined to bow out. In June he decided on a trip to the United States for reasons of health, although Tudor suspected he was going "to avoid being compromised against his will here."[36] By now La Mar and Tudor were close friends, the general receiving extremely flattering encomiums from the consul: "A most gallant soldier and distinguished officer, a pure patriot, with a character public and private unsullied." Furthermore, La Mar was "extremely partial to our country and our institutions, and deserves on every ground, the most cordial reception both as a public and private individual."[37] In such ways are natural predispositions to friendship strengthened and enforced.

When Bolívar left Peru forever in September 1826, La Mar naturally emerged as a major contender. He was elected president in June 1827 by a constituent assembly that next year would ratify a new constitution to replace the despotic one dictated by Bolívar.[38]

Ironically, when La Mar was elected president in 1827, he defeated another friend of the United States, Andrés Santa Cruz. Although some "Pocahontas blood" streamed through this mestizo's veins, Santa Cruz was as much an object of Tudor's diplomacy as was La Mar. In early 1827, during the uncertain hiatus between Bolívar's departure and the complete break between Peruvian nationalists and the Liberator, Tudor sequestered himself with Santa Cruz in a private dinner and blasted away at his favorite tyrant, Simón Bolívar. The constitution dictated by the Liberator should be junked and replaced by one that was more liberal.

"What do you think General Santa Cruz?"

"Well," said the man of Bolivia and descendant of an Inca princess, weighing his words carefully, "I should not be considered as absolutely committed to the administration of General Bolívar. I am, of course, only an instrument of the people and if the public voice calls for a revision of affairs relating to the constitution, then I cannot act otherwise than to summon a Congress to decide."[39]

Tudor considered the thrust of Santa Cruz's thoughts and felt emboldened to attack the Liberator himself. "You must cleanse yourself of his power as rapidly and thoroughly as possible, Sir. He is a tyrant and a despot. Suffer no illusions about his momentary absence from Peru. He shall return to conquer and his authoritarian nature will corrupt us all once again. Now is the time to act!"

But Tudor the Yankee had fallen into an invisible but powerful web woven by the charismatic Bolívar. The Liberator's spirit permeated the souls of many Latin American patriots in a way unperceivable by the consul from the United States. Santa Cruz knew that, rationally, Tudor was correct. But the Bolivarian magic was based on no rational principle.

"You are in errour Mr. Tudor. I know General Bolívar thoroughly. He is only anxious to get rid of all command and retire to private life. He deserves it sir."[40]

Who was right? Bolívar never did return to Peru, but he remained extremely active in the national affairs of Colombia, Ecuador, and Venezuela almost to his death from tuberculosis in 1830. Indeed, within a year of Tudor's dinner with Santa Cruz, Peru and Colombia were at war over boundaries and problems inherited from Bolívar.

In spite of the unsuccessful attempt to disabuse Santa Cruz about the Bolivian threat (a threat of which Santa Cruz may have been well aware but was unwilling to discuss frankly with Tudor), Tudor and Santa Cruz were cordial. When Tudor discovered that Santa Cruz wished to place three of his nephews in schools abroad, preferably in the United States, Tudor took over with enthusiasm, especially as Santa Cruz made it clear that he wished his nephews to be educated with "an American and not European sympathy."[41] Tudor immediately suggested West Point as one of the best schools in the nation. He went further. He offered to ask the president, John Quincy Adams, to place them in the military academy if it was in his power to do so. Tudor assured Santa Cruz that if Adams could, he would. Tudor also asked his good friend, Commodore Isaac Hull, who had replaced Charles Stewart as commanding officer of the American squadron in 1824, if he would be so kind as to transport the three young men on the frigate United States when she returned home in the near future.

Finally, Tudor explained himself to Clay: "I hope I have not been indiscreet in speaking in this measured manner, but it seems to me good policy to encourage the sending of a few of their young men to our country, to maintain hereafter our share of influence with the rising generation of Peru."[42] Periodically, Tudor noted, young men were sent from Peru to England or France to be educated. Tudor could suffer England. Those who went to France, on the other hand, usually received their education at Jesuit schools. Tudor, quite possibly speaking as a good Congregationalist, was appalled at the prospect: "It is our duty on loftier grounds even than those of national policy to counteract the efforts, and assist in producing examples of more liberal instructions."[43] Train the younger generation in your ways, and their sympathies as adults and leaders may very well flow from that experience. One can be sure that Tudor knew he was invoking nothing less than a maxim that had guided the Jesuits for centuries.

Tudor's relations with Isaac Hull were excellent, a fact that made for harmony between the consul and the commodore. The situation contrasted most vividly from an earlier period when the U.S. special agent, Prevost, attacked Commodore Stewart for his allegedly pro-royalist decisions.

Hull, like many captains, brought his wife along during his tour of duty, and she in turn induced her younger sister to come and keep her company. The comely girl made a favorable impression on Bolívar—who always had an eye out for attractive women—which certainly helped to smooth social relations in 1824 and 1825 between the American naval representative and the Liberator.[44] Tudor, an old bachelor, probably frowned on Bolívar the libertine, but in the late stages of the Wars of Independence, Bolívar was still very much preferred over the Spanish by the Americans.

The American insistence on maintaining a strict neutrality was perhaps the greatest single issue in the waning years of the Wars of Independence. Stewart, Hull, and Tudor all objected to the illegality of the blockades erected by the various patriot governments. For a blockade to be effective, they argued, it had to exist in fact as well as in name. This capability the Peruvian navy patently did not possess. One of Tudor's and Hull's constant pleas to Washington was for more ships to protect American commerce from depredations. Tudor was very clear on this point.

> The three vessels we have here are inadequate to the service that is required of them. An instance of it has occurred within the last two days. Admiral Martin Jorge Guise has turned away American vessels [from Callao] and ordered them to Huacho. Come. Hull has no vessel to

send after them as the *Dolphin* is at Valparaiso and *Peacock* at the Inter-
medios (while another sloop of war is wanted to watch Chiloe and one
to protect our commerce at Guayaquil and its vicinity). This conduct of
Admiral Guise is unreasonable, because it is absurd to say that he blockades the port, when he is leaving it half the time.[45]

All the various claims made by Americans caught up in the Peruvian navy's blockades were not settled until 1841 with the conclusion
of a claims convention between the two countries. Therefore, while
the warfare between royalists and patriots effectively ended with
Ayacucho in December 1824 (although General Rodil would hold out
at Callao until January 1826 and thus continue to create problems in
the harbor area), the repercussions of the era persisted for over fifteen
years. They served to remind Americans and Peruvians that serious
differences existed on the nature of blockades and the question of
proper indemnification—legal and financial differences of some substance.

Tudor was not only busy protecting American commercial enterprises but also interested in extending American commerce with Peru
and in building up the forces on naval station to better serve that end.
He traveled about the country after the effective end of hostilities in
December 1824, trekking far back into the Andes to ascertain the state
of affairs for himself.[46] In this he was simply following precedents set
by John Prevost, who also took advantage of the cessation of hostilities to nose about the potential markets in Peru. Early in January
1825, Prevost took passage on the *Dolphin* for the port of Quilca in the
south of Peru. From there he traveled inland to Arequipa and then
up-country to the ancient Inca capital of Cuzco in order to "have some
view of the Interior and its commerce."[47]

Tudor was emphatic on two points regarding the increase of U.S.
commerce with Peru. If "it be an object with the government to expand our commerce with these countries and to increase the consumption of our manufactures, . . . two objects must be attended to:
first, to give every facility to the transportation of specie in our ships-
of-war, and secondly by a new arrangement of our naval force, to
keep a ship constantly going and coming between the U.S. and South
America."[48] As it stood in 1824, American merchants were almost
totally dependent upon English ships of war for intelligence and the
transport of specie, a situation that both Tudor and the American
naval commanders looked upon with disfavor. The sluggish com-

munications between the United States and Peru frustrated Tudor, and he constantly harped on the subject:

> We are yet without any recent intelligence from home, and are looking for some arrivals with anxiety. Since December [1825] we have no regular intelligence and know but little of our national affairs which are more interesting to us than any others. For nearly eight months we have only had a straggling newspaper or letter. To all the officers of our nation here, this want of communication is painful, and extremely injurious to our mercantile interests. I allude to this subject to reiterate in the most earnest manner the expediency of establishing a regular communication thro' the Isthmus, on which I have so frequently written.[49]

In spite of the languorous state of communications and the smallness of the naval squadron, American merchants were doing a good business in Peru in the mid-1820s. Tudor, in fact, found himself stretched by the demands of his consulship and in early 1825 named two young vice-consuls to help him tend to the business. Stanhope B. Prevost, son of Judge Prevost, was appointed vice-consul for Lima while Tudor traveled in the interior. Alfred Cobb took on the same title at the port of Arica. Both men had resided in South America for some years and spoke Spanish fluently, and Tudor had great hopes.[50] At the end of their first six months on duty, young Prevost and Cobb rendered their reports. Tudor, a literary stylist and passionate reporter, was somewhat disappointed: "These reports do not give so many particulars as I could wish, but as the office affords no emolument, I cannot expect of them to employ the time and expense that would be necessary to make it more exact."[51]

By 1826 Peru was emerging as one of the major states of South America, and formal recognition by the United States was in order. Thus, on May 2, 1826, James Cooley of Pennsylvania was named by Secretary of State Henry Clay as the first chargé d'affaires to Peru. Cooley did not arrive in Peru until 1827 and by February 1828 had died of a bilious attack that overcame him in five days.[52] Nonetheless, Clay's instructions to Cooley indicate something of the American character in 1826.

Clay wished to know about Peru's physical condition and about the new nation's moral and political character, personal as well as institutional. What of her foreign relations, boundaries, and relations with Mexico, Colombia, Bolivia, and Chile? Where did her revenues originate? What were the army and navy like? What were the prospects of a republican constitution? What did Peru produce, presently and formerly? What were her relations with Europe, especially Great Britain, France, and Spain? Were the possibilities of increased commerce with the United States strong? Peru possessed a large percentage of Indians (styled "aborigines" by Clay). Had they made advances in civilization? Did they abide by their own laws or those of the former viceroyalty and now republic? Was there a wide distribution of civil rights? Did many or few participate in government? Did the Peruvians have "a taste for and sense of the value of property?"[53] Had progress been made among the aborigines in their conversion to Christianity? Not simple questions, concerned as they were with the nature of property, government, the economy, Indians, and religion—all of great interest if one were to form a realistic impression of this new country.

The instructions Clay issued to Cooley were dated November 1826. Tudor had in fact anticipated one of Clay's questions in the following dispatch, dated August 1826. It was the type of opinion expressed by the consul to which the secretary by now must have become accustomed.

> A predilection for republican governments and a sympathy towards all those in favour of them, is I suppose natural to all Americans: It is however necessary to admit, that Peru is singularly destitute of the requisite character for sustaining an elective republic. The Spaniards and their adherents held all the offices in the country; and these being all dead or banished, few men capable of any branch of administration remain. Most of the leading men are monarchists, and persons who had so long lived under the double oppression of Spanish colonial government and the Inquisition, could hardly be expected to have any republican ideas or habits. The most that could have been done at the outset, would have been to have administered a republican system in a monarchical spirit, preparing the people gradually for the unbiased exercise of the elective franchise and other civil rights. Had General Bolívar been governed by that virtuous ambition, which the world in conformity to his protestations of disinterestedness had given him credit for, such a system might have been safely commenced in Peru. There were several individuals of fine talents and pure character, and popular in the country, who would have been adequate to its administration.[54]

Tudor indulged his anti-Bolivarian prejudice here, but his views on the future of a pacific, republican Peru were prophetic. Similar opinions were voiced by later American representatives to Peru, who were in some instances disgusted by the political chaos swirling about them, in others reflective and genuinely saddened by the plight imposed on the people. None summed up the latter attitude better than James C. Pickett, chargé d'affaires from 1839 to 1845, who wrote to his secretary of state, John C. Calhoun, in 1845:

> I doubt much whether the Spanish Americans have gained anything by their independence, except freedom of commerce, and that they would have had probably before now, even had they continued in a state of colonial dependence. I doubt too their fitness, in general, for a democratic form of government and for democratic institutions; but still they ought to have and might have, something better than the despicable and detestable military despotisms by which they have been so long dishonored and oppressed.[55]

Even though depressed on occasion by these lugubrious reflections on the state of politics, American representatives were almost always quick to offer to mediate Peru's international disputes in the first quarter century after independence. Tudor set the example in 1827 and 1828 when he tried frantically to prevent war between Peru and Colombia.

The feud between these two new countries originated during the viceroyalties, when boundaries between the viceroyalty of Peru and the viceroyalty of New Granada were imprecisely located along the unexplored upper reaches of the Amazon. The Wars of Independence only increased the tension between the two. Colombian troops lent massive assistance in the liberation of Peru, and Colombia wished to be properly compensated. Peru, however, did not agree with the formulas for remuneration. Furthermore, when Bolívar and Sucre were being attacked by the Peruvian press in 1827 for their monarchical, dictatorial tendencies (Sucre being guilty mainly for loyally supporting Bolívar), and Colombians and Bolivians felt an even greater estrangement from Peru. Guayaquil in Ecuador was also a bone of contention between Peru and Colombia, who both claimed territorial rights to the major port and its province. Finally, the liberal faction in Peru was sympathetic to liberals in Colombia who wished to depose the conservative Liberator. What better way to accomplish this end than by defeating him in war?[56]

Tudor threw himself into the widening breach with energy, arguing that a war between Peru and Colombia spelled more hardship for both with little to be gained by either. He lobbied hard with President La

Mar and Francisco Xavier Luna Pizarro, a priest and close friend of La Mar's who was one of the most rabid anti-Bolivarians in Peru. Tudor and Luna Pizarro certainly shared a common view of the Liberator. The consul and the Peruvian leaders met almost daily for a short while in late 1827. Tudor was at his most persuasive, and the Peruvians were vulnerable.

Tudor argued that mediation should be sought not only from the United States but also from England and even Mexico. The ravages of war must be prevented. La Mar balked. Who would listen to an overture from a country whose fortunes had fallen low, which was the victim of such strange disasters, and whose finances were in a shambles? Who would listen to a country that could not even pay her debts and was in the throes of another constitutional crisis?[57] Tudor persisted. Peru had nothing to lose and everything to gain. At length, La Mar and Luna Pizarro reluctantly relented and agreed to submit the dispute to mediation from the United States and England.

The meticulous Tudor oversaw all stages of the proceedings, at one point even suggesting to the Peruvians the name of the most qualified individual in their foreign ministry for drawing up the solicitation for mediation. Even his good friends balked at this level of meddling.[58]

He also lobbied heavily among highly placed friends in England and the United States. Tudor was aware that the initiatives he was taking were extraordinary, but, as usual, he was confident in his stand: "I have taken steps of considerable delicacy, but they must be considered as the acts of a private individual. I hope the President may not be dissatisfied with my conduct; certain, I am, that if the situation of these countries . . . were fully understood, both the U.S. and England would not only offer their mediation, but if necessary accompany it with an alternative that would compel its acceptance."[59]

The United States, however, was unwilling to mediate unless both parties sought their good offices, and Colombia was unwilling to do so. Besides, communication between the west coast of South America and Washington was so poor that it was almost guaranteed to frustrate Tudor's initiatives.[60] By the time Henry Clay formally responded to the Peruvian overture, Colombia and Peru had been at war for half a year.

Thus nothing came of Tudor's effort. By 1830 the war was over, settled largely on a *status quo ante bellum* basis, with the exception that neither Colombia nor Peru received Guayaquil, which joined Quito in separating as the new nation of Ecuador. Tudor sailed for home that same year, stopping in at Rio while his ship replenished. There, within sight of Sugarloaf Mountain, the Yankee from Massachusetts caught a fever. He was dead within a few days.

Chargés and Caudillos

Meanwhile, Samuel Larned, who had served for several years in Chile as legation secretary and then as chargé d'affaires before being transferred to Peru as the new chargé, was kept extremely busy by an ever-changing political situation in Peru. La Mar was overthrown in a coup led by General Augustín Gamarra in 1829, an event initiating a period of military usurpation and caudillismo in Peru that persisted until almost the middle of the century[61] The immediate upshot of Gamarra's coup was born of Gamarra's enmity toward Bolivia's president, Andrés Santa Cruz. Gamarra, *cuzqueño*-born mestizo, resolved to attack Santa Cruz. But before Peru's armies marched, Chile stepped in as mediator in a role that expanded through the nineteenth century—Chile as the arbiter of power in the southern half of the continent.

Larned was injected into this delicate mediation process when asked by the Peruvian foreign minister, Matías León, if the United States would loan the Peruvian government the services of a vessel to transport the Chilean mediator, then in Lima, to Islay in the south. Larned appealed to Commodore Charles C. B. Thompson, who was in command of the Pacific squadron. Thompson agreed to make the *Dolphin* available, and the result of the Chilean mediation was successful, certainly in part due to the timely assistance of the United States representatives. That the Peruvian foreign minister had asked Larned to perform the favor speaks eloquently of Larned's active disposition to help. Long experience in Chile had sensitized the chargé to the Latin American temperament. He noted, by way of self-congratulation but certainly not erroneously, that he had "only to add . . . that the service therein rendered to this government, has been very gratefully felt by it; . . . and which repeated acts of kindness, and manifestations of friendly feelings cannot but have a favourable influence upon our relations here—as well as in conciliating towards us the good will and respect of this people."[62] However, the next time Larned played his hand at mediating, he drew no wild cards.

The occasion was the creation in 1836 of a confederation between Bolivia and Peru and under the leadership of Santa Cruz. The process of coup and countercoup that led to the confederation is tedious to recount and need only concern us here in how it affected the development of United States—Peruvian relations. Basically, Santa Cruz had taken advantage of rivalries among Peruvian caudillos to realize his dream of a united Peru and Bolivia. To this goal Chile objected strenuously. Not only would the confederation upset the emerging balance of power in the continent, but Chile was adamant on two economic issues. First, Peru must pay off old debts contracted during the Wars of Independence, when José de San Martín, with Chilean and Argentine troops, first liberated Peru from Spanish rule and set the stage for the Peruvian declaration of independence. And second, a commercial treaty signed by Peru and Chile in 1835, a treaty which was very favorable to Chile and had been nullified by the Santa Cruz government, must be reinstated.[63]

One of the most incendiary incidents to trigger the war occurred in July 1836. A former president of Chile, General Ramón Freire, was allowed to launch an insurrectionary expedition from Peru against Chile.[64] Whether or not Santa Cruz actively blessed this act of gross interference is a question that, will probably never be entirely settled. That Freire was allowed to purchase and outfit two vessels bought from the Peruvian government and then embark on his expedition for Chile is indisputably true. The expedition proved futile. One of the crews mutinied before reaching Chile, while the other vessel was captured by loyal elements of the Chilean navy conveniently embarked—and disguised—on the ship that had first mutinied.

The Chileans struck swiftly in the face of this brazen attempt to overthrow their government. Two vessels were dispatched from Valparaíso north to Callao with orders to cut out Peru's warships in Callao in retaliation for the Freire raid, however botched its results. The Chilean *Aquiles* and her companion *Colo-Colo* were much more efficient. Showing their colors, they arrived in Callao harbor on August 21 under the pretext of a friendly visit. They were received as such by the Peruvian authorities. That same night the Chileans shucked their disguise and went to work. Several boatloads of armed Chilean sailors and marines easily captured the *Arequipeño*, the *Peruviana*, and the *Santa Cruz* in a surprise attack.[65]

Santa Cruz was outraged. He immediately arrested the Chilean consul general, Fortuno Lavalle, and seized all Chilean property he could lay hands on. Larned was shocked by the Chilean action, and, fearing an imminent threat of war, he dressed at dawn and hurried down to see Santa Cruz as early "as propriety would allow, in order, if possible, to prevent this result, and thus use my endeavours to prevent a rupture."[66] Larned was on excellent terms with Santa Cruz, having dined with the president only a few days earlier in celebration of his inauguration. The "Supreme Protector"—Santa Cruz's title as grand overseer of the confederation—made special mention of his North American friend at the banquet. In the presence of sixty or more guests, including all the members of the diplomatic corps and ministers of state, Larned reported that Santa Cruz expressed "pleasure at seeing [him] still in Peru."[67]

Hurrying in the chill of the early morning, Larned crossed paths with Santa Cruz's private secretary, sent by the president to seek out the American consul. Larned entreated Santa Cruz not to take any hostile acts "calculated to involve the two countries at war."[68] Let the Chileans explain their acts; perhaps cooler heads could still prevail. Santa Cruz listened closely to his friend. The order to arrest Lavalle was already being executed. Did the American have reason to hope? Santa Cruz did not wish for war with Chile. He wished to consolidate his position. Besides, war with Chile would almost certainly mean war with Argentina, which would seize the opportunity to grab some of the Bolivian territory promised to her by Bolívar over a decade ago. Larned's presence forced Santa Cruz to consider the impetuosity of his act. He ordered his aide-de-camp to countermand the order to seize Lavalle. By now the Chilean was already locked up, but he was released soon thereafter as the reverse order from the president came through, perhaps causing the gaolers to wonder about the sanity of their president. Lavalle then demanded his passports and left Lima for Callao. Not finding the *Aquiles* present in Callao roadsteads, Lavalle asked his old acquaintance Larned if he could board an American warship for a short while. The American commodore, Alexander Scammell Wadsworth, was just then on the road from Callao to Lima and thus could not be consulted. Captain Deacon refused Lavalle this permission without express orders from Wadsworth. Larned exploded at this idiocy, although it was well within the prerogatives of naval commanders to act independently. Lavalle slipped aboard a French man-of-war, the *Flora*, before finding the *Aquiles* and returning to Chile.

By late 1836 the mood in Chile was obstinate and bellicose. Yet, even then, Santa Cruz made one last effort to avert the conflict by seeking the mediation of the three major chargés—those from England, France, and the United States—in Lima. Larned was at the heart of this effort as well, although he would have preferred to have been long gone by 1836. He had been applying for leave for several years, and now that it was granted, he could not depart, feeling his presence in Peru was imperative. He should have saved his efforts and gone home. In late December, determined to break up the confederation and the threat it represented to Chilean interests, Chile declared war.

The issues, in fact, went too deep for Larned's intercessions to have any real effect. The boundaries and alliances of the newly emerged nations had not yet jelled, and several major wars in the nineteenth century, including this one, were to plague many peoples before the currents stabilized.

Yet, like Tudor's before him, Larned's efforts to preserve the peace between the warring new "Republiks" represented the familiar mixture of altruism and commercialism that so often motivated American representatives abroad in this period. To preserve the peace was, of course, a noble goal, one that men such as Tudor and Larned were completely sincere in advocating not only by their words but also by their acts. Of no less importance were their efforts to preserve and enhance American commerce with Peru and South America in general. There was nothing inconsistent in these two goals, as Larned cogently observed on the eve of the war: "They [Chile and Peru] may do each other much harm, but no good can come to either, from so mad an undertaking. Foreign commerce will undoubtedly be made to suffer, in such an event, from blockades and embargoes, etc.—and, in fact, such has already been the case in Chile."[69]

What grieved Larned most was the war's threat to his main mission: the cultivation of a good commercial climate between the United States and Peru. The ultimate intention was to conclude between the two countries a commercial treaty based on the most-favored-nation principle. He had originally been transferred in the late 1820s from Chile to Peru for that very purpose. By early 1836, Larned felt he had gone a long way toward fulfilling that mission.

It is a source of gratification to me to reflect, that the principal object of my transfer to this Legation from Chile,—namely, of relieving our cotton fabrics from the prohibition under which they labored, has been accomplished;—and that they now find admission here on more favorable terms than ever. That something, also has been done for our flour;—which, notwithstanding the active opposition and powerful influence of Chile, and her agents and merchants here, has, at no time during my residence in Peru, *in point of fact*, been surcharged with a higher relative duty than the wheat of that country. Attempts of the kind have been repeatedly made, but they have been invariably met and defeated.[70]

The problem was not only wheat and flour but all American commodities and products, such as tobacco and cotton textiles, and their entry into Peru. American merchants—not only in Peru but also in other Latin American nations—felt that they were being discriminated against in favor of nationals from other Latin American countries. The merchants doing business in Peru especially felt the keen competition from Chile and, to a lesser extent, from Mexico and Ecuador. While Larned's objective was to secure the status of most favored nation, Peru's goal was to protect herself from the better-equipped and better-organized merchants of North America and Europe. One way was to create cordial and reciprocal ties with its immediate neighbors, those with whom it truly traded, as opposed to the great commercial powers with whom traffic was commonly one-sided. José María de Pando, a conservative *limeño* serving as minister of foreign affairs in 1832, described this philosophy very candidly to the aggressive American chargé.

According to Pando, Larned said, Peru had nothing to gain from a commercial arrangement with one of the

> great commercial and maritime powers. . . . There could be no real and effective reciprocity between the United States and Peru;—inasmuch as a Peruvian vessel never visited that country, and she [Peru] had nothing for us to take away but silver and gold. . . . Pando maintained that it was not the policy of Peru to form treaties of commerce with the great commercial and maritime powers;—and, more particularly, upon the principles of an equality and reciprocity that would be merely nominal; or of the most favoured nation. Their trade with those countries, being entirely passive, would be best regulated by legislation, agreeably to circumstances.[71]

Pando's intransigence stymied Larned, but he continued to press the case for a treaty and to protect American merchants and their trade as the moments offered.

The competition between Chilean wheat and American flour dominated Larned's attention in the first half of the 1830s. Chilean wheat had certain advantages that Americans could not overcome. One, of course, was distance. American flour had to travel all the way from the eastern coast of the United States, down the length of the Atlantic, round the tempestuous Cape Horn, and then more than halfway back north toward the equator. Furthermore, after the difficult transit from North America to the Pacific, most ships liked to stop in at Valparaíso to rest, refit, and revictual. It was a natural port at which to recoup one's energies, and the Chileans thus tended to control, indirectly, the traffic from Europe and North America to the western coast of Latin America. Furthermore, Peru was a natural trading partner of Chile, selling sugar and other products to her southern neighbor in exchange for wheat and other Chilean commodities. However, Peruvians tended to *prefer* American flour. Larned pointedly asked Mariano de Sierra, the minister of foreign affairs in 1836, to take the taste test. One "has only to appeal to those who have eaten the excellent bread made at Chorillos, during the late bathing season, exclusively of North American flour."[72] But the Chileans got the upper hand in 1834–35, when they negotiated a most favorable commercial treaty with Peru. It was ratified by the renegade government led by the antiforeign Felipe Salaverry (the man who had plunged Peru into the chaos that prompted landing the marines in the incident recalled earlier). When Santa Cruz overthrew Salaverry and defeated all his other enemies, Larned went to work once more.

Santa Cruz was indeed a friend of the United States, and Larned took the main chance. Following his initial instructions, he sought a commercial treaty modeled on an earlier one signed between Colombia and the United States. When the treaty between Chile and Peru concluded in 1835–36 was nullified, the way was opened for one with the United States. Precisely at this "present fortunate juncture," a treaty of peace, friendship, commerce, and navigation was negotiated between the United States and Peru. Larned was extremely pleased and could barely contain his enthusiasm, preferring to draw the evidence of others to throw light on his own actions: "Suffice it to say, that the Treaty is considered, by our commercial fellow citizens here, as (what it really is) a most favorable one; and as essential to the security and advantageous prosecution of our trade to this coast."[73] It was ratified by both nations and was in effect by 1839. Larned finally left Peru in January 1837, exhausted by his endeavors, returning home to Rhode Island after more than two decades on the west coast of South America.

Within two years of his departure, the confederation was cracked apart by Chile, Santa Cruz was deposed, and the treaty of peace, friendship, commerce, and navigation between Peru and the United States was broken by an act of the Peruvian congress meeting at Huancayo on November 23, 1839. That dismaying action highlighted another series of problems plaguing the good relations between the United States and Peru in the 1830s and 1840s: recognition of de facto governments and the validity of their actions through successive coups and revolutions.

When James C. Pickett was assigned to Lima in 1839 as the new chargé d'affaires, he faced a quandary of sorts. Pickett carried accreditation addressed to the Peru-Bolivia confederation, but by the time he reached Lima, Santa Cruz had been overthrown and the confederation was defunct. What to do? Present papers to an entity no longer in existence, or await new orders from the State Department, a matter that could involve a delay of many months or even years? The problem went deeper, for the basic issue was whether Santa Cruz had been a de jure as well as de facto governor of Peru. Subsequent Peruvian governments—and there were many between 1839 and 1845—denied the legitimacy of the Santa Cruz government and thus felt perfectly correct in denying the legitimacy of its acts, such as the commercial treaty concluded between Peru and the United States in 1836. From that principle stemmed the revocation of the treaty in 1839. To the United States, on the other hand, the unilateral revocation of the treaty was unacceptable. Further complicating the differences was the fact that the Peruvian government did not *officially* communicate its revocation of the treaty to the United States until 1847. When Joaquín José de Osma, the first Peruvian minister to Washington, came to the United States in 1846, one of his purposes was to renegotiate the treaty that the Peruvians had renounced seven years before. In fact, a new treaty was drawn up and finally ratified by both countries in 1851, but the United States did not abandon its insistence on the validity of acts committed by de facto governments.[74]

It was through this position that the United States found a way out of having to discriminate between de jure and de facto governments. The solution was fairly simple. *All* governments would be recognized as de facto governments, and the United States would hold all of their actions as legal and binding. This position was defined best by Richard K. Crallé, acting secretary of state, in instructions sent to John A. Bryan, the American chargé who replaced Pickett in 1845.

> The United States claim no right to inquire into, or, in any manner to interfere with the internal affairs of other powers. In their relations with them they look only to the *actual* [my italics] government, as it may exist, without undertaking to inquire into the means by which it has been established, the validity of its title or the tenure of its authority.

Whoever may be in the actual possession and exercise of the supreme power, whether by the consent of the governed, or by force, must be regarded as the government *de facto* of the country, authorized to contract obligations in behalf of the community of which it is the head, and as such, liable for all injuries by its agents or citizens on the rights of others.[75]

Furthermore, said Crallé, "Governments are to be regarded as moral persons whose liabilities remain unimpaired through all the revolutions to which they may be subjected. No change of rulers or modifications of forms can exempt them from their liabilities, or bar the reclamations of the injured."[76]

The delineation of these working principles was meant to guide negotiations on more than the controversial commercial treaty. Also at stake were several hundred thousand dollars in claims against the Peruvian government which had originated during the Wars of Independence. Numerous claims had been filed by American merchants and shippers citing systematic and illegal depredations committed by the patriots during the wars. Some were thrown out, but many were recognized as legitimate, and the United States had been trying to collect on them since the end of the wars.

The claims convention, the first one between Peru and the United States, was finally signed on March 17, 1841. Peru agreed to pay $300,000 in settlement of the debt in ten annual installments of $30,000 each. The convention was not ultimately ratified and proclaimed by both nations until January 18, 1847.[77] Between 1841 and 1847, the two countries sparred with increasing acrimony over this convention: the United States was trying to hold Peru to the original timetable (payments to begin January 1, 1844; interest at 4 percent to begin January 1, 1842), while Peru claimed public penury. The three American chargés in Lima between 1841 and 1847—Pickett (1839–45), Bryan (1845), and Albert Gallatin Jewett (1845–47)—were all bedeviled and frustrated by Peru's failure to comply with the terms of the convention. Compounding the problem were another war—this time with Bolivia, in 1841—and a truly depressing string of coups in the early 1840s that turned Peruvian government into a turnstile.

Jewett, a prickly lawyer from Bangor, Maine, grew so frustrated that he recommended direct action. In October 1845 he sent notes to Stanhope Prevost, by now the consul at Lima, and to Lieutenant Neil M. Howison of the United States Navy, commander of the sloop of war *Shark*, and asked them for an opinion on how seizure of the

Guano islands by the United States might help expedite the payment of the claims. Prevost responded that it would, surely, provide leverage, but the consul had lived long in Peru and was not as impetuous or insensitive as Jewett; he suggested postponing such drastic action. "Let us wait until the Peruvian political situation stabilizes a bit, as I'm sure it is bound to. Then, from political stability will flow economic stability and a natural increase in the prosperity of the country. The payment of the debt will be easily taken care of by this natural increase," the long time Peruvian resident told the Yankee lawyer.

Lieutenant Howison was not as philosophical or wedded to Peru as Prevost. In fact, he went Jewett one step further: "I don't know, Sir, how much could be raised from the Guano islands given the rapid fluctuations in demand for that product and other factors I am only barely aware of as a naval officer. But, I have observed that this government derives most of its revenues from the customs houses. Seize these, Sir, force the government to its knees, and then collect." Although the islands were not seized and the claims later settled amica bly, Howison unwittingly forecasted a forthcoming era in United States foreign policy.

His recommendations however, were not totally out of keeping with the practices of the great powers in the early nineteenth century. England and France tended to behave more forthrightly when their interests were directly threatened, and several U.S. chargés and consuls admired this directness. The fact that English or French actions were reported in great detail testified to the occasional frustrations of the American chargés with the more evenhanded, egalitarian policy that flowed from Washington.

During the last months of the nearly anarchical Salaverry regime in 1835–36, Gallic pride was stepped on, and the Peruvians were forced to abjure. Salaverry's foreign minister, Manuel Ferryros, irritated by the French chargé's arrogance, told the Frenchman that henceforth no further official communications would be received from him. Ferryros soon asked the French government to recall their representative and name somebody "more courteous in his official intercourse, and better acquainted with the duties of his situation."[78] Incensed, the French diplomat left Lima and boarded one of his warships in Callao, whereupon the commanding officer told Ferryros that since he would not traffic with the chargé, he would have to deal with him. Ferryros, not about to submit, curtly informed the French naval officer that a mere commander of a warship had no authority to speak for France, and Peru would not communicate with him either. That was a mistake, as Larned laconically noted: "As it was known to these Authorities, that the French naval force [unlike the American, Larned was most certainly thinking] in this sea is completely subject to the control of the Diplomatic Agent, and that he would enforce the rights of his fellow citizens and action, and was well disposed to do so, if necessary,—this demand brought them [the Peruvians] to their senses."[79] Mollified by the apology, the French chargé withdrew his request for his passports and returned to Lima, no doubt in a high mettle.

The English were equally prompt in dealing with insults and abuses, perceived or real. During the late stages of the war between Chile and the Peru-Bolivia confederation in 1838, a troop of Chilean soldiers jumped an English physician making his rounds near Lima. The Chileans were enforcing a decree to seize all horses, and the good doctor refused. They lanced him and took his horse, leaving him wounded by the side of the road. The English chargé and admiral demanded immediate satisfaction for this outrage. To ensure compliance, the old salt pulled his squadron into the Callao harbor, rolled out the cannon, and dropped anchor alongside the Chilean fleet. The prospect of trading shot with the legendary English fleet was menace enough. General Manuel Bulnes, in command of the Chilean army in Lima, promised immediate measures to punish the perpetrators and make restitution.[80]

Edwin Bartlett, who served as acting chargé in 1838–39 and had been a merchant in Peru for some time, unabashedly admired the use of force: "A display of force and a determination to cause our rights to be respected, will save much trouble; and teach nations which are wanting in a regard for moral obligations, that our maxim is a faithful performance of our conventional stipulations, and an unalterable resolution to exact a strict compliance in return,—*I know this people well.—when turf will not bring them down, we must throw stones* [my italics]."[81] If Bartlett was pugnacious, he still possessed the deftness to be politic. Jewett, on the other hand, was acid-tongued in private and in public. In fact, his behavior was so outrageous that it prompted his recall; he was the only American diplomat to Peru to suffer this indignity in the first half of the nineteenth century.

Jewett's self-righteous arrogance was guaranteed to offend diplomatic sensibilities and etiquette. He spoke intemperately and scornfully of the Peruvian congress, especially vilifying one particular resolution of the claims convention of 1841. He refused to address officials by their proper titles and generally despised Peruvians. He arrived in Lima late in 1845 and was recalled by Secretary of State James Buchanan on March 17, 1847, after repeated requests made by the Peruvian government.[82]

In a letter to Jewett, Buchanan was as explicit as his office would allow. Diplomats loathed by the governments that host them are rendered ineffective, and the Peruvian government's obvious distaste for Jewett made him unfit for the office.

> The Peruvian Minister complains that you have not according to custom, given him the title Excellency. If such be the fact, I regret it. This you may consider as a small matter in itself, but yet such breaches of established etiquette often give greater offence than real injuries. This is emphatically the case in regard to the Spanish race. They have been peculiarly tenacious in requiring the observance of such forms. However ridiculous this may appear to us, it is with them a matter of substance. . . . It is a primary duty of a diplomatic agent to cultivate the good will of the authorities of the country to which he is accredited. Without this, his usefulness must be very much impaired. It is impossible that you can reform either the morals or the politics of Peru, and as this is no part of your mission, prudence requires that you should not condemn them in public conversations. You ought to take its institutions and its people just as you find them and endeavor to make the best of them for the benefit of your own country, so far as this can be done consistently with the national interest and honor.[83]

Buchanan invoked an interesting principle: "It is impossible that you can reform either the morals or the politics of Peru." This principle was subject to some alteration as the century proceeded and finally crumpled when the United States intervened directly in the affairs of Colombia to create the Republic of Panama. But before midcentury, the policy of the United States was clearly to be neutral and noninterventionist, to prefer the almost apolitical and practical recognition of actual governments, with little reference to their means and sources of power. (An exception was, of course, Mexico.)

Bartlett and Jewett represented a fair sampling of American public opinion, permeated as it was by the spirit of manifest destiny that evolved into full-blown imperialism at the end of the century. Still, other American chargés of the period, especially Larned, Pickett, and John Randolph Clay, who succeeded Jewett and served until 1860, were considerably more disciplined and professional as they coped with irregular and frustrating political disturbances. Larned suffered more, personally and officially, than any other chargé, largely because the last period of his service fell during the uproarious year preceding Santa Cruz's takeover in early 1837. Lima and Callao verged on anarchy: "Forced contributions, impressments of men, horses, etc. are actively going on; and every species of vexation being practiced. . . . The roads, even the immediate vicinity, and up to the very gates of the city,—are infested with banditti;—who rob and plunder, indiscriminately, all they meet."[84] Nobody was safe. The British consul general, in company with an English Lord and a French count, was robbed at gunpoint on his way back from a day at the seashore. The "banditti" left the lord, the count, and the consul in their skivvies to walk back to Lima.

In several instances U.S. citizens were seized, sometimes to be conscripted, sometimes for conspiring with one or another of the many revolutionary parties competing for power. Larned managed to spring all of them from their troubles, but he felt that his fellow countrymen were sometimes compromising their neutrality. He warned them against abusing their privileged status, and, with one exception, his admonitions were heeded. The exception was Edwin Bartlett of Alsop and Company, who sold one thousand muskets to the Salaverry government "at a time, too, when they [the muskets] were most wanted by him [Salaverry] . . . and contrary to my earnest advice, recommendation and remonstrance. . . . It is difficult, in view of such conduct, to exact towards our countrymen all the immunities of neutrality."[85] Ironically, in 1838 Bartlett succeeded to Larned's post in an acting status when Larned's immediate successor, James B. Thornton, died in Peru after having served for less than a year. Bartlett had felt he was hewing to the official line that recognized the legitimacy of *all* de facto governments when he negotiated the sale of the muskets to Salaverry. Larned interpreted his acts otherwise. Both were old Latin American hands, and the heated exchanges between the two on this issue singed a few sensibilities.

Larned especially feared the high-handed, demagogic Salaverry, a fact that certainly made the chargé even more critical of Bartlett's sale of arms to the revolutionary. Even Larned's home was pillaged and some of his servants attacked during the worst months in late 1835, just before the marines landed in December.[86] It was not a happy time, and one can little wonder why Larned welcomed Santa Cruz after surviving the Salaverry-induced terror and chaos, much of it directed against foreigners.

Pickett was caught in a similar political maelstrom in 1843–44. The swift changes of government and the resultant economic and political

disorder prompted a rather unusual declaration made by the six leading foreign envoys in Lima, Pickett included. Entitled "Protocol of a
Conference Signed by the Diplomatic Corps at Lima, at the Legation
of New Granada, June 20, 1844," it was signed by the representatives
from New Granada, the United States, France, England, Belgium,
and Brazil. The preface to the protocol reflected the frustrations of the
foreign community: "Peru is plunged into a state of political anarchy
which no longer permits any one of the parties to be recognized as
exercising complete sovereignty."[87] The envoys held the entire Peruvian nation responsible for past and future damages and injuries to their
nationals. All blockades would be disregarded until the state of affairs
became normal, while the diplomats once again reiterated that any of
their nationals voluntarily taking part in the civil strife of Peru "shall be
condemned more than ever and abandoned to the consequences of their
action."[88] It was a remarkable commentary on the times, although it was
certainly consistent with English and French policy in their relations with
Peru, and that fact rubbed Pickett the wrong way.

Pickett did not think the protocol itself improper but admitted his
error of identifying himself "in any manner with European diplomacy."[89] The long-standing American aversion to being associated
with or fear of somehow being entrapped by European politics surfaced dramatically in Pickett's second thoughts about the protocol. He
became convinced of an error when the English chargé casually mentioned that he regarded all signers of the protocol as "allies" who were
each bound to protect the commerce of the others, "even so far as to
use military force, if necessary."[90] Pickett told his English counterpart
quite frankly that he did not see things that way at all. The English
and French could well protect their own commerce, but New Granada, Belgium, and Brazil did not have even a naval force in the Pacific. Furthermore, even if Pickett *had* been willing to use force, he
could not command the American commodore to do so.

Pickett was, indeed, mortified by the implications of his indiscretion: "I
resolved, though internally, to sign no more protocols. I never liked either the things or the name. Europe is governed by them and I expect
that before long, an attempt will be made by the European Powers to
govern this continent by the same kind of machinery."[91] Perhaps Pickett's imagination was overwrought and the result was exaggeration, but
one often acts more on one's perception of conditions rather than on the
conditions themselves, and Pickett's attitude in any case was markedly
different from that of Bartlett, for example, who admired and would have
emulated the methods of the English and French in the Pacific.

The position of foreigners in Peru, alluded to in the protocol, was, of course, one of the principal concerns of diplomats in the country. Foreigners enjoyed certain privileges that irked Peruvians, and justifiably so. Even the old hand Bartlett, who had spent more than fifteen years in Peru making a handsome living, admitted to the impropriety of favoring foreigners in certain aspects. Foreigners, for example, could take part in the retail trade of Peru and be exempt from the regulations and taxes imposed upon Peruvians. To remove this privilege from foreigners "is only justice to their own Citizens; for hitherto foreigners have been exempt from many taxes paid by Citizens, which has enabled the former to undersell, to the prejudice of the latter. The French who are the principal foreign retailers, resist the right of thus taxing Frenchmen, and may butt into another quarrel similar to those at Mexico and Buenos Ayres."[92]

"Butting" into quarrels between one's own nationals and the host governments could sometimes lead to acrimonious exchanges. In one instance, the French chargé and the Peruvian minister of finance (and later president), General Ramón Castilla, argued heatedly about a loan made by a French citizen to the Santa Cruz government a few days before it was overthrown in 1839. The subsequent government, which Castilla served, refused to pay the interest (2 percent per month, 24 percent per year), although it honored the principal of the loan, about nine thousand dollars.[93] Castilla told the French diplomat not to meddle, and the European perceived an insult in the old general's words. He challenged Castilla on the spot. Although the duel was averted, Pickett thought about the circumstances that had nearly caused the duel and reflected on the debt.

> In such cases, foreign Governments and their agents ought not to interfere, for these transactions cannot come within any reasonable definition of regular and legitimate commerce. They are a species of gambling to which lenders are enticed by the promise of exorbitant interest; and it seems to me, that they are not much more entitled to relief against the non-complying government, not a party to the contract, than that government would be, against the usury. And I suppose, besides, that as a general rule, foreigners can have no claim upon their own Governments, to enforce the execution of their contracts with the Government here, any more than when made with individuals.[94]

The distinction Pickett makes between "gambling" and "legitimate commerce" is, of course, one of judgment and not necessarily one

General Ramón Castilla

with which his predecessors or successors would agree. However, the tendency of American diplomacy with regard to Peru in the second half of the nineteenth century was to follow Pickett's discrimination between risk investments and regular commerce. If one took a gamble with eyes wide open as to the possible consequences (revolution, government bankruptcy, and so forth), then the consequences could not be softened or reversed by government intervention. Where one drew the line between gambling and legitimate commerce (such as was disrupted and violated during the Wars of Independence and which finally was settled by the claims commission of 1841) depended upon the individual and the norms of the age. To Pickett, 24 percent per annum was usury.

Pickett's interests, like those of other American diplomats and consuls in Peru, extended beyond the confines of Peru to the adjacent countries of Bolivia and Ecuador, where American representation was lacking or only intermittent. As late as 1842, for example, Pickett noted the lack of an American consul in Bolivia and recommended that Robert S. Meeks, a respectable merchant from the state of New York with long residence in Bolivia, might be suitable. Pickett suggested the cities of Sucre or Cochabamba as two likely locations.[95] Actually, Larned had named a consul to Bolivia as early as July 1835. Alarmed by the revolutionary circumstances then prevailing and by the fact that "the want of a Consul has been for some time felt there," Larned appointed John H. Polhemus of Pennsylvania, a merchant who had resided at the port of Cobija for six years.[96]

Larned was in fact fascinated by Bolivia. In 1832 he offered to visit the remote highland country to negotiate a commercial treaty. Santa Cruz, an old friend from Larned's Chilean days, was then president of Bolivia and very well disposed toward the United States. Larned suggested not only a commercial treaty but also that the United States might recognize Bolivia. It was about time, Larned breezily noted, and he was free to do all of this and perhaps even more.[97] Unless the president, Andrew Jackson, objected, he would proceed on this mission of diplomacy, goodwill, and commercial promise. However, the president did indeed object.

In 1835 Secretary of State John Forsyth stunned Larned with a letter of reprimand that turned the chargé's ears crimson with embarrassment: "The President regrets that your zeal in the public service should have misled you into a belief that you were authorized to negotiate a commercial treaty with Bolivia."[98] Forsyth pointed out that even Santa Cruz could not enter into negotiations until Bolivia's independence had been recognized by the United States and until the necessary powers to treat were given to a duly authorized person or persons. Larned's improper attempts were met with indulgence only because of Santa Cruz's friendship for Larned and the United States. Furthermore, the

> surprize [sic] of the President of the United States is perhaps still stronger than that of the President of Bolivia. . . . It was certainly not expected by him that you would assume to yourself the right of determining for him, whether, and at what time, and on what basis it was proper to negotiate, and what agent it was proper to employ in the negotiation. It is impossible for the President to overlook such a proceeding on your part, and he has directed me to inform you, that, although he does not doubt the uprightness of your intentions, he deems it his duty to express his disapprobation of your conduct.[99]

So much for personal diplomacy. Even given the long delays in communications and the generous discretion afforded to American representatives on the western coast of South America, one was never too far, in time or place, for reprobation and censure. Larned left for home in January 1837. James B. Thornton, Larned's successor, was appointed chargé not only to Peru (in June 1836) but to Bolivia as well (in July 1836). He was the first American diplomat formally accredited to Bolivia.

Peruvian relations with Ecuador had never been as strained or tempestuous as those with Bolivia. Nonetheless, the politics of her northern neighbor were almost always of interest to Peru, especially since their common borders had never been fixed exactly and were the subject of an interminable number of quarrels and treaties.

Then, in 1845 and 1846, rumors abounded in Peru (as well as in other parts of South America and in the capitals of Europe) that Juan José Flores, the first president of Ecuador and then an exile in Europe, was planning an expedition to place a prince of Spain on a new throne in Ecuador.[100]

The United States had no regular legation in Ecuador until 1848, although James Pickett had made an official visit to Ecuador in 1838 on his way to his post in Lima.[101] A special agent was dispatched in 1845 to discuss Ecuador's assumption of her share of the public debts of the former Gran Colombia, but in 1846–47, the crucial years of the Flores expedition, the United States was without formal representation.[102]

The Flores expedition was, in fact, no chimera. The old general had been recruiting actively among Spain's *hidalguía*, and an army of hundreds, collected about the country in several cities, was ready to go. Ships were bought in Great Britain and were waiting to transport this somewhat anachronistic troop to the South American equatorial zone to recreate a portrait of the past. One would be tempted to dismiss the whole lot as touched with a whiff of the incredible if Napoleon III had not later established a European monarchy (albeit a short-lived one) in Mexico.

Peru, under President Ramón Castilla, acted decisively. Her diplomats in Europe clamored at the chancelleries of England and Spain to block this patently illegal and potentially monstrous arrogation of power, while the United States consul in Lima, Stanhope Prevost (first named, one will recall, as a vice-consul by Tudor in 1826), lobbied hard for the United States government's intercession. Prevost, like Larned and Tudor before him, was on extremely good terms with the leaders of Peru, while the United States chargé, Jewett, was busy hating Peruvians and mocking their institutions. Indeed, when Jewett was recalled in 1847, Prevost was appointed interim chargé on July 27, 1847, and served until December 15, when Jewett's successor, John Randolph Clay, arrived in Peru.

Prevost became the conduit of Castilla's appeals to the United States for some kind of intercession with England and Spain to block the further promotion of the Flores expedition. Prevost reminded Secretary of State Buchanan of the Monroe Doctrine and especially of the passages closing the New World to further interference from nations of the Old World.[103] Prevost and Castilla consulted frequently and often informally. Once, while riding, the old consul met up with the president, who insisted that his good friend join him for breakfast to "converse on the all engrossing topic of the day; viz, this expedition of Flores."[104] The great scheme finally came to naught when the English and the Spanish, under great pressure from several South American nations, pressure that had been coordinated by Castilla, interdicted Flores.

The Flores expedition had served to recall once again the Bolivarian dream of a united South America, manifested this time by Castilla's convocation of a general American congress in Lima in 1847. The immediate objectives were to prevent any occurrence of an expedition like that planned by Flores and to arrange for long-term cooperation in making continental policy and protecting the integrity and independence of Latin American nations.[105] The backdrop to this conference, which met from December 1847 until March 1848, was, of course, the United States war with Mexico.

The Peruvians were ambivalent about the war. First, they viewed the conflict as a brazen example of Yankee manifest destiny and territorial aggrandizement, and they condemned it thoroughly. Second, *because* the United States was involved in a war, the dependence of Peru and other nations upon the United States to help prevent intrusions from Europe was sharply undermined, leaving Peru, Ecuador, and others more vulnerable and exposed.[106]

Castilla nonetheless sought official U.S. participation in the congress, which drew representatives from Colombia, Ecuador, Peru, Bolivia, and Chile. While no United States representative came, the new American chargé, Clay, arrived in Lima two days before the initial convocation. His attitudes toward Peru and the congress were sympathetic but guarded, because American participation might have meant abandoning American "principles of non-interference in the affairs of other nations."[107] One cannot help but wonder what Clay thought of the American invasion of Mexico within the context of American "principles of non-interference," but passions more often than not rule reason in the cycles of history.

While the congress produced only some nonpolitical conventions regarding commerce, maritime rights of neutrals, duties and powers of consuls, and postal matters, it did reinforce Peru's position as a leader in South America, a leadership shared, to be sure, with Colombia, Chile, Argentina, and Brazil but highlighted by Castilla's initiatives in 1847–48.

By the late 1840s Peru was passing into another era. Castilla imposed peace and order politically, while economic prosperity was on the horizon, promised largely by the growing exports of guano but also by a gradually widening economic base that included railroads (the first one built between Callao and Lima in 1850), exports of nitrates, and a sugar boom. Castilla reorganized and expanded Peru's diplomatic corps in this new era. Among the expansions was the establishment of a Peruvian legation to Washington, Joaquín José de Osma being the first Peruvian minister to the United States. He arrived in the spring of 1847, landing at a time of exciting events: the war with Mexico, the tumult over Jewett's obnoxious behavior, the Flores expedition, the wrangling over the claims convention of 1841, and the renegotiation of the commercial treaty of 1836. Osma was replaced in March 1848 by Juan Ignacio de Osma, who served as chargé d'affaires ad interim until 1850 and as minister resident from 1856 to 1858.[108]

Meanwhile, the American chargé in Lima, Clay, settled in and proceeded to serve the longest term of any United States chargé, not leaving Peru until 1860. Clay was a true professional diplomat, if one measures professionalism by time and experience in service. He had previously been assigned to Russia, serving first as secretary of legation and then as chargé, between 1830 and 1837, was posted to Austria between 1838 and 1842, returned to Russia in 1845, and was transferred to Lima in 1847. He also became the first U.S. minister to Peru, receiving the title in 1853. He demanded his passports on October 23, 1860, and left the country, temporarily severing relations between Peru and the United States. But that is another story.

During the first twenty-five years of Peru's national existence, American consuls and diplomats behaved forcefully and in some instances had considerable impact on the course of national and international affairs. They acted as much from their own interpretations of what was right or wrong, what was acceptable or repugnant, and what was or was not in the interests of the United States or not as from principles articulated by and orders received from Washington. Some, such as Larned in the early 1830s, acted too independently and suffered rebuke, while one, Jewett, was simply outrageous in his behavior toward Peruvians and necessitated his recall in 1847. However, most, such as Tudor, Larned, and Prevost, were well liked by Peruvian leaders, who not infrequently sought the advice of their North American friends.

The milieu in which the Americans lived was one of general instability, one that Jorge Basadre beautifully described in the following terms: "Lo normal resulto vivir al margen de la normalidad y fueron escasos, cortos y relativos los periodos de legalidad" (Normal was to live on the margin of normality, and the moments of legality were scarce, short, and relative). To unbending, humorless lawyers such as Jewett, the situation was intolerable and worth nothing more than contempt. To longtime residents such as Prevost, one accommodated to the political instability and enjoyed the beauties and perquisites of everything else Peru offered to the foreigner.

United States Chargés d'Affaires and Consuls in Peru, 1825–1850

William Tudor, consul, 1824–29. First consul appointed to Peru.

James Cooley, chargé, 1826–28. First chargé appointed to Peru. Appointment coincided with recognition of Peru by the United

States. Appointed May 2, 1826; died in Peru of bilious attack, February 1828.

Alfred Cobb, vice-consul at Arica, 1825. Appointed by Tudor.

Stanhope B. Prevost, vice-consul at Lima, 1825. Appointed by Tudor. Prevost was the son of John B. Prevost, special agent of the United States in Peru, Buenos Aires, and Chile, 1818–26. Stanhope Prevost later served as interim chargé in 1847. He also was appointed consul on November 25, 1843, and served in that position until at least 1850.

Samuel Larned, chargé, 1829–36. Larned was transferred from Chile. He left Peru in January 1837 for his home state of Rhode Island.

James B. Thornton, chargé, 1837–38. Named chargé to Peru June 15, 1836, and chargé to Bolivia July 7, 1836, the first one appointed to that country. Thornton died January 25, 1838, probably en route from Valparaíso to Callao.

Edwin Bartlett, acting chargé, 1838–39. Had lived and done business in Peru for fifteen years before 1838.

James C. Pickett, chargé, 1839–45.

John A. Bryan, chargé, 1845.

Albert Gallatin Jewett, chargé, 1845–47. Jewett possessed the unenviable record of being the only chargé recalled during this period.

John Randolph Clay, 1847–60. Became the first minister to Peru in 1853. Was minister when relations between Peru and the United States were ruptured shortly over the case of the *Lizzie Thompson* and the *Georgiana*.

Impossible Job, Impossible Man! Thomas Sumter, Jr., and Diplomatic Relations between the United States and the Portuguese Court in Brazil, 1809–1821

Phil Brian Johnson and Robert Kim Stevens

Mr. Madison has spoiled a . . . cotton planter and only made a clumsy courtier of me.

—Thomas Sumter, Jr.

On the morning of November 29, 1807, an exhausted French army commanded by Marshal Andoche Junot marched into Lisbon and secured Portugal for Bonaparte's Continental System. Only hours before, a reluctant Dom João de Braganza, the prince regent of Portugal, had boarded the *Principe Real* and set sail for Brazil, which, finding itself at the center of the Portuguese empire, was to play temporary host to its dispossessed sovereign for the next fourteen years. The United States welcomed the fugitive court to "our Western Hemisphere" and immediately appointed a minister plenipotentiary to the Portuguese court in Brazil. The new envoy was instructed to negotiate a commercial treaty, collect all information pertinent to the commerce between the two countries, submit any intelligence relative to the growing revolutionary movements throughout Latin America, explain the position of the United States on neutral rights, and, finally promote an amicable relationship between the Braganza government and the United States.[1]

Thomas Sumter, Jr., was the man selected by the United States Department of State for its first major diplomatic appointment to Latin America. For a sensitive diplomatic assignment he was an unusual choice, for he was inept, contentious, boorish, barely literate, and only mildly interested in the post. The appointment seems stranger still when one realizes that the envoy's shortcomings were not unknown to his superiors. He had served briefly, in 1802, as secretary of legation in Paris, but after only a few weeks in this position he began showering the minister, Robert Livingston, with a variety of complaints: he was required to work too hard; his office was "scarcely habitable"; Livingston's personal servants neglected to tend his fire and sweep his room; he could not be bothered with keeping the legation office open regularly to the public. In a snit, he quit.[2] With his French bride in tow, Sumter left for London, where he was employed for a few months as private secretary to Minister James Monroe. Then, in the fall of 1803, the couple returned to South Carolina, and Sumter resumed the occupation of a gentleman planter—with disastrous results. During a five-year stewardship, he very nearly drove his father's cotton plantation into the ground. In order to get Sumter off the land before the family was ruined, his father, General Thomas Sumter, the revolutionary war hero, used his influence within the Jeffersonian Republican party to secure a diplomatic post for his son. Rio de Janeiro was it. Far enough away from South Carolina to please the elder Sumter and at the other side of the world from what was really important to the still-fledgling United States—that is, Europe— Rio de Janeiro probably seemed an ideal post for such a thoroughly unpleasant individual. (In modern United States diplomacy there are postings that fulfill the same function today.)

From the standpoint of United States interests, Sumter's mission to Brazil was in no way successful. This was because of a number of difficulties not made easier in the least by Sumter's bumptious and quarrelsome nature. He argued with everybody—with other members of the diplomatic community, with his American subordinates, and, on one occasion, even with members of the Braganza family, with whom he engaged in a public feud over a matter of court etiquette.

During the first two years of his residence in Rio de Janeiro, Sumter spent a great deal of time following Secretary of State Robert Smith's instructions to secure a commercial agreement with the Portuguese court in Brazil. On several occasions when he approached the pro-English minister of foreign affairs Rodrigo de Souza e Coutinho, the Conde de Linhares, on the subject of a trade treaty, Sumter strongly emphasized the benefits that would accrue to Brazil if the United States were to provide an increased market for Brazilian sugar and coffee. But the Portuguese ignored Sumter's blandishments and continued to refuse to negotiate a treaty or even grant to the United States the status of most favored nation—a status that had been promised to Consul Henry Hill in 1808. It should be noted, however, that this had been a verbal promise and never substantiated with documentation. Sumter blamed his lack of success in acquiring commercial concessions from the Portuguese on a lingering suspicion that the United States favored French projects for promoting rebellion throughout Latin America and also on the fact that he had been unable to give these trade negotiations his full attention because of the time and energy expended on quarrels with his subordinates.[3]

Commercial negotiations between the two countries were more or less suspended during the War of 1812 as a result of the controversies that arose over Luso-Brazilian violations of neutrality (although it is interesting to note that U.S. trade with Portugal itself increased markedly throughout the war years). Following the war, the Department of State decided to conduct any future negotiations in Washington. The department was cognizant of the Braganza court's obvious reluctance to grant any commercial privileges to the United States and realized that Sumter, after eight years of presumed effort, was incapable of reaching an agreement with the Portuguese.[4]

Sumter had further been instructed to furnish the Department of State with information on Brazil's commercial resources and potentialities. This was perceived as a necessary prerequisite to the negotiation of a treaty between the two powers. This Sumter failed to do. In 1819, Secretary of State John Quincy Adams informed Sumter's successor to Brazil, John Graham, that the "information possessed at this Department is so slight and imperfect, that it is not possible to found upon it any precise instructions other than that of requesting your vigilant and unremitting attention to the object of collecting, digesting, and reporting, such facts as may prove useful to the public service and tend to facilitate the removal of inequalities injurious to the Commerce of the United States."[5]

Sumter's negligence is certainly an adverse reflection to his ability and interest, but negligence was not uncommon in political appointees to diplomatic posts during this era. It is also indicative of his disinclination to cooperate with and utilize the capabilities of consular officials. But another impression becomes equally clear: perhaps the United States was not overly anxious to conclude a treaty with Brazil, as is evidenced by the Department of State's haphazard correspondence with Sumter, in which commercial matters were only infrequently mentioned. Moreover, at this time the understaffed and overworked Department of State was burdened with European concerns far more pressing than the possibility of commercial relations with a market as yet unproven and with a country less friendly than had initially been supposed. Furthermore, any satisfactory commercial arrangement between the United States and the Portuguese court was rendered virtually impossible by the diplomatic and commercial ascendancy of the English in Brazil.[6] Indeed, while Sumter's admittedly unpleasant and undiplomatic personality would have made any successful negotiation difficult, the failure to obtain a treaty with Brazil was due more to the historical moment than to any personality quirks. He undoubtedly was correct in interpreting the correspondence from Washington to indicate that lack of action on his part was not going to be of great concern back home.

Sumter was also instructed to furnish the Department of State with intelligence relative to the growing revolutionary movements throughout South America. This he did do. Sumter included in his dispatches lengthy statements that detailed the activities of revolutionaries in Buenos Aires, Chile, and Peru and that were based on information he gathered from U.S. special agents who had visited the troubled regions and from naval officers, merchants, and newspaper accounts and broadsides. Unfortunately for his superiors and future historians, however, Sumter's dispatches were poorly written and confusing and, with regard to his information on South America, contained few evaluative judgments. Beyond a curt acknowledgment of their receipt, the Department of State took little notice of Sumter's sketchy reporting. In the instructions issued to special agents and other U.S. officials bound for South America, Sumter's reportage was virtually ignored.

Neutral rights was the most controversial issue occupying Sumter's mission, straining relations between the United States and the Portuguese court almost to the breaking point. Throughout the War of 1812, the United States criticized the Braganza government both for its failure to maintain neutrality and for the aid that it extended to Great Britain. In the years immediately following the war, however, Portugal countered with its own charges that the United States was ignoring its responsibilities as a neutral by not curbing the privateers that were outfitted in American ports and that, under the colors of the Uruguayan rebel General José Artigas, attacked the shipping of Portugal.

The War of 1812 was a minor battleground in the larger context of the Napoleonic Wars, in which the interests of Portugal and its Brazilian colony were tightly joined with those of England. The peninsular phase of the European war was being fought largely by the armies and navy of England. If Prince João and his homesick consort,

Carlota, ever reoccupied their royal residence in Lisbon, it would be thanks to the British force of arms. By declaring war on Great Britain, the United States had for all intents allied itself with France and in Portugal's opinion had become nothing more than an "instrument of France engaged by fear of her in a war which would soon be abandoned from weakness and disunion."[7]

Quite naturally, Prince João and the majority of his ministers actively favored the cause of Great Britain in the War of 1812, which produced the expected hostility toward the United States. Nor had Sumter done anything to counteract this sentiment. Of course, Portugal's favorable attitude toward Great Britain had been guaranteed by the Strangford Treaty, the second of three treaties signed in 1810. By the terms of this treaty, the two powers agreed to defend each other in the event of hostile attack and to provide for mutual defense. Moreover, it stipulated that an unlimited number of British warships could avail themselves of Brazil's ports and that when these vessels were employed for the "benefit and protection" of either party, these warships would be provisioned without charge.[8]

In view of these considerations, the only alternatives available to the Rio government in its relations with the United States were belligerency or a policy of quasi neutrality, either of which would be advantageous to the Portuguese empire and its British ally and offensive only to the poorly represented and commercially insignificant republic to the north. The Braganza government briefly considered declaring war on the United States and entering the conflict on the side of England. This possibility was demonstrated several days after news of the war reached Rio, when Prince João presented the British with a corvette, the *Benjamin*, which was briefly employed as an armed cruiser in Brazilian waters. Prince João decided against belligerency, however, because of the pressure exerted by Lord Strangford, who "in a most decided manner" urged the Portuguese to declare their neutrality. This the court did on September 29, 1812.[9]

If Sumter's official actions in Rio had any influence on these decisions so crucial to his country, he uncharacteristically failed to claim credit for them. In view of his poor relations with the court and his contemporaries, one may assume that Sumter was no more than a bystander, perhaps even a frustrated one, as these decisions were being made around him. For a diplomat there is no greater failure.

Before examining specific instances wherein Portugal violated her neutrality, one should understand that, although at this time there was no universally recognized international agreement regarding the rights and obligations of neutrals, there were certain elemental standards of conduct that a neutral nation was expected to observe. Presumably neutrals abstained from supplying belligerents with the tools of war in the form of ships, naval stores, munitions, and armed forces. Neutrals were obliged to prevent hostilities in their ports and territorial waters and to ensure that their territory was not used as a base for the recruiting of soldiers and sailors by the belligerents. Although a neutral nation could grant asylum or temporary refuge to a belligerent warship, prizes could not be disposed of in neutral ports, nor could an armed belligerent vessel be allowed to remain in a neutral harbor indefinitely; generally, most nations considered a three-day maximum acceptable.

If certain provisions of the Strangford Treaty had been enforced, these rules would have been nullified. Moreover, for several years previous to the treaty and the outbreak of the War of 1812, Portugal's navy and troops had been fighting beside the English in Europe. From a Brazilian standpoint, therefore, the Portuguese declaration of neutrality, limited almost exclusively to prohibitions forbidding the disposition of prizes in her ports, becomes understandable and even sensible. It is not surprising, then, that Portugal violated the rules of neutral conduct, thereby assuring a deterioration in relations with the United States.

In order to understand the nature and effect of Portugal's conduct, one must examine a few of the incidents that so agitated Sumter and the United States. Portugal blatantly disregarded its neutral status and favored the British cause in the matter of the impressment of American citizens. Throughout the war, shorthanded British warships operating in Brazilian waters dispatched press-gangs into the cities to gather up needed crew members. On one occasion a British admiral, with the full cooperation of friendly Portuguese officials, seized four American citizens being detained in a Brazilian prison and impressed them into the service of England. The Portuguese Ministry of Foreign Affairs declined to press any complaints on behalf of the American prisoners, nor did the ministry make any attempt to seek redress from the British at any time during the spring of 1813, when a total of fourteen U.S. nationals were forcibly taken on board British men-of-war.[10] In spite of his frequent and often bitter complaints, Sumter was unable to persuade the Portuguese to curb the British practice of impressment. Sumter waxed eloquent in his dispatches to Washington about the moral evils of impressing American citizens in neutral cities, but this failed to influence the Portuguese, whose higher national interests were at stake.[11] Objectively, there was little that he could have done, but since the only weapon of a diplomat from a weak nation is force of personality, one wonders if perhaps Sumter could have accomplished more (the welfare of fourteen citizens being a minor matter to all parties) had he not been so thoroughly detested by the Rio officials.

Adding insult to injured American national dignity, the Portuguese court in Brazil also gave overt aid to England in the form of armed Portuguese convoys for British merchantmen. Barely six months into the war, Captain Thomas Boyle of the *Comet*, an American privateer cruising off the Brazilian coast, reported an encounter with three heavily laden British merchant vessels that were being convoyed by a Portuguese man-of-war of thirty-two guns. The *Comet* gave chase, and when it overtook the Portuguese warship, the latter requested a conference with the American commander. Captain Boyle was informed that the English merchantmen were under the protection of the Portuguese brig. Boyle ignored the threat, and the ships engaged in battle. The faster, more maneuverable *Comet* succeeded in damaging and driving off the Portuguese brig but could not prevent it from herding two of the damaged British vessels into safe "neutral" waters.[12]

In a variety of other ways Portugal violated the spirit of neutrality and displayed official favoritism toward Great Britain and antipathy for the United States. For example, provincial officials at Bahia compromised Portugal's neutrality by extending excessive protection to the specie-carrying *Bonne Cityonne*, a British brig of twenty-eight guns. The *Bonne Cityonne* was given permission to remain in the harbor at Bahia for as long as the American *Hornet*, under Captain James Lawrence, cruised outside territorial waters in wait for its prey. Despite protests by Consul Hill and several defiant challenges delivered to the British commander by Captain Lawrence, the *Bonne Cityonne* refused to meet the *Hornet* "beyond the neutral limits and the protection of Brazilian guns." Stressing the inequality in Portugal's guarantees of safe harbor for belligerents, William Bainbridge, the commander of the small American force to which the *Hornet* was attached, advised Lawrence not to rely upon similar neutral protection for his ship in the event of the arrival of a superior British force, which would likely "possess sufficient influence to capture you even in port."[13]

It must be concluded that Portugal, albeit for the understandable reasons of national interest, failed to uphold its professed neutrality in the face of British pressure for favoritism. Neutrality, however, is a two-way street: not only must it be enforced by the neutral nation, it must be respected by the belligerent powers. Great Britain was notoriously lax in this respect, but during the War of 1812 the United States was not altogether blameless.

Although the United States officially respected the neutrality of all nations, there were instances during the War of 1812 when the "Champion of Neutral Rights" blatantly disregarded Portugal's neutrality. On several occasions American privateers attacked and looted unarmed Portuguese merchant vessels. In November 1812, the *Revenge* detained the *Triumpho do Mar*, bound from Lisbon to New York, and removed its cargo. In that same year a Brazilian schooner out of Pará was similarly treated. In these and other cases Washington disclaimed any responsibility and advised Joseph Rademaker, the Portuguese chargé d'affaires in the United States, to seek redress through due process in the courts of the land.[14]

More serious than these isolated attacks by privateers, however, was the rumor that American ships had attacked Portuguese Sierra Leone (Guinea-Bissau) and inflicted heavy damage. No evidence was presented to prove or disprove the accusation, but the charge circulated among the inhabitants and officials of Rio and was trumpeted about by those individuals who wanted to believe it by virtue of their sympathy for Great Britain or their antipathy for the United States—an antipathy presumably intensified by their healthy dislike for Sumter.[15]

Illegal recruiting procedures practiced by officials of the United States were another source of irritation between the two countries. In February 1813, José Bernardes, a Portuguese sailor, was enticed into enlisting in a certain Colonel Winder's infantry regiment by "the glittering show of money" and a prodigious quantity of rum. Despite Portuguese protestations, the sailor was kept closely confined in a "Rendezvous House" in Philadelphia and then, with "woeful lamentation," marched off to Baltimore. Antonio João de Feitas was also cajoled or forced into American service, even though the recruiting party knew of his nationality and the contract that bound him to the Portuguese merchant marine.[16]

The Portuguese court was disturbed considerably less by U.S. violations of neutrality throughout the War of 1812 than by the fact that the American government, during the Río de la Plata conflict, declined to prevent American privateers from cruising against the commerce of Portugal and subsequently refused to make reparations. This reluctance on the part of the Madison administration contributed greatly to a feeling of ill will between the two countries which persisted for some years after the end of the Sumter mission.

In 1816 hostilities erupted anew in the Río de la Plata basin. This conflict, which eventually resulted in the establishment of the independent state of Uruguay in 1828, was but a continuation of the centuries-old rivalry between Spain and Portugal for possession of the strategic Banda Oriental, a rivalry intensified by the transfer of the Portuguese court to Brazil. Until 1815, however, English intervention had prevented Prince João from securing control over the Banda Oriental. But in that year Lord Strangford was withdrawn from Rio, leaving the Braganza government momentarily free from English domination to pursue its expansionist goals. By 1815 there were two new claimants to the region: the revolutionary government of Buenos Aires and the party of Jośe Artigas, a native of the Banda Oriental who was determined to make the province independent. In 1816 Brazil confronted Artigas with a land-and-water siege. Having no naval force at his disposal (and no port, for that matter), Artigas reacted by commissioning privateers to prey on Portuguese commerce. The majority of these commissions were granted to Americans, notably residents of Baltimore.[17]

When the Portuguese minister to Washington, José Correa da Serra, learned that citizens of Baltimore were outfitting privateers, he pleaded with Washington to remain neutral and to prevent the Baltimore privateers from committing armed outrages against the shipping of Portugal. It was to no avail. As early as December 1816, an American privateer flying the colors of Artigas captured a Portuguese vessel off the coast to Madeira. Several months later the *Buenos Ayres Patriot*, a Baltimore privateer commanded by J. W. Stephens, captured and ransacked the *Marques of Pombal* and the *St. John Protector*. On October 18, 1818, Correa da Serra complained that another Portuguese ship, the brig *João Sexto*, had been captured by the American privateer *Fortuna* and was presently being fitted in Baltimore to attack Portuguese commerce. In December of the same year the Portuguese minister informed Washington of "depredations and unwarrantable outrages" that had been committed off the Brazilian coast by another Baltimore privateer, the *Vicuna* (alias the *General Artigas*).

In 1820 Minister Correa da Serra estimated that the activities of American privateers had cost his country approximately sixty-five vessels and eighty-one million dollars. In addition to the plundering of ships in a time of peace between the two countries, there were "violations of territory by landing and plundering ashore, with shocking circumstances." Correa da Serra admitted that the American government did not officially countenance what amounted to piracy; nevertheless, these piratical acts were being committed by U.S. citizens who had open recourse to the port of Baltimore, where the populace openly flaunted their support of Artigas by displaying "badges" in their hats. Correa da Serra compared the privateers and their supporters in Baltimore to a "wide extended and powerful tribe of Infidels worse still than those of North Africa," for the North African infidels at least made prizes under the laws of their countries and only after a declaration of war had been issued. But the American infidels attacked the commerce of a nation "friendly to the United States, against the will of the government of the United States, and in spite of the laws of the United States."[18]

While undoubtedly not overly concerned with the fate of the commerce of a nation so lately allied with Great Britain, Washington was not entirely heedless of Portugal's plight. On March 3, 1817, Congress passed an act that clarified and strengthened U.S. neutrality laws. This act prohibited privateers from cruising under a commission granted by "any colony, district, or people," which was an obvious reference to the insurgent governments of Latin America. The neutrality laws of the United States were further reinforced by legislation in 1819 and 1820. But the mere passage of laws was not sufficient to impose neutrality on American citizens, and privateering continued chiefly from "the connivance at violations on the part of the public officials of Baltimore, the privateers' haven, where the federal judges, the collector of customs, the postmaster, the private attorneys, and the populace were culpable either because of selfish reasons or incompetence."[19] Once neutrality legislation had been passed, President Madison professed to have done everything he could to protect Portugal from the Baltimore privateers. However, the disinclination of the United States to curb the privateers with force caused the Portuguese court to disregard many American claims resulting from the War of 1812. Thus, in the opinion of Lawrence Hill, a noted historian of United States–Brazilian diplomatic relations, the neutrality question contributed to bringing the two countries "almost to the verge of actual hostility."[20]

Relations between the United States and Brazil were most seriously impaired, and Sumter's usefulness all but ended, by Washington's favorable attitude toward the rebellion that broke out in 1817 in the northern province of Pernambuco, long a center of republican-separatist intrigue. The Pernambucan rebels hoped to establish a republic independent of the Brazilian monarchy. Their plans were dependent upon the court's being too mired in the Río de la Plata adventure to do more than protest and especially upon assistance and perhaps even official recognition from the United States. To secure the latter, the provisional government of Pernambuco dispatched to Washington Antonio Gonçalves da Cruz, who was instructed to present the Pernambucan cause, obtain diplomatic recognition of the new republic, secure credit for the purchase of war material, and recruit émigré French officers for service in the Pernambucan rebel army. In return for these favors Gonçalves da Cruz was authorized to offer a generous commercial agreement, which, it was thought, would appeal to the spirit of the American people, all of whom were ruled by sentiments of "republicanism and commercialism."

In Philadelphia Gonçalves da Cruz met with Caesar Rodney, the Department of State's unofficial representative, and William Jones, the president of the Bank of the United States. In the name of the acting secretary of state, Richard Rush, Rodney agreed to the following concessions: although the United States would not recognize the Republic of Pernambuco at that time, Pernambucan merchant ships and privateers (but not prizes) could enter American ports; the United States would not respect the Portuguese court's "nominal blockage" of the Pernambucan coast; and, finally, the United States would recognize the belligerent status of the Republic of Pernambuco and would therefore not impede the purchase and shipment of war material.

Acting Secretary of State Rush conferred personally with Gonçalves da Cruz in Washington on June 16, 1817. The Pernambucan representative was told that "precise" recognition of his government was still not possible, but that the United States would do what it could to assist his cause. A cautious Rush then asked Gonçalves da Cruz to establish his formal residence in any other city but Washington, presumably to prevent further deterioration in relations with King João's government. In response to Gonçalves da Cruz's suggestion that the United States maintain a naval force off the Pernambucan coast in order to protect American commerce, the secretary apparently gave the Pernambucan the impression that the United States would act forcibly if circumstances required it. This impression led Gonçalves da Cruz to report to his superiors that there was a real possibility of a confrontation between the United States and the Portuguese court which would all but ensure the independence of the republic.

In Pernambuco itself the United States was represented by Consul Joseph Ray, whose appointment was secured upon the recommendation of Gonçalves da Cruz. Consul Ray openly involved himself in the insurrection. He was suspected of actively plotting with the rebels, and after the revolution was suppressed, Ray harbored some of the leaders of the movement in his house until they were forcibly taken by Brazilian authorities. Although Ray's conduct was condemned by the Portuguese as "criminal to the highest point," out of deference to the United States he was not imprisoned. He was, however, eventually recalled and replaced by James Bennett.[21]

As the preceding demonstrates, there were many obstacles to good relations between Rio de Janeiro and Washington—so many, in fact, that Sumter's mission must be viewed as impossible. For example, there was very little that Sumter could have done to counteract the mutual disregard for the rules of neutrality. Sumter's impossible personality, however, did nothing positive to foster a good understanding or a harmonious relationship between the two governments. Sumter engaged in continual bickering with fellow American officials and with members of the Luso-Brazilian government, whose sensitivities he ruffled on more than one occasion. In a pointed criticism of Sumter's conduct, Secretary of State John Quincy Adams observed that "our relations with Portugal and Brazil have not been well cultivated. Their importance has not been duly estimated. The Minister, who has been there these ten years, was not a fortunate choice. His own temper is not happy. He has been repeatedly involved in quarrels of personal punctilio, even with members of the royal family. He is excessively argumentative, and spins out everything into endless discussions without ever bringing anything to a close."[22] As mentioned above, Sumter even managed to annoy the court. When the Braganzas appeared on the streets, it was customary for people to remove their headgear and for those on horseback to dismount. On several occasions when the less than toothsome Princess Carlota was being driven through the city in her carriage, the American minister refused to get down from his horse. Considering Sumter's behavior to be belligerent and disrespectful, the princess ordered her guards to forcibly detach Sumter from his perch. Sumter responded by drawing his pistols and threatening to fire if touched. Shortly, thereafter, Prince João, who was finding his meddling wife quite a handful, tactfully issued a decree allowing foreign diplomats to remain on their horses in the royal presence.[23]

A less impartial observer, the consul Henry Hill, also berated Sumter for his lack of civility in dealings with the Portuguese government. In Hill's opinion, Sumter had occasionally been treated with courtesy only because of the court's "respect of the government of the United States, the fear of it, and the sincere desire to have its friendship—but not from any respect or fear of the minister—[unless perhaps] originating from his [long] and awful letters, which frequently have never been read, and have often remained unanswered."[24]

Minister Sumter's failure to establish some rapport with the Portuguese court and to accomplish any of the objectives of his mission caused Secretary of State Adams to note that "the state of our affairs with the Portuguese Government at Rio de Janeiro has been entangled in such a snarl of mismanagement and neglect that [nothing can be done] without a review of our political and commercial relations, both with Brazil and Portugal, for the last ten years."[25] Sumter himself recognized the futility of his continued presence in Rio when he admitted that he felt it advisable to "abstain as much as possible, and sometimes altogether, from undertaking to propose anything to the Portuguese government, in which either the interests or reputation of the United States are concerned, . . . lest I should afford it new occasions for treating them with neglect and disrespect."[26] Indeed, by the year 1818, Sumter's influence with the Portuguese court had deteriorated to such an extent that when he routinely submitted several consular commissions to the Portuguese government for approval, the matter was completely ignored. Obviously, by the year 1818 Sumter was unwelcome in Brazil. In August of that year he was recalled, which was not altogether contrary to the minister's wishes. As early as 1816 he had requested that he be relieved of his position.

At the time of Sumter's departure from Brazil in mid-1819, relations between the United States and the Portuguese court, in the opinion of John Quincy Adams, were marked with "so much ill blood . . . that it . . . festered into all but open hostility." In order to reestablish harmony and to renew commercial negotiations, Adams secured the appointment of John Graham—a member of a previous presidential commission to South America and for many years chief clerk of the Department of State—as minister to Brazil.[27] An astute diplomat, Graham set out for his post in the late summer of 1819 with the conviction that his efforts toward conciliation would not be particularly fruitful. Despite his conciliatory attitude, Graham was kept waiting for several months after his arrival in Rio before being received at court. At length, he became so discouraged with the futility of his efforts that he recommended that the United States mission to Brazil be reduced to the rank of chargé. Suffering ill health, Graham returned to the United States after only eight months in Rio. After the departure of Graham, the United States was represented in Rio only by an acting consul, Peter Sarteoris, who remained at that post until the arrival in September 1822 of Consul Condy Raguet of Philadelphia.[28]

In April 1821, King João had yielded to the demands of the Portuguese Cortes and returned to Portugal, leaving his son, Dom Pedro, as regent of the kingdom of Brazil. Chargé John Appleton, Graham's successor, followed the Portuguese monarch to Lisbon, and unresolved disputes over neutral obligations were transferred to the realm of strictly Portuguese–United States affairs. Thus ended thirteen years of unhappy relations between the United States and the Portuguese court in Brazil.

When one traces the relations of the United States with the Portuguese court in Brazil, it becomes obvious that the United States failed to achieve harmonious relations with the Braganza government. With the elevated concerns for neutrality that only a young and weak nation can have, and with the nearly total dependence on the Braganza family on Great Britain, good relations would have been all but impossible to establish or maintain. Given these circumstances, the best that the United States could hope for would have been a "damage-limiting" operation aimed at sufficiently containing the expected strains so that the opportunity for more cordial relations in the future remained possible. Thomas Sumter's mission to Brazil did not attain this limited goal due to the minister's inexperience, incompetence, and lack of fundamental tact—all traits deadly to successful diplomacy.

Individuals, however, are seldom able to rise above the roles in which they are placed and therefore should not be the only ones to suffer opprobrium when they fail. The very fact that the Department of State knowingly appointed an individual so unqualified suggests that the United States was not overly concerned with Brazil and that the post in Rio was regarded as unimportant, even expendable, despite the fact that it represented the only official United States mission in South America. This seeming indifference was further evidenced both by the Department of State's brief and infrequent communications with the minister and by the fact that, in the years following his arrival in Rio, the matter of a commercial treaty was treated with decreasing importance and that little was officially done to promote trade between the two countries. Moreover, even though by 1816 Washington was fully aware that Sumter's usefulness in Brazil had ended, three years passed before he was finally replaced. The pouch in those days was slow, but not that slow.

In a larger context, Sumter's raucous personality was sterotypical of American ideas at a time when differences between European and American customs were much greater than they are now. The incident most often cited to damn Sumter was his disrespect for the prerogatives of the royal family. Yet what could have been more fitting for an official American abroad, representing, as he did at the time, revolutionary republicanism? He was, after all, only one of a number of American representatives who distinguished themselves by refusing to follow court protocol that was intended to degrade those in the presence of royal personages. It is the function of an American representative overseas to truly represent, in both daily life and at official functions, the United States and American ideals and not to "go native" and become merely another courtier. It should be noted, however, that this posture can sometimes interfere with the successful conduct of a diplomatic negotiation and is usually curbed on those occasions. And it is true that Sumter was something of a graceless boor, but we judge him too harshly if we blame the lack of United States diplomatic success in Brazil solely on his poor performance.

Looking beyond Sumter as a personality, one sees that the neglectful attitude of the United States toward Brazil was not exceptional. During the early decades of the nineteenth century, the United States was diplomatically and commercially indifferent toward the whole region. This posture is explained by the fact that domestic and European affairs were regarded as the major concerns of the United States, while Spain's onetime colonies and Brazil were relegated to a tertiary position. Although Latin America was generally viewed as a repository of enormous riches and as a vast future market for American goods, little was done to develop trade with the region; in fact, during the first quarter of the nineteenth century, this trade never exceeded 10 to 12 percent of our total foreign commerce. During the Napoleonic Wars the United States failed to increase its trade with Latin America and challenge its chief rival, England. This opportunity was lost because of restrictions on foreign trade in the United States— the most notable being Jefferson's embargo—and our involvement in the War of 1812. Then, too, the possibilities for development within the United States were tremendous, and this was where most excess capital was concentrated.

Popular sentiment in the United States favored aiding the Spanish American countries in their struggle for independence. The official attitude, however, as expressed by Presidents Adams, Jefferson, and Madison, was one of neutrality, a view that arose from the opinion that the United States stood to gain very little from extending military aid and formal diplomatic recognition to Latin America. It should be remembered that during the Spanish American Wars of Independence the United States was fully occupied in delicate negotiations with Spain for the acquisition of the Floridas, and to have appeared less than neutral toward Spain's rebellious colonies would have endangered these negotiations. It was not until the final exchange of ratifications of the Adams-Onís Treaty in 1821 that the United States could afford, for reasons of its own self-interest, to take an active interest in Latin America and recognize the newly won independence of the young republics.

It is not surprising, then, that a man such as Thomas Sumter, Jr., the first United States representative to Latin America with the rank of minister, was appointed to Brazil or that the men who followed him were of the same low caliber. Nor is it surprising—in view of poor representation in Brazil, the lack of interest displayed by the United States, and the difficult issues that confronted the two countries—that for decades the United States failed to establish close relations with Brazil. Indeed, it remained for Baron Rio Branco, in the early years of the Old Republic (1889–1930), to forge the commercial and diplomatic ties that led to the now "historic" special relationship between the two largest nations in the Americas. Both Portugal and Brazil have traditionally sought to maintain close ties with a protector nation, and it was not until the United States could challenge Great Britain for this role in this hemisphere that the government in Rio de Janeiro was willing—or could afford—to make a meaningful alliance with Washington.

5

Initiating United States Relations with Argentina

Paul B. Goodwin, Jr.

For John M. Forbes, secretary of the United States legation at Buenos Aires, the inclusion in the diplomatic pouch from Washington of President James Monroe's message to Congress of December 23, 1823, could not have been more propitiously timed. Scarcely a month before the news of Monroe's speech had reached La Plata, Forbes suspected that Europe's Holy Alliance had designs on Spanish America, that a despotic plot had been hatched by the Continental forces of reaction to return the rebellious colonies to their rightful mistress, Spain: "The sun of freedom, which has only shone on this Country for a short Winter's day, is fast declining to that horizon whence it will sink into the night of despotism."[1]

It appeared to Forbes, a competent diplomat who maintained the full confidence of Secretary of State John Quincy Adams, that the Argentine people—confronted by the absence of a viable national government and the weak administration of Martín Rodríguez in the country's most important province, Buenos Aires—were deeply troubled by the apparent machinations of Europe's crowned heads. Not surprisingly, Forbes reported that they received Monroe's pronouncement with considerable enthusiasm. On February 5, 1824, Bernadino Rivadavia, the foreign minister, was concerned about the rumors of European intervention in the region and declared to other members of the government that Buenos Aires was prepared to cooperate with any plan that would establish a general peace based on independence and liberty.[2]

Rivadavia's declarations dovetailed nicely with the message of Monroe. The North American president's words were well received by Argentine public officials, and the foreign minister immediately dispatched translations of the document to the governments of Chile,

Peru, and Colombia.[3] On February 10, 1824, Caesar A. Rodney, the first United States minister to Argentina, noted that "this masterly State Paper [which] had inspired us here . . . will have a most extensive influence."[4] Lengthy extracts from the message reproduced in *El Argos*, *La Gaceta Mercantíl*, and *El Avisador Mercantíl*, influential newspapers in the Buenos Aires of 1824, attest to the importance of the news.[5] *El Argos* focused on the portions of Monroe's declaratioan that seemed significant for Buenos Aires: the clauses stating that the Americas were no longer subject to European colonization and that the interference of any European power with the independent nations of Spanish America would be construed by the United States as an unfriendly act inimical to American national interests.[6]

Superficially, then, Argentine-American relations were characterized by a general atmosphere of amity and, apparently, common purpose. Foreign Minister Rivadavia expressed his pleasure at the good relations between the two nations and on May 4, 1824, named General Carlos de Alvear as Argentina's first minister to the United States.[7]

Alvear, however, was ordered to proceed to the United States by way of England—a nation, in Argentine eyes, critical to the realization of Spanish America's independence. In London he attempted to gain recognition for Argentina, but the British foreign secretary, George Canning, demurred. Canning's thoughts were fixed on the situation in Europe, not the periphery of new nations across the Atlantic. Disappointed, Alvear boarded a ship for the long trip to New York. Upon his landfall in early October 1824, the Argentine envoy chanced to encounter the Marquis de Lafayette, the fiery French republican, whom the city of New York was honoring. He declared to Alvear that Buenos Aires, together with other emerging states, could ill afford to look to Europe for support. "The only nation which can offer guarantee by a frank course and identity of principle is that of Washington." These words from such an eminent personage may well have served to "enhance the General's estimate of the Republic of the North."[8] In Washington, Alvear, primed by Lafayette, met briefly with President Monroe and quickly "succumbed . . . to Monroe's sympathetic personality."[9]

The American chief executive explained in greater detail to Alvear the underlying motives of his declaration in a White House conference on October 18, 1824. Alvear was deeply impressed by Monroe's apparent sincerity. But the Argentine agent was either misled by or misunderstood the president, for he felt that Monroe would back his words with armed might. In a dispatch dated October 18, Alvear revealed his belief that this was the case: "[Monroe] expressed firm resolution on what this nation is doing to sustain his message and it will not permit any other nation except Spain to make an intervention in our affairs. He explained how and when the United States have prepared the resources they have, the preventive measures they have taken, the increase of their navy, the fortification of their coasts."[10]

Following his conference, Alvear praised United States policy toward Latin America. He believed, as Monroe suggested, that the United States had already aided the Spanish American republics by its policy of benevolent neutrality and its support of their revolutionary cause in the courts of Europe. Furthermore, Alvear was confident that in the event of war between Argentina and Brazil, which was at that time looming large on the horizon, the United States would favor Buenos Aires "on account of its natural sympathy for republics." Brazil, a monarchy, symbolized to the Argentine statesman an extension of Europe in America, a bulwark of reaction. He naively concluded that the United States perceived Brazil in the same light and, as the protector of the South American republics, would not permit European interference. Alvear, then, "would render his greatest service to the United Provinces by the side of Monroe."[11]

Legislators in the United Provinces also recast Monroe's message so that it conformed with Argentine expectations. At a meeting of the national congress held on December 16, 1824, the governor of Buenos Aires, Juan Gregorio de las Heras, stated: "We have fulfilled a great national duty toward the Republic of the United States of North America. That republic, which from its origin has presided over the civilization of the New World, has solemnly acknowledged our independence. It has at the same time made an appeal to our national honor by supposing us capable of contending single-handedly with Spain; but it has constituted itself the guardian of the field of battle in order to prevent any foreign assistance from being introduced to the aid of our rival."[12]

Despite appearances, too much emphasis should not be placed on the transient impression that the doctrine seemed to produce in Argentina. Rivadavia may have found a symbolic affinity with the United States, but he realized that the safety of Argentina was more secure in the hands of the British fleet.[13]

Forbes's first flush of enthusiasm over the warm reception accorded the Monroe Doctrine had been further nurtured by Rivadavia's rhetorical expressions of common cause with the United States. Rhetoric often produces ephemeral results. On March 22, 1824, Forbes wrote:

> I must frankly say that one of the principal motives of my disgust towards this Country is the overweening partiality of the dominant party and of the highest classes of Society here for the English. I can plainly foresee that all we have done for this people is poorly appreciated and that we are condemned to be in this Country, *"hewers of wood"* and *"drawers of water"* to the English who are daily becoming Lords of the Soil by Proprietorship as well as influence. Your *Splendid Message* at the opening of Congress, so justly classed in point of character and interest with our *Declaration of Independence*, produced an electrical effect on the Republican Party, whose numbers I am sorry to say are few, but was received with an unwelcome apathy by the men in power, because it so far outshone the faint glimmerings of the British Cabinet, the Shrine before which they all bend the knee.[14]

Forbes, acting chargé d'affaires upon Rodney's death in June 1824, repeatedly decried the preponderance of British influence in the United Provinces. He found it difficult to discover "any gentleman of rank or influence, who is not directly subservient to British influence."[15] Virtually everyone of importance courted the British consul general and eagerly pressed him for English recognition of an independent Argentina. By the end of 1824, Argentine gratitude for Monroe's statement was more than offset by the interest expressed in the publication of the Polignac Memorandum, a hands-off South American policy extracted from the French by Canning.[16] Exasperated, Forbes complained that "England derives from this country . . . all the advantages of colonial dependence, without the responsibility or expense of civil or military administration."[17] John Forbes—and this was true of essentially all U.S. diplomatic personnel sent to Argentina during the first half of the century—simply failed to grasp or refused to accept the fact that, to Argentina, Great Britain was far more important than the United States.

If Argentina perceived its relationship with the United States largely in symbolic terms, there were occasions when the United Provinces pragmatically attempted to invoke the Monroe Doctrine to further its own national interests. One such occasion involved the Banda Oriental, present-day Uruguay. Long a source of conflict between Brazil and the viceroyalty of the Río de la Plata, the Banda Oriental again threatened to precipitate warfare. At the convocation of the fourth legislative assembly of the United Provinces, held on May 4, 1824, Governor Las Heras claimed that Alvear had been instructed to suggest to the government of the United States "that none of the new governments of this continent should change by violence its recognized limits at the time of emancipation."[18] The suggestion, if embraced by the United States, would support Argentine claims to the Banda Oriental.[19]

Monroe sympathized with the Argentine position and noted the hostile and unjust desire for conquest exhibited by Dom Pedro I, the Brazilian emperor. But Monroe did not indicate to Alvear that the United States would actively take sides in the quarrel, although he did allow the United Provinces to obtain arms, munitions, ships, and other military material necessary to pursue the conflict with Brazil.[20]

Upon the outbreak of war, several Argentine requests that the Monroe Doctrine be invoked against Brazil went unanswered by the United States. In August 1826, Francisco de la Cruz, President Rivadavia's foreign minister, questioned Forbes on the scope of Monroe's ideas. Were they applicable, he asked the chargé, "in case a European power assisted the Emperor of Brazil to maintain war against the United Provinces, or in case the Emperor sought aid from the Kingdom of Portugal or any part of its dominions to sustain the war?"[21] Similar questions were directed to Forbes by Rivadavia. Summarizing the meeting in a memorandum, the chargé wrote: "[Rivadavia] then touched on the policy of shutting out from this Continent all European power and influence as declared by the late President of the U.S. and noticed the obvious connection of Europe and Brazil, more especially of Portugal (to whose crown he considered Don Pedro's renunciation a mere form) and also of the direct participation of Don Pedro in the views of the Holy Alliance, through his family connection with Austria. He expressed the belief that the President of the United States would feel much disposed to resist this combined influence on this Continent."[22]

President John Quincy Adams was not so disposed. Not until July 1828, nearly two years later, was Forbes prepared to transmit Secretary of State Henry Clay's interpretation of the Adams administration of the Monroe Doctrine to José Rondeau, Argentine minister for foreign affairs ad interim. The United States note was succinct and to the point: "The war cannot be conceived as presenting a state of things bearing the remotest analogy to the case which President Monroe's message deprecates. It is a war strictly American in origin and its object. It is a war in which the Allies of Europe have taken no part."[23]

The United States further declared that no nation could invoke the Monroe Doctrine unilaterally, as it was solely a matter for the American Congress to decide.[24] Bruised sensibilities in Argentina and indifference in the United States to events in the remote United Provinces cooled relations between the two nations.[25] To add insult to injury, Argentine victories came to nothing when Britain mediated the conflict and created Uruguay as an independent state. Thus the coveted territory was forever lost to Argentina.

In the turbulent 1830s relations reached their lowest ebb when the complex controversy over the Falkland Islands led to a virtual cessation of diplomatic relations between Argentina and the United States. The issue directly affected the implementation of the Monroe Doctrine.

The roots of the Falkland Islands question may be traced to the sixteenth century, but it was during the latter half of the 1700s that the question of sovereignty over the islands became a subject of bitter dispute between Great Britain and Spain.[26] The Royal Navy formally took possession of the Falklands in the name of King George III on January 23, 1765, and established a small settlement at Port Egmont. In 1770 a Spanish force sent from Buenos Aires attacked and destroyed the English colony. Madrid eventually disavowed the action initiated by its agent in the Río de la Plata, and Britain regained possession of the islands. The colony, remote and unprofitable, was abandoned in 1774, although the British insisted repeatedly that their sovereignty was still intact.[27] Be this as it may, Spain exercised rights of jurisdiction there after 1774 and until the end of her colonial rule, when, under the aegis of *uti possidetis*, Argentina succeeded to Spain's rights. In 1820 Commander Daniel Jewett of the Argentine navy assumed formal possession of the Falklands, and Luis Vernet was encouraged by the government of Buenos Aires to found a colony on the territory. In 1826 he colonized East Falkland. Two years later he was granted a monopoly of the fisheries in the archipelago and in 1829 was appointed governor.[28] It was Vernet's exercise of authority that brought the Argentine Republic into sharp conflict with the interests of the United States. Trouble ensued when Vernet, in 1829 and again in 1830, warned foreign ships against the use of the shores and harbors and the killing of seals and livestock on the islands and on the coasts of Patagonia and Tierra del Fuego.

Martin Van Buren, secretary of state, informed Forbes in February 1831 that the United States had the right to fish in the area "as they had always done." He complained that "the Government of Buenos

Secretary of State Martin Van Buren (The National Portrait Gallery, Smithsonian Institution)

Ayres can certainly deduce no good title to these Islands, to which those fisheries are appurtenant, from any fact connected with their history, in reference to the first discovery, occupancy, or exclusive possession of them by subjects of Spain."[29]

In spite of Van Buren's statement, of which Vernet was likely unaware, the governor, in July and August 1831, arrested the captains and crews of three American ships for violating the colony's regula-

Juan Bautista Alberdi, Bernardino Rivadavia, and Don Luis Vernet, as portrayed on Argentinian postage stamps.

tions.[30] In an ill stroke of fate, the experienced and temperate John Forbes died several months before the eruption of the Falkland Islands controversy, and he had not been replaced by a new chargé d'affaires. In the meantime, the American legation in Buenos Aires fell into the clumsy hands of the consul in charge of the archives, George Washington Slacum, a man of no diplomatic experience, little tact, and less judgment.[31] Echoing Van Buren, Slacum operated from the premise that the government of Buenos Aires had no legitimate right to the South Atlantic territories in question. This opinion was naturally seconded by the British consul general, who informed the embattled Slacum that England had never abandoned her right to the islands. Particularly nettlesome to Slacum was Vernet's seizure of only American shipping. The governor of the Falklands, according to the consul, admitted that "he could not take *English* Vessels with the same propriety he could American" and then boasted of having made one hundred thousand dollars by "the capture and pillage of American Property." Furious, Slacum described Vernet as an adventurer in charge of vagabonds and demanded prompt action on the part of Buenos Aires for the injustices perpetrated.[32]

Equally callous, Tomás de Anchorena, foreign minister of the United Provinces, implied that Slacum was but a mere consul and did not appear to be authorized to issue a formal protest on behalf of the United States. Later correspondence accused Slacum of ignorance of the issues and cultural insensitivity.[33]

Unsure of himself and apparently bewildered by the extreme displeasure of the Buenos Aires government, Slacum was convinced of the need for a bold stroke. After consulting the United States minister to Brazil, he called on the commander of the USS *Lexington*, Silas Duncan.[34]

Captain Duncan, who had been sent in June by the Navy Department to South American waters to protect the commerce and citizens of the United States, requested on December 7, 1831, that the Argentine foreign minister either turn Vernet over to the United States to be tried for robbery and piracy or arrest and punish him by the laws of Buenos Aires. When Anchorena refused to endorse either suggestion, the *Lexington*, in the company of the USS *Warren*, set sail for the Falklands. The obstreperous commander arrived on the twenty-eighth and spiked the cannon of the small garrison, destroyed the arms and ammunition of the colony, seized the property allegedly taken from the impounded American vessels, ransacked a number of private homes, arrested several settlers, and eventually deported most of the islands' inhabitants.[35]

Argentines were incensed. On February 14, 1832, a public proclamation informed *porteños* of what had transpired in the Falklands. The government pledged itself to secure satisfaction for the outrage. Slacum was informed that in view of the "aberration of ideas and irregularity of language in his official notes, and in view of the recent outrage, the government had judged it expedient to suspend all official communication with him, and requested that he appoint a substitute."[36] Slacum refused to do so, but President Andrew Jackson had already named a new chargé d'affaires, the Massachusetts lawyer Francis Baylies, to negotiate with Argentine authorities. Baylies's instructions demanded that the Buenos Aires government disavow Vernet, restore U.S. property, and pay an indemnity on the grounds that the United States had had actual use of the islands as a fishery for fifty years and that Spain had exercised no sovereignty over the Patagonian and Fuegian coasts of which Buenos Aires claimed ownership.[37]

The explosive mood of the citizenry of Buenos Aires and the rapidly deteriorating relationship between the two nations demanded prompt attention. Baylies was aware of the intensity of feeling but felt that "their point of honour may be satisfied by loud talking and that their anger may evaporate in bluster."[38] When Baylies met with Manuel V. de Maza, the acting foreign minister, both men intransigently maintained their respective positions. Baylies, who, in the words of John Quincy Adams, "stayed . . . just long enough to embroil his country in a senseless and wicked quarrel with the Government [of Buenos Aires]," succeeded only in compounding Slacum's error by attempting to persuade Maza that Vernet was a pirate.[39] Maza at the same time insisted that the *Lexington* raid was unconscionable and demanded immediate and ample satisfaction, reparation, and indemnity for all losses and damages. He declined to discuss any of the issues raised by Baylies until his demands were met. The two diplomats sat at the negotiating table only twice and accomplished nothing of a positive character. Frustrated by the collapse of the talks and the intransigence of Maza, Baylies, without waiting for further instructions, demanded his passports and dashed off an angry note to Secretary of State Edward Livingston: "We have attempted to soothe, and conciliate and coax these wayward and petulant fools long enough. *They must be taught a lesson*, or the United States will be viewed with contempt throughout South America."[40] Baylies and Slacum left Argentina on September 8, 1832, and, anticipating hostilities between the United States and the United Provinces, took with them the legation's archives. War did not eventuate, but regular diplomatic intercourse ceased for nearly a decade.[41]

In his *Memoirs*, John Quincy Adams clearly blamed Baylies for the disastrous mission. It should be noted, however, that Adams and Baylies were bitter political enemies and that Adams's assessment is unduly harsh.[42] Events in the South Atlantic compromised Baylies's mission long before he embarked for Buenos Aires. Livingston's instructions of January 26, 1832, apprised Baylies of the "lawless and piratical nature" of Vernet's acts and said that President Jackson could not for a moment "believe that they were authorized by a friendly power." Baylies was further informed that Commander Duncan, already on station in South American waters, had been ordered to inquire whether Vernet's actions were taken "under the allegation of authority" from the government of the United Provinces; should that be the case, Duncan was merely "to prevent our ships from capture" and "to retake those that have fallen into the hands of Vernet." Only if Vernet's actions were disavowed by the Buenos Aires government was Baylies "to give orders to the commander of the squadron to break up the settlement" and bring Vernet to Buenos Aires for trial.[43]

Just two days after Baylies's instructions had been written, Duncan, on his own authority, anchored in the Falklands and proceeded to destroy Vernet's colony. The action later received the full approval of President Jackson.[44] Events had assured Baylies's failure. When the new chargé finally arrived in Buenos Aires, on June 8, 1832, he was presented with a fait accompli and confronted by an angry Argentine government. Despite the heated atmosphere, Baylies's characterization of Argentine officials as "wayward and petulant fools" was uncalled for, save to soothe his own bruised ego, and reflected a profound misreading of Argentine sensibilities over the controversy. The chargé failed to comprehend that the Argentine government was desperately striving to establish its legitimacy among its own citizenry, that it constantly confronted centrifugal forces that encouraged secession and discouraged unity, and that it was perilously insecure. Captain Duncan's actions demanded a strong Argentine response, even if only to save face and regardless of the legality or illegality of Vernet's activities or his alleged authority as governor. Baylies was not alone in his myopic assessment of the Argentine government. Adams's stinging comments about Baylies's misfortunes revealed his own feelings, and perhaps the feelings of other American statesmen, about the United Provinces: "Nothing but the imbecility of that South American abortion of a state saved him from indelible disgrace and this country from humiliation in that concern."[45]

The embers of resentment toward the United States rekindled in January 1833, when the British corvette *Clio* appeared at Port Luis in the Falklands and her commander announced to the captain of an Argentine naval vessel at anchor in the harbor that he intended to assume possession of the islands in the name of their rightful owner, King William IV. As the government of the United Provinces had not taken the opportunity to reestablish its control over the islands in the confusing aftermath of the *Lexington*'s devastating raid, resistance to the British warship was deemed futile. The flag of the United Provinces was struck and the Union Jack raised in its place.[46] Britain had chosen a "propitious moment" for the reassertion of her claims to sovereignty. British agents in both Washington and Buenos Aires knew of the strained relations between the United States and the United Provinces. His Majesty's government assumed, with good reason, that Washington would neither prevent British occupation of the Falklands nor lend Argentina tangible support in the matter.[47]

News of the *Clio's* seizure of the Falklands reached Washington in late February. Although the British action, in the opinion of Dexter Perkins, was a "clear violation of the Monroe Doctrine" if sovereignty was assumed to rest in the Argentine government, Washington officials said nothing of any transgression of Monroe's principles. It was convenient for the Jackson administration to regard the Falklands as a prerevolutionary possession of Great Britain to which the Monroe Doctrine naturally had no application.[48]

American commercial interests conditioned to a large degree the pro-British stance of the United States with respect to the Falklands. Vernet's seizure of American vessels, which were accustomed to unfettered operations in the region, sparked the incident. American whalers and sealers expressed a decided preference for British sovereignty in the islands.[49] Commercial interests considered Argentine occupation of the islands to be dangerous to all foreign shipping and made known their opinion that, regardless of the claims of the United Provinces, the so-called colony should be destroyed. Secretary of State Livingston wrote that the Argentine colony was composed of deserters from American vessels and renegades from all nations, "governed by no laws but the will of Vernet." It was necessary, in Livingston's opinion, to break up an establishment "so dangerous to our commerce."[50]

Robert Greenhow, noted linguist, physician, and historian, wrote in the influential *Merchant's Magazine and Commercial Review* that, in light of the "depredations" against United States ships, there could be no doubt that Captain Duncan "would have failed in the performance of his duty had he neglected to take measures for bringing to punishment the authors of such acts, and for preventing the commission of them in the future."[51] Greenhow also observed that even though the capture of East Falkland by the British in 1833 was "utterly unjust" and the British had no better claim to possession of the islands than did the Argentines, the government of the United Provinces nevertheless "had . . . placed itself so manifestly in the wrong, by its illegal and arbitrary proceedings with regard to those islands that its complaints excited no sympathy in any quarter. . . . [Their] impudent and rapacious conduct, in attempting to revive the unjust and obsolete prohibitions which Spain had been unable to enforce, drew down upon them the indignation of more powerful states, and subjected them to humiliations for which they have no claims to redress."[52]

The seizure of the vessels, the reasonable doubt surrounding sovereignty over the Falklands, and Argentine intransigence all contributed to the Jackson administration's lack of concern over British moves in the distant South Atlantic. "In such circumstances it was hardly to be expected either that the authorities at Buenos Aires would invoke the aid of the American government or that such aid would be spontaneously offered."[53]

According to some reports, United States citizens resident in Buenos Aires were delighted with the British occupation of the islands. The London *Times* noted in June 1833: "Little is now said of the Falkland Islands' affair, but all are anxiously waiting news from England upon the subject. The Americans here are delighted that they have got out of this scrape, and that the odium now rests with John Bull."[54]

The Argentine government said nothing more about either the attack of the *Lexington* or the British occupation of the Falklands until May 1838, when Carlos de Alvear, again the Argentine minister to the United States, was instructed by Felipe Arana, Governor Juan Manuel Rosas's foreign minister, to secure satisfaction from the United States "for Duncan's depredations and Slacum's effrontery."[55] The timing and tone of Rosas's initiative are curious, for in March 1838 France blockaded Buenos Aires with its fleet. The French action was precipitated by Argentina's unwillingness to extend the privileges of the Anglo-Argentine Treaty of 1825 to French subjects.[56] It would appear that Rosas's best policy with respect to Washington lay in courting the United States, but he chose to revive the Falklands imbroglio.

A possible explanation is that Rosas felt it necessary to press the United States on the issue, for the wounds of 1832 had never healed and remained a barrier to official intercourse. Before the issue of French intervention in the Río de la Plata could be brought to the attention of the United States, Rosas appreciated the need to settle his differences with the American government. Negotiations were eventually opened between Alvear and Secretary of State John Forsyth, but results were slow to develop and were hedged in the most general terms.[57] Alvear also discovered, although it came as no surprise, that in the United States there was little evidence of public interest in events in the Argentine. Only among a few businessmen did Rosas's

Secretary of State John Forsyth (The National Portrait Gallery, Smithsonian Institution)

agent find any support for his country. "The opinion of the businessmen of this country is every day more pronounced against the hostilities of France in Buenos Ayres and Mexico; but however great the influence of this opinion, it will never be consistently strong enough to alter the neutrality constantly observed by this country. One cannot hope . . . to expect any act in favor of the cause which the sister republics sustain except that of official friendship."[58]

Only once was the subject of the French blockade mentioned in Congress. On February 11, 1839, Caleb Cushing of Massachusetts offered a motion to request the president to communicate information on the blockade and the source of the difficulties that plagued relations between the governments of Louis Philippe and Rosas.[59] Nothing came of the motion, and it was forgotten in the business of the day. In the La Plata in April 1839, an American naval officer, Captain John B. Nicolson, made an effort to mediate between the disputants, but his actions were without official sanction and were singularly unsuccessful. In no sense did the United States lend a hand in the final settlement of the conflict. But Rosas never expected American support. Alvear's protestations in Washington were little more than a diversion that may have been calculated to demonstrate to the blockaded citizens of Buenos Aires that Argentina was capable of pursuing an assertive foreign policy. Even more likely is that Argentine "concern" over the Falklands was a mask to still any rumors that Rosas was prepared to cede Argentine rights over the Falklands to Britain in exchange for the cancellation of the debt remaining from the Baring loan of 1824. Such a deal was among the instructions of Manuel Moreno, who returned to London as the Argentine minister in December 1838. Finally, Rosas correctly perceived that effective foreign support against the French could come from only the British. Despite the differences over the Falklands, Rosas cultivated Britain, and ultimately British intervention was instrumental in convincing France to lift the blockade.[60]

Carlos de Alvear finally received from the United States a belated reply about the Falklands dispute in December 1841, more than a year after the Makau-Arana Convention had ended France's intervention. At that time the Argentine minister was advised by Secretary of State Daniel Webster that because the right of jurisdiction over the islands was contested by Great Britain on the basis of claims long antecedent to Duncan's raid, it was "conceived that the United States ought not to give a final answer until the controversy was settled." Such an answer, Webster felt, would under the circumstances involve a departure from a cardinal policy of the United States, that is, nonintervention.[61] This was to remain the fixed policy of the United States on the question of the Falklands.

For North Americans, then, the French intervention in Mexico was more compelling and generated real concern. Washington protested French activity in Mexico; it virtually ignored similar French activity in the Río de la Plata. On a positive note, however, the United States resumed diplomatic relations with Argentina in 1844 with the appointment of William Brent as chargé d'affaires at Buenos Aires. Not long after Brent's arrival, President Rosas again became embroiled

Secretary of State Daniel Webster (The National Portrait Gallery, Smithsonian Institution)

with France and Britain. It appeared that Monroe's principles had again been violated by foreign powers.

Issues involving commercial rivalry, the independence of Uruguay, which was menaced by Rosas's armies, and free navigation on the Rivers Plate, Paraná, and Uruguay precipitated a joint Anglo-French intervention in the region in 1845. When the foreign fleets raised a blockade at Buenos Aires, they appeared to be in violation of the Monroe Doctrine.[62] The intervention did elicit some response from the American press. As early as June 1845, *Nile's Register* commented unfavorably on the Anglo-French actions and mournfully declared that Monroe's words had become a "dead letter."[63] Opinion of another shade could also be found. One author, after establishing Rosas's bloodthirsty personality, wrote: "Must it not seem rather absurd to ourselves, as well as to the rest of mankind, that we should make the change of government in any of those republics . . . a *casus belli* with any nation?"[64]

Washington remained content to admonish the actions of Britain and France in the Río de la Plata.[65] But this low-key policy was undermined by Chargé Brent, who promised the Argentine government the strong support of the United States. Brent wrote to the British minister to Argentina, William G. Ousely, and accorded "no validity at all to the Anglo-French blockade nor the *right* to enforce any such blockade."[66] Enthusiasm is no substitute for measured policy, and the hopes raised by the American agent never materialized. Such unofficial acts on Brent's part were the occasion of his replacement by William A. Harris, who presented his credentials to the government of the Argentine Confederation on July 7, 1846. Harris quickly exploded the bubble of hope created by his predecessor.

The removal of Brent was not lost on Argentines, who received Harris coldly. He was looked upon with distrust "because they had adopted the belief that [he] had not come to make good the extravagant hopes which had been excited by the course of [his] predecessor."[67] Secretary of State James Buchanan left little doubt as to the proper course of United States policy: "Whilst existing circumstances render it impossible for the United States to take a part in the present war, yet the President desires that the whole moral influence of this Republic should be cast into the scale of the injured party. We cordially wish the Argentine Republic success in its struggle against foreign interference."[68]

Harris conveyed Buchanan's sympathy to the Rosas government, and Felipe Arana, the foreign minister, accepted the message with gratitude but "was constrained and cold in his manner."[69] Argentina, to the consternation of Harris and, before him, Brent, was still inclined to treat directly with the British, even though England was a partner in the blockade. Harris noted that when Thomas Hood, a former British consul at Montevideo, was sent to Buenos Aires as a special envoy to propose peace, he was "received with extraordinary marks of respect," which indicated that high government functionaries remained prejudiced toward the United States.[70] Harris apparently did not know that Hood and Rosas had been personal friends for years.[71] Never did American envoys appreciate the character of the Anglo-Argentine relationship. Frustration and incomprehension typify Harris's dispatches: "One of the most unaccountable and strange peculiarities of the Governor [Rosas] and as a necessary consequence also, of all the principal men of note in this country, is an extraordinary partiality, admiration, and preference for the English government, and Englishmen, upon also all occasions and under all circumstances. I characterize this partiality and preference as *unaccountable* and *strange*, in view of the arrogant and selfish policy, and the meddlesome and sinister influences, which the British government and people have always endeavored to exercise in these countries."[72]

What little influence the United States exercised in the United Provinces in the 1840s evaporated with the news of the Mexican War. According to Harris, both the authorities and the inhabitants of the United Provinces "were disposed to sympathize with the Mexicans, and had adopted the British idea that our object was conquest and not a redress of the most aggravated wrongs."[73] Anti-American feeling intensified as the tide of war ran against Mexico. As Harris noted in a dispatch of June 16, 1847: "The strongest feelings and prejudices exist here, with all classes of Spaniards, against our people and government, in regard to the Mexican war. . . . They look upon the war as one of mere conquest, and as an act of the grossest and most cruel oppression . . . so strong has this prejudice become, and so hurtful is it to our interests and standing with these people."[74]

In the meantime, Carlos de Alvear, perennial Argentine minister to the United States, had gradually grown hostile toward Americans and their bellicose ambitions in the Southwest. The United States had become so powerful in relation to the other nations of the Americas that Alvear warned against the invocation of the Monroe Doctrine "except in special cases that may be convenient."[75] Alvear also insisted that Europe had no other option than to refuse to abide by the doctrine, which, if accepted, would grant to the United States a decided superiority in the Americas. Great Britain, in Alvear's mind, was at once a European and an American power, a reality that consistently escaped American statesmen. As such, Great Britain had as much interest "in defending the rights of Mexico from North America as the United States has in defending her from English invasion."[76]

By February 1843, the Argentine minister expressed his intense fear and distrust of the U.S. policy of westward expansion; with the outbreak of the Mexican War, his fears seemed justified. By 1849, he was horrified by the virulent expansionist sentiment in the United States "because it was rooted in the hearts of a whole people."[77]

To Juan Bautista Alberdi, Argentine statesman and author of the 1853 constitution, Mexico was eloquent testimony as to the true character of the Monroe Doctrine—a pronouncement that guaranteed neither independence nor the prevention of conquest. He saw the United States embarking upon a career of expansion and conquest at the expense of Hispanic America. Alberdi, certain of the imperial ambitions of the United States, saw in liberal Europe the best guarantee against American aspirations and menace.[78]

The Monroe Doctrine, so felicitously greeted by Argentines in 1824, eventually proved to be more of an irritant than a balm to the development of relations between the United States and the United Provinces. Poor and not infrequently stormy relations reflected a basic indifference on the part of both nations to the affairs of the other. The United States, in light of its meager military capabilities and the remoteness of the La Plata, did not find events in that quarter of the hemisphere critical to American national interests. And the United Provinces habitually looked to Great Britain for support against the designs of reactionary Europe or aggressive France. Argentines realized that Britain had the capability to defend them, and in the early years of nationhood they deemed the British fleet the great deterrent to European aggression. It was also seen that British economic self-interest proved more effective in the protection of Argentine rights than any principles mouthed by the president of the United States. Despite British actions in the Falklands and even in the La Plata itself, Argentine governments were careful to remain on good terms with England, whereas relations with the United States were often strained.

Alberdi, representative of liberal circles in Argentina, bitterly attacked the Monroe Doctrine. He saw it as opposing indiscriminately all political intervention by Europe, even though such intervention might not be motivated by colonization or the destruction of the independence of the Latin American republics. On the contrary, such interference might have given South America "freedom and orderly self-government, and ended the anarchy to which otherwise those countries were left." The Monroe Doctrine, in Alberdi's view, deprived Argentina and all South America of a source of legitimate aid.[79] But Alberdi's assault must be tempered by Argentina's misguided efforts to invoke the doctrine pragmatically in its own interest—in the war with Brazil, over the British seizure of the Falkland Islands, and over the two blockades of Buenos Aires. United States disinterest produced a corresponding resentment in Argentina.

Much of the ill will between the two nations was created by United States diplomatic personnel. C. K. Webster observed that in Latin America "the United States were on the whole . . . badly served. . . . Their envoys were more liable than those of Britain to clash with the Latin American statesmen and with one another. They were more eager to establish their own reputation."[80] The enthusiasm, ignorance, and perhaps naïveté of Forbes, Rodney, and Brent created expectations in the United Provinces that consistently failed to materialize. The utter incompetence of Slacum, in combination with the aggression of Captain Duncan, destroyed Baylies's mission long before he arrived in the United Provinces. But Baylies also proved inflexible, and he refused to "abandon one tittle of our maratime [sic] rights."[81] Harris was not trusted by the Argentine government because of Brent's unfulfilled promises and because of the actions of the United States at the expense of Mexico. Not a single diplomat, including the capable Forbes, grasped the importance of Great Britain to Argentina in terms of the realities of power politics and trade. In each category Britain had far more to offer Argentina than did the United States, a fledgling, untried power. Exasperated by Argentina's close ties with Britain, American diplomats attempted to operate within a situation that they found incomprehensible and developed a deep-seated paranoia. They constantly spun theories of conspiracy and reported the sinister designs of the English. They saw the British hand everywhere, which seriously compromised their ability as diplomats.

6

The United States and Mexico, 1810–1850

Edward H. Moseley

John Quincy Adams predicted that Cuba would quickly fall into the gravitational pull of the United States, but it was Mexico that was to bear the brunt of Anglo-American expansion and serve as a buffer between the United States and the other nations of Latin America. Some historians and political leaders, both Mexican and American, described the process as a well-organized plan, with the government in Washington in partnership with the forces of slavery. In reality, events were not so well orchestrated; merchants, land speculators, and land-hungry settlers along the Sabine, the Brazos, and eventually the Rio Grande exercised a major influence on the course of international relations.[1] Andrew Jackson, James Tyler, and even James K. Polk were more the followers of the dynamics of private initiative than the shapers of policy and grand strategy. Mexico was the victim of what might be called a natural law of political geometry: proximity breeds suspicion and conflict.

Although Anglo-American forces were anxious to swallow up vast territories, the opportunity was provided by the victim itself. Between 1810 and 1850, Mexico could not solve its basic internal problems. Forces of traditional values clashed constantly with the winds of liberalism, and there was a continual problem regarding the role of the Roman Catholic church within the emerging secular state. Especially influential in foreign affairs was the complex struggle between the central government and a wide variety of regional, state, and local factions. Major centers of discontent included Yucatán, Jalisco, Zacatecas, and Tamaulipas, but it was Texas that brought a rejection of centralized authority into the international arena. Merchants and political leaders in Veracruz resented restrictions that subordinated their

122

interests to those of the capital, and the port city became the spawning ground of the many revolts of an enigmatic caudillo, Antonio López de Santa Anna. The United States simply took advantage of these internal problems, and Mexico became the primary victim of Anglo-American expansionism. Events in Mexico have, in turn, influenced attitudes toward the United States throughout the entire hemisphere.

Colonial Background, 1670–1783

Sir Francis Drake, John Hawkins, and other English sea dogs defied the Iberian monopoly in the New World throughout much of the sixteenth century; after the English colonized South Carolina in 1670, the challenge took on a more decided territorial character. Dr. Henry Woodward organized trading expeditions into the interior of the North American continent, and within a few years, English and Scottish traders won commercial advantages over the Spanish with Cherokee, Creek, and Choctaw chieftains. By 1700, South Carolina commerce was linked with Indian tribes as far west as the Mississippi River, and its success was a primary factor in the collapse of the Spanish province of Guale.[2] When James Oglethorpe attacked Saint Augustine in 1740, he set a precedent for later Anglo-American raids into Florida. North American rivalry mirrored dynastic and national struggles in eighteenth-century Europe; and with the end of the Seven Years' War in 1763, the British flag was raised over Saint Augustine. The acquisition of Florida, along with the withdrawal of France from the North American continent, marked a new phase in Anglo-Spanish competition. At first glance, Louisiana seemed to provide a significant barrier between the English and the silver mines of Zacatecas, but Spain lacked the manpower and organizational skills to utilize the extensive territory that was dumped into its lap.[3] The inevitable clash took a new twist when the English colonies in North America revolted. Spain joined France against Great Britain and in the struggle regained Florida. More importantly, the Spanish Bourbons seemed to have traded a powerful European rival for a set of weak and bickering states. In the long run, the new neighbor was to prove even more threatening than the old, and the ideals and examples of the

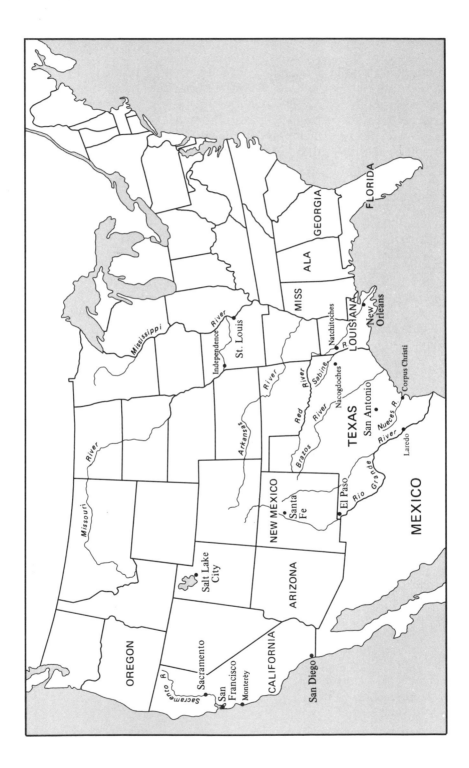

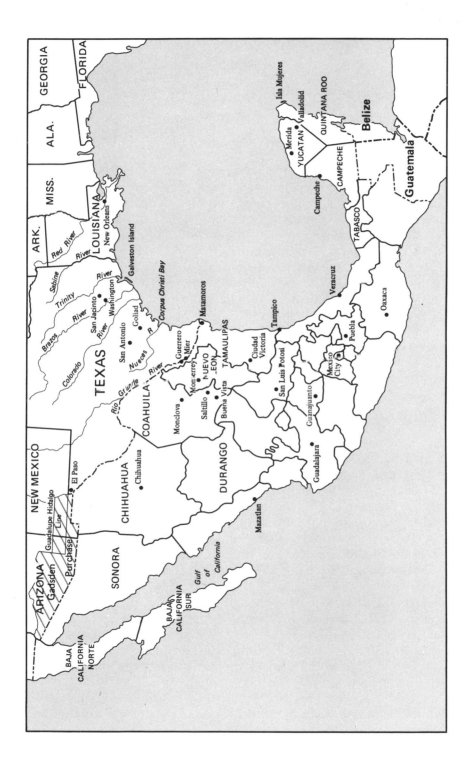

revolting colonists were to influence events that would eventually bring the collapse of Spanish rule in the New World.[4]

The United States and Spain, 1783–1810

Following the American Revolution, Spain established alliances with major Indian groups to block Anglo-American settlers moving south and west. In 1784 it closed the Mississippi River to United States commerce, and from Mexico City Viceroy José de Gálvez established a series of military posts in Texas and strengthened the entire northern frontier of New Spain. It seemed unlikely that thirteen disunited states on the Atlantic seaboard would be able to challenge Spanish rule effectively, especially since the dominant eastern interests in the United States showed little concern for river commerce or other priorities of the westerners.[5]

Both the death of King Charles III in 1788 and the outbreak of the French Revolution the following year weakened Spain's position in the Americas. After the adoption of a new constitution in 1789, the United States was able to establish an effective and stable government under President George Washington. In 1792 Esteban Miró, Spanish governor of Louisiana, expressed alarm at the increasing number of Anglo-Americans pushing into Ohio and Kentucky. Governor Manuel Gayoso de Lemos, on a trip from Natchez to Illinois three years later, reported that most of the trade on the Mississippi was in the hands of the Anglos. As if in resignation to this situation, Spain granted to U.S. citizens the right of navigation on the Mississippi.[6] The decision was made as a result not of effective planning in Washington but of events in Europe as well as relentless pressure from frontiersmen.

As an ally of revolutionary France, Spain was virtually cut off from its empire, which was flooded with contraband British goods. In 1797 a royal order opened ports in Spanish America to neutral shipping, and traders from Baltimore, Boston, New York, and other eastern ports immediately took advantage of the opportunity. In July 1799 a Treasury official at Veracruz reported that of thirty foreign ships in the harbor, twenty-five were from the United States.[7] These commercial contacts contributed to the growing political and economic liberalism in Veracruz, a factor that was to have far-reaching results in domestic and foreign affairs.

In 1803 Napoleon Bonaparte proposed selling the vast and ill-defined region of Louisiana to the United States. Thomas Jefferson quickly accepted the offer, and at once the fledgling North American republic and its restless citizens were face-to-face with Spanish Texas.[8] President Jefferson insisted that the western boundary was the Rio Grande, and a number of intrepid explorers helped to establish claims for the territory in question. Philip Nolan visited Texas perhaps as early as 1785 and then set out from Natchez in 1800 to "hunt for horses" along the Brazos River. Although Nolan was killed by a Spanish force, information from his expedition was of great interest to Jefferson, and authorities in New Spain suspected that the United States was behind Nolan's intrusion into Texas. Following the Louisiana Purchase, Lewis and Clark established U.S. claims in the Pacific Northwest, and Thomas Freeman clashed with Spanish forces in eastern Texas along the Red River. Zebulon M. Pike, one of the most colorful of the Jeffersonian explorers, scouted out the headwaters of the Arkansas and Red rivers during the summer of 1806 and was captured in southern Colorado. Taken to Sante Fe and Chihuahua but eventually released, Pike published an account of his adventures in 1810, revealing to merchants in the United States the lure of profits that awaited them in New Mexico. Many others, including General James Wilkinson and former vice-president Aaron Burr, contrived vague plans to expand into Texas, and even Jefferson seemed caught up in the spirit of expansionism when he hinted that an effort might be made to seize Mexico City. At the time, however, Anglo-Americans were not sufficient in number to carry out the threat, and as war clouds darkened, the attention of national leaders was diverted to Great Britain.[9]

In 1806 Spain and the United States agreed to establish a neutral zone along the Sabine River, a kind of no-man's-land and a haven for adventurers and opportunists. Texas was extremely vulnerable, with only some four thousand inhabitants in the entire province. Most of them were concentrated around San Antonio, leaving a virtual vacuum in the extensive territory eastward to Louisiana. The area farther south (Tamaulipas, Nuevo León, and Coahuila) was almost as open to intrusion as Texas, being more secure primarily because of its increased distance from the Anglo-American menace. The primary threat at the time was not overt invasion but cooperation between traders from New Orleans and Saint Louis on the one hand and Spanish settlers along the frontier who were tempted by the availability and lower prices of contraband goods on the other. As soldiers were sent into Texas to halt the flow of illegal trade, they also succumbed to temptation. Most manufactured goods were cheaper in Nacogdoches than in Mexico City or even Veracruz; thus Texas became an important way station for the eastern interior provinces. In 1808 an official in Saltillo reported that illegal goods from the east were abundant at the annual fair of his city.[10]

Spanish leaders feared the strong mutual attraction between northern Mexican settlers and Anglo traders and merchants across the Sabine. Antonio Cordero y Bustamante, governor of Texas, pleaded for new colonists from the interior of Mexico, but growing factionalism in the viceregal capital made that impossible; in 1808 Spanish-born elements in Mexico City overthrew Viceroy Iturrigaray, replacing him with an aged soldier, Pedro Garibay. The coup was simply the outward manifestation of the deep-seated problems of New Spain. It was the forerunner of a long line of violent actions that were to characterize Mexico for over a half century and to have a profound influence on its relationships with its "Yanqui" neighbor.[11] As Thomas Jefferson left office in 1809, border problems took a backseat to emerging difficulties with the British. Merchants and shippers of the eastern United States were content to enjoy a profitable commerce with Veracruz and other Spanish ports.[12]

The United States and Insurgent Mexico, 1810–1820

Padre Miguel Hidalgo y Costillo issued the *Grito de Dolores* on September 16, 1810, initiating the struggle for Mexican independence. Rooted in Spanish tradition and growing from the dynamics of Mexican politics, the movement shared certain philosophical ideals with the uprisings in Boston and Philadelphia thirty-four years earlier. As Hidalgo swept all Spanish opposition before him in the early months of his revolt, there were strong expressions of support from the United States.[13] Texas governor Manuel Salcedo feared that Anglo-Americans along the Mississippi River would take advantage of the internal strife to seize territory.[14]

By the end of 1810, Hidalgo controlled most of south-central Mexico, including the rich mines of Guanajuato and Zacatecas. On January 7, 1811, his forces took Coahuila without firing a shot, and the governor of Nuevo León immediately capitulated. In Texas, Governor Salcedo was deposed on January 22, and by early February elements loyal to the rebel priest claimed the entire sparsely populated region from San Antonio to Nacogdoches. The news was received with widespread enthusiasm in New Orleans, and Louisiana governor William C. C. Claibourne was especially supportive of José Bernardo Gutiérrez de Lara, rebel leader in Tamaulipas. Despite this encouragement, there was no overt Anglo-American participation in the initial Mexican movement for independence.[15]

Apparently on the brink of victory, Padre Hidalgo turned away from Mexico City and, on January 17, 1811, suffered a major defeat. Remnants of the once proud army under the banner of the Virgin of Guadalupe fled north, reaching Saltillo in early March. Hidalgo planned to continue to San Antonio and eventually to the United States. Two agents were commissioned to proceed with one hundred bars of silver to win support for their cause, but they were captured by royalist forces in San Antonio. On March 21, 1811, the rebel priest and his top aides were also seized as they fled northward. Hidalgo's execution four months later ended the first phase of the Mexican war for independence. By his attempt to gain support from the United States, the ill-fated priest set a pattern that was to be repeated during virtually every uprising in Mexican history.[16]

With the defeat of Hidalgo, leadership of the movement for independence shifted to another priest. By early 1813 the armies of José María Morelos controlled territory south of Mexico City, a wide arc centered in Oaxaca and reaching almost to the port of Veracruz. Morelos declared Mexican independence and in October 1814 sponsored a republican constitution modeled after that of the United States. He appointed José Manuel Herrera to represent his cause in the northern republic. Accompanied by the thirteen-year-old son of his chieftain and an enterprising Anglo-American named Peter E. Bean, Herrera was sidetracked by intrigues along the Texas frontier and never reached Washington. Meanwhile, in the south, Viceroy Felix María Calleja inflicted a series of defeats on the rebels and eventually captured the leader. During his trial in November 1815, Morelos admitted that he had attempted to win support from the United States, but without success.[17]

If one falls into the trap of accepting the traditional interpretation of the Mexican struggle for independence, an interpretation centered on the heroic actions of the priest-warrior in Oaxaca, then it is logical to conclude that the United States contributed little to the movement between 1811 and 1815. If events on the northern periphery are taken into consideration, however, then it becomes apparent that elements of Mexican liberation and Anglo-American expansionism were interwoven in a significant, though often contradictory, way.

José Bernardo Gutiérrez de Lara, having fled Texas at the time of the collapse of the Hidalgo movement, set up a base of operations in New Orleans and recruited volunteers in Tennessee and Kentucky for a projected invasion across the Sabine, apparently with the assistance of Governor Claibourne of Louisiana. During a visit to Washington, Gutiérrez was warmly received, though Secretary of State James Monroe avoided any official recognition. In late March 1812, the chieftain returned to New Orleans, where he was joined by two other soldiers of fortune, Don Simón Tadeo Ortíz and José Alvarez de Toledo. Governor Claibourne once again offered his encouragement. Also favoring the cause were William Shaler, a recently appointed U.S. commercial agent to Mexico, and James Wilkinson, a veteran intriguer. President James Madison proclaimed neutrality, but no effort was made to enforce that official position along the Louisiana-Texas frontier. This was made quite clear in June when Lieutenant Augustus Magee of the United States Army resigned his commission and organized a "volunteer" Anglo-American force, the Republican Army of the North. From his post in Washington, the Spanish minister Luís de Onís loudly denounced these expansionist activities.[18]

With a combined force of about 130 men, Gutiérrez de Lara and Magee pushed across the Sabine and on August 12, 1812, captured Nacogdoches. Volunteers streamed in from the United States, and Louisiana merchants and speculators dispatched hundreds of supply wagons. In mid-October the invaders camped west of the Trinity River and by the following February prepared to attack San Antonio with a force of some 2,500 men. They soundly defeated the small Texas force under Governor Manuel Salcedo, and on March 29, 1813, Gutiérrez declared the region to be independent.

It is significant that the proclamation in Texas came seven months before the declaration of Mexican independence made by Morelos in the south. Although Gutiérrez insisted that his only objective was to liberate Mexico from Spain, many of the participants in the fighting anticipated that Texas would be annexed by the United States and that they would receive extensive land grants. As Gutiérrez prepared to push into Coahuila and Nuevo León, serious dissatisfaction was expressed by the Anglo-American faction. Magee had died in February, and his associates were disgruntled when they failed to receive political offices in the newly established Texas government. Yankee troops in San Antonio revolted in August 1813 and forced Gutiérrez to surrender his command to Alvarez de Toledo.

From his headquarters in Monterrey, Brigadier General José Joaquín Arredondo, virtually independent of the authority of the viceroy in Mexico City, was responsible for the vast region called the Interior Provinces of the East, which comprised the present-day states of Tamaulipas, Nuevo León, Coahuila, and Texas. Arredondo took advantage of the dissension in the ranks of the invasion force and on August 18, 1813, recaptured San Antonio. In an orgy of celebration, the royalists returned to Monterrey with fifty-two human ears laced together as a trophy. Although a number of Anglo-Americans were killed, most fled eastward beyond the Sabine. If President James Madison had ever entertained any ambition of utilizing the Gutiérrez-Magee expedition to expand U.S. territorial holdings, he abandoned the idea and took no action regarding the Americans executed by royalist order.[19] Despite the failure of the ambitious invasion, private elements in the United States had contributed greatly to the destabilization of northeastern New Spain, a situation that was to have serious long-term consequences for the region and for all Mexico.

By the end of 1815, central New Spain seemed to be once again under firm Spanish control. Although a few guerrilla leaders such as Guadalupe Victoria and Vicente Guerrero continued to hold out in mountain retreats, Viceroy Juan Ruíz de Apodaca was rather successful in his efforts to win the support of the Mexican people. Most of Mexico returned to relative peace and security but continued to suffer severe economic dislocations brought about by years of conflict and destruction. A primary concern of Viceroy Apodaca, however, centered upon the continuing problems on the northeastern frontier.[20]

General Arredondo had few resources for meeting an overwhelming challenge: the economy of the entire eastern interior provinces was in shambles from long years of neglect, and Indian bands roamed across the desert region in ever-increasing numbers. Eastern Texas, long the scene of invasion and uncertainty, was virtually uninhabited and posed an open invitation for renewed Anglo-American adventurers. Arredondo concluded that the only solution was to open the region to colonization, preferably from Mexico or Spain. From Washington, Luís de Onís suggested that it might be possible to persuade a small group of French settlers to move from Demopolis, Alabama, to Texas. Though it never went beyond this initial suggestion, the plan was strongly criticized by Secretary of State John Quincy Adams.[21] In 1817 another threat from the east made it even more clear that a buffer was necessary to maintain Spanish control in the Texas region.

While serving as agent to the United States for Padre Morelos, José

Manuel Herrera negotiated with a small faction on Galveston Island to open a port of the Mexican republic but abandoned the scheme when he failed to win support from New Orleans merchants.[22] Soon after Herrera's departure, however, another ambitious adventurer sought to utilize the Galveston base. Francisco Xavier Mina, though born in Spain, became an advocate of Latin American emancipation soon after leaving his homeland in 1815. In England he met Servando Teresa de Mier of Nuevo León, who spoke of the vulnerable northern flank of New Spain. Mina reached the United States in June 1816, quickly gained backing from a group of prominent businessmen, and transferred his base of operations to Galveston. He organized an expedition of some 350 men, mostly Anglo-American volunteers, and appointed Colonel Henry Perry as assistant commander. From his Washington observation post Onís denounced the Texas events as a blatant violation of United States neutrality. On April 7, 1817, with nine small vessels, Mina departed from Galveston. He stopped briefly at the mouth of the Rio Grande and then divided his force into two separate units. Perry marched northwest toward San Antonio. On June 19, Texas governor Antonio Martínez attacked the column, killing Perry and twenty-five of his men and capturing most of the rest. The primary invading force under Mina fared no better and was completely crushed near Guanajuato. Mina was taken prisoner, tried, and executed.[23]

Despite U.S. public opinion, which strongly favored the filibusters in Texas, the Monroe administration maintained a policy of official neutrality. Secretary of State John Quincy Adams was negotiating at that time with Onís over the Florida question, and by the terms of the treaty completed on February 22, 1819, the United States recognized the Sabine River as the legitimate border between Louisiana and Texas. In exchange for the transfer of Florida by Spain, the Monroe administration abandoned the claims for territory to the Rio Grande which had been set forth by Thomas Jefferson. Senator Thomas Hart Benton, a voice for the frontier, denounced the eastern establishment for "giving away . . . the region west of the Sabine."[24] Secretary Adams was surely aware that the dynamics of settlers and adventurers would soon override this formal agreement. He was concerned, however, when the frontiersmen took matters in their own hands before Spain could ratify the treaty.

James Long, backed by New Orleans financiers, led a force into Texas in June 1819, taking with him the venerable revolutionary Bernardo Gutiérrez de Lara. In Nacogdoches, Long once again declared

Texas independent, organized a government, and promised land to those loyal to his cause. He appointed the pirate leader Jean Lafitte as governor of Galveston Island. In February 1820, Texas governor Antonio Martínez defeated the raiders and captured Long. During the following several months, however, filibuster leaders continued to carry out hit-and-run attacks. The United States denounced the adventurers, undoubtedly because they posed a threat to the Adams-Onís Treaty still being debated in Madrid.[25]

Liberal factions in Spain moved against Ferdinand VII in January 1820, forcing him to reestablish the constitution of 1812. At the same time, a land law of January 4, 1813, which offered titles to open lands in the colonies, was also reestablished and was to have a major impact upon the northeastern Mexican frontier. Both General Arredondo and Governor Martínez favored the measure, which promised assistance against the ever-increasing Indian raids.[26] Aware of the new policy, Moses Austin visited San Antonio in December 1820 and assured Governor Martínez that, if granted the right to colonize in Texas, he would accept all Spanish laws and customs.[27] As preparation began for the establishment of a peaceful settlement of Anglo-Americans, fundamental political changes occurred in central Mexico.

Iturbide and the United States, 1821–1823

Augustín de Iturbide, an ambitious Creole officer who had staunchly supported royal authority against Hidalgo and Morelos, reversed his position on February 24, 1821, and joined with rebel leader Vicente Guerrero in the Plan of Iguala calling for Mexican independence and the continued religious preeminence of the Roman Catholic church. After the acceptance of the plan by the newly arrived viceroy, Juan O'Donojú, the Army of Three Guarantees moved triumphantly into Mexico City. Iturbide "reluctantly" accepted the crown as emperor on May 19, 1822, and promised to build an orderly and stable society.[28] He seemed to have achieved an impossible task, that of bringing widely divergent factions into the support of a new national effort. James Smith Wilcocks, United States consul in Mexico City at the time, praised the new government and declared that the people of Mexico supported it. Secretary of State John Quincy Adams favored the establishment of commercial relations and dispatched consul agents to Veracruz and other key cities.[29]

On January 8, 1822, Iturbide expressed to President James Monroe

Joel R. Poinsett (The National Portrait Gallery, Smithsonian Institution)

his hopes that Mexico be able to purchase ships from the United States. Following his coronation, the emperor appointed Manuel Bermúdez Zozaya as envoy to the North American government, where he was received by president Monroe. Iturbide considered friendly relations with the United States to be an important part of his efforts to bring stability to his fledgling empire. Washington officials, on the other hand, were reluctant to rush into a close alliance with the newly established Latin American monarchy. President Monroe dispatched Joel R. Poinsett, an experienced veteran of South American affairs, on a fact-finding mission. Poinsett met with Iturbide on November 3,

1822, and continued to observe conditions in the Mexican capital. The following January, he expressed serious doubt that the emperor had the support of military leaders or of the general Mexican population. Acting upon his advice, the United States delayed in appointing an envoy to Mexico for the next three years. Monroe's decision has often been labeled a costly mistake which gave Great Britain a virtual monopoly of influence at the court of Iturbide.[30] The lack of formal relations did little, however, to hinder the ever-increasing pressures by the North American private sector.

From his headquarters in Monterrey, General Arredondo rejected the Plan of Iguala, declaring his continued loyalty to Spain. On July 2, 1821, he was forced by factions from Saltillo to reverse his position and to accept Mexican independence. Within a short time Iturbide replaced Arredondo with an ardent republican and longtime advocate of independence, Colonel Gaspar Antonio López. The new commander invited Gutiérrez de Lara to return to Mexico and ordered Governor Martínez to release James Long, referring to the filibuster leader as a fellow champion of Mexican independence. Furthermore, López removed Martínez and named as governor of Texas a close associate of Long, Félix Trespalacios.

In the midst of the confusion, Stephen F. Austin arrived in San Antonio on August 10, 1821, claiming the territory that had been granted to his father the previous year by Spanish officials. Despite some opposition, the following December Austin was allowed to bring his first colonists into the region between the Brazos and Colorado rivers. The legal status of the holding was still in question in early 1822, when a commission appointed by Iturbide recommended to the Chamber of Deputies that approval be given to the continuation of the Spanish colonization law upon which the Austin grant had been based. Austin traveled to Mexico City in April to assure Iturbide and members of the legislative body that his colonists would be good citizens of the Mexican empire. Much to Austin's disgust, debate over the measure dragged on and became enmeshed in the growing hostilities between the emperor and various factions in the assembly. As might have been expected, one of the strongest advocates for Austin's cause was the deputy from Tamaulipas, José Bernardo Gutiérrez de Lara. Valentín Gómez Farías, an ardent liberal from Zacatecas, denounced the scheme on the basis that it would introduce slavery into Texas. In late November 1822, following a purge of the legislature by the emperor's armed forces, the measure was approved by the remnants of that body, and the emperor signed it on January 4, 1823.[31]

Austin was aware that the fate of his enterprise was dependent upon the ability of the Mexican nation to provide a stable and workable government. By 1823, however, it seemed doubtful that the empire could provide that security.

Although Texas was the most important focus for Anglo-American activity in the early days of Mexican independence, significant developments were also under way farther west. As early as 1812, Yankee traders dreamed of establishing profitable commercial links with Chihuahua and Zacatecas through New Mexico. Spanish representative Onís denounced the early efforts as a trap to lure away the loyal subjects of New Spain. It was after the Plan of Iguala, however, in the summer of 1821, that Captain William Becknell escorted a party of some twenty-five traders from Saint Louis, Missouri, to Santa Fe. Governor Facundo Melgares of New Mexico, who had accepted the proclamation of Iturbide, welcomed the Yankee merchants and their highly desirable wares.[32]

Thus while Iturbide attempted to consolidate his political rule against powerful odds and the United States government held him at arm's length, the Anglo-American private sector was engaged in agricultural settlements and commercial ventures on the northern fringe of the empire. This was not a part of a coordinated plan to promote republicanism or expand slavery, but was based upon the widespread desire in the private sector to acquire rich lands and gain profits. From his lonely vantage point in Washington, Iturbide's envoy José Manuel Bermúdez Zozaya warned: "In time they will be our sworn enemies, and foreseeing this we ought to treat them as such from the present day."[33] The validity of that prophecy in late 1822 was due in large part to the continuing internal problems of the Mexican nation.

Relations between Two Federal Republics, 1823–1828

Iturbide's façade of national unity was quickly stripped away. Creoles despised *peninsulares* who retained lucrative posts and influence, republicans denounced the monarchy, and provincial leaders chaffed under central rule. In Veracruz, Jalisco, and Yucatán, ambitious politicians criticized the emperor, and in Coahuila Miguel Ramos de Arizpe declared that the best solution was to be found in a federal republic. The problem was to be solved not by debate but by force of arms:

Antonio López de Santa Anna proclaimed the Plan of Casa Mata, which was endorsed by various elements throughout the nation. On March 27, 1823, Guadalupe Victoria marched into the capital, declaring the monarchy to be at an end. While the question of national rule was debated, municipal and provincial authorities assumed control. Guatemala led Central America in what proved to be a permanent break from Mexico and entered into its own era of conflict. Yucatán, too, considered complete separation from the central region of Mexico but agreed to retain its association if certain local privileges could be guaranteed. In the interior provinces to the north there was also an important tendency toward self-rule, and it was at this time of uncertainty that Coahuila and Texas adopted a colonization law that bestowed legal recognition of the claims of Stephen F. Austin and other newly arrived settlers.[34]

In 1824 Mexico adopted a new federal constitution that granted extensive powers to the individual states, including control of their public lands. Padre Mier of Nuevo León denounced the document as a mere translation of the Constitution of the United States, unsuited for Mexico. Since that time, critics of the federalist system have alleged that its principal author, Ramos Arizpe, was strongly influenced by his friend, Stephen F. Austin. To credit Austin and the U.S. model for the Mexican constitution of 1824 is to ignore Spanish influences and the strong convictions of leaders such as Ramos Arizpe and Lorenzo de Zavala, who viewed centralization as a primary factor in the ills of their newly independent nation. The alternative to federalism in 1824 may not have been an efficient, centralized republic but the complete splintering of the former Spanish colony. As has been demonstrated by several detailed studies of New Spain, there were important precedents for Mexican federalism.[35] The chaotic nature of the Mexican nation after 1824 was not due to the form of government but stemmed primarily from political and military leaders who refused to accept any restrictions on their personal ambitions.

Guadalupe Victoria, the first president of Mexico, expressed optimism regarding relations with the United States. The brilliant young Yucatecan who entered his cabinet, Lorenzo de Zavala, was a great admirer of the northern neighbor, and at that time even the more conservative Lucas Alamán seemed favorably disposed toward the United States. On November 18, 1824, Pablo Obregón, Mexican minister to the United States, met briefly with President James Monroe in a cordial setting. Obregón was to provide a listening post on the Potomac for almost four years, but his contributions to his nation were to be limited by ill health, constant financial problems, and a lack of ability in the English language.[36]

Events surrounding the first United States envoy to Mexico were much more lively and were to have significant influence on relations between the two countries. Joel R. Poinsett was appointed minister to Mexico after many delays. He reached Mexico City in June 1825, finding that much of the initial enthusiasm for republican solidarity had faded. Poinsett initiated discussions relating to the boundary but, under instructions from Secretary of State Henry Clay, exercised caution in pressing territorial claims. Poinsett emphasized broad friendly relations and the development of commercial links. Within a short time after his arrival, however, the Yankee envoy was caught up in the internal factionalism that erupted after Mexico's brief "era of good feeling." Supportive of Lorenzo de Zavala and other members of the York Rite Lodge, he came to be distrusted by Lucas Alamán and the more conservative factions. President Victoria gave much greater emphasis to the establishment of ties with Great Britain, represented in Mexico City by Henry George Ward, who had arrived almost two years before Poinsett. Ward not only warned against the threat of United States expansionism but also offered the lure of loans and investments from the English business and banking community, especially in the long-neglected mining industry.[37]

Late in 1826, Haden Edwards proclaimed the Fredonian revolt against Mexican rule in eastern Texas. Despite the fact that Stephen F. Austin and other loyal Anglo-Americans supported the Mexican authorities and that Henry Clay denounced the uprising, the events around Nacogdoches triggered concern among Mexican officials. From his vantage point in Washington, Pablo Obregón observed the enthusiasm of the common citizens and newspaper editors in the United States over the events west of the Sabine. Ambassador Ward, always happy to give unsolicited advice, suggested that Mexico conduct an investigation of the Texas borderlands.[38] In the following year, Manuel Mier y Terán carried out an extensive inspection of conditions in the northeast.

At the same time that settlers moved into Texas, there was a major increase in the trade from Missouri across the eight hundred miles of wilderness to Santa Fe. Merchandise from Saint Louis was much cheaper than goods sent northward from Mexico City and Chihuahua. Value of imports expanded from about $15,000 in 1822 to some $150,000 by 1828. The trade not only provided citizens of New Mexico with scarce items but produced considerable revenue for the local government. Although considered desirable by officials in Santa Fe, these activities were viewed with suspicion by the administration in Mexico City. Concern must have increased when the governor of Chihuahua reported in 1825 that the Yankee traders were better acquainted with New Mexico than were Mexican authorities. Obregón also expressed concern that the trade would weaken Mexico's hold on her northern provinces.[39]

By 1827, as the term of President Victoria drew to a close, there was a growing suspicion of U.S. motives. Much of that suspicion was directed against the American minister, who dabbled constantly in internal politics. Poinsett was denounced by even some of his Yorkist associates, and Secretary of State Henry Clay stated that it would be perfectly understandable if the South Carolinian would choose to return home.[40] Poinsett has often been branded a failure, the victim of his own ideology and zeal. His shortcomings, great though they may have been, were not the fundamental reason for his failure to establish harmonious relations with the sister republic. British commercial and investment objectives as represented by Ward were compatible with the interests of Mexico as perceived by its leaders at the time, especially Lucas Alamán. Anglo-American objectives, represented primarily by private elements rather than the national government, were territorial and commercial. The treaty that Poinsett finally signed in 1828 actually sacrificed United States claims west of the Sabine.[41] That document, yet to be ratified by both parties, might have been the final act in Anglo-Hispanic territorial rivalry in North America. The fact that this was not to be the case had little to do with Poinsett or his successors, but was to be altered by the continuing movement of settlers westward from the United States. More importantly, Mexico was to enter another period of internal conflict that would eventually involve the Anglo-American citizens of the north and would, in turn, set the stage for increased tensions with the United States.

Mexican Relations in the Age of Jackson, 1828–1835

Having been denied power in 1824, Andrew Jackson and his partisans swept into office in 1828 and were to dominate United States politics for the next twelve years. Jackson's victory over South Carolina nullifiers in 1832 was hailed as a triumph of nationalism over narrow sectional interests, but it also foreshadowed conflicts that would eventually influence Mexican relations. The Indian Removal Bill forced some sixty thousand native Americans west of the Mississippi, thus adding to problems along the Texas border.[42] Despite the many political battles that raged throughout his presidency, Jackson remained a strong and dynamic leader and projected an image of stability and dynamism.

By contrast, Mexico faced grave difficulties in 1828. Loans that had been secured from British bankers in the early years of the republic had been squandered, and the suspension of interest payments virtually eliminated all sources of further credit. When Scottish Rite candidate Manuel Gómez Pedraza won the presidential election of 1828, Yorkist opponents refused to accept defeat. The Chamber of Deputies, pressured by regional military chieftains and in blatant disregard for the established electoral mechanism, awarded the prize to Vicente Guerrero. When that Yorkist champion took office on April 1, 1829, he found the treasury empty and the nation in shambles. Accused of scheming with Joel Poinsett for the sale of Texas, the old hero was deserted by many former supporters, including Antonio López de Santa Anna. By the end of the year, he was expelled from the capital and was soon after executed as a traitor to his nation.[43]

In 1831 a relatively stable government was established under General Anastasio Bustamante, who was assisted by one of the most able individuals in the nation, Lucas Alamán. Many regions, especially those distant from Mexico City, rejected centralized authority, and in early 1832 Valentín Gómez Farías raised the cry for federalism in the silver-rich state of Zacatecas. His movement was soon echoed throughout much of the nation: Santa Anna, always prepared to join a popular wave, championed the rebellion in Veracruz. By the end of the year, Bustamante resigned, and the rebels, seeking to give their coup an air of legitimacy, brought Gómez Pedraza back to the presidency on January 3, 1833. New elections were held, and to the surprise of no one, Antonio López de Santa Anna was declared the winner.[44]

Proclaiming the virtues of federalism, the caudillo took office on April 1, 1833, but immediately stepped aside, leaving the troubled nation in the charge of his vice-president, Valentín Gómez Farías. The Zacatecas liberal not only made a sincere effort to reestablish the constitution of 1824 but also initiated a series of measures to curb the wealth and power of the Roman Catholic church. The resulting polarization of Mexican politics was to reach its high point some twenty years later in the War of the Reforma. The early *puro* experiment was cut short in December 1834, however, when Santa Anna switched sides, ousting Gómez Farías in the name of religion and order.[45] The nation was once again plunged into conflict and disorder.

Internal divisions and the resulting instability formed the background for Mexico's relations with the United States from 1828 to 1835. Conditions in Coahuila and Texas were the major influence in U.S.-Mexican relations throughout the Jackson administration. There was a widespread fear that President Jackson was plotting to seize the region west of the Sabine.[46] Secretary of State Martin Van Buren declared in 1829 that the administration had no intention of invading its neighbor and warned Anthony Butler, Poinsett's successor as minister to Mexico, to stay out of the internal politics of that troubled nation.[47] The president did desire to readjust the border and instructed Butler to strike a bargain for additional territory. The mere suggestion that Vicente Guerrero might sell Texas was an important factor in his overthrow and death.[48]

General Manuel Mier y Terán conducted his inspection of Texas in 1828. He reported that most Mexican officials along the frontier were ignorant, venal, and corrupt, while the Anglo-Americans who made up the majority of the population were a mixture of vagabonds, criminals, and honest laborers. Mier y Terán admired Stephen F. Austin as a man of great vision and energy but concluded that he and other colonists posed a grave danger for Mexico. Most of the commerce was linked to New Orleans merchants. The commander was further alarmed by the constant rumors that an Anglo-American force was massing along the Sabine to invade Texas.[49]

Acting upon his observations, Mier y Terán submitted a plan of action reminiscent of the energetic measures taken by the Spanish Bourbons in the eighteenth century. He recommended a system of fortifications across eastern Texas, the introduction of German and Swiss colonists, and the opening of commerce between Texas and other Mexican ports on the Gulf of Mexico. When the plan was submitted in the capital city, Lucas Alamán added an article that prohibited the further entrance into the border area by colonists from the United States. The measure was passed by the Mexican congress on April 6, 1830.[50]

The following October, construction was initiated on a Mexican fort at Anáhuac on Galveston Bay, under the direction of Virginia-born John Davis Bradburn. Ironically, the small force of thirty men representing the authority of Mexico on the northeastern frontier was dependent for its survival upon supplies from the United States. Anglo-Americans resented the establishment of customs duties and regularly ignored them. The flood of emigrants from east of the Sabine, now officially illegal, continued virtually unchecked. When he attempted to interfere in that process, Bradburn was denounced not only by the emigrants but also by state officials from Coahuila, who accused him of usurping their right to make land grants. In May 1832 Bradburn arrested William B. Travis, a recent arrival in Texas and an outspoken critic of Mexican policy. This triggered a rebellion under the leadership of John Austin, and by the end of the year, Bradburn and his small force were expelled from Texas. Seeing the collapse of his ambitious plan, General Mier y Terán committed suicide.[51]

Mexican officials denounced the United States for its involvement in the events along the frontier. When the Mexican minister José María Tornel arrived in the United States in early 1830, he became fully aware of the desire on the part of many Americans, including President Jackson, to acquire Texas. He insisted to Secretary of State Van Buren that the Mexican laws against emigration to Texas should be enforced by the United States, but the secretary contended that citizens of his nation had a right to go where they chose and pointed out to Tornel that there was no pressure on them from the United States government. Tornel also complained of intrusions into Mexican territory by "United States Indians," but Van Buren rebuffed that argument. The Mexican ambassador wanted to secure a firm boundary along the Sabine, but the volatile conditions on that border and the weakness of his home government defied his efforts.[52]

In Mexico much of the criticism of U.S. plots centered upon Anthony Butler. Ramón Múzquiz, a prominent Mexican citizen of San Antonio, saw the American minister as an ally of the proslave interests so prominent among the Anglo emigrants in eastern Texas and branded him as a proponent of separation of Texas from Mexico. Other citizens of northern Mexico also warned that Texas would be lost and identified the flood of emigrants from the United States as the basic force in the process of deterioration.[53] In Mexico City, Butler found the climate so hostile that he advised President Jackson that it would be best to delay efforts to purchase the Texas territory. Following the overthrow of Guerrero, despite the pro-British leanings of Alamán, Butler felt that there might be a possibility of striking a bargain.[54] Before this dream could be fulfilled, however, the federalist forces came to power.

With the overthrow of Mexican authority in Galveston, there were renewed rumors of an invasion from the United States. The triumphant elements in Galveston proclaimed, however, that their movement was not an overthrowing of Mexican authority but an integral part of the federalist effort for the reestablishment of the constitution of 1824.[55] The struggle between centralists and federalists gave the Anglo-Texans the perfect excuse to carry out their quest for power within the context of Mexican nationalism. In 1833 they joined with federalist elements in Coahuila to transfer the capital of the vast state from Saltillo to Monclova. Encouraged by the repeal of many of the restrictions that had been enacted in 1830, Stephen F. Austin traveled to Mexico City in the spring of 1833 to meet with fellow federalist Valentín Gómez Farías. He must have been surprised and disgusted when he was forced to wait two months before being received by the acting president. Upon his return trip, Austin was arrested on the charge that he advocated the separation of Texas from Coahuila. After nearly a year in prison, he was finally allowed to return to Texas. There he found that the elements of separatism had gained a powerful spokesman in Sam Houston, former governor of Tennessee and a close friend of President Jackson.[56]

The activities of Anthony Butler were carried out in the shadow of events in Texas, and the Mexican press continued to link him with the most sinister of plots. Always lacking in basic understanding of Mexico and its people, the United States envoy assumed in 1833 that he would be able to acquire Texas through an agreement with Gómez Farías. The federalist leader was no more anxious to barter away the northern territory than were his centralist predecessors. Butler, though at first cautious in his approach, grew hostile and sarcastic by early 1834, convinced that his enemies were plotting against him and his nation.[57] By the end of 1834, Santa Anna returned to center stage, this time a champion of *fueros* and centralism. Butler demanded of the new foreign minister that Texas be recognized as rightfully belonging to the people of the United States.[58] Privately, he bragged to President Jackson that he could bribe officials under Santa Anna to readjust the border.[59] When Butler returned to the United States in June 1835, he was convinced that through secret negotiations with Santa Anna, the United States could acquire not only Texas but New Mexico and California as well.[60]

The official position taken by the Jackson administration was one of aloof neutrality. Throughout the period each of the secretaries of state emphasized their desire to maintain cordial relations with Mexico. In answer to complaints of violations of the border, however, they claimed that it was impossible to limit the movements of free citizens.[61] President Jackson wanted to expand national territory but at the same time vowed to remain at peace with Mexico.[62] He seemed content to allow private forces to bear the brunt of expansionist activities. Jackson lost contact with his intrepid ambassador to Mexico between July and November of 1835 but was soon to learn of his new intrigues and insults against Mexican officials.[63]

Mexican observers in the United States stood by in frustration, convinced that the Jackson government as well as the vast majority of the American people supported rebellion beyond the Sabine border. Juan N. Almonte, who made a detailed study of the frontier, warned of impending dangers.[64] Joaquín Moreno, a young assistant to Lorenzo de Zavala who arrived in New York in 1834, was shocked to hear constant speculation relating to rebellion in Texas and became even more concerned when he realized that his mentor was in the thick of these plots.[65] By 1835 United States relations with Mexico were to be totally intertwined with the rebellion in Texas.

Texas Rebellion and United States Neutrality, 1835–1837

By June 1835 the centralists had triumphed in Mexico City; Gómez Farías and Lorenzo de Zavala were in exile. Strong federalist sentiment continued in the remote regions of Sinaloa, Sonora, and Yucatán. It was in the northeast, however, that Santa Anna's new system faced the most serious threats. Colonel José María González defied central authority in Tamaulipas and maintained communications with elements in Texas. In Coahuila the factionalism was a question not so much of political ideology as of the continuing struggle for power between Saltillo and Monclova. Leaders in Saltillo charged their opponents with hiding Gómez Farías in Monclova, while Governor Agustín Viesca called upon citizens of Texas to join in the fight against the tyranny of Santa Anna and his Saltillo agents. Viesca was captured in June 1835, but when he escaped the following October, he fled to Texas.[66]

General Martín Perfecto de Cos, observing events in Texas, reported that exiled federalists led by Gómez Farías maintained important links with the dissidents. When delegates from various Texas towns met on October 15, 1835, the well-known Yucatecan liberal

Lorenzo de Zavala was a delegate from Harrisburg. General Vicente Filisola suspected that Zavala had every intention of fomenting rebellion.[67] In many ways, the civil unrest in Texas was an extension of the instability that affected the rest of Mexico in 1835.[68] The situation there was unique, however, within the setting of Mexican politics. First of all, Texas bordered on the United States, and, more importantly, it had a vigorous and expanding Anglo-American population. The force under William B. Travis that seized Anáhuac in June 1835 was almost totally Anglo.[69] Despite his long-standing loyalty to Mexico, Stephen F. Austin returned from prison prepared to join the forces of resistance if Santa Anna moved into the region.[70] It might be noted that when Austin had gone to Mexico City to plead for Texas rights, he had found little sympathy from his fellow federalist Gómez Farías. When its convention ended on November 14, 1835, Texas was fully under arms, poised to fight. The conflict that followed was much more than an internal rebellion; it was also a clash of cultures. A few native Mexicans such as Juan N. Seguín took up the struggle against the centralist forces, but the overwhelming majority of those under arms were from east of the Sabine. On November 21, an armed force arrived from Louisiana, changing its name from the New Orleans Greys to the San Antonio Greys. They played a prominent role in a victory over General Cos on December 11, 1835, which forced him to retreat south of the Rio Grande.[71]

Santa Anna abandoned the presidential chair vowing to crush the Texas rebels. Formidable on paper, his army suffered greatly from disorganization and inadequate supplies. After stopping briefly in San Luis Potosí to extract loans from the clergy and propertied class, the commander in chief pushed into the desert plain of northern Coahuila by late 1835. General Vicente Filisola advanced from Monterrey toward Laredo, while the main force under Santa Anna reached the outskirts of San Antonio by February 22, 1836.[72] The Texas force that had reveled in victory only three months earlier had been weakened by desertions and internal bickerings.[73] The capture of the Alamo on March 6, 1836, was hailed by Santa Anna as a glorious triumph for the Mexican nation over its enemies. Federalists such as those in Tamaulipas became convinced that the Anglo elements of Texas were not a proper ally, thus strengthening the concept of Mexican nationalism.[74] On the other hand, the stories of cruelty and brutality associated with the fall of the Alamo were fixed in the minds of the Anglos and became intertwined in the history of Texas and the United States with a negative image of Mexico and especially of Santa Anna. That concept was deepened by the execution of 445 defenders of Goliad on March 27.[75]

In the midst of a series of Mexican victories, Texas representatives met at Washington on the Brazos. On March 2, 1836, they declared their independence and two weeks later adopted a constitution strongly resembling that of the United States. Only three Mexicans signed the declaration of independence, illustrating the preponderance of Anglo-Americans in that process. When a provisional government was established, however, the Yucatecan federalist Lorenzo de Zavala was appointed vice-president to serve with the provisional president David G. Burnet.[76]

The Texas cause seemed doomed in its inception: Santa Anna's forces seized San Felipe de Austín on April 7 and continued the march eastward. The Mexican press hailed the triumph of the cause of their nation and boasted that the victorious army would soon be on the Sabine line.[77] The thrill of victory was short-lived; on April 20–21, 1836, General Sam Houston routed the army of Santa Anna at San Jacinto. At Velasco on May 14, the Mexican commander signed two treaties not only ordering all Mexican forces to retreat south of the Rio Grande but also promising to promote Texas's independence after his release. Knowing the strong public opinion against Santa Anna, the Texas officials kept him securely shackled, and there was widespread talk of his execution.[78] While the hero of the Alamo and victim of San Jacinto languished in a Texas jail, the Mexican nation sought an explanation for its humiliation. It is only natural that they came to view their northern neighbor as a basic factor in their defeat.

Mexican charges against the United States began long before San Jacinto. *El Anteojo* of Mexico City charged in November 1835 that the citizens of the United States were "the natural enemies of Mexico."[79] The *Diario del Gobierno* denounced the Jackson administration for its support of Texas rebellion on May 7, 1836, and in the following month Anthony Butler reported that *El Nacional*, "a dirty little Newspaper," advocated war against the United States.[80] Mexican officials also blamed much of the unrest in Texas on the United States: José María Ortíz Monasterio, acting minister for foreign affairs, blamed the private American elements for many of the difficulties in Texas.[81] The most avid critic of the United States was José María Tornel y Mendívil, minister of war and former ambassador to the United States. He lashed out at the overt anti-Mexican activities in the northern republic: "From the state of Maine to Louisiana a call has been made to the public squares to recruit volunteers for the ranks of the rebels in

Texas. Everywhere meetings have been held, presided over, as in New York, by public officials of the government, to collect money, buy ships, enlist men, and fan that spirit of animosity that characterizes all the acts of the United States with regard to Mexico."[82] Powhatan Ellis, who had arrived in Mexico City in May 1836, felt that Tornel wished to incite the Mexican population against the United States.[83]

In June 1835, the dissident forces of Texas declared that their cause was supported by their brothers to the east.[84] When Lorenzo de Zavala arrived in Texas on October 15, 1835, reports circulated that he had been given promises of assistance by President Andrew Jackson.[85] Similar rumors were spread concerning Stephen F. Austin. The significance of the United States in the plans of Texas was clear by November 25, 1835, when Austin resigned as commander in chief in order to head a commission to the sister republic.[86] Even before the formal declaration of independence from Mexico, there was a widespread assumption among Texans that Texas would soon be annexed by the United States.

Public opinion in the United States was strongly in favor of the Texas rebels. Not only were the Texas fighters related to families east of the Sabine, but the new republic took the United States as its political and economic model. Support for the Texas cause was especially strong in the South and in border states. The lure of land and the prospects of a quick profit simply strengthened the ideological and kinship ties. Texas agents traveled freely in the United States to seek loans and recruits to support their struggle.[87] Their efforts were quite successful, and streams of volunteers joined the army of Sam Houston and other Texas leaders.[88] The American press was strident in its condemnation of Mexico and its praise for the new republic. They openly published calls for volunteers, especially in Tennessee, Kentucky, and Louisiana. Mexican officials were most incensed, however, over the pro-Texas articles in the *Globe*, a paper that they considered to be reflective of the government of the United States.[89] Former president John Quincy Adams was the most distinguished spokesman for a small faction that opposed the Texas cause; he warned against a war for the annexation of Texas and expansion of slavery.[90]

It was widely known that President Jackson had strong ties with Sam Houston and other leaders of Texas, but his official position was one of continued neutrality. Secretary of State John Forsyth made a special point to inform Anthony Butler of this stand.[91] The intrepid minister paid little attention to his instructions and, upon his return to Mexico, openly praised the Texas rebels. The Mexican foreign minister Joaquín M. de Castillo y Lanzas accused Butler of directly involving himself in a fraternal quarrel.[92] On Mexican insistence, Forsyth recalled Butler, and Powhatan Ellis was named chargé d'affaires in January 1836. In his instructions, the secretary of state stressed the policy of neutrality and informed Ellis that he was to convince the Mexican government that the United States was not involved in the actions of any of its citizens in Texas.[93] Ellis encountered not only distrustful Mexican authorities and citizens but also, upon his arrival in Mexico City in May 1836, an uncompromising and hostile former ambassador. Butler denounced Forsyth for blocking the true intentions of President Jackson, the annexation of Texas to the United States. He insisted that the president had given him verbal instructions to work for that purpose and that now the secretary of state was countering that objective. He threatened to attack General Tornel and continued to speak out as if he were still representing his country. He became a constant embarrassment for Ellis and the ready symbol for Mexican charges that the United States was engaged in an expansionist plot against their territory. Finally, accusing Mexican officials of plotting his assassination, Butler departed for Texas.[94]

Powhatan Ellis brought a sense of dignity to his position but reported continuing suspicions and hostilities against the United States. He felt that Mexico, due to its chaotic internal affairs, could not recapture Texas without outside assistance. He suspected that Mexican leaders were working to gain British support for their cause through an appeal to the antislavery sentiment that prevailed in England at that time.[95] Ellis charged that U.S. citizens in Mexico were being mistreated through forced loans and other actions against their rights and property. On September 26, 1836, he offered a strong protest: "The Flag of the United States has been repeatedly insulted and fired upon by the public armed Vessels of this Government."[96] The question of claims would eventually lead to the termination of his mission, but even in the course of rather heated discussions, Ellis maintained a sense of dignity and diplomacy. In a coded message of September 24, 1836, however, he too revealed a hint of expansionist sentiments: he praised the riches of California and the importance of San Francisco Bay and told Forsyth that they would be of great importance for the United States.[97]

Don Manuel Eduardo de Gorostiza, an outstanding literary figure who had served as a Mexican diplomat in Europe, was appointed ambassador to the United States in January 1836. He arrived in Washington in early April, at the high tide of Santa Anna's Texas campaign. Secretary of State Forsyth assured Gorostiza that the United States was neutral in Mexico's squabbles, but the newly arrived minister denounced the open recruitment of men for the Texas cause. The secretary of state promised to have the U.S. attorney of the Tennessee and Kentucky district investigate these matters but made no promise that the advertisements would be halted. Events along the Sabine line brought the pledges of neutrality into serious question.[98]

General Edmund P. Gaines was stationed at Natchitoches, Louisiana, when the Texas rebellion erupted. In late March, Gaines suggested that he cross into Texas, and on May 4, 1836, the secretary of war gave him permission to advance as far as Nacogdoches, Texas. When Forsyth first discussed the matter with Gorostiza, he was evasive about the moves, simply stating that *if* Gaines moved into Texas it would be merely to protect citizens of both the United States and Mexico against hostile Indians and would not be contrary to U.S. neutrality.[99] The news of the defeat of Santa Anna at San Jacinto arrived during their discussions and must have increased the frustration of the Mexican minister, who rejected the pretensions of Forsyth and denounced the actions of Gaines as open hostility by the United States against a friendly neighbor.[100] Gorostiza reported to the Mexican minister of foreign relations that his "friends" in the government in Washington furnished him with documents, including letters from General Gaines relating to troop movements along the Sabine. Gorostiza concluded from the documents that the movement of Gaines was calculated to bring the United States into the war on the side of Texas.[101] It was not necessary for him to reveal the source of his information in order to point to clear evidence of territorial violations in eastern Texas. On May 8, the entire matter was openly discussed in the *Globe*; editors stated that the incursion was justified because Nacogdoches was, in effect, United States territory.[102] Though he continued to show restraint in his dealings with Forsyth, Gorostiza, in confidential reports to his home government, accused the Jackson administration of lying.[103]

Although the Gaines affair furnished the central point of action for U.S.-Mexican relations during most of 1836, a number of other matters occupied Gorostiza's attention. He was painfully aware of anti-Mexican popular opinion in the nation to which he was assigned and reported that after news of San Jacinto many left for Texas "marching off to the tune of My Old Kentucky Home."[104] He criticized any discussion in the Congress of the possible recognition of Texas and strongly protested the arrival of a commission from "the so-called government of Texas." Furthermore, he stringently rejected any notion that General Santa Anna retained any authority to speak for Mexico.[105] The minister was encouraged that the opponents of recognition of Texas continued their strong objections. In addition to the antislavery forces of the North, the ranks of the "pro-Mexican" elements were strengthened by the support of Henry Clay. On July 6, 1836, Gorostiza praised Clay and proudly stated: "Así nada han ganado los Texanos con sus intrigas en el Senado."[106] He faced continual frustrations, however, in his attempts to win concessions from the Department of State. When he objected to reports of a large force moving to Texas from Tennessee, Forsyth simply stated that the Mexican ambassador should not put any faith in newspaper reports.[107]

By October 1, 1836, Gorostiza dropped all pretense of diplomatic finesse; in an indignant statement, he charged that all of the claims of Indian attacks in eastern Texas were merely an excuse to utilize United States troops to support the Texas rebellion.[108] Assistant Secretary of State Asbury Dickins delivered a sharp rebuke on October 13, stating that Gorostiza was in error about President Jackson's reasons for sending troops into the territory "formerly claimed by Mexico."[109] Two days later, the minister informed Dickins that he considered his mission to be terminated and requested his passport. He charged that the statements of the Jackson administration were merely a pretense at neutrality while United States forces violated Mexican territory.[110] As he departed, Gorostiza turned over documents relating to the Gaines affair to a French publisher in order "to reveal the hypocrisy of the United States in its position regarding Texas and Mexico." Part of the correspondence was published in Philadelphia, much to Jackson's disgust. Upon returning to Mexico, Gorostiza was greeted as a champion of the national cause as he informed his fellow citizens that the United States had fully supported the Texas rebels "con sus brazos, con su dinero, con sus escritos, con sus consejos y con su odio hacia México."[111] He was praised by another former Mexican ambassador to Washington, José María Tornel y Mendívil, who in 1837 lashed out at both private and public figures in the United States for their overt enmity toward Mexico. He accused President Jackson of courting slaveholders and land speculators and manipulating events to annex Mexican territory for the United States.[112] The Mexican embassy in Washington seemed to be the best breeding ground for anti-U.S. sentiments.

Powhatan Ellis faced difficulties similar to those of Gorostiza. He attempted to gain redress for grievances of American citizens in a nation hopelessly bogged down in internal bickering and financial ruin. Foreign Minister Ortíz Monasterio not only refused to acknowledge most of the claims placed before him but also denounced many merchants from the United States as "notorious smugglers." Furthermore, he demanded that Ellis give a full explanation of the violation of Mexican territory by the forces of General Gaines. When Ellis demanded his passport, Ortíz accused the envoy of unbecoming conduct but granted his request on the afternoon of December 27, 1836. Although Joaquín M. de Castillo y Lanzas was to remain as Mexican chargé in Washington for several more months, diplomatic relations between the United States and Mexico were almost completely severed by the end of 1836.[113]

Meanwhile, President Jackson continued to show an active interest in the affairs of Texas. On June 28, 1836, he appointed Henry M. Morfit as special agent for the United States in the new republic. Secretary Forsyth instructed the envoy to gather as much information as possible, especially that regarding sentiment toward annexation to the United States. Morfit was to maintain secrecy at all times and to report his findings to the Department of State. The Texans received him warmly, and a majority favored joining the United States. By September 1836, rumors circulated that a Mexican army of four thousand men was massing for a campaign north of the Rio Grande, but Morfit doubted that Mexico was capable of mounting such an attack. He was convinced that the greatest strength of the new republic came from the continuing flow of emigrants from the United States and warned that several European powers were showing an interest in Texas's affairs.[114]

On July 4, 1836, Antonio López de Santa Anna wrote to President Jackson, apparently on the advice of Stephen F. Austin. He sought assistance in winning his release from prison and implied that he would cooperate with the United States to bring about a peaceful settlement of the Texas question. The former dictator seems to have discussed these matters with both Morfit and Gaines, but it was not until September 4 that Jackson responded to the request. He expressed doubt that any meaningful settlement could be carried out, since Santa Anna had been repudiated by his own government. On November 25, however, Texas president Burnet released the prisoner, possibly upon a request from Jackson. On January 18, 1837, the caudillo reached Washington and was escorted to the White House by Secretary of State Forsyth. No official records were made of his meeting with Jackson, but according to Waddy Thompson, who witnessed the affair, Santa Anna proposed the cession of Texas "for a fair consideration." The president refused to take the bait but provided his guest a fine dinner and passage to Veracruz on the USS *Pioneer*. After arriving in Mexico in February, Santa Anna charged that Jackson had misunderstood some of his statements and denied that he had ever made any offer that would compromise the territorial integrity of Mexico.[115]

By the time his mysterious guest had left Washington, Jackson's term of office was nearly over. In response to strong public opinion, and no doubt because of his personal feelings, the old general extended recognition to Texas on March 3, 1837, his last day in office. He also selected Alcée La Branche to represent the United States as chargé d'affaires, but the activation of his mission was to be left to the administration of Martin Van Buren. Jackson, though described by Mexican leaders at the time as an unrestrained expansionist, was actually quite hesitant. He was aware of the great internal tensions and party divisions inherent in the Texas question.

A Different Kind of Neutrality, 1837–1841

Davy Crockett said that comparing Martin Van Buren to Andrew Jackson was like comparing dung to a diamond, yet Old Hickory selected the New Yorker as the Democratic presidential candidate in 1836.[116] Upon taking office the following year, Van Buren faced grave economic problems, the panic of 1837. The Whigs, anticipating the election of 1840, placed total blame for these conditions at the feet of the Democrats. John C. Calhoun, still chaffing under the rebuffs he had received from Jackson and his lieutenant, plotted the latter's overthrow. Both Daniel Webster and John Quincy Adams delighted in the opportunity to accuse Van Buren of cooperating with sinister southern interests for the expansion of slavery.

Despite having served as secretary of state, Martin Van Buren was much more interested in domestic politics than in foreign affairs. The issues of Texas and Mexican relations were barely mentioned during the presidential campaign of 1836.[117] Scorning early rumors that he might resign, John Forsyth continued as secretary of state under the new administration. Although a former governor of Georgia, Forsyth was by no means an advocate of the expansion of slavery and was anxious to promote sectional harmony within the Democratic party. Due to a strong personal friendship and agreement on policy objectives with Van Buren, Forsyth was to exercise a much more independent role in foreign policy than he had under Jackson. He faced a number of difficult problems. On the northern border, Canadian rebels who sought assistance and a safe haven in the United States threatened to damage relations with Great Britain. The most serious diplomatic challenge continued to be in the Southwest, where Texas pressed for admission to the United States and Mexico demanded recognition of its sovereignty over that alienated territory. A new wave of Anglo emigrants, stimulated by the severe economic problems back east, pushed into Texas between 1837 and 1841.[118]

In early 1837, Mexico faced rumors of a military uprising under the leadership of the recently returned Santa Anna.[119] When presidential elections were held in March, General Anastasio Bustamante defeated all other candidates and took office on April 19, 1837, slightly more than a month after Van Buren was inaugurated in Washington. The bureaucracy was in disorder, the economy was in shambles, and the entire Mexican nation suffered the stigma of defeat at the hands of the Anglo-Americans. Although denounced in many quarters as an ultraconservative centralist, Bustamante was actually rather moderate on many issues and sought to bring national unity and stability. He remained in office until 1841, thus holding power longer than any other Mexican ruler since Guadalupe Victoria. Bustamante vowed to bring Texas back into its rightful position within the nation. He might have had a chance to accomplish that task, had not constant problems plagued his administration.[120]

French citizens blamed Mexican authorities for economic losses suffered during the civil strife and turned to Paris for assistance. On April 26, 1838, a French naval force blockaded Veracruz and on November 27 seized the fortress of San Juan de Ulúa. Former ambassador to the United States Eduardo Gorostiza, having recently been appointed Mexican foreign minister, expressed confidence that Mexico would receive help from Great Britain, but that assistance failed to materialize. On December 4, Antonio López de Santa Anna stepped back into the limelight and attacked the French position in Veracruz. Although he lost a leg in the action and never dislodged the enemy force, Santa Anna declared the operation to be a significant victory and returned once again to his hacienda. Mexico promised to pay some six hundred thousand dollars in claims, and by early March 1839 the French abandoned their beachhead.[121] Though in the long run it would play a part in the emergence of Mexican nationalism, the foreign invasion did nothing to promote national unity at the time. In fact, throughout the entire episode, internal dissension continued without interruption.[122]

Gómez Farías, philosophical and symbolic leader of the emerging Liberal party, was living in New Orleans in 1837. The conservatives of Mexico charged that he and other liberal exiles were linked with Masonic forces in the United States to support Texas separatists. Although the evidence for these charges was not convincing, the exiles did contribute to the disruption of the national system. The high point of the plots of Gómez Farías came on July 15, 1840, when his partisans captured the national palace and for a short time held Bustamante prisoner.[123] The primary driving force in the chaotic politics of Mexico between 1837 and 1841, however, was federalism in its more pragmatic and splintered forms.

The distant and isolated peninsula of Yucatán had joined Mexico in the pact of 1824 on an assumed basis of equality. Yucatán's philosophical base was linked with Texas through the personality of Lorenzo de Zavala. Although there was a bitter rivalry between Mérida and the port of Campeche, leaders of both cities denounced economic burdens imposed by President Bustamante and the drafting of their citizens to fight in Texas and other "foreign" regions. In late 1839, Captain Santiago Imán, scheduled to embark on a campaign against Texas, raised the standard of rebellion and on February 10, 1840, occupied the important city of Valladolid. Rebellion spread rapidly throughout the peninsula, and in June of that year Texas sent most of its navy to assist its Yucatán friends. When John Lloyd Stephens arrived to explore Mayan sites, he found Campeche blockaded and Mérida in a state of alert against the central government. On September 6, 1840, federalist Santiago Méndez Ibarra was selected as governor. When he failed to go far enough in his anticentralist policies to satisfy those who wanted a complete break with Mexico, a group of radicals invaded the Mérida municipal hall on March 16, 1841, demanding independence. Among them was a young politician from Campeche named Miguel Barbachano, who later played an important role in the affairs of the region. Governor Méndez promulgated two months later a new constitution that declared internal sovereignty for the state within the federal system. The region was operating independently from Mexico City, and by the summer of 1841 Gómez Farías prepared to transfer his base of operations to Yucatán.[124] The stage was also set for direct diplomatic relations with the United States.

Chiapas was not as closely linked to the liberalism of Gómez Farías as was Yucatán, but plots against the Bustamante regime in San Cristobal de las Casas took on a decided international dimension. Guatemala claimed the region, and Charles G. Dewitt, United States chargé d'affaires in Central America, reported that the conflicting claims in Chiapas helped to produce a favorable attitude toward the United States in Central America.[125]

California, like Yucatán and Chiapas, was on the periphery of the Mexican nation. Ambitious plans to populate the region never materialized, and morale in the scattered garrisons continued to decline. On November 7, 1836, the California assembly proclaimed its support for the reestablishment of the federalist constitution of 1824. Juan B. Alvarado emerged as the leader of the movement and found support from an Anglo-American distiller named Isaac Graham. The arrival of a United States ship in Monterey Harbor, although seemingly unrelated to the proclamation, caused alarm among officials. The most significant cause for concern by Mexican authorities, however, was the growing number of Anglo-Americans settling on the coast or pushing south from Oregon. John Sutter, though not from the United States, was identified as a part of the overall threat; in 1839 he established his headquarters in the Sacramento valley and by 1841 expressed confidence that he could resist any force the Mexican government might send against him. Juan N. Almonte, an astute observer of the frontier with long experience in the United States, warned that the Anglo-American colonists represented a distinct danger to Mexican control.[126] As if in response to that warning, Mexican officials in California in the spring of 1840 arrested about ninety foreigners, most of them from the United States. In Mexico City, Ambassador Powhatan Ellis demanded their release, accusing Mexico of high-handed acts of tyranny and oppression. The matter dragged on through September, contributing to increased suspicion and distrust. Secretary of State Forsyth denounced the entire affair and instructed Ellis to demand not only the immediate release of those arrested but the restoration of their property and indemnity for losses.[127] President Van Buren did not attempt to use these incidents to acquire territory on the Pacific. Ellis, who had in earlier years attempted to convince the White House of the desirability of California, in 1841 merely recommended that Thomas O. Larkin, a U.S. citizen in Monterey, be appointed as consul in that port city.[128] By that time, however, President Bustamante realized that California presented a vulnerable flank.

In New Mexico a band of Pueblo Indians occupied Santa Fe in August 1837 and murdered Governor Albino Pérez. Rumors circulated that the United States was involved in the clash, but most of the Anglo-Americans residing in New Mexico, fearful of the consequences of a general Indian uprising, actually supported the reestablishment of Mexican authority. The government of New Mexico, aware of its dependency upon the Anglo traders, did nothing to prohibit their continued residence there. In Mexico City, officials were legitimately concerned, however, when Texas president Mirabeau B. Lamar claimed that his republic's boundary extended into New Mexico and Texas agents encouraged citizens of the region to join their newly established nation.[129]

Uprisings in Yucatán, Chiapas, California, and New Mexico all had strong international dimensions, and within the next decade much of that periphery would be lost to Mexico. Between 1837 and 1841, however, problems in those regions were primarily due to chaotic domestic conditions. Although justified by noble ideals of federalism and liberalism, they were fomented by ambitious regional politicians or disgruntled military commanders whose primary objective was to seize power. Similar movements occurred in Sonora and Sinaloa and in the internal states of Jalisco and San Luis Potosí. These outbreaks kept the government of Anastasio Bustamante in a state of constant imbalance, thus making impossible a coherent foreign policy or a sustained campaign to regain Texas.[130]

In no section of Mexico was hostility to central authority more ingrained than in the vast and sparsely populated region formerly known as the Interior Provinces of the East. It was in Coahuila and Tamaulipas that the regional revolts between 1837 and 1841 had the most significant impact upon the political fate of the North American continent.

In Coahuila the destructive rivalry between Saltillo and Monclova, which had deprived the state of any sense of stability before 1837, continued unabated. General Juan Pablo de Anaya led a federalist revolt in January 1839 and turned to Texas for volunteers and supplies. He promised to recognize Texas's independence in return for support against central Mexican authorities, but President Lamar rejected the overtures. When Anaya was defeated in late 1839, a new effort emerged under former Coahuila governor Francisco Vidaurri y Villaseñor, who proposed a loose confederation of northern states stretching from Tamaulipas to the Californias. He also advocated an alliance with Texas, but once again Lamar refused to participate in the scheme. Hopes for the grand design were dashed on January 30,

1840, when centralist forces in Coahuila defeated those of Vidaurri y Villaseñor.[131]

Tamaulipas had never been a cohesive political unit. Its traditional northern boundary was the Nueces River, not the Rio Grande, as Texas claimed. The desolate territory between Corpus Christi Bay and Matamoros, which had never been effectively colonized, became the scene for a complex struggle for power. To complicate matters further, the provincial capital of Ciudad Victoria exercised little control over the ports of Matamoros and Tampico. General Vicente Filisola in 1839 organized a military force in Tamaulipas to carry out the reconquest of Texas, but he had to abandon these plans in order to crush a federalist uprising in Tampico. In the following months, local factionalism in Tamaulipas merged into an ambitious political scheme. On September 30, 1839, in the vicinity of the Nueces River, General Antonio Canales raised an army that included about 180 Anglo-Americans. In the next months, he conducted raids throughout Tamaulipas, Nuevo León, and Coahuila. On January 7, 1840, he suffered a major reverse and retreated north of the Rio Grande. On January 18, he proclaimed the establishment of the Republic of Rio Grande, to be composed of a vast territory encompassing most of the former Interior Provinces of the East, including Texas. With Colonel S. W. Jordan and a number of other Anglo-American supporters, Canales occupied a string of border towns along the Rio Grande, including Laredo and Camargo. He marched through Nuevo León during the summer and was received with open arms in Ciudad Victoria.[132]

Rumors spread in Mexico City that between two hundred and three hundred Texans supported the federalists, who were preparing to attack San Luis Potosí. As Canales moved into Coahuila, however, his force was weakened by growing hostilities between Mexican and Anglo elements. On October 23, 1840, a centralist army defeated him near Saltillo, and the chieftain retreated north of the Rio Grande. On November 9, Canales came to terms with the Bustamante government, thus ending his dreams of the Republic of Rio Grande.

Despite their failure, the uprisings along the Rio Grande increased the apprehension of Mexican leaders relating to Texas. Gorostiza, former Mexican ambassador to the United States, in 1840 serving as foreign minister, advocated a campaign against Texas in part to protect the contiguous region of Tamaulipas and New Mexico.[133] That threat was never as great as it seemed from Mexico City. Although Canales and other caudillos called for a joining of all the forces along both sides of the border to oppose the central government, there was always an uneasy relationship between their Mexican followers and volunteers of United States origin. Victims of plunder and destruction in the small towns along the Rio Grande developed strong suspicion of those forces of cultural and linguistic differences. The events between 1837 and 1841 worked more to divide the Texans and the northern Mexicans than to unite them.[134] Furthermore, Texans north of Corpus Christi Bay looked toward the United States for their political alliances.

Texas as a Buffer State

At the time General Sam Houston was elected president, Texas voters expressed an almost unanimous desire to join the United States.[135] William H. Wharton and Memucan Hunt were cordially received by President Jackson, but with the inauguration of Van Buren, the atmosphere in Washington turned decidedly cool toward the Texas representatives. Not until four months later was Hunt recognized as the accredited representative of his government.[136] The chagrined agent warned Secretary Forsyth that if the United States did not accept the offer for annexation within a short time, then Texas might be forced to seek other alliances.[137] Forsyth assured Hunt that the president was seriously weighing the matter but was concerned that acceptance might damage United States relations with Mexico.[138] Alcée La Branche was appointed by President Jackson as chargé d'affaires to Texas, but he did not take his post until late October 1837. He found that citizens of the Lone Star Republic were still anxious to join the United States but by the end of the year warned that the Houston government might turn to Great Britain if the United States did not act soon.[139]

Despite the international implications of the Texas question, the primary basis for policy was found in domestic politics. The national Democratic party, which Van Buren had helped to forge, was threatened by sectional divisions. Many southerners, including John C. Calhoun, accused the president of blocking the will of the American people by his continued delay in embracing Texas. The Alabama state legislature, in December 1837, adopted a resolution calling for annexation.[140] On the other hand, former president John Quincy Adams denounced Van Buren for even contemplating the measure and charged the Democratic administration with plotting the expansion of slavery.[141]

On June 25, 1838, Anson Jones replaced Memucan Hunt as the Texas representative in Washington. He met equal frustration in his efforts to gain annexation and in October of that year announced that his government was withdrawing its request. Rumors circulated that President Houston had decided to seek British assistance, but he later stated that his desire to join the United States had never faltered. When his term ended in December 1838, however, his successor, Mirabeau B. Lamar, was less devoted to these efforts. In fact, Lamar declared that Texas was neutral in the internal conflicts below the Rio Grande and expressed hope that Mexico would recognize his nation's independence.[142] Van Buren and Forsyth seemed willing to accept Texas as a buffer state on the southern border of the United States while avoiding the slavery issue in the presidential election of 1840.[143]

Between 1838 and 1841, the United States carried on diplomatic relations with the Texas republic in a friendly, though at times rather strained, manner. The boundary between Texas and Arkansas, an issue with Mexico in earlier years, became a point of difference with the new republic. President Lamar insisted that U.S. troops remaining in Nacogdoches should be withdrawn east of the Sabine. The questions of boundary encroachments and conflicting claims were further complicated by constant Indian raids along the sparsely settled border. Texas claimed that most of these problems were caused by "United States" Indians, especially the Cherokee who had been moved west by Jackson. Forsyth refuted this claim and in turn charged that Texas forces that pursued Indians across the border were guilty of illegal encroachment into United States territory. Indian hostilities and claims continued to be a bone of contention in the following years.[144] Texas authorities insisted, however, that the most significant aspect of the question had its foundation in Mexico. Lamar contended that the Bustamante government was purposefully inciting Indian hostilities along the border, hoping to sow seeds of discord between the United States and Texas.[145] The Texas president, on the other hand, sought the assistance of the United States in reaching a settlement with Mexico.[146] Forsyth was willing to mediate between the two, but only if the Mexican government requested it.[147]

Upon taking office, President Martin Van Buren expressed hopes that friendship and mutual respect could be established between the United States and Mexico. He tried to show that the recognition of Texas independence was in no way an unfriendly act toward the Mexican nation.[148] In May 1837 the president sent Robert Greenhow as special agent to the Bustamante government, a first step in the reestablishment of diplomatic relations.[149] Upon his arrival in Mexico City in July, Greenhow found conditions in a state of confusion. Although Foreign Minister Luis G. Cuevas was most courteous, the envoy sensed widespread hostility against the United States for its role in the Texas revolt and its recognition of the independence of the republic. Central to the hostility was Eduardo Gorostiza, former minister to the United States, who divided his time between political intrigue and managing the Mexico City opera. Upon his return to the United States in early August, Greenhow characterized the former ambassador as "one of the most violent of the fanatic party" and confided to Forsyth that he felt that President Bustamante would probably be pleased to send Gorostiza's head to the United States but could not afford to alienate the strong faction that he represented.[150]

Bustamante, while continuing to insist upon Mexican sovereignty over Texas, took steps to reestablish diplomatic relations with the United States. On October 16, 1837, Francisco Pizarro Martínez reported as Mexican minister to Washington, a post he retained until his death in February 1840. He was frustrated by the difficulties in maintaining communications with his home government, especially during the French occupation of Veracruz. Pizarro objected to U.S. commercial relations with Texas and was critical when the Van Buren administration negotiated a boundary settlement with the republic.[151] Forsyth insisted that in recognizing Texas his government was in no way being unfriendly to Mexico. Due to continued differences, however, full relations were further delayed.

On June 24, 1839, Powhatan Ellis returned to his post as ambassador to Mexico after an absence of almost two and a half years. President Van Buren hoped that he might persuade Mexico to recognize Texas and allow the United States to mediate between the two to bring a peaceful settlement on the North American continent.[152] Upon his arrival in the Mexican capital, however, Ellis faced hostility from Gorostiza, who had assumed the post of foreign minister the preceding January. Just six days prior to the arrival of the U.S. envoy, furthermore, José María Tornel, another former representative to Washington, delivered to the Chamber of Deputies a fiery speech calling for a renewed campaign against Texas.[153] Any chance that Ellis might have had to mediate between Mexico and Texas was destroyed by the involvement of Anglo-Americans in the conflicts along the Rio Grande. Many Mexican leaders continued to blame the United States for the loss of Texas and assumed that the Van Buren administration still had ambitions for expansion.[154] Actually, Secretary of State Forsyth made every effort to avoid getting involved in the frontier clashes. He threatened to bar all Texas ships from U.S. waters, for example, when the commander of the Texas brig *Colorado* carried out recruitment activities in the southern states.[155] He was especially anxious to avoid interference with Mexico's treatment of Anglo-American prisoners captured in the raids against Matamoros in 1840.[156]

Despite Van Buren's sincere efforts to develop friendly relations with Mexico, many problems persisted. When Robert Greenhow reached Mexico in the spring of 1837, he presented a list of fifty-seven claims to the Bustamante government, including the demand for an apology for the actions of Gorostiza. Most of the claims were for incidents involving individual citizens, but they also included attacks against U.S. consuls in both Matamoros and Tabasco.[157] Bustamante was hesitant to respond to these demands since they carried far-reaching political implications. By 1838 there was a tentative agreement to submit the matter to the king of Prussia, but the French invasion of Veracruz delayed the process further.[158] Forsyth was especially frustrated by the lack of commitment on the part of the Mexican minister, Francisco Pizarro. On April 11, 1839, however, a draft treaty of friendship was signed in Washington, and Powhatan Ellis initiated discussions on the matter in June upon his return to Mexico.[159] By September he was optimistic that the measure would be approved, but after a month of waiting his expectations waned.[160] In January 1840 Foreign Minister Juan de Díos Cañedo informed Ellis that the Mexican assembly had accepted the treaty and that it had met the approval of President Bustamante.[161]

In early June 1840, however, the hopes for a meaningful settlement were suddenly disrupted by reports of the apprehension of United States citizens in California. Ambassador Ellis reacted angrily, denouncing the arrests as acts of tyranny and oppression.[162] Forsyth shared his minister's indignation, calling the Mexican actions "barbarous and unjustifiable."[163]

By November 1840 President Van Buren seemed quite willing to see Texas remain independent. Having received his party's nomination, the candidate wished to avoid the issue of annexation, seeing it as harmful to the nation as well as to his political chances.[164] Henry Clay, confident of receiving the Whig nomination, was equally determined to avoid exposing the Texas question to American voters. Though he did receive the greatest number of votes on the first ballot, it was not sufficient for a victory. His opponents succeeded in diverting enough support to give the nomination to General William Henry Harrison and selected John Tyler of Virginia for the second spot on the ticket. In the campaign that followed, the Whigs emphasized the heroism of their candidate in Indian wars and praised him for living in a log cabin and drinking cider from a barrel. Few issues were discussed, and the Texas question was taken completely out of the contest. Harrison's victory over Van Buren seemed to have few implications for United States relations with Mexico.[165]

When the Democrats left office in March 1841, there seemed to be a good possibility that Texas would remain an independent republic. Not only had the leaders of both political parties seemed to accept that situation, but the Texans had good reason to expect European support. In early 1837 Joseph T. Crawford, a British agent in Texas, encouraged the British ambassador in Mexico, Sir Richard Pakenham, to promote Texas independence. In the following years additional observers repeated the advice, pointing to the lucrative trade opportunities in the region. Such a step had been taken in 1833 in the Río de la Plata, where Uruguay was established as a buffer state between Brazil and Argentina. However, Lord Palmerston hesitated to follow a similar policy on the Rio Grande, partly because of the slavery issue but primarily because of the lack of the approval by Mexico. British authorities hoped to convince President Bustamante that it would be in the best interest of his nation to recognize Texas independence and establish a new boundary agreement.[166]

Anastasio Bustamante was a moderate and inclined to compromise on many issues. To have done so on the Texas question might have prevented a bloody war and the loss of an extensive part of Mexico's national territory. It was simply impossible for him to take that action: opposition factions were waiting for an excuse to topple his regime, and a hint of compromise on the northern frontier would have offered the perfect cause. His enemies within a very short time would find other reasons to renew the fraternal struggle.[167] Meanwhile, changes in Texas and in the United States would remove the option for a buffer on the Rio Grande.

From Neutrality to Annexation, 1841–1845

William Henry Harrison seemed content to continue the policy of neutrality toward Mexico and the acceptance of Texas independence which had been designed by Van Buren and Forsyth. Daniel Webster, the newly appointed secretary of state, had dabbled in Texas land

President John Tyler (The National Portrait Gallery, Smithsonian Institution)

speculation and feared British ambitions in the region, but in general he favored a "truly independent" Texas. As Harrison's architect of foreign affairs, he seemed well suited to continue the policy of neutrality which had prevailed from 1837 to 1841.[168]

On April 4, 1841, President Harrison died, only a month after his inauguration. He was succeeded by John Tyler, a former Jacksonian Democrat who was an avowed expansionist. There was, however, no immediate change in policy. The new chief executive faced strident opposition from Henry Clay, who considered himself the rightful leader of the Whig government and even attempted to deny Tyler the presidential title. The Kentucky senator persuaded most of the cabinet to resign, but Webster remained, in part because of his dedication to important foreign policy objectives but also to assert his independence from Clay. Tyler was in almost constant conflict with Clay and his associates in Congress throughout his term. They clashed over tariff questions and the Whig efforts to recharter a national bank, and on many occasions the president vetoed measures passed by the legislative branch. The Whigs finally became so exasperated that they expelled the president from their party.[169]

It was against this stormy domestic background that Tyler attempted to enact a major change in foreign policy. He informed his secretary of state in October 1841 that he hoped that the slavery issue would not be used to thwart annexation and asked that his cabinet work in harmony on the matter.[170] Webster, on the other hand, was primarily interested in constructing a compromise with Great Britain on the boundary between Maine and Canada and opposed any decision in the Oregon territory or in the Southwest that might jeopardize his negotiations.[171] Throughout his tenure the secretary of state instructed U.S. representatives in both Texas and Mexico to work for mediation and peaceful settlement of the differences between those two parties.[172] President Tyler, continuing to face major political problems from Henry Clay and other Whigs, was willing to give Webster a relatively free rein in foreign policy for over two years, delaying his own ambition for westward expansion. The failure to annex Oregon resulted in the bitter dissatisfaction of Senator Thomas Hart Benton of Missouri.[173] Many citizens of the slaveholding regions of the United States were equally harsh in their criticism at the failure to annex Texas. Once the eastern boundary was settled, Daniel Webster would step aside, allowing Tyler to appoint a new secretary of state and chart a new course of action. Meanwhile, developments in both Mexico and Texas helped to shape the ultimate outcome of the question.

Madame Calderón de la Barca, wife of the Spanish ambassador, reached Mexico in February 1841. The nation still suffered the ravages of internal strife; highways were in disrepair and subject to frequent banditry, but Mexico City possessed an air of sophistication and culture. The most popular attraction in the theater that season was the play "Contigo, pan y cebolla," by José Eduardo Gorostiza, former ambassador to the United States. General Anastasio Bustamante continued to give to the government a slight sense of stability and continuity based on compromise and conciliation.[174]

The uneasy peace was shattered when General Mariano Paredes y Arrillaga rebelled in Guadalajara on August 8, 1841; in the following weeks regional chieftains throughout the nation joined the movement. Some demanded the restoration of federalism, and in Veracruz Antonio López de Santa Anna called for a return to honor and national pride. The basic motivation behind most of the uprisings, however, was personal ambition and a quest for power. Bustamante held out for a short time, but when the garrison in the capital defected on August 31, he capitulated. In September, a military junta proclaimed Santa Anna commander in chief and provisional president of the nation. The caudillo marched triumphantly into Mexico City on October 7, 1841.[175] He assured clerical leaders and the upper classes that he had no intention of tampering with their wealth or privileges. Courting key military officials, he appointed General José María Tornel as minister of war and marine. Not until June 10, 1842, was a constituent congress convened, and that body debated for almost a year before the "Bases Orgánicas" was adopted. A carefully controlled election conferred the trappings of legitimacy on Santa Anna on June 13, 1843. All told, he ruled as supreme authority of the nation from October 10, 1841, to December 6, 1844, attempting to mediate all of the petty jealousies and factional concerns that were an integral part of the Mexican system. When Waddy Thompson, Tyler's newly appointed ambassador, arrived in April of 1842, he felt that Santa Anna represented the only element of stability in the nation but that his control could last only as long as he could pay his army.[176] The strong man squandered scarce resources on rich decorations and ceremonial functions and, as on previous occasions, left affairs of state in the hands of subordinates.[177]

Opposition to Santa Anna broke out in many sections of Mexico, especially on the periphery of the nation. In Coahuila, Chihuahua, and Sonora, hostile Indian raids created constant problems, and in California, factionalism was rife. The most serious challenges of sectional revolt, however, were centered in Yucatán and Texas. The two rebellious provinces formed a close relationship, and both looked to the United States for assistance. This brought Daniel Webster and John Tyler more deeply into what the Mexican authorities considered to be their domestic affairs.

On October 1, 1841, the Chamber of Deputies of Yucatán declared that state to be once again independent of Mexico. The Senate refused to endorse that drastic step, but for all practical purposes the region resumed its autonomy. When American envoy and Mayan sleuth John L. Stephens reached Mérida at the end of the month, he found the city in a state of confusion and Texans involved in many affairs of the region. Stephens quickly put the cares of modern politics behind him and returned to exploring Mayan ceremonial centers. However, in early 1842, when he reached the island of Cozumel on the eastern coast of the peninsula, he found that Texas influence was as great as ever. Rumors of an impending invasion of Mexico by the United States circulated widely.[178]

On December 28, 1841, Santa Anna, with the assistance of Andrés Quintana Roo, granted Yucatán its traditional position within the Mexican nation. Generally, the state was as autonomous as it had been during much of the colonial period and was exempted from most of the national tariffs and taxes. By March 1842, however, the peninsula was racked by an internal factionalism that also had its roots in the colonial era. Miguel Barbachano represented the interests of Mérida, linked commercially with Cuba and the United States. Opposing him was Santiago Méndez, backed by the port city of Campeche, where the merchant class relied more upon trade with Mexico City through Veracruz. When Méndez led a revolt against the state authorities in March of 1842, Santa Anna moved to cancel his pledges. On May 7, he declared Yucatán to be an enemy of the Mexican nation, primarily because of its failure to break relations with Texas. Barbachano countered with a promise to distribute land to all Yucatecans who opposed Mexican aggression, and on March 27, 1843, he concluded a pact to that effect with Mayan leader Cecilio Chí. He also sought assistance in Texas and the United States.[179]

Mexican historians have charged that during this time the Tyler administration channeled money and troops into Yucatán through Texas.[180] There were links between the United States and Yucatán, but there was by no means a well-plotted course to undermine Mexican authority. When Ambassador Waddy Thompson first arrived in Mexico City, he was very interested in the events in Yucatán, but he was cautious about dealing with the separatist forces there. He feared that such action on his part would result in a harsh reaction by Mexican officials. Two months later Thompson seemed more inclined to favor separatist elements, expressing his hope that he might be assigned to a post in Mérida.[181] The secretary of state opposed this move, however, and warned Thompson to exercise the greatest caution toward Yucatán and to give his primary attention to affairs in

Mexico City.[182] In the spring of 1843, Charles Thompson was appointed United States consul to Mérida and Sisal, where he assisted American citizens in a brisk trade with the region. He was aware of many intrigues that were under way, but seemed to have little part in them.[183]

The quarrel between Yucatán and Mexico was temporarily patched up by December 1843; the Creole ruling class soon forgot the promises they had made to the Mayan leaders. The resulting bitter struggle, known as the Caste War, would bring a renewed effort on the part of Mérida authorities to seek U.S. assistance. Meanwhile, it was the close relationship between Yucatán and Texas that irritated Santa Anna.

Texas president Mirabeau B. Lamar dreamed of expanding both the commercial and the political power of his fledgling nation. In June 1841, Hugh McLeod led an expedition of over three hundred soldiers, merchants, and adventurers into New Mexico, proposing to develop commercial ties and extend an invitation to the people of Santa Fe to join the Texas constitutional system. Unprepared for the harsh environment and attacked by hostile Indians, many of McLeod's followers abandoned the venture. The remaining members of his force were captured near Santa Fe and eventually sent to Mexico City, where they became the object of much curiosity and a source of great embarrassment to the United States.[184] Daniel Webster, anxious to avoid being linked to the event, instructed Joseph Eve, his envoy in Texas, to gather information on the U.S. citizens who had been involved and to attempt to determine who shared responsibility for the enterprise and who had simply gone along for the adventure.[185] Despite Webster's caution, the United States became identified with the affair both at home and in Mexico.

In September 1841, Sam Houston was elected president of Texas for a second time, and, in his address to Congress the following December, he called for a policy of "armed neutrality" with Mexico. He felt that this would give Texas an opportunity to overcome serious Indian problems, address economic difficulties, and consolidate its sparsely populated territory. Santa Anna had no intention of allowing Texas to retain its independence, especially since it was linked to the rebellious faction in Yucatán. The struggle along the Rio Grande in 1842 was to be the most vicious since the battle of San Jacinto.[186] In early January, General Mariano Arista issued a proclamation to the people of Texas, demanding that they accept the rightful authority of the Mexican government. When Houston rejected this ultimatum,

Santa Anna prepared his forces for action; on March 5, 1842, General Rafael Vásquez led a force of five hundred dragoons against San Antonio, capturing the city without a struggle and pushing on to Goliad and El Refugio. It soon became apparent that the Mexican army was incapable of any long-term occupation of Texas territory. Houston denounced this act of aggression and shared his criticism with the United States, Great Britain, and Yucatán. Some six hundred volunteers from Louisiana and other southern states poured into Galveston within a few months after the initial clash, and that number was greatly exaggerated in Mexico City. By the end of July, however, the Anglo-American volunteers along the Nueces had dwindled to less than two hundred.[187] Houston also faced harsh criticism from members of the Texas legislature who blamed him for not taking the fight to the enemy.[188]

General Adrian Woll, with a Mexican force of two thousand men, once again took possession of San Antonio on September 10, 1842, capturing a number of prisoners. By November, Santa Anna developed a comprehensive plan to crush the rebels in Yucatán and then to strike against Galveston. Although this scheme was never carried out, rumors of an impending Mexican strike continued to pester Houston and cause internal strife among his followers and opponents.[189]

President Houston ordered the Texas militia to retaliate against the Mexican incursions, and an offensive was mounted along the Rio Grande line. On December 9, 1842, General Alexander Somervell captured Laredo; despite his efforts to restrain his followers, a number of them proceeded to plunder the town. Following the capture of the pueblo of Guerrero, Somervell commanded his small force to withdraw to north of the Rio Grande. Colonel William S. Fisher, in defiance of those orders, pushed across the river to the town of Mier, where on December 22 he was crushed by General Pedro Ampudia. Virtually the entire force of 261 men was captured, and when some escaped they were recaptured and 17 of them executed. The following April the prisoners were transferred from Matamoros to Mexico City, where they were to play an important role in the relationship between Washington and Mexico City, but that issue was overshadowed by the question of the political status of Texas.[190]

Though long an advocate of joining the United States, Sam Houston was aware that such a union faced stiff resistance in Washington. Opponents included not only Henry Clay and John Quincy Adams but Secretary of State Daniel Webster himself.[191] Texas representatives did not press the question of annexation but attempted to convince the Tyler administration and the American public that Mexican authorities were guilty of extreme cruelty against the prisoners taken at Santa Fe and Mier. Isaac Van Zandt, the Texas chargé in Washington, insisted that Mexico violated all Christian principles of warfare.[192] Webster denounced Mexican predatory raids but also condemned similar violations by Texas forces. He wished to convince Mexico that he was fair and impartial in these matters.[193] The secretary felt that he could remain neutral in the struggle raging along the Rio Grande and at the same time protect the commercial interests of powerful elements in the United States.[194] He was willing to cooperate with Texas to control predatory Indian raids along the border, and he apologized when United States deputies crossed the Sabine to seize escaped slaves.[195] This concept of neutrality and impartiality remained the basis of United States policy until the resignation of Webster in May 1843. He was soon to learn, however, that his formula for an independent Texas attracted uninvited and dangerous supporters. Although Daniel Webster did not wish to see Texas fall under European control, his policy of neutrality seemed to support that effort.[196]

François Guizot, French premier and foreign minister under King Louis Philippe, advocated cooperation with Great Britain and Mexico to guarantee Texan independence.[197] British officials preferred to follow a unilateral policy but hesitated to recognize the Texas government, despite strong pressures from members of the private sector anxious to compete in the lucrative commercial opportunities there. Diplomatic recognition was finally extended in 1841, and Captain Charles Elliot was appointed chargé d'affaires. His assignment was delayed for a year, however, while the treaties of friendship and commerce were being debated.

When Elliot finally reached Galveston on August 23, 1842, he reported that the forces for annexation to the United States were on the verge of success.[198] The chargé developed an elaborate plan to block such a move and to tie Texas into the British commercial and financial system. England was to pressure the Mexican government to accept Texas independence while London banks were to extend credits to the Houston government, allowing commercial expansion and the abolition of slavery with compensation. Elliot urged Richard Pakenham, British minister in Mexico, to work toward those same objectives.[199]

By the end of 1842 Lord Aberdeen endorsed most of Elliot's scheme and instructed Pakenham to promote Mexican recognition of Texan independence. He was careful, however, to warn Elliot not to take any action that might seem to show British favoritism toward Texas.[200] It was clear that Lord Aberdeen still wished to avoid steps that might alienate Mexico or produce open conflict with the United States.

Elliot was convinced that President Houston was willing to accept British protection, especially if Santa Anna could be persuaded to accept Texan independence.[201] The old warrior later contended that he was merely using the British threat to goad the United States into action. A careful examination of the record, however, seems to indicate that in 1842–43 Houston simply wanted to keep his options open and to protect the interest of his vulnerable republic.[202] After all, there was no assurance that Santa Anna would yield to British persuasion, even when it was linked to financial promises.

If Houston's objective had been to alarm and confuse United States officials, he certainly succeeded. In the spring of 1842, American merchants in Galveston were quite concerned when Texas extended favorable trade terms to French and British interests.[203] William S. Murphy, who arrived in Galveston on June 3, 1843, to replace Joseph Eve as U.S. chargé, was convinced that President Houston, influenced by Elliot, would make an agreement with Santa Anna. This would be done, he felt, in defiance of overwhelming sentiment for annexation to the United States by Texas citizens.[204] At the same time, Duff Green, Tyler's confidential agent in England, warned that the Texas government seemed willing to accept the abolition of slavery in return for British loans and protection against Mexico.[205] By then, however, changes in the Tyler administration brought a dramatic shift in policy.

Daniel Webster resigned as secretary of state on May 8, 1843, and the president appointed as his successor Abel P. Upshur, a southerner whose ideas on expansion were very close to his own.[206] From Galveston, William S. Murphy warned that Houston was inclined to give in to temptations offered by Charles Elliot.[207] Upshur took the warnings seriously, charging that Great Britain was involved in a conspiracy against both the United States and Texas. In contrast to Webster, the new secretary was deeply concerned that the "British wolf" would not only block United States annexation of Texas but also convince the Houston government to abolish slavery. Upshur defended his position, declaring that the very preservation of the Union depended upon annexation. Instructing Murphy to oppose Houston in his schemes with the British, the secretary worked to convince the Texas envoys in Washington that he and President Tyler were making

Secretary of State Abel P. Upshur (The National Portrait Gallery, Smithsonian Institution)

every effort to persuade the Senate to approve annexation and at the same time would do everything necessary to defend Texas territory against a Mexican invasion.[208] Upshur's actions were strongly denounced in the Senate by Clay and the Whigs and in the House of Representatives by John Quincy Adams. In his private correspondence, former secretary of state Daniel Webster also expressed grave doubts about the policy of his successor, fearing that it would bring southern domination in the House of Representatives and bitter sectional conflict.[209]

In Texas, President Houston continued to equivocate on annexation, but by Christmas 1843, Murphy reported that he was on the best of terms with the old general.[210] Houston sent J. P. Henderson to assist Van Zandt in Washington, instructing the envoys to establish an alliance with the United States if annexation seemed to be unattainable.[211] Houston's action was probably influenced in part by the persuasion of his old friend Andrew Jackson. At the same time, he was encouraged by the willingness of John Tyler to move a military force along the Sabine border and a fleet into the Gulf of Mexico.[212] Despite continuing opposition in Congress, Tyler's program for expansion seemed to be on the verge of success.

The Texas strategy was interrupted on February 28, 1844, when Upshur and a number of other officials were killed in an accidental explosion aboard the sloop of war *Princeton*. The acting secretary of state, John Nelson, criticized Murphy for promises of military protection to Texas.[213] The interlude to expansionism was short, however, for on March 16, 1844, President Tyler appointed John C. Calhoun as secretary of state. Taking office on March 30, the South Carolina Democrat was even more energetic than Upshur in working for annexation. He assured Houston's agents that U.S. forces would protect Texas against any Mexican attack while the treaty was being discussed, and the president gave his full approval to this promise.[214] When a draft treaty was signed on April 12, 1844, Calhoun notified Mexican minister Juan N. Almonte of its completion, as if to inform him that Mexico had no choice but to accept the action.[215] Needless to say, the treaty would be a central issue in the growing Mexican hostility against the United States. At the time, however, Tyler and Calhoun were more concerned with opposition closer at home.

When the president submitted the proposed treaty to the Senate on April 22, he praised it as beneficial to the nation as a whole. Much of the opposition was on the basis of party lines, but the sectional implications were readily apparent. Secretary Calhoun openly admitted that one of his primary objectives was the preservation and strengthening of slavery. Senator Thomas Hart Benton of Missouri, an outspoken opponent of the treaty, characterized it as "an act of unparalleled outrage on Mexico."[216] On June 8, 1844, the Senate defeated the proposal by a vote of thirty-five to sixteen. Though bitterly disappointed by the rejection, Calhoun assured Van Zandt that the United States would continue to honor its commitment to protect Texas against Mexican aggression.[217] By this time expansion had become the central issue in the presidential election of 1844.

John Tyler hoped to win the Democratic nomination, but most party leaders seemed to favor Martin Van Buren. In late April 1844, the former president published a letter expressing his fear that the annexation of Texas would lead to war with Mexico. At the same time, Henry Clay issued a similar pronouncement, thus causing some to suspect that the two candidates had agreed to eliminate the Texas question from the campaign, just as had happened in the election of 1840. When the Democratic convention met, pro-Texas forces conspired with other opponents to defeat Van Buren. After protracted maneuvering, James K. Polk of Tennessee, a protégé of Andrew Jackson and an outspoken expansionist, was nominated.[218]

There was never any doubt that Clay would be the Whig candidate: party leaders selected the Kentucky senator on May 1, 1844, without a formal vote.[219] His opposition to the annexation of Texas was well known, and voters at last seemed to have a choice between candidates with strongly opposing views on the issue. During the course of the campaign, however, Clay attempted to moderate his position in order to appeal to southern voters, stating that he had no objection to the annexation of Texas but feared that such action would disrupt the Union. This statement alienated antislavery Whigs, possibly providing the key to the Kentuckian's defeat.[220]

Proponents of expansion hailed the election of James K. Polk as a triumph of the democratic process. President Tyler called upon Congress to accept the decision of the American people for the annexation of Texas. By a joint resolution, annexation could be carried out with a simple majority in both houses of Congress rather than the two-thirds vote necessary for the ratification of a treaty in the Senate.[221] The measure was approved on March 1, 1845, at the very end of Tyler's term. Supporters shouted for joy, and opponents predicted that the action would result in sectional splits and a war with Mexico.[222]

Most members of Congress assumed that implementation of the legislation would be left to Polk, but Tyler and Calhoun did not intend to wait. On March 3, 1845, the secretary of state instructed Andrew Jackson Donelson, recently appointed chargé to Texas, to urge President Anson Jones to accept annexation as quickly as possible.[223] By that time, however, the question had been further complicated by international maneuverings and Texas politics.

When the United States Senate defeated the treaty of annexation on June 8, 1844, Lord Aberdeen, the British foreign minister, proposed a "Diplomatick Act" guaranteeing the independence of Texas. Abandoning his earlier stance, Aberdeen sought to win French approval for the measure.[224] He also attempted to convince Tomás Murphy, Mexican minister in London, that any attempt on the part of Mexico to block Texas independence would merely plunge his nation into a disastrous war with the United States.[225] Murphy was concerned that France might side with the United States in such a conflict but received assurances that Guizot was in complete accord with the British. Aberdeen pressed even more strongly for Mexican acceptance of his scheme when he received news from the United States that Tyler's joint resolution was meeting with success. The United States minister in England, Edward Everett, was aware of the discussions between Aberdeen and Guizot, but he was convinced that neither would go to the extent of supporting Mexico in a war with the United States.[226]

Returning to Texas in late December 1844, Charles Elliot worked to convince Texas officials to come to terms with Mexico. Assisted by French envoy Alphonse de Saligny, Elliot prepared a draft proposal wherein Texas guaranteed that it would not join any other power in return for Mexican recognition of its independence. With this document in hand, the British chargé traveled to Mexico City in the spring of 1845. Santa Anna had been deposed the previous December, and the new government of José Joaquín Herrera was still attempting to establish a meaningful base of power. Foreign Minister Luis G. Cuevas kept Elliot waiting for three weeks but finally agreed to discuss the proposal. On May 19, 1845, the foreign minister tentatively approved the document but insisted that any final agreement would have to be guaranteed by both England and France. The British envoy returned to Texas with the treaty on June 4, 1845.[227] By that time it was simply too late for Aberdeen's grand scheme to be accepted in the Lone Star Republic.

President Houston, disgusted by the defeat of the treaty of annexation by the United States Senate, actually instructed Ashbel Smith, the Texas representative in England, to embrace the offer of Lord Aberdeen.[228] This was not carried out, however, since the old warrior's term was drawing to a close and his orders were delayed by President-Elect Anson Jones.

Jones, the Texas minister to the United States in 1838 and 1839 and then Houston's secretary of state, had taken the view that his nation should not beg for annexation. He maintained a close relationship with the British envoy, in the fall of 1843 naming one of his sons Charles Elliot Jones.[229] After he entered the race for president of Texas, the secretary was accused of being under British influence. In the election of September 2, 1844, however, he defeated the more militant Edward Burleson.[230]

Andrew Jackson Donelson arrived in Texas on November 10, 1844, and was confident that he could persuade both Houston and the president-elect to keep the door open to annexation. Elliot, on the other hand, was convinced that both leaders preferred Texan independence if it could be guaranteed by England and France. In his inaugural speech of December 9, 1844, Anson Jones seemed to support the British envoy's hopes: he did not mention joining the United States but instead emphasized his desire for peace with Mexico. These remarks once again triggered speculation that the new chief executive was opposed to annexation.[231]

During his first three months in office, Jones played a cautious diplomatic game. When Donelson informed him of the joint resolution for annexation on March 20, 1845, the president gave no immediate response. When Elliot and the French minister Alphonse de Saligny appealed to him the following week to accept the mediation of Great Britain and France, Jones was willing to delay a decision for ninety days while they negotiated with Mexico.[232]

During this time of uncertainty, a number of influential individuals from the United States went to Texas to assist Donelson in persuading politicians and the general public. George W. Kendall, former Santa Fe prisoner and editor of the New Orleans *Picayune*, and Archibald Yell, former governor of Arkansas, were among the most effective. With their encouragement, proponents of annexation denounced Jones as an enemy of the true interests of Texas. By early May, Donelson remained suspicious that Jones might still be willing to give in to English bribes. Through the entire time Jones seemed simply to be trying to keep open viable diplomatic options for his nation.[233]

Elliot returned from Mexico with the draft treaty on June 4, 1845. President Jones called the Congress to debate the matter, but the final decision was to be made by a special convention elected by the people. On June 16 the Senate rejected the measure by an overwhelming vote and made public the terms of the negotiations, thus exposing Jones to severe criticism. The Texas congress then passed a joint resolution favoring annexation, and that action was ratified by the convention on July 4, 1845.[234]

Formal annexation was not completed until February 19, 1846, but for all practical purposes Texas was part of the United States. Commodore Stockton anchored four American ships at Galveston, and President Polk strengthened the army along the border.[235] Rumors circulated that the British had promised to declare war on the United States in exchange for the transfer of California and New Mexico.[236] Donelson rejected the rumors but harshly criticized Charles Elliot's efforts to provoke a war between the United States and Mexico. He urged Secretary of State James Buchanan to prepare to counter a Mexican attack.[237]

United States diplomatic relations with Mexico between 1841 and 1845 were carried out in the shadow of the Texas question. As long as Daniel Webster was secretary of state he was sincerely dedicated to the concept of neutrality and favored the continuation of a buffer along the Rio Grande. He attempted to convince Santa Anna that the United States wanted to be an impartial friend to both of the contending parties and pointed to the fact that the United States was not alone in recognizing Texan independence.[238]

On February 10, 1842, President Tyler appointed Waddy Thompson of South Carolina as minister to Mexico. Reaching his post on April 16, the envoy remained for just over two years.[239] Extremely overconfident and naïve during the early days of his assignment, Thompson felt certain that he would be able to deal effectively with the issues facing the two nations. He felt that Santa Anna was genuinely interested in establishing friendly relations with the United States and that members of his cabinet were "gentlemen of polished and kind manners." Thompson's optimism quickly faded as it became clear that there was a fundamental difference of opinion regarding the United States position of "neutrality."[240]

José María de Bocanegra, Mexican minister of foreign affairs during most of the period from 1841 to 1845, admitted that the United States government had not openly promoted the Texas insurrection, but it had allowed private citizens to furnish arms, troops, and money without restraint. Bocanegra pointed out that many public officials in the United States openly encouraged the invasion of Mexican territory and concluded that the assistance to the Texas rebels could not have been more effective if the United States had actually been at war with his country.[241] José María Tornel, a former ambassador to Washington who was very influential with Santa Anna, joined in the criticism, as did many other political leaders representing all segments of the political spectrum.[242]

In September 1842 General Juan N. Almonte was appointed to fill the long-vacant position of Mexican ambassador in Washington. He presented his credentials on October 27, 1842, and was to remain in Washington until March 6, 1845. From his post in Mexico City, Waddy Thompson praised Almonte as a fine patriot and gentleman with a favorable view of the United States.[243] Actually, the newly appointed envoy was one of the most outspoken critics of Anglo-American expansion into Texas and California.[244] He faithfully noted the speeches of John Quincy Adams and other opponents of Texas annexation and reported the strident statements regarding expansionism appearing in the American press and in the halls of Congress. These pronouncements were often hostile to Mexico, its culture, and its religion.[245]

Daniel Webster reacted strongly against the Mexican criticism: he informed Bocanegra that the government of a democratic society could not restrict freedom of expression or even prohibit trade in materials of war. Furthermore, individual citizens who wished to leave the United States and take up residence in Texas were perfectly free to do so, although they would lose the protection of their former home-land.[246] Thompson concluded that many of the belligerent statements by Bocanegra were for domestic political purposes, and he felt that Santa Anna would be willing to deal with the United States and even make territorial concessions.[247]

Although Daniel Webster sincerely wished to remain neutral in the conflicts between Texas and Mexico, he had no intention of abandoning what he perceived to be the basic interests of his country and its citizens. He insisted that Mexico pay all legitimate claims owed to United States citizens.[248] Ambassador Thompson, after spending only eleven days in Mexico City and filled with a sense of superiority, was convinced that he could persuade Santa Anna to cede both Texas and California to clear up those obligations.[249] Thompson's optimism faded in the following months, however, as Bocanegra delayed the negotiations.[250]

One claim is of special interest: William S. Parrott, a dentist and trader on the west coast of Mexico who was reported to live in an extravagant manner, turned to influential friends in Washington, including President Tyler, for assistance in his demands that the Mexican government pay for certain losses. Thompson expressed disgust at the pressures being brought upon him and agreed with the Mexican negotiators that Parrott's claims were excessive.[251] It is important to note that unpaid claims would eventually be cited by James K. Polk as a justification for war with Mexico and that Parrott would be used by that president as a special agent to Mexico.

Despite the difficulties, Thompson and Bocanegra signed a claims treaty on January 30, 1843. The first two payments were made on time, but after that, Mexico's internal problems and bitter public resentment brought a moratorium on further payments. When Daniel Webster resigned as secretary of state, the question was still a bone of contention between the two nations.[252] Meanwhile, other issues

arose to challenge Webster's efforts to establish neutrality and friendship.

In December 1841 around 160 prisoners who had been captured in
the abortive Santa Fe expedition were transferred from Chihuahua to
Mexico City. Many of them were American citizens, and although
most had regarded the expedition as a commercial enterprise or
merely as an adventure, they had illegally entered Mexican territory.
Madame Calderón de la Barca described them as objects more of curiosity than of hatred, yet rumors of brutality against these captives
circulated widely in Texas and in the United States.[253] Daniel Webster
knew that Mexico was justified in holding the prisoners, but he was
forced to react to strong political pressures at home. Friends of George
Kendall, editor of the New Orleans *Picayune*, asked for political intervention on his behalf, and General Leslie Combs of Kentucky sought
the release of his son. James Buchanan, within a few years to be appointed secretary of state, joined with other Pennsylvania political
leaders to call upon Webster to assist in the release of John Holliday, a
native of their state.[254]

The secretary instructed Powhatan Ellis to make every effort to secure the release of those who had not been involved in armed revolt
against Mexico and to insist upon humane treatment for all of the
prisoners. Webster approached the Mexican authorities in a conciliatory manner, fearing that hostilities generated by the incident would
disrupt his efforts to establish peaceful relations.[255] After Waddy
Thompson replaced Ellis, Webster reminded him that he should protest the "indignity and suffering" of innocent prisoners but should
not challenge the right of Mexico to hold them.[256] This approach
seemed to succeed; Santa Anna ordered their release on June 20,
1842. In his accustomed style, Thompson reported this event as a
great personal achievement.[257]

In less than six months, Thompson was once again forced to defend
neutrality and seek the release of prisoners in the wake of Texas politics. United States citizens were among the raiders captured at Mier
on Christmas Day 1842 and paraded in chains through the streets of
Mexico City. New political pressures were brought to bear in Washington: Senator John J. Crittenden of Kentucky, whose son had been
captured, demanded action by the Tyler administration. Suspicions
and animosities were once again heightened on both sides. The prisoners were eventually released, but Webster was painfully aware of
the impact this situation had on his policy of neutrality.[258]

Conditions in New Mexico seemed much more peaceful by 1842,

and trade along the overland route between Saint Louis and Santa Fe increased. In the spring of 1843 Webster worked out an agreement with Ambassador Almonte whereby an American escort would be allowed to protect the convoy against hostile Indians and outlaws, even within Mexican territory.[259] In July, however, an armed force headed by a "Colonel" Snively carried out a series of robberies in New Mexico. Foreign Minister Bocanegra pointed out that it had set out from Independence, Missouri, and that the majority of the participants were from the United States. Mexican newspapers branded the affair a "new invasion of Santa Fé." The alarm was placated when American troops arrested Snively.[260] Yet the uncertainties and suspicions generated by the incident weakened the efforts of Webster.

It was on the most distant periphery of Mexican territory that Daniel Webster's policy of neutrality suffered its greatest frustration. Shortly before taking his post in Washington, Juan N. Almonte warned that the increasing numbers of emigrants from the United States posed a serious threat to Mexican authority in the region, and Santa Anna ordered California closed to settlers.[261] As has been indicated, Waddy Thompson advocated the acquisition of California and felt that it could be arranged through peaceful negotiations. He assured both Webster and President Tyler that he would be able to convince Santa Anna to surrender the valuable region. He warned that if the United States failed to act quickly, then the valuable territory on the Pacific would be ceded to the British or French.[262]

Daniel Webster, though a sincere advocate of peace with Mexico, was lured by the great value of California. He privately revealed an interest in acquiring the territory, but he took every precaution in discussing the matter. During his negotiations with Lord Ashburton over the Canadian boundary, the secretary raised the question of San Francisco. When Ashburton did not object to the possibility of Mexico's selling the region, Webster assumed that Great Britain would not block an American move in that quarter.[263]

All hopes for a peaceful acquisition of California were rudely dispelled on October 19, 1842. Commodore Thomas ap Catesby Jones, apparently believing that war had been declared between the United States and Mexico, sailed into Monterey Bay and forced the surrender of the small garrison there. The next day, upon learning of his mistake, Jones restored Mexican authority and wrote a letter of explanation to Waddy Thompson.[264]

Bocanegra reacted harshly against the violation of Mexican national territory, and newspapers were filled with inflammatory statements.

Thompson expressed regrets for the incident and promised payment for any damages that had been inflicted, but he stopped short of an apology. He then took the offensive in the verbal battle, denouncing Bocanegra and other officials for their vehement statements against the United States.[265]

The incident took Daniel Webster by surprise. He informed Thompson that the attack had not been authorized and that the president regretted it greatly.[266] Almonte called the raid a scandalous infraction of the treaty of friendship and demanded that Jones be punished. Webster expressed "deep regret" for the incident and told the Mexican minister that he hoped that it would not disrupt good relations between their nations.[267] President Tyler, on the other hand, was incensed by the tone of Almonte's letters.[268] Despite the president's feelings, on March 3, 1843, Webster informed Almonte that Jones had been recalled from his command, thus illustrating the United States' desire to maintain its friendship with Mexico.[269]

By the time he left office on May 8, 1843, Daniel Webster's policy of neutrality and moderation had failed: Bocanegra viewed the secretary's expressions of friendship as a façade for territorial aggression, and the Mexican press charged the United States with racial and religious prejudice. Waddy Thompson concluded that the general population of Mexico had a "bitter and unchanging" hatred for his country.[270]

Upon taking office, Abel P. Upshur continued much of the rhetoric of neutrality, but he was much less concerned than his predcecessor about Mexican sensitivities. Some initial progress was made on outstanding claims, but payments were suspended within a few months.[271] Santa Anna was unsuccessful in his attempt to close the Santa Fe trade. By the spring of 1844, New Mexico was more closely tied to the commercial system of the United States than ever before; Yankee trade expanded in Chihuahua, Durango, and Sonora. Santa Fe was also a major way station for Anglo-American traders and adventurers on their way to California.[272] Santa Anna failed in his effort to block that movement, and some eight hundred new immigrants moved into California during 1843–44.[273] Yucatecan governor Miguel Barbachano once again asserted independence in the spring of 1844, declaring neutrality in the war between Mexico and Texas.[274] As in the past, Santa Anna suspected U.S. involvement in most of Mexico's regional problems. However, it was the Anglo-American private sector, rather than the Tyler government, that shaped most of those events on the periphery.

The major change in policy with the arrival of Upshur was the administration's open effort to annex Texas.[275] In reaction to this change, Bocanegra warned that Mexico would consider any U.S. treaty for the acquisition of Texas to be a declaration of war.[276] When General Almonte delivered that message in Washington, Upshur retorted that Mexico had absolutely no voice in questions between Texas and the United States.[277] The tensions continued, and on November 3, 1843, Almonte warned that if Congress approved the treaty under discussion, Mexico would be forced to declare war.[278]

Bocanegra seemed to modify his hard line in the spring of 1844, in part due to his growing difficulties with Great Britain and France.[279] At about the same time, Upshur attempted to convince Almonte that Mexico could never hope to reestablish its rule in Texas. The secretary was guardedly confident that annexation might be carried out peacefully.[280] If there had been any cause for optimism, however, it soon faded with the death of Upshur and the arrival of an even more ardent expansionist as secretary of state.

John C. Calhoun, while promoting the treaty for annexation in the Senate, utilized the armed forces to protect Texas against the threatened Mexican invasion. He promised to extend generous terms on the boundary once annexation was completed but declared that Mexico had no alternative but to accept the loss of her former state. At the same time, he demanded that the rights of American citizens be respected, especially in California.[281]

Waddy Thompson resigned as minister to Mexico in the spring of 1844. The chargé d'affaires, Benjamin Green, who temporarily represented the Tyler administration, faced harsh criticism from Bocanegra and speculated that these abuses were the direct result of speeches in Washington by Henry Clay and John Quincy Adams. Santa Anna threatened to crush the Texas rebels, but his plans were thwarted by regional unrest, administrative confusion, and the chronic shortage of funds. The strong man was further weakened in August with the resignation of Bocanegra as minister for foreign affairs.[282]

Wilson Shannon, former governor of Ohio, was appointed ambassador to Mexico by President Tyler and reached his post in September 1844. Shortly after his arrival, Santa Anna released 120 of the Mier prisoners, seemingly in an effort to win over the new envoy. Manuel Crecencio Rejón, a Yucatecan with a reputation for liberal views, was appointed as foreign minister by the dictator. If Shannon had any illusions that friendly relations might be established, however, they were quickly shattered when Rejón vigorously attacked United States policy toward Mexico. The Yucatecan was especially critical of proslavery forces that supported annexation and insisted that President Tyler would be personally responsible for all of the evil consequences that would evolve from that policy. Rejón was greatly encouraged when the United States Senate rejected Tyler's treaty of annexation.[283] Shannon was discouraged and considered abandoning his post, but he agreed to remain through the last months of 1844.[284]

The election of James K. Polk in November 1844 greatly strengthened the Texas policy of President Tyler and his secretary of state. They defended annexation as the true product of the democratic process and denounced any attempt on the part of Mexico to interfere with the free choice of the people of the sovereign nation of Texas. Virtually every political faction in Mexico denounced the expansionist policies of the United States. At that crucial time, however, they refused to cooperate in the face of increasing foreign pressures. In November General Mariano Paredes revolted against Santa Anna in Guadalajara; factions throughout the nation quickly supported the rebellion. The garrison in the capital defected on December 5, 1844, and a mob dragged the statue of the dictator through the streets. Although Santa Anna continued to resist for several weeks, the nation was once again in a state of confusion and disorder.[285]

General José Joaquín Herrera was appointed provisional president and was to serve for the following year. Luis G. Cuevas was named secretary of foreign affairs, but for all practical purposes foreign relations were suspended in the midst of continuing factionalism. Congressional leaders, in an effort to condemn Santa Anna, published materials showing that the dictator had attempted to cede California to the British in exchange for financial assistance.[286] Shannon attempted to take advantage of the internal strife and confusion, hoping that Herrera might be willing to abandon the strident position that the previous government had taken about Texas.[287]

On February 28, 1845, while Mexican factionalism and regional revolt continued, President Tyler succeeded in pushing through Congress the joint resolution for the annexation of Texas. The Mexican reaction was immediate: Juan N. Almonte denounced it as a willful usurpation of Mexican territory and demanded his passport. When news of the resolution reached Mexico City in late March, Cuevas notified Shannon that diplomatic relations would be severed, blaming the decision on United States aggression.[288]

President James K. Polk (The National Portrait Gallery, Smithsonian Institution)

Annexation to Conquest, 1845–1848

On April 24, 1846, a small force of General Zachary Taylor's army clashed with troops of General Mariano Arista north of the Rio Grande, initiating a conflict that would drastically alter the geo-political and cultural balance of the North American continent. Mexican officials and editors denounced President James K. Polk for having deliberately provoked the war to seize their rightful national territory. One of the most outspoken critics was Juan Almonte, recently returned from his mission in the United States.[289] Many of Polk's opponents in Washington echoed the Mexican charges, branding the struggle as a deliberate act of aggression to expand slavery.[290] Since that time historians have examined in great detail the events leading to the "Mexican War." Most citizens of the United States have very little understanding or interest in the conflict, which was a significant one in the nation's history. In Mexico, however, the perception of the war as a deliberate act of aggression by the United States against a weak and defenseless neighbor is virtually unquestioned.[291]

When James K. Polk came to office, he readily accepted the Texas claim that the Rio Grande was the legitimate boundary with Mexico and dispatched the army of Zachary Taylor to defend that newly acquired territory. It is significant, however, that Taylor remained at Corpus Christi for almost a year before pushing to the Rio Grande. John Slidell was appointed as minister to Mexico with instructions to reestablish diplomatic relations and discuss the differences between the two nations. Secretary of State James Buchanan instructed him to press for the long-overdue claims by United States citizens against Mexico and to ascertain if the Herrera government might be willing to sell California as a means of satisfying those claims. Buchanan was convinced that there was strong public support in the United States for these steps and that any break in relations would be blamed on Mexico.[292] President Polk attempted to persuade influential senators, including Thomas Hart Benton and Sam Houston, to appropriate the funds necessary to make the proposed purchase but wished to avoid making the scheme public.[293] He wanted to settle the differences with Mexico peacefully, but only if his dreams of territorial expansion could be satisfied.

When Slidell reached Mexico City in the fall of 1845, the government of José Joaquín Herrera faced major internal pressures. The president did not dare risk the ire of the Mexican populace and dissident political factions by recognizing an envoy who insisted that the question of Texas's annexation was a closed subject. Foreign Minister Manuel de la Peña y Peña charged that Slidell's mission was merely to mask the efforts of the United States to provoke a war.[294] The U.S. envoy seemed sincere in his effort to reach a negotiated settlement, but William Parrott, who was still serving as confidential agent, actually hoped that Mexico would declare war, thus opening the way for the United States to acquire additional territory.[295]

Peña y Peña maneuvered to gain the support of Great Britain for the protection of Mexican interests in California, but Tomás Murphy reported from London that Lord Aberdeen would never risk war with the United States to protect Mexican possessions in the Pacific.[296] Despite his refusal to receive Slidell, President Herrera was overthrown by a military uprising in December 1845, in part on the charge that he was planning to alienate national territory. When General Mariano Paredes took power in January 1846, some speculated that he might be willing to make a deal on both the claims and the territory in exchange for desperately needed funds. Secretary Buchanan instructed Slidell to make every effort to gain recognition, thus shifting the blame for any rejection of compromise to Mexico. Slidell, aware that his mission would probably fail, maintained contact with Commodore John D. Sloat, commander of the U.S. naval force in the Pacific port of Mazatlán.[297]

Polk, while attempting to discuss a settlement with Mexico, strengthened military forces that might be utilized in case the negotiations failed. He not only ordered Taylor to the Rio Grande but also increased naval forces in both the Gulf and the Pacific. Commodore Sloat was instructed to seize San Francisco if war broke out. The president was also involved in the "surveying mission" of John C. Fremont into California just before the outbreak of hostilities in that region.[298] Ironically, Polk's decision to use force was advocated by a messenger from Santa Anna who stated that this was the only way to achieve success with Mexican politicans.[299]

By the end of April 1846, the president had decided to ask Congress to declare war on Mexico and was prepared to justify that request on the basis of long-overdue claims. Word of Taylor's clash allowed him to amend his message to accuse Mexico of aggression.[300] Secretary of State Buchanan felt that the United States should deny any intention to acquire California in the course of the war, stating that such a denial would ease tensions with England. Polk indignantly rejected Bu-

Secretary of State James Buchanan (The National Portrait Gallery, Smithsonian Institution)

chanan's suggestion, insisting that the conflict, which was initiated by the wanton attack against the United States, warranted the expansion of the nation to the Pacific at the expense of Mexico.[301]

The struggle quickly evolved into a war for major territorial acquisition, manifest destiny at its most aggressive. Zachary Taylor crossed the Rio Grande and captured Matamoros and, by late September 1846, the key city of Monterrey. He narrowly defeated Santa Anna at Buena Vista the following February, virtually securing the vast region of northeastern Mexico for the United States. Taylor's plan to march south to Mexico City was discarded due to logistical and strategic con-

General Zachary Taylor (The National Portrait Gallery, Smithsonian Institution)

siderations and a dash of party politics. The landing of Winfield Scott at Veracruz and his march to the central valley of Mexico was a feat that rivaled the invasion of Cortés over three hundred years earlier. The Anglo-American force occupied the Halls of Montezuma on September 14, 1847. The battles of Taylor and Scott captured the public imagination in the United States and served as a training ground for the officers and men who would later face each other on the battlefields of Fredericksburg, Gettysburg, and Antietam.[302]

The campaigns on the northern periphery, though less spectacular, were even more significant. Colonel Stephen W. Kearny gathered volunteers from Missouri and quickly advanced against Santa Fe, taking the city without a struggle. A force of nine hundred men under Colonel Alexander W. Doniphan continued south to capture El Paso, and by July 1846, New Mexico was under Anglo control. Kearny pushed westward to California.[303] Long before his arrival, that rich province had been declared a part of the United States by Fremont, and on July 9, 1846, Commodore Sloat raised the Stars and Stripes in San Francisco. Within four months of the declaration of war, the vast region from Texas to the Pacific was under United States dominance.[304] The Treaty of Guadalupe Hidalgo simply ratified an accomplished fact.

The victories at Buena Vista, Churubusco, and Santa Fe were not the product of an efficient U.S. military organization or sinister political intrigue in Washington. They were achieved primarily because of the constant internal strife within the Mexican nation and especially on the far-flung northern periphery, which was so vulnerable to Anglo-American pressures. President Herrera attempted to unify the Mexican population through an appeal to national honor.[305] He faced severe financial problems but did not dare mention the possibility of compromise. Internal factionalism was so rife that there was little ability to organize any effective opposition to the occupation of Texas.[306] Mexico City was more a prize to be captured than an administrative center from which to plan and execute a national defense.

Despite Herrera's refusal of Slidell, General Mariano Paredes pronounced against the elected president on December 14, 1845, and was quickly joined by a wide range of dissident factions. It was in the midst of this confusion that John Slidell reached the outskirts of the capital. Herrera was overthrown, and a handpicked junta elected Paredes president on January 4, 1846. The general faced an empty treasury, but having risen to power on the cry of territorial integrity, he had to reject the promise of funds dangled before him by Slidell.[307]

Paredes was no more successful than his predecessor in his appeals for unity. The outbreak of the war increased denunciations of the United States but did nothing to reduce internal intrigue. Ideological lines were blurred as the federalists of Gómez Farías joined the conservatives and other dissident groups in a revolt against Paredes in August 1846. The rebels gained an unlikely supporter when President Polk ordered his navy to allow Santa Anna to slip through its blockade.[308] Reaching the capital in mid-September, the caudillo was elected president on December 23, 1846, with Gómez Farías given the second spot on the ticket.[309]

When Santa Anna marched north at the head of the Mexican army to challenge Zachary Taylor, new waves of conflict arose in the capital. This was in part simply a continuation of the usual intrigue, but it also involved a conflict of political ideology that would eventually enflame the nation in bitter civil war. The interim president Gómez Farías declared that in the face of a foreign invasion Mexico was justified in calling upon the Roman Catholic church to support its national defense. Rejecting this as an attempt to remove one of its most valued privileges, the Mexican clergy supported a coup against the Zacatecas liberal. As he returned from the disastrous campaign against Taylor, Santa Anna joined the supporters of religious privilege and assisted in the ouster of Gómez Farías at the very time General Winfield Scott marched virtually unopposed from Veracruz.[310]

In June 1847, Moses Y. Beach, a United States confidential agent in Mexico City, remarked that Catholic leaders would be willing to accept United States dominance in Mexico if they could be assured that church property would be protected.[311] His opinion seemed to be proven when clerical leaders in Puebla cordially received General Scott. After the American commander entered Mexico City, he developed a friendly relationship with Archbishop Juan Manuel Irizarri y Peralta.[312] Liberals angrily blamed the clergy for the humiliating defeat at the hands of the Yankee invaders. Conservatives, on the other hand, charged the liberals with a lack of patriotism and stressed their philosophical kinship with the North American Protestants. After 1848, following the humiliation of defeat, mutual accusations continued and eventually led to another destructive fraternal conflict, the War of the Reforma, and to renewed foreign invasion.[313]

The power struggle in central Mexico was reflected also in the provinces. Although President Herrera attempted to moderate the centralism of the *basis orgánicas*, regional unrest continued, and by the time Paredes seized power in January 1846, rebellions raged in Zacatecas, Veracruz, Nuevo León, Michoacán, and Querétaro. Yucatán once again proclaimed independence and after April declared its neutrality in the war between Mexico and the United States. It was in the far northern periphery, however, that the breakdown in central control had the most devastating effects, paving the way for rapid conquest by the neighboring power. In Sonora, Chihuahua, Durango, and Coahuila, much dissatisfaction centered upon the failure

Arrival of Caravan at Santa Fe, circa 1840 (Denver Public Library, Western History Department)

of the central government to offer protection against hostile Indian incursions. New Mexico and California also charged Mexican authorities with neglecting their security and economic interests.[314]

The Anglo-American private sector played a highly significant role on the Mexican northern periphery during the war and helped to determine the political fate of those regions by 1848. The value of trade between New Mexico and the United States jumped from $200,000 in 1844 to $342,000 in 1845. A large caravan was on its way from Saint Louis to Santa Fe in May 1846, when congress declared war against Mexico. Rather than attempt to stop the traders, Secretary of War William Marcy incorporated them into Kearny's invasion. The traders were quickly joined by an additional one thousand mounted Missouri volunteers. The combined force that moved into Santa Fe in early summer was merely following a well-worn commercial path, and the decision by New Mexico officials to surrender was greatly influenced by long-established dependence upon American trade goods. James Magoffin of Kentucky, who had been in the region for a number of years, helped to pave the way for the transfer of authority when Colonel Kearny arrived. By the end of 1846, trade between the United States and New Mexico reached $1 million, more than double the total for the previous year.[315]

California was an even more attractive prize: Fremont and Sloat were able to take advantage of internal divisions and the long-standing distrust toward Mexico City. Their small military and naval units would have been inadequate, however, had it not been for the Anglo-American private sector. Merchants, whalers, trappers, and adventurers were the true vanguard of the conquest, and most of them did not cost the Polk government one penny. In the fall of 1845, between three hundred and four hundred new settlers arrived, and in the following year many of the volunteers who made up Kearny's army were discharged on the coast, further increasing the ranks of the private sector.[316]

Buffalo hunters, trappers, and fur traders pushed into the vast area between New Mexico and the Pacific coast. By 1845 the region was dotted with small trading posts linked to the commercial system of the Santa Fe and Oregon trails. Just as war with Mexico was about to break out, the region also witnessed a unique Anglo-American migration. Mormons throughout the Middle West faced an increasing wave of hostility by 1844. Rising to leadership in the movement after the murder of founder Joseph Smith, Brigham Young announced that he would lead the congregation westward to a new "Kingdom of Zion." During 1845 and 1846, thousands of families from Ohio, Illinois, and states farther east crossed the Missisippi River into Iowa. By the summer of 1846, a body of Mormons numbering some fifteen thousand, together with their cattle, sheep, mules, horses, wagons, and implements of agriculture, camped along the Missouri River. They were planning to move into territory claimed by Mexico, but Young realized the importance of gaining permission and support from the United States.

Special envoy Jesse C. Little arrived in Washington on May 21, 1846, just nine days after the declaration of war. He assured President Polk that the Mormons were loyal to the United States and offered to supply thousands of volunteers to support the struggle against Mexico. President Polk and Secretary of War Marcy were skeptical regarding the patriotism of the sect but eventually agreed to accept five hundred recruits to assist in Kearny's campaign. The "Mormon battalion" was quickly organized and reached Santa Fe in early October 1846. It marched south to El Paso, then across the desert regions of New Mexico, Arizona, and southern California, reaching San Diego in January 1847. The battalion met very little resistance but carried out one of the most remarkable military marches of history. More important was that the Mormon volunteers furnished a valuable Anglo-American presence in the Southwest at a crucial time.[317]

Samuel Brannan sailed from New York with 238 Mormon settlers in

February 1846, their destination being the Mexican province of California. He reached San Francisco Bay the following July, just three weeks after Sloat proclaimed United States rule. The well-equipped and highly disciplined Mormon faction acknowledged United States authority and, at a very critical point, was a significant American presence in the San Francisco region. Brannan suggested that California be made headquarters for the Mormon Zion, but Brigham Young rejected that proposal, deciding instead that his religious state would be in the isolated fastness of the Great Basin. Many of Brannan's followers eventually migrated to Utah, but some remained in California along with many discharged members of the battalion, forming an important core of Anglo-American agricultural settlers not only in California but in Arizona and Nevada as well.[318]

Meanwhile, thousands of Mormon migrants prepared to move west. Brigham Young led an advance party into Nebraska, Wyoming, and northern Utah, planting crops, building bridges, and laying out lots for his future capital city. The main body was under way by early 1848, its movement patterned after the march of Moses from Egypt. By December 1848, some five thousand pilgrims had settled in and around the valley of the Great Salt Lake.[319] They were not trappers and hunters but farmers and husbandmen seeking land for their crops and pasture for their cattle and sheep. These migrants shared many of the characteristics of settlers who had moved into Texas some two decades earlier, but with one major difference. Coming primarily from the Northeast and Middle West, they were not slaveholders. Though they remained the target of suspicion and hostility for years to come, the pilgrims of Brigham Young served as a significant vanguard of United States settlement in the West.[320]

Limits of Expansion, 1848–1860

Secretary of State Buchanan assigned Nicholas P. Trist to accompany General Scott's invading army and to negotiate with Mexican officials. Trist was to insist upon the extended Texas boundary and the payment of outstanding claims. At the same time, he was to offer $15 million for New Mexico and California, absorbing the claims in the process. After settling his personal differences with General Scott, the envoy negotiated an armistice with Santa Anna on August 20, 1847, just as the American forces neared the gates of Mexico City. Critics charged that he and Scott were duped by the crafty Mexican caudillo.[321] The war was renewed in September, and the Yankee army occupied the capital. Trist resumed his efforts to negotiate in early 1848 but had difficulty finding a Mexican official willing to risk the stigma of signing away national territory. After the ouster of Santa Anna, however, a moderate faction rose to power: Luis G. Cuevas met with Trist at Guadalupe Hidalgo and on February 2, 1848, signed a preliminary agreement that contained most of the terms that had been in Buchanan's original instructions to Trist.[322]

When the treaty arrived in the United States, President Polk hesitated to submit it for ratification, although it gave him all he had anticipated at the beginning of the war. The military victories throughout Mexico and the rapid occupation of the northern territories raised expectations. The president made little effort to hide his desire to expand U.S. holdings south to the Sierra Madre Oriental, and it was widely rumored that he intended to annex all of Mexico. Trist reported that many influential citizens in the capital would actually prefer United States rule.[323]

Abolitionists and their allies accused Polk of deliberately scheming to expand slavery. Henry Clay, with one eye on the presidential election of 1848, spoke out strongly for the establishment of a "just boundary."[324] A number of prominent political leaders, including Senator Lewis Cass and John C. Calhoun, warned that the United States should not annex regions in which cultural and racial identities were markedly different from those at home.[325] From Mexico, both General Scott and Trist advised against annexation, partly because of the military and logistical problems but mainly because they felt that such an action would pose grave dangers to the institutions of the United States.[326]

In a climate of tensions and mixed emotions, the president submitted the Treaty of Guadalupe Hidalgo to the Senate. After debate behind closed doors, the measure was approved on March 10, 1848, and signed by Polk six days later. Mexico accepted it on May 30, 1848, and on that same day José Joaquín de Herrera was again chosen president. He faced all of the problems of working out the terms of the pact and of rebuilding the nation.[327]

The Treaty of Guadalupe Hidalgo was by no means a guarantee that Anglo-American expansion would cease. Many westerners wished to expand into the provinces of Tamaulipas, Nuevo León, Coahuila, Chihuahua, Sonora, and Baja California. As in the previous decades, Texas volunteers joined ambitious regional caudillos in northern Mexico who opposed the central government. In September 1855, when

Captain James H. Callahan led a Texas force into Coahuila, ostensibly to pursue renegade Indians and escaped slaves, Mexican authorities branded the raid an attempt to expand the Texas border.[328] Filibustering expeditions from California, including that by future "president" of Nicaragua William Walker, threatened Baja California and Sonora.[329] Between 1853 and 1860, Presidents Franklin Pierce and James Buchanan attempted to acquire additional territory in northern Mexico by treaty but were blocked by strong congressional opposition. In 1853, James Gadsden did purchase some nineteen million acres in southern Arizona for a railroad route, but all other schemes for territorial transfer along the border were abandoned.[330]

One other region of the periphery literally thrust itself into the arms of the United States during the Mexican War. Maya chieftains of eastern Yucatán rebelled in July 1847, threatening to push the white ruling classes into the sea. Governor Santiago Méndez appointed his son-in-law, Justo Sierra O'Reilly, as special envoy to the United States. Arriving in Washington in November 1847, the young Yucatecan made an impassioned plea for assistance against the "barbaric hordes" and called for North American settlers to migrate to his "nation."[331] Secretary of State Buchanan, though willing to discuss the issues, never recognized the sovereignty of Yucatán.[332] In the spring of 1848, while the Treaty of Guadalupe Hidalgo was being debated, Justo Sierra attempted to gain the support of influential congressmen, including Sam Houston and John C. Calhoun.[333] By April, after the Senate had approved the treaty, Governor Méndez realized that drastic steps would be necessary. He offered to have Yucatán placed directly under the protection and sovereignty of the United States. He made it clear that if the United States rejected the offer, his "nation" would seek support from Great Britain and Spain.[334]

President Polk met privately with Justo Sierra on April 22, 1848, and shortly thereafter submitted the "Yucatán bill" to Congress. The measure described the plight of the inhabitants of the peninsula and the threat of European involvement in that strategic region but did not advocate annexation.[335] Debate on the bill lasted throughout most of May and tended to revolve around sectional and party politics. Many northern Whigs denounced the measure as a part of Polk's overall expansionist ambitions. A number of Democrats, especially southerners, were sympathetic with Yucatán, but very few actually advocated annexation. In keeping with his concerns about central Mexico, John C. Calhoun stressed the dangers of attempting to incorporate into the Union people with such strong cultural and political differences.[336]

In June the Yucatán bill was defeated, and Justo Sierra ended his mission in despair. His native land seemed doomed. Just as the Maya armies seemed ready to take Mérida, they ended the siege and withdrew to the southeast. Miguel Barbachano, having replaced Méndez as governor of Yucatán, had little choice but to once again join the Mexican nation. President Herrera accepted the wayward province and immediately asked the United States for some three thousand to four thousand troops to assist against the rebellious Indians. Buchanan, though sympathetic, denied the request.[337] Although Yucatán would retain its strong sense of regional pride and separatism, it would never again desert the Mexican nation.

With the exception of the Gadsden Purchase and a few minor border adjustments, the United States did not expand further into Mexico after 1848. This was in part due to the bitter sectional strife within the union: the Civil War was in many ways an outgrowth of the absorption of new western territories gained from Mexico. At the same time, the farmers, cattlemen, and traders who had pushed into Texas, California, New Mexico, and Utah simply did not penetrate Tamaulipas, Chihuahua, or Yucatán; they turned instead to the gold mines of California and the rich valleys of Oregon and Washington. Mexico, as vulnerable as it was in the years following the war, was not the target of the private sector, which was the primary force of Anglo-American expansion on the North American continent.

The Heritage of Expansion

The conflict-filled relationship between the United States and Mexico between 1821 and 1848 has had profound influences upon both nations. Sectional strife aggravated by the problems of the Mexican cession brought the United States to the verge of destruction. With the end of the Civil War, however, the nation, a great continental power, was poised to assume a leadership role in the hemisphere and eventually in the world. The industrial and commercial success of the United States was based to a great extent upon the agricultural lands of Texas and California, the vast mineral resources of the Southwest, and the seaports of the Pacific coast.

Mexico emerged from the war and from the Treaty of Guadalupe

Hidalgo a broken and humiliated nation. Factionalism and party strife plunged the country into another civil war followed by another foreign invasion, this time by Europeans. After 1872, a new sense of pride and nationalism emerged. The liberal regime of Porfirio Díaz looked to the United States as an economic model and linked its agricultural and mineral production with the North American system. As a sense of Mexican nationalism developed, however, it was based in part upon the humiliation suffered at the hands of the northern neighbor. Resentment toward and suspicion of the United States were always to remain only slightly below the surface.

Mexico suffered the brunt of Anglo-American expansion and territorial aggression. The other nations of Latin America, however, were very much aware of the Mexican experience and came to share many of Mexico's suspicions about United States policy within the hemisphere.

Early United States Recognition of Colombian Independence and Subsequent Relations to 1830

Eugene R. Huck

What started out as a whirlwind romance ground to protracted boredom in less than a decade. The early excitement of being the first nation to recognize any of the successes of the Latin American revolutions soon turned the United States from the position of a model and a mentor to a manipulator trying to manage minor commercial concessions. The fault of it all can be divided among many factors, including the internal problems of Colombia in her struggle between centralism and federalism, the preoccupation of the United States with its own West, the former Spanish colonies' inexperience in democracy, the pressures of England and France in the diplomatic arena, the conflict of alien ideologies, the quality of United States diplomats, the impact of an accelerating Industrial Revolution, and the scramble for the mind and markets of a virgin territory.

The United States, enjoying its Era of Good Feelings after the novel but indecisive War of 1812, was viewed as the model of a successful government by all of the Latin American colonies who were struggling for independence. After all, the United States not only had won its freedom from a major world power but had sustained that break in the second contest. Moreover, after the renowned XYZ Affair, which brought the country to the brink of war with France shortly after 1800, the United States had been fairly successful in avoiding entanglements with Europe. The country was looking to the West generally as a result of the Lewis and Clark expedition of 1804 and was trying to plan the occupation of the Louisiana Territory, whose purchase in 1803 had doubled the size of the nation. Businesses using machinery were beginning to thrive after 1815, and the country was self-absorbed and, if not hostile, at least indifferent toward foreign affairs. The intrigues of the Congress System of Europe were not as interesting to the populace as utilizing steam power and watching the growth of a canal network and macadamized roads. Perhaps some of the calmness of life in the United States was envied by the Spanish American insurgents who, in a seemingly endless round of battles, strived for freedom. That envy caused them to emulate the example of the United States.

Socially and religiously, Latin American life changed little after the wars. When peace came to the bulk of the lands in revolt, religion remained unaltered, and social changes did not appear significant. Politically, intellectually, and commercially, however, Latin American life changed immensely. The Creoles, who had always been a part of the social elite, maintained their positions and elevated themselves to political power after the departure of the natives of Spain and Portugal. This situation was a basis for some of the political complications still evident in the twentieth century.

In northern South America, where Simón Bolívar[1] won victories for the antimonarchical revolutionaries, political destinies were not soon resolved. Before and after his death on December 17, 1830, many suspected Bolívar of having monarchical tendencies. Even more important than the question of monarchy was the struggle between the centralists and the federalists. The first few decades after the 1810 declaration of independence were a time of nominal victory for the federalists.[2]

By 1813, the Colombian representative in Philadelphia, although not officially received, gave this compliment to the government of the United States: "From this day on we may ventilate our views and open our ports to the other nations, among which we will be glad to distinguish the inhabitants of New Albion, who have presented us with a standard of wise government."[3] Many citizens of Colombia[4] were in sympathy with the form of government of the United States. There were those, however, who thought that its brand of republicanism was not suitable for northern South America. One such person was General Antonio Nariño, who gained notoriety (and imprisonment by the Spanish for ten years) for translating and printing the historic document of the French Revolution, the Declaration of the Rights of Man and Citizen. Speaking in favor of a centralist government, which he tried to produce as president, Nariño stated his views upon giving up the title of dictator-president on June 13, 1813:

> [You may consider] the example of North America, but I will answer a hundred times, if necessary, we cannot be compared to peoples who

were always free, and who also had the aid of France and Spain to defend themselves. These fine unworkable constitutions will ruin us if we do not pretty soon open our eyes to reality and learn from experience. . . . As the famous Smith has pointed out in his *Wealth of Nations* . . . , what works perfectly for one economy, will not necessarily work in a very different one. Plans which flourish in the north die here, and vice versa. There is no government equally suitable to all climates and parts of the world. No man should expect a universal system equally suitable all over the world.[5]

Two modern Colombian historians have characterized both the lack of political experience and the interest in modeling the new government after the United States in this manner: "The deplorable situation which the country presented was due to the interpretations of the so-called federal system advocated by many of our prominent Colombian men who were honest in purpose but little versed in governmental affairs. They had learned their theories in books, and the prosperity of the United States attracted and deceived them. They believed the progress of that country was owing to its constitution, and without stopping to observe conditions at home, reached the conclusion that a federation would have the same results here."[6] Colombia, indeed, was to experiment with various forms of republicanism in the first half of the nineteenth century.

Our task, then, is to look at the interaction of the United States diplomats to Colombia, to see how successful they were, and to compare them with those of Great Britain and other competing nations. Since commerce was the overriding interest of most major powers in their relations with the Latin American republics, one can perhaps assume that fostering it was the most compelling duty of the diplomats. This was true of the United States.

In the area of commerce, Colombia stagnated internally and almost completely depended on outside assistance. Having practically no navy, she commissioned ships from the United States and from other countries for privateering action during the independence movement. She took aid where she could find it and promised favorable trading concessions to the nations that would help her in her struggle. As early as 1797, almost a generation before the wars began, Francisco de Miranda, the Precursor of Independence, pointed out to the British cabinet that he was eager to forge a defensive alliance between Great Britain, the United States, and South America. He also wanted to secure the opening of navigation between the Atlantic and Pacific by cutting across the Isthmus of Panama and a guarantee of the freedom of such a channel from the British nation.[7] Despite the preoccupation of the United States and Great Britain with the intrigues of the Napoleonic era and with the War of 1812, both nations competed for the trade and markets of Latin America. That competition eventually led to recognition of Colombia's independence and to the signing of treaties granting commercial concessions.

British policy toward the United States was altered after the War of 1812, and she became quite friendly. "She not only showed a sincere desire to refrain from any unseemly meddling with American affairs, but even displayed a real anxiety to avoid all chances of future trouble."[8] She postponed differences and winked at such violations as General Andrew Jackson's high-handed treatment of Arbuthnot and Ambrister in Florida. By 1818, Richard Rush, from his post as minister to Great Britain, reported that William Wilberforce of the House of Commons had said that the United States "was one of the . . . great powers of the world." James McIntosh, also of Parliament, had said that the United States was a country "which had long been the abode of public felicity, and which [he hoped] was also to become the model of legislative wisdom"; he added that it was "already notoriously the second country in the world in commercial wealth." At a meeting of the British and Foreign Bible Society, Chancellor of the Exchequer Nicholas Vansittart emphasized that Great Britain and the United States were "the two greatest maritime states in the world."[9] Rush did note, however, that the newspapers of London maintained an "unjust and even angry manner" toward the former English colonies. Two reasons may be proffered for the animosity of the British press. First, public opinion was not as easy to change as official opinion toward a former enemy, and, second, the press was more nearly reflecting the opinion of the merchants, who continued to be unfriendly toward an ever-growing commercial rival.

By 1819, official opinion was still friendly. Lord Castlereagh, British foreign secretary, said, referring to the signed but not ratified treaty between the United States and Spain concerning Florida: "Let me deal candidly. [We] prefer Spain's owning the Floridas, to their fall into your hands. Spain is weak, you are strong. But the treaty has been made and we now prefer its ratification to the possibility of any serious disturbance to the pacifick relations between the United States and Spain."[10]

On the question of recognition of the independence of Latin America, the same division of opinion existed. Official opinion was against recognition, but public opinion generally favored it. The same situation prevailed in the United States. John Quincy Adams, as minister to England in 1816, made this observation: "The National Sentiment in England is . . . strong in favor of the South Americans and the prevailing opinion is that their independence would be highly advantageous to the interest of this country. A different and directly opposite sentiment is entertained by the government. Their disposition is decided[ly] against the South Americans; but by a political obliquity, not without example, it is not so unequivocally, in favour of the mother country."[11] Adams then delineated the reasons for Great Britain's wishing that the insurrection in the New World would be suppressed:

(1) They have a deep-rooted and inveterate prejudice, fortified by all the painful recollections of their own unfortunate contest, against any revolution by which colonies are emancipated and become independent states.

(2) They have a forcible *moral* impression, like that of their antipathy to the slave trade, that it is *wrong*, to assist or encourage colonies in the attempt to throw off the yoke of their mother country.

(3) They dread the influence of example, and always remember how many colonies they themselves still possess.

(4) They fear the consequences of South American independence upon the whole system of European colonial policy. Their attachment to this has been amply displayed, in their anxious and preserving efforts to draw the Braganza family back to Lisbon [from Brazil, where England helped to take them to avoid Napoleon].

(5) [They also maintain] . . . the mystic virtues of legitimacy. It is impossible to write with proper gravity upon this subject, but it has no small operation against the South American independents.

(6) And last but not least, they look with no precipitous eyes to the relations which will naturally arise between Independent governments on the two American continents. They foresee less direct advantage to themselves, from a free commercial intercourse with South America, than indirect injury, by its tendency to promote the interests of the United States.[12]

The British position, as stated by Adams, remained opposed to recognition of independence of any of the Latin American states until the combined pressures of the Monroe Doctrine, the recognition of independence by the United States, and the mounting force of the British merchants worked to reverse the policy.[13] All of this despite the fact that British ex-soldiers from the Napoleonic Wars were using all sorts of excuses to come to Colombia to serve under Bolívar and that unemployment was rife in England in 1817. The time and circumstances were not ripe just yet.

While Britain was having some difficulty reconciling official policy with popular sentiment, the United States was not having much more luck. Like the merchants in Britain, the merchants of the coastal areas were eager for new markets. The government, although in complete sympathy with revolutions, could not afford to support the movement until the negotiations over the purchase of Florida from Spain had been completed. Once this was done in 1821, the way was clear for recognition the following year.

Far fewer U.S. citizens than British citizens went into service for the Latin American insurgents because unemployment in the United States was not as pronounced as that in Britain. The frontier was available for any unemployed veteran who wanted a job farming. Those who did go came, in the main, from Massachusetts,[14] Kentucky, and Tennessee.[15] Most of the states had some representation. The maritime states contributed seamen and captains to Latin American insurgents who desired their services.[16] Jackson's role in weakening the Spanish hold on the New World is well known: his capture of Pensacola in the summer of 1818 helped to undermine Spain, but the action backfired because it caused maritime insurance rates to be increased by one-half percent. The reasoning behind the increase was that there were rumors of war between the United States and Spain and increasing accounts of ships to America being depredated by pirates under Spanish American colors.[17]

United States assistance was also in the form of supplies. When the Liberator, Bolívar, was in the campaign to capture Bogotá in December 1819, he decided that he would need additional muskets. He sent one hundred thousand dollars to Angostura to be forwarded to Britain to purchase twenty thousand muskets. Because the two contractors were able to raise only fifteen hundred, Colombia's unofficial representative to the United States, Manuel Torres, was asked to supply the rest. After inspecting fourteen thousand in Baltimore, Philadelphia, New York, and Boston and finding four thousand suitable, Torres applied to the president of the United States for twenty thousand weapons "on terms and conditions that the President may think most proper."[18] There is no record that the deal was completed. Chances are that the request was given serious consideration because the United States was on the eve of recognition of Colombia's independence.

The protracted struggle within the United States to win recognition for Colombia was spearheaded by Henry Clay.[19] He had been a champion of the recognition since his War Hawk days. During 1817 and 1818, when he was in competition with Calhoun as heir apparent to Monroe, there was constant bickering over the question of independence. Clay, in retaliation for the inhospitable treatment afforded the recognition attempt, threw cold water on the administration's efforts to bring about the amalgamation of the parties and even satirized with severity the attentions received by the president from the old Federalists. When the turn of events indicated that public opinion was hostile to delay in recognition, the program was taken from Clay's hands. Calhoun, in alluding to the recognition message, said, "Yes! the fruit has now become ripe and may be safely plucked!" and the whole matter served to deprive Clay of credit for the venture.[20]

The ruse to take from Clay the credit for the struggle for independence may have been accepted by some in the United States. Such was not the case in Colombia. As early as the very important 1821 congress of Cúcuta, which established the constitution for Colombia for over ten years, official public appreciation was tendered to Clay. As the congress closed in October of that year, a resolution honoring Clay in the following words was approved: "The Honorable Henrique Clay, President of the House of Representatives of the United States of America, animated by a most pure and sincere love for his brothers of the South, has upheld their rights with a neighborly eloquence, and profound diplomacy that brings together the noble sentiments of the heart with the interests of the country . . . [and we therefore honor him]."[21] The U.S. House of Representatives' resolutions for more information on the status of the struggle in Latin America as well as the details of the congressional debates on Colombian independence were carried in English and Spanish on the third page of the April 7, 1822, issue of the *Gaceta de Colombia*. Since Colombia's independence had not been recognized, there was extreme interest in what favorable action the United States was taking.

When the recognition did come on March 30, 1822, it was greeted, almost universally, with enthusiasm. Many had thought that victory for the insurgents was assured as early as 1819, and now, with the United States recognition, victory seemed definite. The Abbe de Pradt of Malinas wrote, in reference to the New World struggle, "I will not decieve anyone when I say that [Spain] is going to lose its army and money and will not recover America."[22]

The U.S. minister to Great Britain, Richard Rush, spoke of how England was receiving the news. He said that the recognition "formed a foundation point around which the judgment of the world can rally, undistracted by the uncertainties and contradictions [in] which the destinies of those new empires seem hidden."[23] Rush pointed out in an interview with Mr. Onís, ambassador from Spain, that he hoped no offense would be taken by Spain, and "he replied that he thought Spain ought to follow the example."[24] The dispatch went on to conclude, "If the commercial penalties which a French newspaper states as those which the Republic of Colombia designs to inflict upon the nations withholding a recognition be correctly stated, and if the new Republic do the same, it may be presumed that the example of the United States will not be long without imitators."[25] The reaction in Paris, as described by an avowed friend of the United States, the Marquis de Lafayette, was what one might expect; in writing to Henry Clay, he said: "You have had the pleasure, in which I was long ago ready to sympathize, of the acknowledgement of Colombian independence by the United States. May every part of that continent be also free, independent and universally acknowledged!"[26]

By 1822, although England had not formally recognized the new governments of Spanish America, she afforded them all the courtesies of de facto governments. She had recognized the revolutionists as bona fide belligerents and had respected the rights of blockade. When the news of the announcement of United States recognition arrived, there was already in the hopper a bill by a Mr. Robinson concerning foreign trade with the insurgents. The announcement by the United States inspired the merchants of London to hold a meeting to consider the "means of opening a beneficial commercial intercourse with the countries of South America *formerly under the domination of Spain.*"[27]

The announcement of recognition of Colombia proved timely. Its leaders had known since 1818 that the official community of Great Britain would not oppose such a move with force. Rush had sent a confidential message in cipher stating that "it will be enough that I repeat with increasing confidence that the belief which I have heretofore expressed that Great Britain would not consider our recognition of the independence of any of the colonies as in itself cause of war."[28] By 1822, England was moving out of the Holy Alliance and was serving as a checkmate to it on the continent of Europe. The eve of the

General Francisco de Paula Santander

Monroe Doctrine was at hand, and England was found in the commercial doldrums.

From the time that the United States recognized Colombia until the British finally did so on January 11, 1825, the diplomatic advantage belonged to the United States. At a banquet given by Vice-President Francisco de Paula Santander for the British commissioners Colonel J. P. Hamilton, P. Campbell, and James Henderson, a Mr. Robinson of the United States took the opportunity to propose a toast. He said that "the United States, which had been the first on the American continent to proclaim liberty, and the first that had recognized the independence and sovereignty of Colombia will be the last to abandon the cause of liberty of America."[29] This was a double insult to British pride. In his report the following year, James Henderson, a British commissioner, informed George Canning that the current opinion of the British was none too high in Bogotá: "A considerable degree of ill-found distrust as to the policy of His Majesty's Government in respect to the Recognition of the Independence of Colombia has recently crept in here upon the public mind, having its origin mainly in some articles in the Colombian Gazette, said to have emanated from the Vice President. And being exceedingly anxious that a feeling so incompatible with the generous proceedings of the British Cabinet should not gain ground amongst a people easily misled, I conceived it not only expedient but strictly just that the question should be exhibited in its true colours, which I hope I have not wrongly portrayed in an article in the accompanying paper."[30]

Aside from the question of recognition, the complications within the British possessions over the loss of trade in the early 1820s commanded attention. The most lucrative portion of the British empire by the turn of the nineteenth century was the British West Indies. They accounted for about one-third of the export-import trade of England. By 1830, England exported goods worth £2,800,000 to the British West Indies as against £1,900,000 to British North America.[31] West Indian exports to England did not nearly match imports. The early 1820s, however, witnessed a glut of West Indian sugar on the market which was responsible for the extremely unfavorable balance of trade. In 1822, the ban on direct trade with the West Indies was lifted with the object of alleviating the crowded market conditions. Since all of Europe could buy sugar cheaper from Brazil or Cuba, the crisis in the islands did not abate. In the following year, after a quarrel between the British colonies and the United States, the restrictions on the islands were reimposed. By 1830, when they were finally removed, the West Indian planters were beyond redemption.[32] This trade competition eventually figured into the maritime problems that complicated diplomatic relations between Colombia and the United States.

England accelerated its shipping to and investment in Colombia. An upswing in business in 1824 and 1825 and the encouragement of Canning's American policy prompted some to contemplate "sending the steam engine and the machine to delve for American gold." A number of reasons for the movement of British capital were apparent. Leland H. Jenks mentions several: (1) the deflation connected with the postwar collapse had entirely run its course; (2) business life had stabilized; (3) the bank note circulation in England's banks had doubled since 1822; and (4) commerce and industry gave such abundant employment that political agitation almost ceased.[33] To these reasons may be added several more: (5) wars for Latin American independence were all but over; (6) active trading competition with the United States was in order; and (7) the whole of Latin America was clamoring to sell raw materials and to buy manufactured goods. British loans and investments in Colombia were to prove only a temporary aid, and when the notes came due, Colombia's credit rating in England plummeted and British capitalists began foreclosure pressures. This also created more problems to impede smooth trade relations between Colombia and the United States.

Early U.S. recognition had, then, an effect on prompting Great Britain to follow suit. By December 1825, the Colombian minister José María Salazar thanked the United States for persuading the Russian emperor to interrede with Spain for possible recognition.[34] On February 1, 1826, John Quincy Adams sent to the Senate of the United States, upon its request, the correspondence and documents relating to the intervention of the emperor of Russia for Spain's recognition of the independence of the South American states.[35]

The overt attempts of the United States to gain Spanish recognition for the South American states began to influence Colombia's attitude toward Britain. In a confidential message from the British observer to the congress of Panama, Edward J. Dawkins, to George Canning, Colombian lack of confidence in Britain was cited.[36] Dawkins explained that he was at a loss to account for the coolness shown to him by Colombia's Pedro Gual until he found, among the papers presented by the president of the United States, a dispatch from the U.S. minister at Madrid, Alexander Everett. The papers had been received by Gual, and the one dated October 25, 1825, read as follows:

No offer of formal Mediation has been made by England since her recognition: indeed her interest as a commercial and manufacturing country is now on the other side. The longer the war continues, the longer she enjoys a monopoly of the Spanish American market for her fabrics, and the more difficult will Spain find it to recover her natural advantages upon the return of peace.

England will therefore probably be very easy in regard to this matter [mediation], and will leave Spain to pursue unmolested the course she may think expedient.

I suggest this point both to Mr. Zea and to the Russian Minister, and was inclined to think from what they said that it had more weight with them than any other consideration in favor of Recognition. They both admitted the justice of my remarks.

I learnt nothing from Mr. Lamb [British minister to Spain] except the fact that the British Government is now quiet in regard to this matter, and makes no attempt to influence the decision of Spain.[37]

Dawkins immediately set about to counteract the communication. He explained to Canning that since his post as an observer to the congress of Panama was "unofficial" and he was therefore not to convey anything by official correspondence, he wrote a private note to Gual to explain the British side of the situation: "I told him in answer to Mr. Alexander H. Everett's first assertion, [that] I possessed proofs of Mr. Lamb's exertions which I should be happy to lay before him whenever he could make it convenient to receive me, and with respect to the second, I left him to judge whether England, the strenuous opposer of the principles which the United States are urging this congress to adopt, that 'free bottoms make free goods' can possibly be a gainer by the war between Spain and her Colonies."[38] Gual thanked Dawkins and expressed the wish that the congress would not disband without establishing a basis upon which the Latin American states would solicit the mediation of Great Britain.

The records consistently show that the Liberator, Simón Bolívar, always favored Great Britain over the United States and that he was at times openly hostile to the latter. In response to a letter from his vice-president, Francisco Santander, who was usually a supporter of the United States, and to being informed of the progress of the congress of Panama and of the negotiation of a commercial treaty with England, Bolívar declared: "We will join the soul and the body to the English to conserve at least the form and the advantages of a civil and legal government. . . . The Holy Alliance trembles completely before Great Britain and how can we ourselves exist if we do not join ourselves to her . . . ? Unfortunate is he who opposes her, yet unfortunate will he be who is not allied nor joined with her fortune."[39] Was Santander beginning to forget his United States model, or was he already trying to placate Bolívar, with whom he was to have an open quarrel that culminated by 1828 in an assassination attempt in which he was implicated?

A more damaging commentary on Bolívar's affinity for Great Britain came from one of the British commissioners to Bogotá in his communication to London in November 1826. Colonel Campbell told of a social meeting in which Bolívar "proposed the health of Mr. Adams, and in a short speech mentioned the advantages the citizens of the United States had in being English descendants, and hoped they would continue to imitate the virtues of the parent State."[40] Afterwards, Campbell stated that Bolívar's "partiality had always been notorious, but not so to the United States."[41]

General Andrew Jackson was a bit kinder to Bolívar than Bolívar was to be toward the United States. At a party on March 21, 1825, to honor the triumph of arms in South America, Jackson made this toast referring to Bolívar's offer to give up his position after the Battle of Ayacucho: "Bolívar—Inspired by the same dignity that guided our country in the revolution, has given liberty and independence to his country. That he resigns his commission before the people as a unique legitimate bridge to power will be compared with our immortal Washington."[42]

Colonel J. P. Hamilton, also a member of the British commission to Colombia, had good words for Bolívar. He said that Bolívar had the fine trait of "unbounded generosity, which is the more remarkable as the Creoles are in general mean and extremely fond of Money."[43]

All Britishers did not paint exactly the same picture, but the following account of the Colombian by the famous English admiral Thomas Alexander (Lord Cochrane), who carried the bulk of the naval action for the Latin American insurgents, is a good summary of all views:

> They have certainly a desire to adopt English manners and give a decided preference to everything English. This may be thus accounted for: first, that for a long period England was the country that furnished them, through Jamaica [by means of contraband trade] with all the comforts and luxuries of life, and consequently gave them a relish for everything English, and engendered a kindly feeling towards the inhabitants of a country which supplied all their wants: and secondly, because the natural turn of the native Colombian much more assimilates with the character of an Englishman than that of any other nation in Europe; for he is reserved, thoughtful, and fond of commercial pursuits, yet, like an Englishman, he becomes intimate, and then you find him to be an excellent and valuable friend.[44]

During the 1820s, Colombia negotiated commercial treaties with Great Britain and the United States. From the above, one might expect that

President Andrew Jackson (The National Portrait Gallery, Smithsonian Institution)

the British would enjoy certain advantages over the citizens of the United States. The work of the United States diplomatic representatives was obviously going to be difficult.

Colombian governmental officials, concerned with encouraging their new nation in the development of the arts and sciences, had a parallel interest in the growth of trade and commerce. Aside from the fact that the offering of commercial treaties to foreign powers was a good exchange in return for recognition, the nation was truly interested in the development of its commercial intercourse. Probably the first official mention of a commercial treaty was in a communication from Manuel Torres, representative to the United States residing in Philadelphia in 1820. Torres suggested discussions "which have for their object, the more effectual consolidation of the interests of the two governments by means of a Treaty of Friendship and Commerce."[45] On February 20, 1821, Torres wrote to John Quincy Adams that his government had empowered him to negotiate "treaties of navigation and commerce, founded upon the bases of reciprocal utility and perfect equality, as the most efficacious means of strengthening and increasing the relations of amity between the two Republics."[46]

John Quincy Adams was at first not particularly inspired by the proposal of a treaty. Shortly after receiving Torres's overture, Adams confided to Henry Clay: "I have little expectation of any beneficial result to this country from any future connection with them [Colombia], political or commercial. We shall derive no improvement to our own institutions by any communion with theirs. Nor is there any appearance of a disposition in them to take any political lesson from us. As to the commercial connections, I agree with you that little weight should be allowed to arguments of mere pecuniary interest; but there is no basis for much traffic between us. They want none of our productions, and we can afford to purchase very few of theirs."[47]

By 1823, after the United States had recognized Colombian independence, Adams had reappraised his thinking on the desirability of a treaty and was considering the terms that should be in the pact. What the United States wanted in such an agreement was a guarantee of the status of most favored nation for its commerce. In his instructions to Richard Clough Anderson, the first United States minister to Colombia, Adams said, "The only object we shall have much at heart in the negotiation [of a treaty] will be the sanction by solemn compact of the broad and liberal principles of independence, equal favors, and reciprocity."[48]

The new Colombian nation prepared to comply with Adams's wishes and to open her ports "to the commerce of all people." On July 30, 1824, Colombia outlawed one of the last vestiges of the restrictions of the preindependence period when she repealed the obligation that foreigners consign goods only to national businessmen.[49]

Everything pointed toward a liaison between the United States and Colombia. As part of his instructions to Anderson, Adams singled out Colombia as the most advanced of the Latin American republics: "The Republic of Colombia is, of all the nations which have arisen from the ruins of the Spanish power in America, . . . that which amidst the convulsions of the revolutionary tempest has assumed the most encouraging appearance of consistency and stability; and that in which the principles of civil liberty have apparently made the most successful progress towards a final triumph over the prejudices of inveterate ignorance, despotism, and superstition."[50]

The stage was set for the negotiation of a commercial treaty. The discussions got under way in the summer of 1823. Anderson was instructed by the Department of State to point out that Colombia, as the United States saw it, was bound to acknowledge certain features of treaties made by Spain while Colombia was in the colonial status. It seemed that the United States was particularly concerned about the concept of "free ships make free goods." Adams's instructions went on to state: "Is it asserted that by her declaration of Independence, Colombia has been entirely released from *all* the obligations by which as a part of the Spanish Nation she was bound to other nations? This principle is not tenable. To all the engagements of Spain with *other* nations affecting their rights and interests, Colombia, so far as she was affected by them, remains bound in honor and in justice."[51] A considerable amount of time and talk was spent on the question. Pedro Gual, negotiating for Colombia, was also concerned about the concept, in view of the war that was still going on between some of the colonies and Spain. He felt that if enemy goods could be transported in neutral ships, this right tended to work a disadvantage upon Colombia in her struggle. However, after much discussion, Gual accepted the United States' contention, which was written into the treaty.[52]

An apparent quid pro quo in the treaty was the inclusion of a most-favored-nation clause, which, however, did not go all the way to reciprocity. The representatives concluded the treaty and signed it in October 1824; the United States Senate ratified it on May 7, 1825. After José María Salazar, the Colombian minister in the United States, was notified by Clay on March 21 that the treaty had cleared,[53] the formal exchange took place on May 27.[54]

The treaty seemed to make the two signatories happy. Complications occurred, however, over an unwritten discrimination that amounted to a 5 percent tariff against United States trade. This was, in the words of William Henry Harrison, briefly the minister to Colombia in 1829, "a thing which would constitute a complete prohibition" of trade with the United States.[55] The nature of the prohibition was a 5 percent tariff on goods brought into Colombia on ships other than those of the nation that produced the goods. As the United States viewed it, this created for U.S. trade a definite hardship since much of its produce brought in was handled by merchants involved in the "carrying trade." The purpose of the discrimination in favor of

European trade was to eliminate the West Indian merchants, who were making tremendous profits from the carrying trade. Their aid had been useful during the Wars for Independence, but when the struggle was over the service was too expensive.[56] The United States, by the 1820s, was not yet producing enough manufactured goods for export. Britain and France, however, were not hurt by this tariff because only a minute portion of their trade to Colombia involved nonnational goods. When the United States examined the subsequent treaty between Colombia and the United Provinces of Central America and noted that it provided for complete reciprocity, she lodged a protest. Colombia countered by explaining that the treaty was based on an "alliance" with the Central American area and that it drew those nations closer together. On his return to Colombia in January 1826, after a visit to the United States, Anderson experienced little difficulty in obtaining from Santander an executive order placing his country on the same basis as Great Britain.[57] As soon as this arrangement was made, the United States Congress passed legislation that equalized the duties on Colombian vessels and even offered a refund of all discriminating duties on their cargoes after January 29, 1826.[58]

The internal difficulties of Colombia and the region caused U.S. merchants to be suspicious of trade.[59] As early as 1823, before the treaty was arranged, J. M. MacPherson, the United States consul at Cartagena, complained of the 5 percent discriminatory tariff: "It appears from all the information I have been able to obtain, that the trade from the United States is extremely limited; and it is with such suspicion I find, that the cargoes of vessels coming from the United States are subject to five percent additional duties over and above what is paid by vessels from ports in Europe. It is impossible to conceive how such a marked distinction in favor of *all the powers* in Europe and the manifest injury of the trade of the United States should have originated."[60] A year later, the consul, still arguing against the discrimination, noted that "the trade with the United States is much distressed. This is to be attributed principally to the excessive duties on North American production which bear no proportion whatever to the imports on European manufactures."[61]

Actually, the trade with Colombia was not large by the end of the 1820s. The same consul reported in 1826 that not a single ship from the United States had entered the harbor.[62] It was noted in the minutes of the Colombian cabinet (*consejo de estado*) that the United States minister, R. C. Anderson, had made an observation to the minister of foreign relations that, as the duties stood, they favored Great Britain.[63] The treaties were slightly different in construction and in date of signing (the United States signed in October 1824, Great Britain in April 1825), and the British did have an advantage. Great Britain's rested on reciprocity, the United States' on the concept of most favored nation. The council saw the justice of Anderson's request and granted the modification by an executive decree on January 30, 1826.

In referring to this decree, President John Quincy Adams, after explaining the arrangement to the United States Senate, noted that since the Colombian government had made a concession, Congress should "secure to the citizens of the Republic of Colombia the reciprocal advantages to which they are entitled by the terms of the convention, to commence from the 30th of January last."[64]

It seems apparent that Colombia, too, viewed potential trade with the United States with an optimistic eye. As early as 1823, Salazar made his first provisional nominations for consular posts in various cities. Manuel Torres, Salazar's predecessor, had pointed out earlier how extensive the trade goods required by Colombia could potentially be.[65] That extensive trade did not seem to materialize.

One solution to the slump in trade to Colombia in general and to Cartagena in particular was offered by the consul, MacPherson. He claimed that the solution might rest in the added prestige of an American warship in Colombian waters. In May 1826, he wrote, "The commerce of the United States with this country is not of great magnitude, but still I hope there is a man of war on the coast to look after the interests of our merchants. I have not seen one of our ships of war at the place since my arrival, now nearly three years ago."[66]

In 1829 MacPherson continued to note the depression in trade to the port of Cartagena. He said that trade was limited to a "line of monthly packets of small tonnage." Even these had difficulty in processing freight at New York, the port to which they belonged. As to the items involved in the trade, the exports were mainly hides, dye weeds, and cotton, most of which was sent to Europe. The imports from the United States were flour and candles, "to which may be added occasional invoices of India and China goods and small parcels of French and Spanish brandies." From January 1824 to December 1826, the tonnage from the United States to Cartagena was 13,723. The value of the goods is unknown since the shipmasters did not have to declare it.[67]

The consul at Cartagena summarized the reasons for the decline in trade as follows:

The great falling off of the trade between this port and the United States is to be attributed in the first place to direct trade established with Europe, which did not exist in the years 1824 and 1825 except in a limited degree. Another powerfull cause, is to be found, in the long credits given by the British merchants, which extend to six, nine and sometimes twelve months; and as punctuality is not much attended to, two or three months may be added to each of the above periods before the money is collected. This mode of doing business few shippers in the United States can support, and they have wisely withdrawn their business from this post rendered more perilous to mercantile transactions by the hitherto unsettled state of the country.[68]

MacPherson claimed that he had no reason to suspect clandestine activities from United States merchants to that port but stated that he would keep a sharp vigilance.

If the United States could not stimulate much trade with Colombia, it could at least provide a service to some of the Colombian nationals. Lieutenant Colonel Tomás Cipriano de Mosquera, who was later to be president, was sent to the United States by the Colombian cabinet to be treated for a "grave illness" caused by a wound received while defending Barbaracoas. He was officially the intendant of Guayaquil but was located in Panama when the illness occurred.[69]

World trade with Colombia flourished from 1821 to about 1826. The reasons for this activity can be found in the temper of the times. The ending of the Spanish monopoly made it easier for trading activities, and the loan that had been arranged with Great Britain in 1824 made money available to the government, which directly encouraged commercial activities. It can also be assumed that the illegal operations of the colonial times did not stop overnight. All of this meant that Colombia bought more than it sold. The loan from the British in 1824 had been initiated with suspicion, and it ended two years later with the default of Colombia and the subsequent collapse of the banking house that made the loan.

The loan negotiations caused much excitement among the bankers of London. Colombian minister Manuel José Hurtado announced that bids were to be open until five o'clock on a given evening. He then proceeded to close at two o'clock in favor of Messrs. Goldschmidt. A protest concerning the transactions was made to the congress at Bogotá. The money from the loan was to be placed by Hurtado in public securities, but he left it in the hands of contractors who caused it "to be employed in stock exchanges and other speculations." When the Colombian government failed to pay off the loan, the loss to the British public was estimated as $2.5 million. The effects of the situation were summarized by Consul MacPherson:

(1) Of the effects likely to be produced by the . . . [failures, will be the] tending to retard the great object of this country in obtaining a peace with Spain . . . ,

(2) that the annual expenditure of the state far exceeds the present revenue, or indeed any revenue they can hope to raise for years to come,

(3) [that] foreign loans are now out of the question,

(4) that the failure of the contractors, has caused a decrease to the Colombian navy of a line battleship and a frigate, which puts the long talked of invasion of Cuba, out of the question, [and]

(5) [that] people [will] take advantage of Colombian trade.[70]

MacPherson's forecast was only partly correct, because the United States had made a large loan to Colombia two months before the consul sent his dispatch. He should have known of the loan since the official newspaper cited it about two months before MacPherson's communication. The loan was for 10.4 million pesos with interest at 4.5 percent. It was to be repaid in two parts, one on January 1, 1829, and the other on January 1, 1830. The loan was to be used for the repayment of Colombia's old loans, which carried 6 percent interest.[71]

Speaking generally, Arthur Whitaker's summary of the trading situation between the United States and Colombia from 1820 to 1830 applies well to the period ending in 1826.

Until the independence of Latin America was established, all classes alike in the United States—farmers, merchants, shipowners, manufacturers—could, and many of their members did, hope that the independence of Latin America would open up a bonanza to them. This was a hope that all could share. For while farmers continued to find a modest market in some parts of independent Latin America, what they sold there was an insignificant part of their total product and, above all, the hope of further increase had vanished; and the manufacturers suffered an even more complete disillusionment, for they could not compete with English and other European manufacturers in foreign markets.[72]

If one were to look at the commercial situation in 1826, one would predict a pleasant and prosperous future for both nations. Nothing could be further from the case for the next two decades. United States commerce with Colombia did not increase. After Bolívar reassumed control of the government of Colombia in 1827, the legislation on trade with the United States was modified.

In 1826, the commerce of Colombia hit a low point due in part to the political disturbances and the European depression. One historian views the leveling off as simply the natural position reached by Colombia's inability to pay.[73] At Cartagena, MacPherson had his own views on why Colombia was not prospering commercially or developing her human and material resources. He had visited Colombia in 1814 and had spent eighteen months touring the country before his official assignment to the port of Cartagena in 1822. In 1826, he wrote:

> My experience has convinced me, that nine hundred and ninety nine out of a thousand of the inhabitants [of Colombia] are altogether incapable of appreciating the value of that liberty for which their rulers have been contending. . . . Instead of a race jealous of political rights, he [a viewer] finds a people absolutely indifferent to everything, but the privilege of indulging in idleness, with all its train of vices. This applies to every section of Colombia. . . All they care for is to be allowed the unrestrained indulgence of their appetites, and to pass their time, in revelry, dancing and gaming. The Sundays and fiestas devoted exclusively to pleasure and amusement and not only enjoined by their priests, but unfortunately enforced by their magistrates to be so spent, occupy nearly, if not entirely, one half of the year. The system of impressing or rather kidnapping for the army and the navy—and by the way, men were never procured otherwise since I knew the country—is a source of discontent.[74]

A cursory look at the native business enterprises in Colombia tends to support some of MacPherson's extremely critical observations. Little mention of native business is to be found in the newspapers of the 1820s. At this time Colombians had almost no experience in commerce because trade was carried on almost exclusively by foreigners.

One of the high-ranking Colombian officials who did have an eye toward private business was José Manuel Restrepo, secretary of the treasury during most of the 1820s, director of the mint during the 1830s and 1840s, and ultimately one of Colombia's most renowned historians. Restrepo, while traveling in the United States after 1816, was extremely concerned with new manufactures, how they were established, and how they were operated. While in Philadelphia he obtained letters of recommendation and traveled to Wilmington, Delaware, where he met with Victor Du Pont and a Marshal Grouchy, late of Waterloo, apparently to talk about business. In Philadelphia, Restrepo wanted to learn the art of dyeing cloth, but he could not find an instructor at a moderate price. He did attempt to learn about the tanning and dyeing of leather, because he thought this would be useful in his country. According to Restrepo, he was hopeful "that his studies on manufactures and tanneries would be very useful but he never reached the day in which his hopes were realized."[75] When he returned to Bogotá, he and other insurgents were accused by the Spanish of belligerent activities. They said "that they [Restrepo and his friends] had been to North America to make themselves more radical in republican principles and to be more insurgent."[76] In 1825 and 1826, he retired to his domestic businesses and at that time bought some mines to sell to the eager British. However, after he sold his interest of twenty thousand pounds, he found himself disgraced and bankrupt when the checks proved to be worthless.[77] During the administration of Tomás Cipriano de Mosquera in the 1840s, two of Restrepo's sons were in Europe—Ruperto as a partner of Montoya, Sáenz, and Company of Colombia and Manuel "to complete his practical mercantile education."[78]

Restrepo seemed to be an admirer of the United States and suggested to the Colombian government that the way to improve the roadway system of Colombia was to copy that of the United States, which was using the new McAdam system and was charging tolls to cover the costs. In his "Memoria" as secretary of interior in 1823, Restrepo reported: "Such a matter [of building roads] is of great importance. . . . We should follow the example of the United States in conceding tolls to special companies that undertake expensive and spacious roads. They have today excellent groups almost from one extreme of the Union to the other. The traveler pays, but travels speedily and comfortably."[79]

Although the liberal government of Santander was attempting to break the policies and practices of restricted trade and monopolies, it did not have much success in the 1820s. "The economy of the nation continued within the shackles of monopolistic concessions and government monopolies. Foreign trade was burdened by preferential protective import duties and by export duties. Interest rates increased constantly until the 1830s and the government was paying its own citizens at the rate of 2.5% a month."[80]

The period from 1826 to 1830 was tempestuous for Colombia.

Bolívar returned from the wars to take over the government from Santander, his elected vice-president, because the Liberator thought the government had become too liberalized. Before the abortive assassination attempt on Bolívar's life on September 25, 1828, measures were taken to tighten up the government. The result was that United States shipping, already declining, almost stopped. It is also during this period that vocal United States ministers such as General William Henry Harrison alienated Bolívar's government. Bolívar lashed out.

Bolívar reviewed the national income from importation taxes and realized that frauds and scandals were depleting the economy. He also found that "the relaxation of public morale; the considerable diminishing of the income of the treasury; and the common and scandalous frauds" that were being perpetrated forced him into action. By 1826, it has been noted, the trade boom that had lasted for five years was dying down. Bolívar spelled out the culprits as the following persons:

(1) those who imported, exported, or held, foreign merchandise products, or effects eluding their presentation to customs to avoid payment of the established tariffs,

(2) those who introduced into the ports of the Republic, merchandise, products, or effects that were prohibited,

(3) those who, against the prohibition of the laws, slyly export prohibited metals,

(4) those cultivators, sellers, or dealers in tobacco who against the instructions of the branch of the government or without the requisites, deal in tobacco, and

(5) those clandestine distillers and retailers of aguardientes [native liquors] without a license as determined by law.[81]

The punishment for being caught defrauding the government was loss of all the goods possessed. Those apprehended were to pay the costs of the trial as well as the costs of importation of the goods.

Bolívar continued to be concerned with the financial status of his country. The credit of Colombia was lagging in the countries of the world, and, in an effort to pay off some of Colombia's obligations, Bolívar issued a decree about the floating debt. He said that "each day it is more urgent to diminish the debt that weighs heavily upon the Republic."[82] The decree instructed that an eighth of all import tariffs was to be diverted to the payment of the floating debt. The rest of the decree dealt with the mechanics of the payment.

On May 8, 1829, Bolívar issued a decree concerning trade. In light of his known hostility toward the United States, its content was not surprising. The decree led to the issuance, on June 21, of a tariff that almost tripled the duty on the principal import from the United States by raising the flour duty from three dollars to eight dollars per barrel. In addition, a 5 percent import tax was placed on all products not of the origin or manufacture of the shipping country.[83] The struggle to obtain trading concessions equal to those accorded to Europe and particularly England was thereby set back to its pre-1826 status. Rectification did not come until midcentury with the Bidlack Treaty.

Bolívar did have certain provocation for his action. In 1828, the United States adopted the so-called Tariff of Abominations, which effected certain restrictions against Colombia. Several of the tariff rates were adjusted upward, and one that seemed to work a particular hardship on Colombia was that on indigo. Although indigo was produced in Venezuela, that area was still part of a unified Colombia, and as an export indigo followed only coffee and cacao in importance. The *Gaceta de Colombia*, the country's official newspaper, noted that the tax of fifteen cents per pound was raised to twenty cents until June 30, 1829, when it would be increased by ten cents a year until it reached a half peso.[84] Not long afterward, the newspaper took cognizance of the poor reception that the tariff was receiving in the cities of the United States. It quoted an article that appeared in the *Investigator* of Maine, under the caption of "The Death of Commerce," saying: "It is supposed that when New York adopts the tariff they will fire volleys of cannon every minute as they do in a shipwreck, and they will lower the flags to half mast as a sign of mourning. The authorship of the bill is generally attributed to Mr. Quincey [sic] Adams, and the opinion has it that his reelection to the presidency is compromised."[85]

The tariff on flour created a real hardship on U.S. shipping. Thomas P. Moore, the United States chargé d'affaires at Bogotá, spoke of it and the 5 percent tariff in a letter to the minister of foreign relations, Felix Restrepo, and noted that trade had been "monopolized by one nation only [Great Britain] and that though France, Britain and Spain sometimes pay forty percent on imports, we pay 174 percent on barrels of [flour]. . . . It would be very easy to prove that this tariff so constituted, has been prejudicial to Colombia, diminishing the consumption of bread."[86] Moore added that the United States had reduced its tariff on coffee and cacao to "a nominal sum" to show that it was desirous of improving trade relations. Since these two items ranked first and second in total exports from Colombia, a favorable impression was created.

The Colombian government took action on the matter on November 21, 1831, promulgating a decree that stated, in the first article: "The vessels of the United States of America, and their cargoes, *whether of the growth or manufacture of the United States, or of any other country* [italics mine], proceeding directly from the ports of that Republic, shall pay, on being entered at the custom-houses of Colombia, no duties of import, anchorage, tonnage or other, higher than those which are, or hereafter may be, laid on Colombian vessels, in conformity with the provisions expressed in the eleventh article of the treaty concluded between Colombia and the United Provinces of Central America."[87] The imposition of this decree of November 21, 1831, was not of long duration. The United States had, in May 1832, made adjustments in its tariffs "for giving effect to a commercial arrangement between the United States and the Republic of Colombia," but the Colombian government repealed its decree on December 17, 1832, on the grounds that the Colombian president had exceeded his constitutional powers.[88] This situation existed until the arrangement of the Bidlack Treaty of 1846, despite the continuing efforts of the United States chargés to modify it. Diplomatic agents were an important support for commerce even when commerce lagged.

Colombia always realized the importance of having qualified representatives abroad so that her interests were handled as expeditiously as possible. Although sometimes they ran afoul of the host government—as did Antonio Francisco Zea in England over the question of loans—for the most part they did an adequate job of representation. Manuel José Hurtado, who replaced Zea, managed to obtain a gigantic loan in 1824, just at the time when Colombia needed it. In the United States, the aged and infirm Manuel Torres was the tireless agent for his country's interests. His replacement, José María Salazar, was an energetic correspondent on behalf of his government. He held his post for four years, preferring to work out of Philadelphia or New York, where he had commercial contacts, rather than Washington. In early 1831, with the recognition of independence by France, Colombia sent one of her experienced men, Colonel Leandro Palacio, to Paris as representative and to arrange a "treaty of amity and most favored nation."[89] Leandro Miranda was subsequently named to England because of his experience and because he was a native Colombian (Zea, and some others, were natives of Caracas). Apparently they voiced no complaints about their salaries. In 1826, the secretary of foreign relations read to the council a decree that provided for the naming by the executive power of *agentes secretos* to the foreign courts. They have to have an annual salary not to exceed five thousand pesos. A closing comment to the discussion of the decree was "that this clause would be a bit scandalous if it were to be published."[90]

The caliber of the United States agents to Colombia seemed, for the most part, adequate. They did not always give the most gracious of compliments to the host country, but most of them served the interests of the United States well. A summary of the service and tenure of the U.S. agents in Colombia would begin with those of Colonel Charles S. Todd. Todd, who served from 1820 to 1823, was officially designated only as "commercial agent" since his tour in Colombia predated recognition. While his observations on the character of the struggling insurgents seem fair, tactful, and accurate, his appraisal in a letter to Secretary Clay concerning Spanish and British influence reflects contemporary prejudices: "I might refer you to Colonel Duane for detailed information with respect to the state of affairs here; . . . if he were to meet with you, . . . he would tell you that though the country is separated from Spanish Dominion and misrule, yet that Spanish duplicity in the Governors, and Spanish superstition in the people are but too painfully prevalent; while the hopes of the public councils are directed to Europe, and especially Great Britain, in the vain delusion, that is by those powers alone, their interests can be promoted."[91] Todd's purpose in Colombia was to explore commercial possibilities and to perform, in the absence of recognition, quasi-consular duties in aiding United States trade there.

Richard Clough Anderson was the first officially appointed minister to the Latin American states. He served from 1823 until his death in 1826. His instructions were explicit. He was to develop Colombian interest in trade and commerce. Adams, in giving Anderson the commission, explained the destinies of the two countries by encouraging Colombia to "look to commerce and navigation, and not to empire, and her means of communication with the rest of the human family. These are the principles upon which we hope our sisters of the southern continent will ultimately perceive it to be for their own welfare, no less than for that of the world, that they shall found themselves."[92]

Anderson's arrival in September 1823 was viewed with caution by Santander because his government had at that time no inkling of Monroe's policy toward the Quadruple Alliance. Writing to Bolívar, Santander stated: "The minister of the United States, Mr. Anderson, is already in LaGuayra; we wish to see him here because we want to understand the intentions of his government. I have an anxiety to know what the cabinet in Washington thinks of the secret treaty made in Verona by the four allied potencies. Its tenor embraces the whole world where there is a representative government and freedom of the press."[93] Anderson's tour in Bogotá was productive for the United States in the completion of the treaty of "trade, peace, commerce and amity" of 1825.

Anderson's successors were not nearly as successful as their predecessor in carrying out their assignments. Beaufort T. Watts (1826–28) and William Henry Harrison (1828–29) were both individually accused of dabbling in the internal politics of Colombia. Watts's involvement was the most pronounced because he expressed himself in writing and could be readily quoted. He was probably sincere in his views of the Bogotá government in the middle of 1827, but he heaped great coals of fire on the Santander regime when he wrote to Bolívar, "All is lost without you, the three nations which you alone have created and rescued from a mass of chaos will soon return to their original darkness without a continuation of your services to sustain them."[94] By 1827, with the Santander-Bolívar feud underway, Bolívar published the letter as a "new proof of the interest of the United States in the 'prosperity of Colombia.'"[95] When the government at Bogotá learned the contents of the letter, José Manuel Restrepo, the foreign minister, informed Watts that an explanation of his actions would be demanded from Washington.[96] Washington had heard of the incident through the press, and since Bolívar approved of Watts's actions, Washington did likewise.

Watts was finally replaced in 1828 by William Henry Harrison, a future president of the United States and the most inept of all of the ministers to Colombia before 1850. Adams did not want to send Harrison, for the post required a man of tact and finesse. He considered him, in fact, a man of a "lively and active, but shallow mind, a political adventurer, not without talents, but self-sufficient, vain, and indiscreet." He acceded, however, and appointed Harrison, not as "the best adapted to the place" but as "the most suitable appointment."[97] Harrison had been at his post for less than a month when Jackson recalled him.[98]

Because Jackson had built up a reputation for filling offices with spoils-seekers, the removal of General Harrison prompted an immediate reaction. One source of complaint was a Mr. Ritchie, a newspaper editor from Virginia. In a letter to Secretary Martin Van Buren complaining of the replacements, Ritchie asked for an explanation and requested that the substance of the letter be conveyed to the president. Jackson's reply, through Van Buren, informed Ritchie that his objections were ill founded and that the only publically visible man removed from office was General Harrison. Jackson, explaining his action, stated:

> There has been as yet no important case of removal except that of General Harrison; and I am sure if Mr. Ritchie has read the instructions given to our Ministers, who were sent to Panama, he must think the recall of General Harrison not only a prudent measure but one which the interest of the Country makes indispensably necessary. I have referred to the case of General Harrison only, because I cannot suppose Mr. Ritchie has any allusion to the auditors and comptrollers, who were dismissed not so much on account of their politics as for the want of moral honesty.
>
> The gentleman who has been selected to supply the place of General Harrison is, I believe, as well qualified, if not better, than any other who would have undertaken the mission to that country.[99]

Jackson went on to reiterate that if appointees are qualified they should not be refused positions just because they are his friends.

In Colombia, the major complaint against Harrison was that he sided with the opponents of Bolívar and that he was indiscreet in his contacts with government officials. He had had no foreign experience, possessed and publicized ultrarepublican ideas, associated with disgruntled foreigners, and was even accused of masterminding an insurrection. Jackson sent his replacement hurriedly, an action that undoubtedly saved Harrison from being declared persona non grata.

Thomas P. Moore replaced Harrison in 1829 and did a creditable job in getting the claims questions and the discriminatory tariff temporarily worked out. When he arrived he stated that he "would very scrupulously abstain from any direct or indirect intervention in the domestic policies and negotiations of Colombia."[100] As the United States minister until 1833, he witnessed the departure of Bolívar and the arrival of Santander in the office of president. If one were to judge from the number of his dispatches to his government and the number of his letters in the records of the Colombian cabinet, he seemed to have been a hard worker for the interests of the United States.

When Bolívar died on December 17, 1830, Minister Thomas P.

Moore wrote a lengthy letter of sympathy to the Colombian government. It read, in part:

> In the Liberator, Colombia has lost a benefactor and a father, society one of its most distinguished ornaments, the human race a skillful and successful defender of civil liberty. . . . His name is that of a patriot and a hero; and although his exploits encompass a hemisphere his reputation has spread to all nations and will reach to the extremes of posterity. They can win or lose empires, establish or destroy them, wipe out his memory in the whirlpools of revolutions, but as long as the holy cause of liberty has an advocate in the land, the name of Bolívar will not be forgotten.
>
> The undersigned relates to this government the hope that in spite of the recent calamity, the friendly relations between Colombia and the United States will be continued without interruption or curtailment and I trust that a united and peaceful Colombia will continue strongly her march toward glory and national happiness.[101]

Among Moore's other functions were the acceptance of a general invitation of the Colombian government to occupy a gallery reserved for the diplomatic corps at the constitutional convention of the republic;[102] a contribution to the fund for the invalids, orphans, and widows of the battle at Santurario;[103] and the delivering of speeches on notable occasions. An example of the last is the statement that Moore made on hearing of the new constitution of 1832: "[Peace and Providence] . . . cannot fail to obtain and assure to this very favored land all the advantages that constitute national prosperity. Agriculture and commerce will balance the present and past discouragement. You will receive new and efficacious impulses of industry and the spirit of business and fountains of national and individual riches will develop."[104]

Moore entertained the members of the government at the celebration of independence of the United States. The vice-president and the presidents of the council of state and the supreme court as well as various cabinet members, foreign agents, and some private citizens were in attendance. The vice-president in charge of executive power tendered the following toast: "To the United States of the North, our teachers in Liberty. They have served as a model for New Granada to follow for her independence."[105]

One of the tasks of the representative to Colombia was to recognize the formation of new governments as they came into power, provided they gained control in legal ways. In 1831, the fall of the dictatorship of Rafael Urdaneta was characterized by Moore as "not merely satisfactory but delightful," for the English party that had the support of Bolívar and Urdaneta was discredited "forever."[106]

The life of United States consuls in Latin America in the early nineteenth century was generally an unenviable one. It was very difficult to get volunteers to accept the living conditions and the poor pay that the posts offered. As a result, those who took the posts were, in most cases, businessmen who had reason to be in the area. Very often it was impossible to get a citizen of the United States to represent his country. There was no representation in Venezuela in 1834, and Robert B. McAfee while at Bogotá had to perform a service for a U.S. citizen in that country.[107] A classic commentary on the plight of the consular post at Santa Marta was made by a U.S. traveler in December 1835: "There were but seven foreign residents when we were there, only two of whom were of any consequence; the one an Englishman the other an American. The American consul is a Frenchman and one who takes little interest in the welfare of the States; nor can it ever be otherwise when foreigners hold these offices abroad which should alone belong to native citizens of the country they are intended to represent."[108]

In the period from independence to the dissolution of Gran Colombia by 1830, one notes that Colombian trade with the United States did not thrive, especially in the last half of the decade. The 1825 treaty of commerce and friendship set an encouraging pace, but, for various reasons, by 1826 the trading enthusiasm of Colombia had died down. Then, too, United States merchants labored under the hardship of a 5 percent discriminatory tariff that was inherent in the treaty and that was designed to cripple the West Indian carrying trade. It worked no hardship on European countries, but it caused no end of trouble for United States traders. From 1826 to 1830 trade languished. Despite a temporary removal of the discrimination during 1831, it continued and was a constant source of irritation to United States merchants. It remained in force until a change of attitude took place in the early 1840s.

Once the independence era passed with Bolívar's death in 1830, Colombia's internal turmoil dominated her history. As the struggles to gain political maturity pitted federalists against centralists (now called liberals and conservatives), the liberals made some advances. The diplomatic activity of the United States began to focus on an interoceanic connection through Panama, part of Colombia's territory.

The Biddle mission failed to acquire permission for the connection, but it was secured by the Bidlack Treaty of 1846. Despite the turmoil and Colombia's disappointment when Teddy Roosevelt took Panama from her, the nation of Bolívar and Santander has generally supported and appreciated the United States. In the long run, Bolívar's affinity for Great Britain was supplanted by Santander's admiration for the United States. Both democracy and friendship for the United States have played a major role in the international relations of Colombia.

8

Personnel Diplomacy: The United States and Chile, 1812–1850

T. Ray Shurbutt

Surprised, flattered, and perhaps even a little embarrassed by the pageantry and celebrations that accompanied his arrival in Chile in April 1824 as the U.S. chargé d'affaires, Heman Allen seemed to adjust easily to such deference. The fact that he so grossly underestimated the importance Chileans attached to U.S. de jure recognition of their young republic indicates just how little Allen understood about his mission to commence formal relations with Chile. Unfortunately, his successors, except for Samuel Larned, shared this lack of preparation and understanding; they did not speak Spanish, most were passionately anti-Catholic, and they knew next to nothing of Chile's traditions and expectations. Indeed, political favor and sinecurism appear to have been the usual requisites for the appointment to head the Santiago legation.[1]

Considering their lack of diplomatic training, perhaps one should not be too hasty in criticizing these envoys for their professional deficiencies. And not only was the State Department's appointment policy suspect, but, once the chargés were at their posts, Washington seems to have ignored their requests for additional instructions and advice on a variety of matters, some of which were urgent. Chargé Allen's twenty-second dispatch, written nineteen months after his arrival in Santiago, despondently stated that since he had not received "any communication from his government . . . [he was] unable to determine whether or not [his] conduct corresponded to its views, hoping however, that no essential variations [had] intervened."[2] And there is no evidence that Washington undertook any measures to remedy the cause of similar complaints from Allen's successors. Twenty-six months passed before Samuel Larned received *any* communications from the State Department. Then, when at last the long-awaited dispatch did arrive, he found it devoid of the specific instructions he had sought; the dispatch merely informed him that he was being transferred to Lima.[3] A few years later, in 1831, Chargé John Hamm lamented Washington's neglect, stating, "Here I am—completely isolated—not a single American of intelligence and standing in the whole city—No one . . . can form any idea of the embarrassments [one] has constantly to encounter in all his transactions with [this] Government and people speaking nothing but a foreign language."[4] A year later, still with no news from Washington, Hamm complained, "Not a single letter, the President's messages, or a Newspaper!! Most astonishing!! Do you imagine, my dear friend, that I am dead?"[5] In July 1837, Chargé Richard Pollard rather sarcastically informed Washington that "by a stray paper . . . I saw that Mr. Van Buren had been chosen . . . President."[6] Pollard's replacement, John Pendleton, in 1843 regretfully referred to his Santiago post as "the most remote position in the whole line of Diplomatic service."[7] And although his less assertive successor, William Crump, seldom made any complaints, he did inform Secretary of State James Buchanan that he thought it appropriate to request an American flag and official seal for the legation; after all, at the time of his request (1846), the legation was in its twenty-third year of operation.[8] Crump's replacement, Seth Barton, who was far less reticent about complaining, categorically chided Washington's neglect and tardiness in forwarding official and personal mail. In April 1848, Barton cynically stated that he had recently received dispatches, addressed to Crump and dated August 1846, that "had crossed both oceans and rounded Cape Horn four or five times" before finally reaching Valparaíso.[9]

Such feelings of isolation and neglect were exacerbated when these envoys were required to make important, quick policy decisions. Commercial treaties had to be negotiated and amended; U.S. merchants sought their assistance in gaining the release of vessels impounded or confiscated for allegedly smuggling contraband or violating Chilean port regulations; U.S. squadron commanders needed clarifications to determine the legality of Chilean naval blockades and port quarantines during her squabbles with Bolivia and Peru; and American citizens and commercial houses constantly demanded that these chargés be more aggressive in their efforts to settle indemnity claims against Chile worth hundreds of thousands of dollars. And due to Washington's lackadaisical—indeed, one might even say cavalier—attitude regarding their pleas for particular instructions, it fell to these men to make their own judgments. Then, too, in the absence of adequate training and experience, it was often personality traits, unschooled opinions, and even moods of melancholy and depression resulting from ill health that proved to be determinants for important decisions.

Although 1823 marked the initiation of formal U.S. relations with Chile, commercial intercourse—clandestine and illegal—with this *situado* of the old Peruvian viceroyalty began in the 1790s, when the crest of Castile and León precariously struggled to hold sway. Renowned historian Diego Barros Arana remarked that both English and "Bostonnes" smugglers were frequent visitors to Valparaíso and other ports, regularly bribing royal officials in order to transact their lucrative ventures. From 1788 to 1796, only twenty-six American vessels are known to have traded in Chilean ports, but from 1797 to 1809, their number increased by two hundred. Twenty-two of these, including the *Belle Savage* and the *Hazard*, were seized and confiscated for illicit activities, though the majority were released upon appeal. One should take particular note of the fact that Spain's policy concerning foreign trade to her colonies during this period was scarcely consistent. Her frequent status changes dictated by the vicissitudes of the French Revolution and the Napoleonic Wars found Spain issuing decrees that at times permitted neutrals to trade with her colonies and at other times prohibited such trade.[10] Once the patriots declared independence and established their junta on September 18, 1810, all Chilean ports opened to American trade.[11]

Of course, this freer trade produced effects and stimuli that proved to be political as well as economic in nature. Actually, the seeds of U.S. republicanism had been sporadically sown among Chile's liberal-minded elite for nearly three decades, for the writings of Jefferson, Washington, John and Samuel Adams, Madison, and others were known and admired by many of Santiago's new ruling class. Merchants such as William Shaler, who in 1802 smuggled contraband into Valparaíso, introduced Spanish translations of the Declaration of Independence and copies of several state constitutions.[12] And in December 1811, the U.S. Congress passed a joint resolution recognizing Chile's patriot forces as "belligerents," a de facto status that the junta hoped would soon be elevated to a fully legal recognition. The José Miguel Carrera regime eagerly embraced newly arrived special agent Joel Roberts Poinsett that same month. Poinsett's credentials also extended to the juntas in Buenos Aires and Peru, and he had been instructed "to promote the most friendly relations, and the most liberal intercourse between the inhabitants" of these areas and the United States.[13]

On July 4, 1812, Poinsett staged an elaborate banquet for three hundred guests in celebration of American independence. At this gala affair many toasts of mutual admiration were offered, as the new blue, yellow, and white Chilean flag proudly waved next to Old Glory. This was probably the high point of early U.S.-Chilean relations. *La Aurora de Chile*'s editor, Camilo Henríquez, who had published translations of *Common Sense*, Washington's farewell address, and Jefferson's inaugural speech, debuted "a patriotic hymn" at Poinsett's banquet, intoning the hope that the arms of Washington would extend to his brothers to the south, perhaps establishing a confederation of the whole New World. Unfortunately, this ambience of camaraderie was spoiled when several overly intoxicated Americans began a fistfight with a few Chilean soldiers.[14]

Much of Poinsett's early success in establishing goodwill for the United States was lost through his indiscretions involving the intra-junta bickering between the Carrera and Bernardo O'Higgins factions. While Juan José Carrera referred to him as "the guardian angel of union, peace, and domestic happiness" for Chile, several O'Higgins supporters wished to relegate the often meddlesome Poinsett to a spot far removed from the celestial sphere.[15]

It must be remembered that Poinsett's actions were based entirely upon his own personal interpretations of the current, fluctuating political conditions in Santiago. In an August 1813 letter to a friend in Charleston, South Carolina, he mentioned that he had not received any instructions from Washington in two years. Indeed, he was not aware of the U.S.-British hostilities until months after they had begun, and then he was unsuccessful in attempting to gain Carrera's moral support against the British. Chile remained strictly neutral, even after Poinsett had Commodore David Porter entertain Carrera on board the U.S. frigate *Essex* in Valparaíso.[16] Perhaps the reason Poinsett thought he could gain Chile's support was based on his own misconception of what it really meant to be neutral. His own actions certainly had been questionable concerning U.S. neutrality. In an "advisory position," Poinsett had traveled with Carrera to Concepción to inspect and modify its defenses in anticipation of an expected attack from the royalist stronghold at Talcahuano. Poinsett proposed that Carrera's troops launch a preemptive offensive, recapturing Chillán and thus dividing the royalist forces. This plan failed miserably, and the royalists were soon marching northward toward Santiago, where the junta swung its backing to O'Higgins before again dissolving in its chronic factionalism. The junta soon healed its self-inflicted wounds, but Carrera never regained his predominant position, and Poinsett's loss of prestige signaled an opportunity for England to usurp the role of influence peddler in Santiago.[17]

In late April 1814, Poinsett left for Buenos Aires via the arduous Andean passes, and soon afterward Commodore Porter's *Essex* left Valparaíso on its homeward voyage, for all practical purposes ending direct U.S. influence in Chile for the next three and a half years. Both men were determined to lobby for increased interest in Spanish America's struggles for independence. Before being reassigned to sea duty in 1818, Porter promoted a group of political writers whose influence was directed "in favor of our taking a decided stand in the affairs of S. America . . . to make it appear that the interests of the U.S. are jeopardized by the machinations of England, . . . that we are the *natural* allies of S. America, that unless we aid them they will throw themselves into the arms of our worst enemy . . . England [which] has been long at work to effect her [hegemony]." This quote is from Porter's October 23, 1817, letter to Poinsett, in which he lavished praise on Henry M. Brackenridge's pamphlet *South America: A Letter on the Present State of That Country, to James Monroe.* This letter also lauded the editorials of Joseph H. Skinner, under the byline "Lautaro," which were widely circulated in the newspapers of Washington, Richmond, and Baltimore and were reprinted in Santiago, Buenos Aires, and elsewhere in Latin America.[18]

One may consider January 26, 1818, as the date when the United States renewed its official presence in young republican Chile. On that day the USS *Ontario*, under Captain James Biddle, arrived at Valparaíso with John B. Prevost, who had been empowered to act as the American diplomatic representative in Chile and Peru. Momentous political changes had transpired in Chile since Poinsett's departure, but Chile was not yet wholly the master of her own destiny. True, Spain's restored Bourbon king, Ferdinand VII, had failed in his attempts to gain the aid of the Holy Alliance in recapturing his rebelling colonies, but Viceroy Joaquín de la Pezuela still resided, threateningly, in Lima; royalists still controlled Talcahuano; a Spanish naval force blockaded Valparaíso and Coquimbo, holding at anchor ten U.S. merchantmen, among others; and several thousand royalist land forces would represent an ominous menace to Chilean independence until their rout on April 5 in the decisive battle on the plains of Maipú.[19]

The turbulent and unsettled conditions of these years had not, however, deterred U.S. merchants from plying their profitable trading along the Chilean coast. Much money could be made by neutrals, whether their goods were traded to patriots or to royalists, and Agent Prevost reported that American cargo in the blockaded port of Valparaíso alone was valued at over $1 million. The merchantmen, along with the forty or so New England whalers that regularly operated in these waters, frequently attempted to run the Spanish blockades to sell munitions and other contraband and, when caught, usually had their cargoes confiscated as legal prize. Before Prevost's arrival there was no one to officially represent them in their appeals to Viceroy Pezuela for the release of their seized ships and cargo.[20]

Both Prevost and Captain Biddle recommended the establishment of a permanent U.S. naval presence "to secure proper respect for our commerce in every port and from every flag," as President Monroe had stated.[21] But there was another reason for an increased show of U.S. naval power—desertions by, and/or impressment of, American seamen. During 1817 and 1818, Chile began building a navy, acquiring ships wherever and however possible and manning them as best she could, particularly through luring American seamen to join the patriot cause. The arrival of the *Ontario* was welcomed by many merchantmen as a deterrent to such activities. But the promises of higher wages, quick promotions, and a share in the disbursement of booty when a royalist prize was taken were formidable enticements indeed. Nearly every U.S. vessel in Valparaíso reported the loss of seamen through desertion, with some crews so depleted that their ships were unable to continue their voyages. Captain Biddle acknowledged that the *Ontario* itself had not escaped the loss of a few crewmen.[22] And in all candor, some of the actions of Biddle and Prevost were more than likely responsible, albeit indirectly, for some U.S. seamen joining the patriots. The *Ontario*'s chief carpenter was "volunteered" to aid in refitting Chile's flagship, the *Lautaro*; U.S. consul Henry Hill, in Valparaíso, had accompanied Chilean officers as they boarded American vessels with their enticements to serve the new republic;[23] and, as Prevost stated on March 20, 1818, "our warships are carrying freight for the belligerents, and are so interested in making profits that they forget their real purpose in these waters."[24] While Prevost's statement is certainly exaggerated, it is true that neutral merchantmen (American and others) did entrust specie to the *Ontario*, and later to the *Franklin*, for either deposit or safe transshipment from one port to another. This was a common practice during the independence struggles, for neutral warships passed through blockades with impunity; also, it was profitable for U.S. squadron masters. The normal fee for deposits was 1 percent, for transshipments, 2.5 percent, some of which totaled tens of thousands of dollars.[25]

When the *Ontario* cleared Valparaíso harbor on April 12, 1818, to continue northward to Callao, Biddle and Prevost felt their brief stay had been successful in establishing a favorable rapport with the budding republic's newly selected officials and in regaining respect for the United States in general. Biddle was as confident as the Chileans were that their independence would soon be a fait accompli. In a letter to his brother Nicolas, he prophesied that it "is certain [America] might secure great commercial advantages by being before hand with the British in coming out in favor of this people, especially if we had an intelligent, discreet agent on the spot. . . . [There] is a strong sentiment of sympathy and kindness toward our government here and in all classes of people, and we are in fact greatly preferred before all other foreign nations. This sentiment, I can flatter myself has not been weakened by the presence of this ship."[26]

When Prevost returned to Valparaíso a year later, he was disappointed to find that during his absence the British had supplanted the Americans in nearly all facets of commerce and perhaps even in respect. Prevost's findings were not erroneous. Over the next four years, 1819–23, British exports accounted for about 80 percent of Chile's total collections on foreign duties, and, as English traveler Maria Graham observed in 1822, Valparaíso bustled with English merchants and vessels, making "one fancy Valparaiso a coast town in Britain."[27] Substantiating the observations of Miss Graham were those of U.S. special agent Jeremy Robinson, who reported to Secretary of State John Quincy Adams:

> it is due to candor to state that there has been a leaning towards European connexions and habits, English and French, particularly the former, generated in their extensive intercourse (manufactures, numbers and power) with this people. . . . The English will take the lead of every other nation. . . . The trade of the United States on this side of the Andes will be very limited and comparatively inferior to that of the British. . . . Things must continue in this state until the United States

can manufacture and send commodities which this people want, as cheap and as good as the Europeans—especially the English.[28]

The April 1824 arrival of Chargé Heman Allen, representing the first non-Latin American de jure recognition of independent Chile, automatically placed the United States in a preferential status and was considered a major step in counteracting recent British gains. Allen had been instructed to seek most-favored-nation status for U.S. trade through a commercial treaty, and within a month his preliminary talks with Foreign Minister Rafael Egaña offered such assurances. Indeed, acting on behalf of Supreme Director Ramón Freire, Egaña even promised that Chile would consult Allen before entering "into any stipulations [treaties] with other powers . . . [and] if she granted advantages to any nation, . . . that nothing would be granted to others, which was not yielded to us."[29] There were four successive ministers of foreign relations during the first year of Allen's mission, and he gained identical assurance from each of them.[30] Such verbal assurances did not, however, negate the fact that English merchants and commerce continued to dominate Chilean imports. Allen was astounded to find that British wares "inundated" Chilean markets, that British mercantile houses were being established in nearly every Chilean port, and that English "merchants [would even] intermarry with the natives."[31] The last part of this statement is an unfortunate example of Allen's patrician attitude and superior air, which often worked to preclude many commercial and diplomatic advantages that might have enhanced U.S. interests. Of course, Washington's neglect of his requests for advice and additional instructions only exacerbated his ineffectualness.[32]

From the outset of his mission, Allen's attitude toward Chileans and his lack of understanding of Chile's heritage and cultural traditions proved counterproductive. His actions were frequently condescending, as when he lectured Chilean officials on topics as diverse as international law, democracy, and economics. Soon after his arrival in Santiago, he referred to Chile as "a rude and uneducated state . . . [in need of] the hand of civilization to entitle them to the proud appellation of freemen."[33] Nine months later, in February 1825, Allen categorized Chile as a nation "without money, credit, or capacity, and the constitutional apathy, so peculiar to all classes of people, seems rather to incline them to indolence and sleep, than to exertion, either of the body or mind, particularly the latter."[34] Yet, as dangerous and undiplomatic as these statements seem, they are mild when compared to the vitriolic comments he reserved for the Catholic church. Allen lamented that "priests [have] complete Supremacy, in State as well as Church. It is said there are no less than eight hundred of *these miserable beings*, who are prominading in every part of the city; certainly, a great portion of time is devoted to *their* ridiculous ceremonies. But, time it is hoped, and the consequent improvement which it may create will in some measure eradicate these evils, and that the redeeming spirit, which has as often guarded the destiny of other nations, may yet, have much in store for Chile."[35]

According to Allen, the blame for many of Chile's problems—social, political, and even economic—rested squarely on the cassocked shoulders of the clergy. Why, questioned the chargé, had Chile maintained Catholicism as the state religion, when any intelligent observer could see that she should "shake off this *incubus*, which stifles her growth, [or] it would be impossible for her to proceed in the march" toward true freedom?[36] However, Allen optimistically informed Washington that Freire and his liberal-minded new foreign minister, Antonio Pinto, had initiated several controversial measures aimed at curbing the church's power: the recently arrived nuncio had been ordered to return to Rome, since "his presence . . . was degrading to a people pretending to be free;"[37] several royalist-sympathizing priests had been banished;[38] the number of feast days, including Sundays, was reduced to seventy;[39] and Minister Pinto had informed Allen that all foreigners would be permitted freedom of worship and rights of interment in their separate cemeteries.[40] Allen's opinionated optimism proved premature. Within a year and a half, Chile's brief flirtation with attempts to diminish the church's power had all but ended, as the aristocratic elite succeeded in molding the conservative coalition that would dominate the nation's politics for the next three decades.

Allen had also expressed early optimism concerning the settlement of several private and commercial claims that U.S. citizens had filed against Chile, most of which emanated from ship seizures and detainments during the Wars for Independence. During 1821, Captain Biddle had been successful in negotiating settlements of similar claims against royalist actions, but some of the claims against Chile would drag on for decades, becoming chronic sources of frustration and irritation for Allen and his successors. The simple truth is that even if Chile had recognized her liability for these claims, her state of near bankruptcy in the mid-1820s would have precluded any regular reparation payments anyway. And, of course, Allen's problems over these claims were multiplied by the fact that until 1825, the royalists maintained their control within the port of Callao and Chile's navy continued its blockading actions there, resulting in new claims being filed by U.S. merchants. The situation at Callao was complex, to say the least. Commodore Isaac Hull and the USS *United States* had arrived at Callao in April 1824 to command the U.S. naval forces comprising the Pacific squadron and had found that U.S. merchantmen were being harassed by royalists and patriots alike: ships had been detained, cargoes had been confiscated or damaged, and there had even been threats of impressments. Hull's orders specifically stated that he was to consult Allen on "all difficult cases,"[41] and since Agent Prevost (in Lima) had "invariably declined" to assist Hull "in the execution of his arduous duties," Allen's counsel would be a necessity. Concerning the legality of Chile's patriot blockade, Allen advised Hull that he could use force to defend the U.S. shipping against these "paper blockades." Quoting President Monroe, Allen told the commodore that "paper blockades of fifty degrees of latitude, or a thousand leagues of coast [are] illegal throughout [their] whole extent, even for the ports which may be in actual blockade: otherwise every capture itself would be proof of the blockading force."[42]

Prevost died in March 1825, after which time Allen's opinions became even more significant for Hull, as they represented his only official source for advice on these delicate matters. Hull's primary concern was with the recent seizure of a U.S. merchantman, the *General Brown*, by the patriot blockade. According the Hull, the government in Lima, newly recognized by the U.S., had declared the *General Brown* a legal prize for carrying royalist goods and had ordered its cargo and rigging confiscated and its crew imprisoned. There were even reports that several of its crewmen had been tortured. Hull's protests to Peruvian officials had been futile, and the press in Lima had been quite critical of Hull's interference in the affair. Allen assured the commodore that his protestations had been justified and that Peru's intimidating attempts to silence him were nothing more than bravado. Indeed, Allen commended him for his diligent efforts on behalf of the *General Brown*'s crew, stating that "if you are restricted in the exercise of your pen, you have only to represent the fact to your government, and in the meanwhile, administer justice with your guns." Then, perhaps caught up in the eloquence of his own martial rhetoric, Allen concluded his supportive dispatch to Hull by saying that the guns of the USS *United States* should be used to protect *all* U.S. merchantmen "from the fangs of such unprincipled marauders."

How easy it must have been to dispense such ultimatums from the quiet and safety of distant Santiago.[43]

Perhaps Allen's self-righteous air and bellicosity regarding Hull's trials and tribulations in Callao may be attributed partially to frustrations over his failure to accomplish his own goals with the Chilean government. He had made little progress in gaining acceptance of Chile's liability in the claims cases; his negotiations for a commercial treaty had gotten nowhere; and, to add to his problems, from mid-1825 until he ended his mission in 1827, he suffered from lingering fevers and a general weakness that forced him to leave Santiago and reside in Valparaíso. Samuel Larned, Allen's secretary, remained in the capital to keep the legation open and for all practical purposes took care of U.S. concerns during those two years.[44]

In Larned the United States possessed a unique opportunity to enhance its interests. Unlike Allen, Secretary Larned was fluent in Spanish, made friends easily, and had actively involved himself with the social and political elite of Santiago. His inroads of influence were especially strong among the emerging moderate wing of the conservative *pelucón* party. Referring to Allen's voluminous correspondence with the Chilean foreign ministry as "tardy" and "ineffectual," Larned began a more direct course of action based upon his personal contacts.[45] While "old guard" *pelucones* led by Mariano Egaña and others were usually Anglophiles, progressive *pelucones* openly sought Larned's advice on political and economic policy matters and began to cite the United States as the role model for their emerging republic. And perhaps without fully understanding the possible negative repercussions that might result from his actions, Larned—still Allen's secretary, with no official status—found himself involved in *pelucón* intraparty disputes. Egaña had authored two newspaper articles, "Memoria Política" and "Abeja Chilena," criticizing U.S. political and religious institutions, and Larned replied with countering polemics of his own, entitled "Observations in Reply."[46] Joaquín Campina, a close friend of Larned and a vocal leader of the progressive *pelucones*, encouraged him to continue defending U.S. policies, and soon Larned's publications were being reprinted in Lima, Buenos Aires, and even Bogotá. Antonio Pinto, governor of Coquimbo and former foreign minister, distributed reprints to all the schools in his province and ordered that all pupils commit these articles to memory.[47]

Chargé Allen never commented about Larned's public defense of U.S. policies, but he was certainly wary of England's prestige among most Chilean officials. In an April 1826 dispatch to Secretary of State

Henry Clay, he reiterated his Anglophobia by informing Washington that if a pending Peruvian-sponsored Panama conference resulted in an "American Confederation," he feared that England would become its dominant ally. Allen predicted that if this occurred, the new Spanish-American republics would be little more than "de facto" colonies. He concluded his dispatch by saying that though some might consider his opinions as "visionary, and perhaps absurd," "these peoples [Spanish Americans] are still like children," and "it cannot be denied that there is a total want of character amongst them, that even their *nominal* liberties are still held by a very feeble tenure, and that they would very easily fall a prey to the snares of some artful foreign power."[48] Allen remained condescending and negative, while Larned's influence became substantive and positive.

Larned's effective use of personal diplomacy had already proven successful with the Chilean judiciary. In February 1825, the U.S. schooner *Chile* had entered the port of Talcahuano to buy supplies and allow her sailors a brief spree on shore. Unfortunately, some of the crew had brought in tobacco and cigars—a Chilean monopoly and therefore considered contraband—and a district court ordered the *Chile* seized and confiscated, along with her cargo of five thousand sealskins. Secretary Larned was able to have this judgment overturned by the Chilean supreme court by convincing the justices that the small quantity of tobacco in question was simply the crew's personal rations. The *Chile* and her cargo were restored to their owners. An obviously proud Larned later acknowledged that the high court judges were "all [his] personal friends."[49]

His prestige and reputation among Santiago's political elite were further exemplified during the summer of 1826, when he served as the "observer-member" of the Chilean congressional committee charged with framing a new constitution. José Ignacio Cienfuegos, president of the congress, personally asked Larned to advise this committee; Cienfuegos was yet another close friend.[50] Apparently Larned was far more than an observer, for he was credited with having authored much of this "Constitutive Act." Their federalist proposal was too liberal and too progressive for the *peculón* majority and was subsequently rejected by the conservative solons.[51]

Also during 1826, Larned reopened preliminary talks with Foreign Minister Carlos Rodríquez concerning a formal commercial treaty. One should remember that Chargé Allen was still in Valparaíso— though he was ill and had requested to be replaced—and that Larned had no *official* diplomatic status.[52] But Rodríquez had asked for

Larned's advice on several economic matters, and this seemed to be a good opportunity for Larned to pursue a trade agreement. Although no formal negotiations resulted from his discussions with Rodríquez, Larned did receive verbal assurances that U.S. trade would be granted most-favored-nation status when a commercial treaty was signed; of course, Allen had received similar promises from Rafael Egaña and every subsequent foreign minister since 1824.[53]

In any event, when Allen took homeward passage on board the French merchantman *Charles Adolphus* on September 25, 1827, Larned could at last begin functioning in an official capacity as the new U.S. chargé.[54] Over the next year and a half he and Rodríquez conducted several conferences aimed toward finalizing a tentative treaty. There was a degree of urgency in these conferences by late 1828, for Larned discovered that Chile was negotiating similar agreements with Buenos Aires, Mexico, and Peru, each of which sought to include reciprocal provisions guaranteeing that Spanish-American commerce would receive preferential treatment over that of all other nations. Rodríquez was reminded of his promises that U.S. goods would be given most-favored-nation status, without exception.[55] During these conferences, Larned also renewed discussions of several claims cases filed by U.S. merchants seeking compensations for losses suffered during Chile's independence struggles. Owners of the *Macedonian*, the *Warrior*, and the *Garret* had combined reparation claims that totalled tens of thousands of dollars by 1828. Chile had denied that these cases were legitimate, claiming that these seizures had been conducted lawfully under the rules of wartime blockades and that her naval prize courts had validated these actions. Larned hoped to persuade Rodríquez to reconsider the merits of these claims and treat them under a "special convention" as part of a commercial treaty.[56]

Perhaps because of his perseverance, Larned was informed that Chile had decided that any future trade negotiations should take place in Washington, not Santiago, and in January 1829 he forwarded a detailed treaty proposal to the State Department. Composed of thirty-six articles, three of which (articles 2, 3, and 31) contained the most-favored-nation principle, his proposal was fashioned after the recent U.S.-Colombian commercial agreement.[57] Also included in this dispatch was an analysis of current U.S.-Chilean trade, complete with an itemized, descriptive account of imports and exports, to assist Washington in completing negotiations. According to Larned, chief U.S. exports to Chile were cotton, household furniture, and flour, along with foreign goods—transshipped by U.S. merchantmen—sugar, "herb of Paraguay, China and India goods, and some French and German fabricks." Principal Chilean exports to the United States were pig copper and bullion. Larned was optimistic that U.S. exports would continue to expand due to Chile's lack of skilled labor and the capital necessary to establish specialized manufacturing.[58]

Feeling quite pleased with his efforts, Larned was confident that Washington could utilize his proposal to complete the trade negotiations quickly and would certainly commend him for his recent accomplishments. How disillusioning it must have been for him when he eagerly read Secretary Clay's long-awaited response. Not only was Clay's reply void of any praise for the chargé's successes on the treaty proposal, for his publications of "Observations in Reply," or for his expert handling of the case of the merchantman *Chile*, but this July 1829 dispatch simply informed Larned that he was being transferred to Lima as the first U.S. chargé to Peru. Larned did not reject his new post, but he did appeal for a reconsideration of his transfer, for he knew that his influence and reputation would make his service far more effective in Santiago than in Lima. He wondered if perhaps the newly inaugurated Jackson administration felt that his political preferences might not be compatible with its philosophies and was therefore transferring him to a less important position. Swearing his loyalty to Old Hickory's regime, Larned professed that he actually had no party affiliation and, indeed, had never even "made use of, on a single occasion, the electoral franchise."[59] The new secretary of state, Martin Van Buren, ignored Larned's appeals, and on October 15, 1829, Larned took leave of the Chilean government to begin his voyage to Lima, where he would remain as U.S. chargé until 1837.[60]

Larned's last few months in Santiago seemed filled with despondency and depression. He made several failing attempts at gaining Minister Rodríquez's acknowledgment of Chile's accountability for indemnities from the seizures of the *Macedonian*, the *Warrior*, and the *Garret*, but his "good friend" refused to treat with the then lame-duck chargé. So frustrated had Larned become that he actually implied that if Rodríquez continued to ignore his diplomatic overtures, the United States might be compelled to impose other methods—even military ones—to gain a favorable response from Chile.[61] Yet why should Rodríquez rush to reconcile these claims and other problems? Would it not be logical to anticipate that Larned's replacement would know less of these matters than his predecessor did? And would it not also be logical to assume that the new chargé would be more like the sinecure Heman Allen than the forceful, productive Larned? Hindsight clearly answers these questions in the affirmative. Certainly, Washington's lackadaisical attitude toward replacing Larned reflects no urgency in settling the claims cases or even in maintaining uninterrupted relations: the new chargé, John Hamm, was not appointed until May 1830;[62] he did not leave for his mission for another seven months;[63] and he did not present his credentials in Santiago until May 26, 1831, nineteen months after Larned's departure for Lima.[64]

Chargé Hamm, a native of Zanesville, Ohio, had been instructed to continue efforts to resolve the claims cases and to resume negotiations for a commercial treaty, since it had been decided to shift these discussions back to Santiago. Following Larned's initiatives, Hamm hoped to incorporate the claims cases as a "special convention" of the proposed trade agreement; had Chile accepted this concept, it would have been a major concession, for several additional claims had been added to those dating from the independence era.[65]

Hamm's arrival in Santiago coincided with the beginning of Chile's thirty-year "Conservative Era," with the election of President Joaquín Prieto signaling the nation's passage from toddling infancy to the exuberancy of adolescence. And although real national maturity still remained for the future, Hamm was optimistic that Chile's fledgling self-confidence would convince her to accept responsibility for the claims cases and see the desirability of finalizing the pending commercial treaty. Hamm's optimism seemed warranted, for within a month after his arrival Andrés Bello was appointed as Chile's minister plenipotentiary and commissioned to complete the trade negotiations and resolve the claims cases. Had Hamm been aware of his counterpart's brilliance and prowess in diplomacy, he certainly would have tempered his optimism with at least a little caution.[66] They initialed on May 16, 1832, a preliminary draft for the treaty, which, except for the goods of Spanish-American nations, did give U.S. trade the most-favored-nation status (article 2). And although Hamm's instructions had not authorized such an exception, he categorized his actions as a minor compromise necessary to pave the way for Chile's eventual acceptance of the U.S. position on the claims cases.[67]

Hamm also expressed great personal pride and satisfaction concerning article 11, which guaranteed U.S. citizens freedom of religious conscience and the right of burial in Chilean (Catholic) graveyards. He boasted that even though a "host of influential Priests" had vehemently opposed this section of the treaty—delaying its adoption until October—many liberal thinkers had applauded the measure as an "entering-wedge for the attainment of other desirable objects of . . . religious [freedom] . . . in such a bigoted country."[68] Ironically, Hamm's great expectations for the growth of liberalism in Chile were dashed in mid-1833, when a new, strongly centralized constitution was promulgated. Not only was Catholicism—a "wild beast," according to the chargé's definition—again designated as the state religion, but the new law of the land expressly forbade the public exercise of all other faiths.[69] Hamm lamented that once again "*ecclesiastical influence*" would dominate every aspect of society[70] and that "kingcraft and priestcraft . . . [would] sit like an incubus on their senses."[71]

Ironically, there is evidence to support the theory that the 1833 constitution actually helped to foment the emergence of a schism between the moderate and the old guard within the *pelucón* party. Moderates such as Bello, Manuel Renjifo, and Joaquín Tocornal chose to remain with the party during its factional struggles, capitalizing upon the influence of their governmental positions to help bring about several progressive measures. By 1835, the National Institute had formally separated from the seminary in Santiago, thus fostering more freedom in education for Chile's young elite. Then, too, the liberal polemics of Francisco Bilbao and José Lastarria, though condemned by the church, found more sympathy and supporters than one might have thought. Of course, the Catholic hierarchy did not simply turn the other cheek when targeted by such open criticism. And by the 1840s, church-state controversies were being argued and debated in the congress, in the newspapers, and even in the streets of Santiago and Valparaíso. Naturally, Chargé Hamm and his successors openly and freely offered their advice and opinions against the antiquated institutions of the "incubus."[72]

On November 27, 1833, the *Lady Adams* cleared Valparaíso harbor, and Hamm ended his three-and-a-half-year mission, able to claim at least a degree of success: he was homeward bound with the final draft of the commercial treaty and was personally escorting to Washington Manuel Carvallo, Chile's first minister to the United States.[73] Also, although Hamm had been unsuccessful in settling the six claims cases already filed by U.S. merchants (the *Macedonian*, the *Warrior*, the *Garret*, the *Trusty*, the *Franklin*, and the *Good Return*), he had persuaded President Prieto to agree that the executive branch—not only the judiciary—had the power to resolve these matters, thus removing the major delaying tactic Chile had been employing.[74]

And speaking of delays: seventeen months passed between Hamm's departure and the arrival of his replacement, the Virginian

Richard Pollard, in March 1835. Chargé Pollard would choose to adopt a more openly aggressive attitude in dealing with his Chilean counterparts, constantly pressing to fulfill his instructions to resolve the claims cases and to eliminate any exceptions to the U.S. most-favored-nation status in the new commercial treaty.[75] From the day of his arrival in Valparaíso, which unfortunately fell on the eve of a devastating earthquake and an accompanying tidal wave, most Chileans found Pollard's personality and actions both irritating and condescending. During his initial meeting with Prieto, he committed the diplomatic faux pas of referring to the United States as Chile's revered political and philosophical role model and great "benefactor." Such an air of superiority could not have gone unnoticed.[76]

Pollard's patronizing demeanor soon surfaced again during his discussions with Foreign Minister Joaquín Tocornal concerning amending the commercial treaty so that goods from the U.S. would receive parity with those from Spanish-American nations. Chile was currently finalizing a similar treaty with Peru, whose sugar exports would be allowed to enter Chilean ports at one-half the duty rate imposed on U.S. sugar. Pollard reminded Tocornal that the 1823 U.S. formal recognition of Chilean independence and issuance of the Monroe Doctrine had undergirded the young republic's existence and had "said to all Europe stand aloof—thou shall not aid in replacing those manacles of slavery upon these heroic people who had broken them asunder."[77] And although Tocornal could have responded that the as yet untested Monroe Doctrine still represented form, not substance, he could not diminish the importance and credibility that Chile had gained from the early U.S. recognition. Then, too, in 1834 U.S. minister plenipotentiary to Madrid, John Van Ness, had been instrumental in persuading Spain to open communications with her former colonies. Certainly, Pollard reasoned, economic discrimination was not the proper way for Chile to demonstrate her friendship and thanks for all the United States had done for Chile.[78] Pollard also reminded Tocornal that both Mexico and Colombia had recently signed trade agreements with Washington and had granted U.S. products most-favored-nation status without exception.[79]

Neither the chargé's reasoning nor his polemics was sufficient to carry his arguments, and the pending Chilean-Peruvian treaty was ratified in August 1835.[80] Yet, fortunately for U.S. trade interests, the new treaty became moot the following May, when the junta of Lima's Felipe Santiago Salaverry was overthrown and this treaty was numbered among the coup's casualties.[81] Salaverry's ouster had been manipulated by Bolivian dictator General Andrés Santa Cruz, who reestablished Peru's ex-president, Luis José Obregoso, as a puppet to help accomplish Bolivia's true goal—the absorption of Peru as part of the Bolivian Confederation. Santa Cruz next planned to use those consolidated forces to subjugate Chile and even Argentina.[82] During the next year tensions increased steadily, and war seemed inevitable. In August 1836, Santa Cruz sponsored a filibustering landing of Chilean exiles at Chiloé under ex-president Ramón Freire, but with no real effect. Freire's ill-prepared forces consisted of two aging vessels, one of whose crew mutinied off the coast of Valparaíso and surrendered to the Chilean navy in exchange for amnesty, and soon afterward Freire and the remainder of his ragtag band were captured, brought to Valparaíso, tried, and banished for ten years. Pollard had privately favored Freire, owing to his antichurch reputation, and he expressed disappointment concerning the ill-fated venture: "There is nothing like the fidelity among the soldiery of this country. They pass from one chief to another and from one side to the other as percussionary prospects prevail."[83] Luckily, Pollard's personal preferences did not, however, alter the U.S. stance of strict neutrality during the course of Chile's ensuing war with Santa Cruz; English and French merchantmen cavalierly ran Chile's inadequate blockades along the Peruvian coast. Many contemporaries considered England's attitude as pro–Santa Cruz, and France indignantly dismissed the Chilean efforts as mere "paper blockades."[84]

It is interesting to note, however, that while Pollard was officially neutral in his actions, his personal anti-Chile leanings must have been obvious to Prieto and his regime. On February 12, 1837, Pollard volunteered his opinions on Chile's involvement in the war. These unsolicited opinions, penned to Vice-President Diego Portales, blatantly accused Chile of meddling in Peru's internal affairs and of pursuing the war solely for the personal aggrandizement of Chile's merchant elite, including Portales himself—this, emanating from an envoy avowing strict neutrality![85] Pollard's lack of tact cannot be excused, but it is true that much of what he wrote reflected a growing disapproval of and frustration over Chile's entrance into the conflict: taxes had been raised, the press censored, and mandatory conscription enacted, and the uncovering of a "revolutionary plot" had resulted in the summary sentencing and execution of four of its leaders. Portales, Chile's "Ajax Telamon," as Pollard labeled him, was the target of most of this growing criticism.[86]

By June 1837, this general dissatisfaction over the war had manifested itself as discontent at the Quillota staging area near Valparaíso, where Chile's expeditionary forces were being readied for their embarkation for Peru. There, on June 3, while conducting an inspection tour to boost morale among the recruits, Portales and his staff were taken prisoner by a mutinous faction of draftees and a few leftist officers. Although the mutiny was easily suppressed by loyal forces from Valparaíso, the relief forces arrived too late to save Portales, who had been unceremoniously executed. Pollard, whose personal dislike of Portales was well known, committed the diplomatic faux pas of neglecting to send a letter of condolence for the nation's loss to President Prieto.[87] This unpardonable breach of protocol was probably the reason that Prieto rejected Pollard's offer of the USS *North Carolina* as the neutral site for peace negotiations between Chilean and Peruvian representatives the following December. By that time Pollard had conveniently forgotten his own actions and was outraged that Prieto had selected an English vessel at Callao for the peace talks. According to Pollard, Chile's "ingratitude" and snubbing of the "Eldest Sister of the American Family" further evidenced the young republic's inability to sever the ties with its monarchical past. In reality, these talks proved no more than a ruse to gain time for Chile to complete its invasion preparations.[88]

Eleven months later, in November 1838, General Manuel Bulnes left Valparaíso with a large force, effectively blockaded Callao, and soon was advancing on Santa Cruz's armies.[89] By April the combined Bolivian-Peruvian forces were routed, and Santa Cruz had sought sanctuary in the British consulate in Arequipa. From there, one hundred British marines escorted the fallen dictator to the safety of an awaiting ship of war, under whose Union Jack Santa Cruz sailed to Guayaquil and exile. Surely, Pollard reasoned, when these pro-Peruvian English actions were juxtaposed to his own adherence to strict neutrality, the "Eldest Sister of the American Family" would at last be guaranteed the economic and diplomatic advantages she deserved.[90]

The chargé's optimistic supposition proved fallacious: the war's end occasioned no substantive trade losses for British merchants in Chile, and Britain's official agents certainly suffered no diminution in rank or status. This inconsistency in Chilean attitude was incomprehensible to Pollard; he never understood or accepted it. His disgust over this turn of events peaked in September, when he and all of the other diplomats in Santiago were the honored guests at the annual banquet commemorating Chile's independence. Pollard was seated at the right of Foreign Minister Tocornal, with the Brazilian chargé at the minister's left—an arrangement that seemed to meet the approval of the ever-protocol-conscious Pollard. Then he observed, to his utter disbelief, that the Bolivian minister plenipotentiary sat at Prieto's right, while at the president's left sat the British admiral who had ordered the safeguarded passage of Santa Cruz into exile. Pollard refused to allow such an obvious slight to go unchallenged, naturally, and after the serving of the first course he curtly left his seat, walked straight to Prieto's table and "turning indignantly went out of the room and left the house."[91] Apologies were later offered by the banquet hosts, but Pollard refused to accept them or forgive this purposeful indignity against himself and the honor of the United States.[92]

Pollard's actions—indeed, one might even say performance—at this banquet were of a piece with the general emotional depression and feelings of uselessness reflected in his dispatches from 1838 to the end of his mission in 1842. His personal letters are filled with references to his chronic ill health, his despair stemming from his contention that Chilean officials consistently worked to prohibit him from accomplishing his goals, and his belief that Washington neither appreciated his efforts nor bothered to support him. For five years he had sought to gain reparations for the 1831 seizure and detainment of the whalers *Franklin* and *Good Return* for entering Chilean ports with small quantities of tobacco, but each time success seemed within reach, the skillful Andrés Bello would find yet another reason to postpone the negotiations or counter Pollard's positions on these cases.[93]

Pollard was successful, however, in gaining Chile's recognition of liability concerning the cargo seizure and crew impressment of the U.S. merchantman *Warrior*. This case, dating from the independence period, involved a clear-cut violation of international law when Chilean officers authorized the seizure of a neutral vessel for trading with royalist forces. The claimants had sought $15,868 in indemnities, but Pollard settled for a principal of $15,000, plus $1,500 in arrears of interest, payable over a seven-year period and bearing 5 percent interest. Pollard carried the first installment ($3,741.43) with him when he ended his mission in June 1842.[94]

In stark contrast to the simplicity of the *Warrior* case stand the complexities of the famous—or perhaps infamous—April 1819 *Macedonian* claims case, which occupied most of Pollard's energies during his last three years in Santiago. It is more difficult to fathom the bizarre, multifaceted intricacies of this case than to divine safe passage through a Byzantine labyrinth. This is not the place to chronicle the puzzling issues of this legal quagmire, yet a partial listing of the case's main points of contention provides one with an idea of the problems that Pollard faced: Some doubted the trustworthiness of the *Macedonian*'s captain, who was generally known to engage in smuggling and other illicit trade activities; the *Macedonian*'s confiscated cargo was purported to have been owned by American merchants, or by Spanish merchants, or by both, according to whose affidavits one believed; a large amount of money had been seized from a royalist, on board the French brig *Gazelle*, who claimed to have held the sum on consignment from the *Macedonian*'s captain; the legality of the Chilean blockade of Peruvian ports had to be substantiated; the conduct of Chile's Admiral Lord Cochrane had to be validated by precedence in international law; Chilean prize courts had initially rendered decisions in favor of the *Macedonian*'s owners, then the same courts had overruled their own verdicts; and counterclaims had been filed by Spanish merchants. There was even a discrepancy over exactly how much money and/or cargo had actually been seized—was it $140,000, or was it $142,000? Is it any wonder that, from 1839 to 1842, Pollard had time for little else than laboring over these complexities? And then how frustrating it must have been when, just as he and a special Chilean commission had finally reached agreement on a compromise settlement of $104,000, Pollard received word that the *Macedonian*'s owners had decided to combine their original claim with a second, similar claim of $70,400 dating from an 1820 seizure of their ship. Totally frustrated and aware that the Chilean congress was currently debating the merits of the compromise settlement, Pollard wisely decided not to jeopardize the affair by muddying the waters with the additional claim.[95]

Early 1841 certainly was not an appropriate time to pursue any new negotiations. Santiago was in the midst of a heated, intra-*pelucón* rivalry for its presidential nomination, and everything else would be subordinated to near obscurity until after the July elections. Pollard was more than a curious observer; the minority progressive faction was led by Foreign Minister Joaquín Tocornal, with whom Pollard had reached the pending *Macedonian* agreement, and his election probably would have led the way to the settlement of other U.S. claims cases. However, fearing an irreparable split within his party, Tocornal withdrew his candidacy shortly before the election, thus assuring the success of the *pelucones*' old guard choice, General Manuel Bulnes. Bulnes, called the Victor of Yungay for his victories over the Peruvians in the recent war, was the nephew of President Prieto and had promised to continue his uncle's conservative policies.[96] Tocornal had resigned his cabinet post during the campaign, being replaced first by Ramón Luis Yrarrazaval, whose illness forced his resignation, and then by Manuel Renjifo.[97]

In the fall of 1841, Pollard began a lengthy correspondence with Renjifo concerning the second *Macedonian* claim, but a careful reading of these documents indicates that the chargé was simply going through pro forma motions, with no hopes of gaining a settlement. Indeed, the Chilean solons still had not authorized the payments of the first claim, and Pollard knew that because he was soon to be replaced, Chile was under no pressure to finalize anything with the lame-duck envoy.[98] Ironically, had the Chileans been able to foresee the fiery, abrasive disposition of Pollard's replacement, they would have rushed to resolve all U.S.-Chilean differences at once.

John Strother Pendleton, a thirty-nine-year-old Virginia lawyer, arrived in Santiago in May 1842 to assume his duties. During late May and early June he met with Pollard, who was awaiting the arrival of the USS *Saint Louis* for his homeward passage, and from these meetings Pendleton was made fully aware of the frustrations the former chargé had experienced in his negotiations over the *Macedonian* case and other matters. Pendleton determined to be more assertive in his dealings with his Chilean counterparts.[99] On September 1, he met with Foreign Minister Yrarrazaval, who had reassumed his duties following his illness, and warned him that if Chile did not begin payment on the initial *Macedonian* claim within four months (by January 1, 1843), he would take "the strongest ground authorized by [his] instructions" to seek reparations; Commodore Thomas ap Catesby Jones's flagship, the USS *United States*, was currently anchored in Valparaíso harbor.[100] Whether perceived as an idle threat or as a not so veiled militant innuendo, Pendleton's statement had the desired effect: the Chilean congress soon authorized payment, and on January 2, 1843, Pendleton pridefully acknowledged receipt of the first installment, $32,634. Twenty-four years had passed since Lord Cochrane's seizure of the *Macedonian*.[101] In Valparaíso, *El Mercurio*'s report of this payment created quite a bit of anti-American feeling, especially since the infamous vessel and its disreputable captain, Eliphalet Smith, were still remembered for their smuggling activities.[102]

Given this anti-American sentiment, it was probably fortunate that Pendleton was unable to rush immediately into negotiations for the second *Macedonian* claim ($70,400). Minister Yrarrazaval was again ill, and the second round of talks were postponed until August 1843.[103]

Then, once commenced, these negotiations proved to be nothing more than tedious reflections of the first claim's history—a disputacious series of delays grounded upon rumors of impending "new evidence" in Lima, counterclaims, "lost records," and other pretexts by which Pendleton refused to be deterred. Pendleton reasoned that since his adamant, threatening stance concerning the first claim had brought success, an even more determined attitude and posture were called for now. In a sharply worded letter dated January 9, 1844, he criticized Yrarrazaval for his unwarranted procrastinations, reminding him that President Bulnes had promised "Perfect Justice"—and justice should be swift—in this second settlement. The chargé concluded:

> The government of the United States does not wish Chile to pay one farthing which is not justly due. Show that this money was *not* taken— or that it has been returned—or that it was lawful prize—and there is an end of the demand. Or . . . show that this doctrine of *prescription*, which has been attempted to be applied, has been recognized by any respectible Government in the World, in a case like this—and there is again an end of the matter.
>
> It is the option of His Excellency's Government to proceed with the discussion—or to pay the money—or to refuse to pay it.

If Chile refused an immediate settlement, Pendleton said, Washington would be notified that all diplomatic avenues had been exhausted and force (undefined) would be necessitated.[104]

Confident, the expectant chargé was sure his letter would bring results, yet Yrarrazaval's February 2 reply was scarcely what Pendleton anticpated. Chile regarded Pendleton's letter as a threat, as inconsistent with relations deemed "proper between representatives of two friendly nations." Furthermore, Yrarrazaval considered the tone of the letter to have been personally slanderous and without dignity, and if Pendleton persisted in such tenor, the foreign minister promised to direct a formal protest to Secretary of State Daniel Webster.[105] Of course, Pendleton denied that he had breached any diplomatic protocol. He stated that if Yrarrazaval had read anything offensive in the letter, this was simply the fault of an incompetent Chilean translator, who obviously had been unable to convey the charge's true feelings. Pendleton then demanded that Yrarrazaval retract his erroneous accusations. With both men claiming that their honor had been impugned and with neither willing to accept responsibility for the resulting impasse, any further attempts at negotiation proved futile. Ironically, Pendleton's actions had brought about exactly what Chile had desired—more delays on the second *Macedonian* claim.[106]

Pendleton ended his mission that June, but not before Yrarrazaval could fire off one last parting shot. His June 12, 1844, letter expressed Chile's total displeasure over the unstatesmanlike conduct displayed by the chargé throughout his stay in Santiago.[107] And then to underscore his opinion and concern, the foreign minister addressed a similar note to the newly appointed secretary of state, John C. Calhoun. Secretary Calhoun, himself not known for an overabundance of patience and tact, did not censure Pendleton for his behavior, but he did decide that the new chargé should adopt a more conciliatory tone in seeking claims settlements.[108]

George William Crump received his appointment as chargé to Chile on April 15, 1844, but did not arrive at the Santiago legation until June 1845, nearly a full year after Pendleton's departure.[109] A Virginian, Crump held a law degree from Princeton and had studied medicine at the University of Pennsylvania. In addition to his law practice, his experience included two terms in the Virginia House of Delegates and one year of service in the United States Congress, completing the term of John Randolph following the illustrious solon's resignation in 1827. Then from 1832 until his appointment as chargé, Crump was chief clerk of the Pension Bureau.[110]

Crump's two-year mission coincided with a period of general anti-Americanism in Latin America, a mood heightened by U.S. involvement in Mexican affairs and other ramifications of the evolving concepts of manifest destiny. Indeed, President Bulnes' June 1, 1845, message to the Chilean senate referred to the second *Macedonian* claims case as yet another example of the recent, aggressive U.S. policy of intimidating weaker nations. Pendleton's attitude had certainly seemed forged from just such a philosophy, and Crump hoped that his genteel and patient manner would restore more amicable relations. His hopes were shared by Chile's new foreign minister, Manuel Montt, and more especially by Montt's assistant, Andrés Bello, upon whose counsel both Bulnes and Montt greatly depended.[111]

From September 1845 through March 1846, Montt and Crump carried on lengthy negotiations over the complex 1821 *Macedonian* case, but, as with their predecessors, their labors prove futile. And doubtless it was with appreciative relief that Crump received the news that Manuel Carvallo was being reassigned as Chile's plenipotentiary to Washington, with specific orders to conclude the *Macedonian* affair.[112]

Ironically, just after this case's venue had shifted to Washington, Crump was called upon to act on behalf of two U.S. merchantmen recently seized in Chiloé for violating Chile's 1836 revenue laws. The *Pantheon* and the *Leader* were accused of smuggling and illegal seal fishing in Chilean territorial waters. Their masters, Captains Dimon and Prey, pleaded innocence on the grounds that their ships had been driven into Chilean waters in search of safe haven from an approaching storm. Chiloé's San Carlos tribunal found in their favor, but the local prosecutors—likely caught up in the augmenting tide of anti-Americanism—had appealed to the supreme court in Santiago, where the cases were retried in May 1847. Captain Dimon and the *Pantheon* were again exonerated on all charges, but the San Carlos decision concerning the *Leader* was overturned, and the ship and its cargo were ordered confiscated for tobacco smuggling.[113] Crump categorized this penalty as draconian to say the least, and he determined to gain executive clemency from President Bulnes. The new foreign minister, Manuel Vial, agreed to aid Crump in preparing his appeal, which proved successful on the condition that Captains Dimon and Prey drop their counterclaims for damages to their cargoes incurred during their ships' detentions. This cooperative effort would have been out of the question had not Crump accomplished his goal of recementing cordial relations with Santiago. Pendleton's "stick" diplomacy may have forced Chilean compliance on the *Macedonian*'s first claim, but Crump's "carrot" method offered its own obvious and more amiable advantages.[114]

Then, just as Crump was beginning to enjoy the fruits of his patient, cooperative diplomacy, the increasing number of disputes between the United States and Mexico finally ran their inevitable course and matured into hostilities, thus reviving anti-Americanism and again loosening the building blocks of friendship that the chargé had so meticulously sought to mortise. Chile's exports to Mexico diminished as U.S. blockading forces sealed off Mexican ports, and Crump was soon reporting that the only Chileans sympathetic to the American cause were German, English, and French immigrants.[115] The Chilean press was, of course, openly criticial of the U.S. aggression. There was really nothing Crump could have done to reverse these sentiments, so he received the news of his replacement with no regrets and quickly arranged his homeward passage aboard the USS *Columbus,* sailing from Valparaíso on November 1, 1847.[116] Among the packets of correspondence carried by Crump was a personal letter from Minister Vial to Secretary of State James Buchanan praising the departing chargé's effective mission and hoping that his replacement would possess a similar cordiality. The tensions of the period certainly warranted Vial's desires, but his hopes would be in vain.[117]

President James Polk had already appointed Colonel Seth Barton as the new chargé to Santiago. Barton, whose appointment was a classic example of political sinecure, had faced a difficult confirmation hearing in the Senate, where his qualifications had been hotly debated and where Chilean envoy Carvallo had failed in his lobbying attempts against the appointment.[118] Barton's experience consisted of a successful law partnership with the renowned Judah P. Benjamin in New Orleans and a 1845–47 stint as Polk's solicitor of the treasury—a background more or less consistent with those of his predecessors to the Santiago post. Why, then, was there such an uproar over his selection? The answer seems to be personality: Washington gossip cliques characterized Barton as arrogant, indiscreet, and so witlessly uncouth that he was surpassed by few of his contemporaries. Indeed, except for his friendship with Polk and his staunch support from the naval secretary, John Mason, his appointment would never have been confirmed.[119] But this was the era of manifest destiny, and the aggressive posture of the United States in inter-American diplomacy could scarcely be personified by shrinking violets when tiger lilies seemed more in vogue. Barton's reputation preceded his arrival in Valparaíso on Christmas Day, 1847, and his subsequent reception in Santiago with Minister Vial and President Bulnes was professionally polite though obviously cautious and apprehensive.[120]

Part of Barton's instructions included a directive to review all Chilean commercial agreements signed after 1832 to ensure that U.S. trade continued to receive most-favored-nation status, excepting Latin-American commerce, of course. During his inquiries, he heard rumors that the 1845 Chilean-Spanish treaty placed Spain's trade on an equal footing with that of Latin-American nations. According to the 1832 agreement, if this were true, U.S. goods would also have to receive this same status; if denied this privilege, the Spanish treaty would have to be amended to allow for the Latin-American exception as specified in the U.S. treaty. Since Barton was on friendly terms with the Spanish envoy, Salvador de Tavira, he acquired a copy of the 1845 treaty and found that article 10 did indeed substantiate what he had heard. Article 10 not only violated the 1832 U.S. treaty but also, according to Barton's investigations, stood in direct contradiction to· an 1834 Chilean law that forbade the signing of *any* commercial agreement that did not grant Latin-American trade priority status. The timing of the chargé's discovery was most fortuitous. Chile was then negotiating a new commercial treaty with Peru to allow her flour exports to enter Peru at a very low import tax rate, while she would reciprocate by granting similar low import taxes for Peruvian sugar. U.S. merchants had already approached Barton with estimates of their losses that such an agreement would cause. Barton's approach to Minister Vial on this matter was quite simple: if the 1845 Spanish treaty guaranteed Spain trade equality with Peru, he demanded trade equality with Spain and therefore also equality with Peru.[121]

The end result of Barton's demand was that Chile choose to exercise article 31 of the 1832 U.S. treaty, terminating the agreement a year following notification; Chile's pacts with Spain and Peru were not amended.[122] After several rounds of ineffectual negotiations to extend the treaty, on January 20, 1850, the 1832 agreement was at last canceled, and for the next two years no subsequent commercial talks were held. However, an 1852 trade proposal was signed, though never ratified, that would have placed the goods of the two countries on most-favored-nation status with no exceptions. The Chilean senate rejected this new treaty, when the U.S. Senate insisted upon deleting an article requiring the United States to safeguard Chilean miners who had migrated to the gold fields of California.[123] By 1851, over three thousand Chilean forty-niners had found their way to California, and Chilean newspapers frequently carried reports of discrimination and even open brutality by U.S. rushers against their South-American counterparts. These reports had created yet another atmosphere of anti-Americanism, especially in Valparaíso.[124] Ironically, many Valparaisian merchants had grown wealthy from the increased trade to the new boomtowns in California.[125]

Contemporary with Barton's initial negotiations with Vial concerning the commercial treaty, several unrelated incidents occurred that Barton felt were purposely carried out to harass him and render him less efficient in his official duties. As was the case with each of his predecessors, his feelings of isolation and the lack of regular communication and support from Washington caused him to view even a trivial incident as a major personal affront; paranoia seemed to envelop each chargé as he reached Santiago. There were three such incidents for Barton, each of which did affect his official performance, his personal reputation, and consequently Chile's attitude toward the United States. The first incident may have been a misunderstanding; the second was ludicrous, absurd; and the third became a cause célèbre resulting in his recall.

The misunderstanding began on February 11, 1848, when Barton received from the Santiago police department a "preemptory order" telling him that the legation's official flags were to be displayed the following day in commemoration of Chile's 1817 victory over the royalists at Chacabuco. Barton felt that the order had been delivered by mistake, because his records indicated that the legation had voluntarily flown its flags for this and all other Chilean holidays. Then, two months later, on April 4, another "order" was sent to the legation, this time concerning flying official flags to celebrate the anniversary of the patriot victory at Maipú on April 5, 1818. Barton immediately assumed that both orders had been sent as deliberate attempts to harass him and even try to usurp jurisdiction over the U.S. flag and legation. He addressed to Minister Vial a scornfully worded note detailing his irritation, and to Barton's surprise—indeed, to his embarrassment as well—Vial's reply was most apologetic and conciliatory, placing the blame on the ignorance of the Santiago police and assuring the chargé that no such mistakes would occur in the future. An uncharacteristically contrite Barton graciously thanked Vial and offered his own apology for his earlier note.[126]

Yet the flags controversy was to be unfurled once again, and this time one would be hard-pressed not to fault Chilean authorities for deliberately attempting to provoke Barton. On February 11, 1849— exactly one year after the delivery of the first preemptory order— another police directive arrived at the legation, again concerning the Chacabuco celebration.[127] Barton was absolutely enraged. He and Vial were then engaged in correspondence over two other controversies, and Barton vented his wrath in a letter that was scornful, sarcastic, and maybe even justified. Why was it, he asked, that only the U.S. legation was honored with these "orders"? Were the Santiago policemen so stupid as to be unable to distinguish one legation and/or flag from another? The coup de grace came when Barton discovered that the chief of police, who had signed each of the three orders, was none other than Vial's father-in-law. Vial never replied to Barton's letter, and Barton refused to unfurl the legation's flags during the remainder of his mission.[128]

The second incident indirectly affecting Barton's performance was an accident involving his two carriage horses. On June 10, 1848, his coachman, James Sylvester, hitched the horses to their barouche and was exercising them along Santiago's main promenade, La Canada, when the reins suddenly broke and the startled horses ran away with the barouche in tow. After running some distance, the frightened animals darted between two trees, lodging and damaging the barouche, then raced through Santiago's crowded streets before at last being caught and controlled by a mounted policeman. Sylvester, who was uninjured, identified himself and asked permission to return the horses to the legation. But the policeman insisted upon confining the horses at the police stables while the accident was investigated, and he actually threatened to arrest Sylvester, who had become a bit too persistent in his demands to retain the horses.[129] Barton considered the police actions toward Sylvester a breach of diplomatic immunity, yet he delayed filing a formal protest to Minister Vial because he expected that the police department would apologize for this "outrage."[130] To his dismay, however, not only was no apolgy offered, but three days later (June 13) a policeman "paraded" the horses along the street fronting the legation in what Barton perceived as mockery. Then, on June 17, the chief of police—Vial's father-in-law—came to the legation to inform Barton that their investigation was completed and that the horses would be returned as soon as Barton came to the police stables and signed for them. But this was no apology. A bristling Barton refused the chief's verbal offer, informing him that since the whole affair had become a public joke at Barton's expense, any further treatment of the matter would have to come directly from Vial through formal diplomatic channels and only after an official apology was received at the legation.[131]

Vial refused to become a player in this comedic horse opera being enacted in the streets of the capital, and act two's locale was transferred to Washington, where envoy Carvallo was asked to reach a settlement with Secretary of State John M. Clayton. Clayton, who had already received Barton's voluminous description of the affair, displayed a rather uncharacteristic stance of complete support for the distant chargé, telling Carvallo that if Chile expected the United States to appoint qualified ministers to Santiago, the very least she could do was to guarantee a chargé's diplomatic immunities.[132] Barton was replaced by Balie Peyton before the curtain descended on the final scenes of this drama; the horses remained in the police stables for nearly two more years, until June 1850, when they were auctioned off to compensate for their sizable feed bill.[133] The profits from the sale—$41.72—were forwarded to Washington as a draft payable to the secretary of state. The State Department considered the affair a "private matter," and because ex-chargé Barton refused to accept the money without an official apology, the draft is still on file in the archives of the Library of Congress.[134]

The third and most publicized incident involving Barton was his marriage controversy—the dispute that resulted in his recall and that must be analyzed within the broader context of Chilean internal politics and the growing anti-Americanism of the late 1840s. During Bulnes' two administrations (1841–51), there was a growing undercurrent of dissatisfaction concerning the power of the Catholic church in Chilean politics. This movement came not only from the liberal *pipiolos* but also from the increasing number of moderate *pelucones*, many of whom had gained national prominence. The church was not prepared to stand by idly and watch its influence and *fueros* diminish, of course, and in 1848 Rafael Valentín Valdivieso was appointed archbishop of Santiago to lead the church's opposition to the liberal trends. It was into this atmosphere of church-state friction that Barton and his marriage were unwittingly interjected, indirectly affecting U.S.-Chilean relations.[135]

In September 1848, Barton met and quickly fell in love with Isabella Astaburuaga, an aristocratic, twenty-six-year-old maiden of one of Santiago's leading families. Then, after a brief, though intense, two-month courtship, the couple announced their plans to marry, openly flouting tradition and creating a whirl of excited gossip in Santiago.[136] The fifty-two-year-old chargé was not only Protestant but a widower, with two grown daughters, who had remarried and then divorced his second wife.[137] Also, rumors were circulating that there were "questions" concerning his divorce; one report stated that his previous wife, now living in New Orleans, still maintained the legality of their marriage.[138] These rumors were untrue, but Archbishop Valentín publicly announced his opposition to the marriage and prohibited any Chilean priest from solemnizing the wedding. Barton's sworn affidavits disproving the rumors were rejected by Valentín, prompting Barton to state that it had been "a sad mistake to have looked for Christian justice at his Reverence's hands." If Valentín persisted in his slanderous opposition, Barton would ask Minister Vial to intervene and thus "vindicate [his] honor . . . so grossly and flagrantly insulted by [the] report in circulation."[139]

Vial stayed out of the affair, and after Isabella's personal appeals for the prelate's dispensation were denied, the chaplain of the USS *Independence* was summoned from Valparaíso to conduct the wedding at the legation on December 28, 1848. Of the many who had been invited, only Isabella's anguished family, a few close friends, and several members of the diplomatic corps chose to defy Valentín's scorn by attending the ceremony. Barton considered the conspicuous absence

Rafael Valentín Valdivieso, the uncompromising Archbishop of Santiago.

of invited Chilean officials as a personal slight and as impugning the honor of the United States. Sarcastically, he wondered if perhaps some "Delphic revealing of a cabinet credence" had visited their august assemblage and warned the ministers not to attend.[140]

On January 2, Valentín sent to Barton a condemnatory letter accusing him of bigamy and perjury and describing Isabella (referred to by her maiden name) as a fallen woman who had forfeited her virtue and who would multiply "the number of [her] sins, as often as she availed [herself] of the privileges of a wife." Several small demonstrations supporting the church's position had already been staged in front of the legation, and although Barton's fears that these demonstrations might become violent were probably exaggerated, he sent a formal protest to Vial. His protest letter demanded police protection for the legation and a governmental censure of Valentín, "the insolent bigot," for his inflammatory accusations and lies. Barton threatened to ask for his passports and close the legation if Vial ignored his demands.[141] But what could Vial do? The old guard of his party was firmly behind Valentín, and even the slightest hint of support for Barton would have widened the intra-*pelucón* schism. More important was that the irrepressible ex-dictator Ramón Freire, like the legendary phoenix, was once again attempting to rise from the ashes of earlier liberal-based filibusters and raise an invasion force against the Bulnes regime. Freire promised that if he succeeded, he would obtain full apologies and reparations for Barton, including the exiling of Valentín. In exchange, Barton sent to Freire an unofficial secret communication offering U.S. recognition and support. The coup never matured beyond the planning stages. But even the possibility of its success underscored the reason why Vail and Bulnes could not afford to undercut their political power or party unity by offering any concessions to Barton during his marriage controversy.[142]

On May 22, 1849, a dejected Barton officially closed the legation and, with his now-pregnant wife, left for Valparaíso and a long, perilous voyage to New Orleans.[143] Soon afterward, Vial published a 103-page pamphlet, entitled *Memoria sobre las incidencias occurridas en la matrimonio del H. señor Barton, encargado de negocias de los E. V. de América*, stating the Chilean government's position on the whole affair. Vial's publication basically supports Valentín's stand and probably was instrumental in maintaining the church's backing of the conservative party.[144]

When Barton left Santiago, the first generation of U.S.-Chilean relations came to a close. The six chargés d'affaires of this period had served with varying degrees of expertise, success, and failure: trade and commerce between the two countries had grown; several claims cases had been settled, though a few remained unresolved; and Chile's perception of the role the increasing power of the United States would play in international affairs had been formulated. The missions of the productive Samuel Larned and the patient William Crump would be remembered favorably in Santiago; Heman Allen, John Hamm, and Richard Pollard would be recalled as condescending and overbearing; and surely the missions of the unyielding John Pendleton and Seth Barton left memories of adamancy and controversy. The selection of each of these men, except perhaps for Larned, was based upon political reasons, with little regard for their training and experience or lack thereof. Once at his post, each chargé was on his own, nearly neglected by Washington, thus assuring that the personalities and attitudes of the chargés would be major determinants of U.S.-Chilean relations. This was certainly an era of "personnel diplomacy."

Notes

Chapter 1
Origins of United States–Latin
American Relations

1. José de Onís, *The United States as Seen by Latin American Writers* (New York: Hispanic Institute in the United States, 1952), p. 7.

2. Pedro Henríquez Urena, *A Concise History of Latin American Culture* (New York: Praeger, 1966), p. 33.

3. Harry Bernstein, *Making an Inter-American Mind* (Gainesville: University of Florida Press, 1961), p. 4; Onís, *United States*, pp. 8–9, 12–15. One can trace, century by century, European interest in Latin America in A. Curtis Wilgus, *History and Historians of Hispanic America* (New York: Cooper Square Publishers, 1965).

4. Arthur P. Whitaker, *The Western Hemispheric Idea* (Ithaca, N.Y.: Cornell University Press, 1954), pp. 14–15. Whitaker edited *Latin America and the Enlightenment* (New York: D. Appleton-Century, 1942).

5. Onís, *United States*, pp. 13–14. See Wilgus, *History and Historians*, for a chronological compilation of the various works published by Iberians and others about the New World.

6. Harry Bernstein, *Origins of Inter-American Interest, 1700–1812* (Philadelphia: University of Pennsylvania Press, 1945), pp. 66–71; Onís, *United States*, pp. 15–16; Whitaker, *Western Hemispheric Idea*, p. 15; Bernstein, *Making an Inter-American Mind*, p. 609.

7. Bernstein, *Making an Inter-American Mind*, pp. 53–56.

8. Whitaker, *Western Hemispheric Idea*, p. 12; Kenneth R. Maxwell, "Enlightenment (Brazil)," in *Encyclopedia of Latin America*, ed. Helen Delpar (New York: McGraw-Hill, 1974), p. 219; J. Manuel Espinosa, *Inter-American Beginnings of U.S. Cultural Diplomacy, 1936–1948*, Department of State Publication no. 8854 (Washington, D.C.: U.S. Government Printing Office, 1976), pp. 30–31.

261

9. Bernstein, *Origins of Inter-American Interest*, pp. 55–56.

10. Maxwell, "Enlightenment (Brazil)," p. 219; Asunsión Lavrin, "Enlightenment (Spanish America)," in *Encyclopedia of Latin America*, ed. Helen Delpar (New York: McGraw-Hill, 1974), pp. 219–20; Whitaker, *Western Hemispheric Idea*, p. 13.

11. Whitaker, *Western Hemispheric Idea*, pp. 17–19; Onís, *United States*, pp. 16–17, 37, 29; Bernstein, *Making an Inter-American Mind*, p. 22.

12. For a detailed summary of pre–American Revolution trade, both legal and illegal, between the Iberians and others, see Bernstein, *Origins of Inter-American Interest*, chap. 2.

13. William Spence Robertson, *Hispanic-American Relations with the United States* (1923; reprint, New York: Kraus Reprint Company, 1969), p. 186; Bernstein, *Origins of Inter-American Interest*, pp. 34–35.

14. Bernstein, *Origins of Inter-American Interest*, pp. 26–27, 33–34; Anthony H. Hull, *Charles III and the Revival of Spain* (Washington, D.C.: University Press of America, 1980), p. 253; Edwin Lieuwen, *U.S. Policy in Latin America* (New York: Praeger, 1965), p. 4.

15. Bernstein, *Origins of Inter-American Interest*, pp. 15–25, 35.

16. See John Lynch, *The Spanish-American Revolution, 1808–1826* (New York: W. W. Norton, 1973), pp. 12–16, for a summary and a convincing analysis of these reforms and their effects.

17. The term "United States" will hereafter be used to refer to the thirteen colonies in revolt against England.

18. Arthur P. Whitaker, *The United States and the Independence of Latin America, 1800–1830* (New York: W. W. Norton, 1964), pp. 3–4; Hull, *Charles III and the Revival of Spain*, pp. 251–53; Bernstein, *Origins of Inter-American Interest*, pp. 35–36; Samuel Flagg Bemis, *The Latin American Policy of the United States* (New York: W. W. Norton, 1967), p. 25.

19. Bernstein, *Origins of Inter-American Interest*, pp. 26, 30, 36–39; Robertson, *Hispanic-American Relations*, pp. 186–89; Whitaker, *United States and the Independence of Latin America*, pp. 4–6.

20. Javier Cuenca Esteban, "The United States Balance of Payments with Spanish America and the Philippine Islands, 1790–1819: Estimates and Analysis of Principal Components," in *The North American Role in the Spanish Imperial Economy*, ed. Jacques A. Barbier and Allan J. Kuethe (Manchester, Eng.: Manchester University Press, 1984), p. 28; Barbier and Kuethe, "Introduction," in ibid., p. 2; Manuel Lucena Salmoral, "The Commerce of La Guaira with the United States during the Venezuelan Revolutionary Juncture, 1807–1812," in ibid., pp. 171–76; Jesús Miguel Lorente, "Commercial Relations between New Orleans and the United States, 1783–1803," in ibid., pp. 117–91.

21. Bernstein, *Origins of Inter-American Interest*, pp. 30–31, 47–48; Whitaker, *United States and the Independence of Latin America*, pp. 7–16; Robertson, *Hispanic-American Relations*, pp. 187–90; Cuenca Esteban, "United States Balance of Payments," p. 28.

22. Bernard Moses, "The Neglected Half of American History," cited in Lewis Hanke, ed., *Do the Americas Have a Common History?: A Critique of the Bolton Theory* (New York: Knopf, 1964), p. 54; Robert A. Alexander, *Latin American Politics and Government* (New York: Harper and Row, 1976), p. 15; Charles Bell, "Constitution of Apatzingán (1814)," in *Encyclopedia of Latin America*, ed. Helen Delpar (New York: McGraw-Hill, 1974), p. 164. C. K. Webster postulates that the French Revolution had more influence than the United States on the development of Latin American republics: see C. K. Webster, ed., *Britain and the Independence of Latin America, 1812–1830: Select Documents from the Foreign Office Archives*, vol. 1 (London: Oxford University Press, 1938), p. 6. Jay Kinsbruner, in his *Spanish-American Independence Movements* (Hinsdale, Ill.: Dryden Press, 1973), pp. 77–78, contends that the early leaders of the Spanish American independence movements were rarely irrevocably committed to either monarchism or republicanism and could have lived with a moderate form of a monarchical or a republican government.

23. Glen Dealy, "Prolegómena of the Spanish American Political Tradition," *Hispanic American Historical Review* 48 (February 1968): 37–58. The Dealy thesis has two aspects: the assumptions underlying Spanish American constitutional norms stemmed from the Spanish colonial experience, and the founding fathers of Spanish American independent governments were not lacking in political experience. William Spence Robertson has demonstrated that there was some rather pronounced U.S. influence in the framing of early and later Latin American constitutions: in *Hispanic-American Relations with the United States* (New York: F. S. Crofts, 1923), pp. 176–77, he characterizes Latin Americans' perception of U.S. constitutional developments as impractical idealism with regard to applying the lessons to themselves. But one must remember that Latin American liberals of the nineteenth century were obviously influenced by Western liberal political thought on such issues as church-state relations, and in this area the liberals generally won out over time.

24. Robertson, *Hispanic-American Relations*, pp. 65–66.

25. Bemis, *Latin American Policy*, pp. 48–49; Whitaker, *United States and the Independence of Latin America*, pp. 178–80; J. Lloyd Mecham, *A Survey of United States–Latin American Relations* (New York: Houghton Mifflin, 1965), p. 35; Whitaker, *Western Hemispheric Idea*, p. 21.

26. Bemis, *Latin American Policy*, pp. 37, 182, and quote from John Randolph on p. 183; Mecham, *Survey*, p. 36.

27. See text and n. 23 above.

28. From *Memoirs of John Quincy Adams*, ed. C. F. Adams, as quoted in Bemis, *Latin American Policy*, p. 44; Dealy, "Prolegómena," pp. 45, 48, 53, 54.

29. Dealy, "Prolegómena," pp. 49–51, 58.

30. Harold Eugene Davis, "The Origins and Nature of Latin American Foreign Policies," in *Latin American Diplomatic History: An Introduction*, ed. Harold Eugene Davis, John J. Finan, and F. Taylor Peck (Baton Rouge: Louisiana State

University Press, 1977), pp. 4–6. Davis identifies the other axis as east-west and mainly cultural, linking the New World nations to their European "countries of origin."

31. Harold Eugene Davis, "International Aspects of Independence," in *Latin American Diplomatic History: An Introduction*, ed. Harold Eugene Davis, John J. Finan, and F. Taylor Peck (Baton Rouge: Louisiana State University Press, 1977), p. 37; Bemis, *Latin American Policy*, pp. 16–17; Abraham P. Nasatir, *Borderland in Retreat: From Spanish Louisiana to the Far Southwest* (Albuquerque: University of New Mexico Press, 1976), pp. 19–35.

32. Julius W. Pratt, *A History of United States Foreign Policy*, 2d ed. (Englewood Cliffs, N.J.: Prentice-Hall, 1965), pp. 24–27.

33. Bemis, *Latin American Policy*, p. 18.

34. Ibid., p. 19; Whitaker, *United States and the Independence of Latin America*, pp. 27–28.

35. This support continued until the pro-French administration of Thomas Jefferson. In addition, a new treaty of 1800 with France did not commit the United States to aid in protecting French New World possessions. See Davis, "International Aspects of Independence," pp. 39, 51.

36. Ibid.; Bemis, *Latin American Policy*, pp. 21–22.

37. Bemis, *Latin American Policy*, pp. 22–23.

38. Ibid., p. 34.

39. Whitaker, *United States and the Independence of Latin America*, pp. 42–43; Bemis, *Latin American Policy*, p. 27.

40. Davis, "International Aspects of Independence," p. 49; Bemis, *Latin American Policy*, pp. 27–30; Mecham, *Survey*, pp. 26–27.

41. Whitaker, *United States and the Independence of Latin America*, p. 43.

42. Ibid., pp. 47–49. Whitaker pointed out that the new market in Latin America substantially compensated the British for that temporarily denied them in the United States, thus defeating the purpose of the embargo.

43. Ibid., pp. 52–53.

44. William Spence Robertson, *France and Latin American Independence* (Berkeley: University of California Press, 1939), p. 69; Whitaker, *United States and the Independence of Latin America*, pp. 57–60, 63–78; Webster, *Britain and the Independence of Latin America* 1:8–12.

45. Robert L. Ferrell, *American Diplomacy: A History*, 3d ed. (New York: W. W. Norton, 1975), pp. 136–37; Bemis, *Latin American Policy*, p. 33; Whitaker, *United States and the Independence of Latin America*, pp. 94–99.

46. Webster, *Britain and the Independence of Latin America* 1:11–12; Bemis, *Latin American Policy*, pp. 35–36.

47. Whitaker, *United States and the Independence of Latin America*, pp. 193–99; Bemis, *Latin American Policy*, pp. 34–35.

48. For the development of this story, see Philip C. Brooks, *Diplomacy and the Borderland* (Berkeley: University of California Press, 1939). Another aspect of the treaty was renewal of the Pinckney Treaty but minus free navigation of

the Mississippi, now, as Bemis put it, a "one hundred percent American River" (*Latin American Policy*, p. 37).

49. The essential works for this period are Harris Gaylord Warren, *The Sword Was Their Passport* (Baton Rouge: Louisiana State University Press, 1943), and John Ryjord, *Foreign Interest in the Independence of New Spain* (Durham, N.C.: Duke University Press, 1935), in addition to Bemis, *Latin American Policy*, and Whitaker, *United States and the Independence of Latin America*.

50. Samuel Flagg Bemis et al., *A History of the Monroe Doctrine* (Boston: Little, Brown, 1963), provides the necessary structuring and filling in of these events.

51. See Whitaker's chapter on recognition in his *United States and the Independence of Latin America* and Bemis, *Latin American Policy*, pp. 43–47.

52. These various interpretations are examined in Armin Rappaport, ed., *The Monroe Doctrine*, American Problem Studies (New York: Holt, Rinehart, and Winston, 1964).

53. Whitaker, *United States and the Independence of Latin America*, pp. 179, 334–35.

Chapter 2
United States–Central American
Relations, 1824–1850

1. The best general account of Central America is Ralph Lee Woodward, *Central America: A Nation Divided* (New York: Oxford University Press, 1976). For a discussion of the ideological background of the constitution of 1824, see Virgilio Rodríguez Beteta, *Idologías de la independencia*, 4th ed. (Guatemala: Secretaría de Información, 1965), and Andrés Townsend Ezcurra, *Las Provincias Unidas de Centro-América: Fundación de la república* (San José: Editorial Costa Rica, 1973). Spanish influence on the constitution of 1824 is amply discussed in Mario Rodríguez, *The Cádiz Experiment in Central America, 1808–1826* (Berkeley: University of California Press, 1977).

2. Joseph B. Lockey, "Diplomatic Futility," *Hispanic American Historical Review* 30 (August 1930): 265–94.

3. Mary Wilhelmine Williams, *Anglo-American Isthmian Diplomacy, 1815–1915* (Washington, D.C.: American Historical Association, 1916).

4. Robert S. Smith, "Financing the Central American Federation, 1821–1838," *Hispanic American Historical Review* 43 (November 1963): 483–510; Rodrigo Facio, *Trayectoria y crisis de la federación centroamericana* (San José: Imprenta Nacional, 1949).

5. For a full discussion of British influence, see Robert A. Naylor, "The British Role in Central America prior to the Clayton-Bulwer Treaty of 1850," *Hispanic American Historical Review* 40 (August 1960): 361–82. For the standard

Central American view, see Virgilio Rodríguez Beteta, *La política inglesa en Centro América durante el siglo XIX* (Guatemala: Ministerio de Educación Pública, 1963).

6. A possible exception is George W. Montgomery, *Narrative of a Journey to Guatemala in Central America in 1838* (New York: Wiley and Putnam, 1839).

7. Henry Dunn, *Guatimala, or The Republic of Central America in 1827–1828* (New York: n.p., 1828). For travel literature, see Franklin D. Parker, *Travels in Central America, 1821–1840* (Gainesville: University of Florida Press, 1970).

8. John Quincy Adams, *Memoirs*, vol. 6 (Philadelphia: J. B. Lippincott, 1875), pp. 325–26.

9. A good contemporary comparison of interoceanic routes is Alexandre Holinski, *La Californie et les routes interocéaniques* (Brussels: Meline, Cans, 1853). For scholarly analyses, see John H. Kemble, *The Panama Route, 1848–1869* (Berkeley: University of California Press, 1943), and David L. Folkman, Jr., *La ruta de Nicaragua: El tránsito a través de Nicaragua* (Salt Lake City: University of Utah Press, 1972).

10. Relevant correspondence concerning the Cañas mission is in William Ray Manning, comp., *Diplomatic Correspondence of the United States concerning the Independence of the Latin American Nations*, vol. 2 (New York: Oxford University Press, 1925), pp. 881–83.

11. J. Lloyd Mecham, *A Survey of United States–Latin American Relations* (Boston: Houghton Mifflin, 1965), pp. 87–89.

12. The following discussion of United States diplomats in Central America to 1848 is based on Lockey, "Diplomatic Futility," pp. 265–94.

13. John L. Stephens, *Incidents of Travel in Egypt, Arabia, Petraea, and the Holy Land*, 4th ed. (New York: Harper and Brothers, 1838), and *Incidents of Travel in Greece, Turkey, Russia, and Poland* (New York: Harper and Brothers, 1838).

14. John L. Stephens, *Incidents of Travel in Central America, Chiapas, and Yucatan*, 2 vols. (New York: Harper and Brothers, 1841).

15. Charles L. Stansifer, *Ephraim George Squier: Diversos aspectos de su carrera centroamericana* (Managua: Revista Conservadora del Pensamiento Centroamericana, 1968).

16. Consular dispatches from Central America as well as diplomatic dispatches are available in the United States National Archives, Washington, D.C. Microfilm copies of these were studied by the author in preparation for this article.

17. Louis E. Bumgartner, *José del Valle of Central America* (Durham, N.C.: Duke University Press, 1963), pp. 215–16.

18. William J. Griffith, "Juan Galindo, Central American Chauvinist," *Hispanic American Historical Review* 40 (February 1960): 25–52.

19. Carlos García Bauer, *Antonio José de Irisarri, diplomático de América* (Guatemala: Editorial Universitaria, 1970), pp. 10–11.

20. Naylor, "British Role in Central America," pp. 370–80; Mario Rod-

ríguez, *A Palmerstonian Diplomat in Central America: Frederick Chatfield, Esq.* (Tucson: University of Arizona Press, 1964), pp. 116–17.

21. For an account of British policy on the Bay Islands, see Davis Waddell, "Great Britain and the Bay Islands, 1821–1861," *Historical Journal* 2 (March 1959): 59–77.

22. An excellent general account of British Honduras in its early years is O. Nigel Bolland, *The Formation of a Colonial Society: Belize, from Conquest to Crown Colony* (Baltimore: Johns Hopkins University Press, 1977). Relations between Guatemala and British (and other) entrepreneurs are fully developed in William J. Griffith, *Empires in the Wilderness: Foreign Colonization and Development in Guatemala, 1834–1844* (Chapel Hill: University of North Carolina Press, 1965).

23. Robert A. Naylor, "The Mahogany Trade as a Factor in the British Return to the Mosquito Shore in the Second Quarter of the Nineteenth Century," *Jamaican Historical Review* 7 (1967) (Published Spring 1970): 40–67.

24. José Dolores Gámez, *Historia de la Costa de Mosquitos hasta 1894* (Managua: Talleres Nacionales, 1939), pp. 174–85.

25. Naylor, "British Role in Central America," p. 371.

26. M. Rodríguez, *Palmerstonian Diplomat*, passim.

27. The best exposition of this view is Naylor, "British Role in Central America," pp. 361–82. Mark Van Aken challenges Naylor's interpretation in his "British Policy Considerations in Central America before 1850," *Hispanic American Historical Review* 42 (February 1962): 54–59.

28. Clay to Anderson and Sergeant, May 8, 1826, 30th Cong., 2d sess., H. Rept. 145, p. 331. See also Theodore E. Burton, "Henry Clay," in Samuel Flagg Bemis, ed., *The American Secretaries of State and Their Diplomacy*, vol. 4 (New York: Knopf, 1929), pp. 152–53.

29. Buchanan to Hise, June 3, 1848, William R. Manning, ed., *Diplomatic Correspondence of the United States: Inter-American Affairs, 1831–1860* (Washington, D.C.: Carnegie Endowment for International Peace, 1933), 3:33.

30. Clayton to Squier, May 1, 1849, Manning, *Diplomatic Correspondence . . . Inter-American Affairs* 3:50.

31. Stansifer, *Ephraim George Squier*, pp. 12–14.

32. Ibid., pp. 14–15.

33. Ibid., pp. 17–20.

34. Paynter to Santos Guardiola, December 26, 1849, Manning, *Diplomatic Correspondence . . . Inter-American Affairs* 3:489.

35. Carcache to Clayton, December 31, 1849, and Clayton to Carcache, January 2, 1850, Manning, *Diplomatic Correspondence . . . Inter-American Affairs* 3:497, 57.

36. Hunter Miller, ed., *Treaties and Other International Acts of the United States of America* (Washington, D.C.: U.S. Government Printing Office, 1937), 5:671–72.

37. These negotiations are fully discussed in Dean Kortge, "The Central

American Policy of Lord Palmerston, 1855–1865" (Ph.D. diss., University of Kansas, 1973).

38. Charles L. Stansifer, "The Central American Writings of E. George Squier," *Inter-American Review of Bibliography* 16 (1966): 144–60.

Chapter 3
Steps of Considerable Delicacy:
Early Relations with Peru

1. Larned to Forsyth, November 16, 1835, Lima, William R. Manning, ed., *Diplomatic Correspondence of the United States: Inter-American Affairs, 1831–1860* (Washington, D.C.: Carnegie Endowment for International Peace, 1938), 10:373.

2. Clements R. Markham, *A History of Peru* (1892; reprint, New York: Greenwood Press, 1968), p. 308.

3. Compiled from a Report of the Committee of Foreign Affairs pursuant to H.R. 28, reprinted in Committee on Foreign Relations and the Committee on Armed Services, *Situation in Cuba*, 87th Cong., 2d sess., 1962, pp. 80–87, and reprinted in C. Neale Ronning, ed., *Intervention in Latin America* (New York: Knopf, 1970), p. 27.

4. Robert Erwin Johnson, *Thence Round Cape Horn: The Story of United States Naval Forces on Pacific Station, 1818–1923* (Annapolis: United States Naval Institute, 1963), p. 6.

5. Markham, *History of Peru*, pp. 278–80.

6. Tudor to Adams, December 22, 1824, Lima, Manning, *Correspondence* 3:1775.

7. Johnson, *Thence Round Cape Horn*, p. 3; Edward Baxter Billingsley, *In Defense of Neutral Rights: The United States Navy and the Wars of Independence in Chile and Peru* (Chapel Hill: University of North Carolina Press, 1967), p. 14; Lawrence A. Clayton, "A History of United States Naval Forces Operating in the Pacific off the West Coast of the Americas between the Years 1812–1852" (Master's thesis, Tulane University, 1969), pp. 1–9.

8. Timothy E. Anna, *The Fall of the Royal Government in Peru* (Lincoln: University of Nebraska Press, 1979), pp. 170–74.

9. Johnson, *Thence Round Cape Horn*, pp. 28–29.

10. Ibid.

11. Ibid., p. 34; Billingsley, *In Defense*, p. 193; Clayton, "History of United States Naval Forces," pp. 33–34.

12. Clayton, "History of United States Naval Forces," pp. 33–34.

13. Much of the material on Tudor was gathered from various correspondence appearing in Manning, *Correspondence*, and from the *Dictionary of American Biography*, vol. 19.

14. Billingsley, *In Defense*, p. 184.

15. Tudor to Adams, May 3, 1824, Callao, Manning, *Correspondence* 3:1750–51.

16. Ibid.

17. Jorge Basadre, *Historia de la República del Perú*, 6th ed. (Lima: Editorial Universitaria, 1968), 2:315; Jay Monaghan, *Chile, Peru, and the California Gold Rush of 1849* (Berkeley: University of California Press, 1973), pp. 91–92.

18. Johnson, *Thence Round Cape Horn*, pp. 1–2.

19. Monaghan, *Chile, Peru*, p. 92.

20. Tudor to Adams, September 18, 1824, Lima, Manning, *Correspondence* 3:1766.

21. Ibid.

22. Tudor to Clay, March 21, 1825, Lima, Manning, *Correspondence* 3:1780.

23. Ibid.

24. Markham, *History of Peru*, pp. 281–82.

25. Tudor to Clay, May 17, 1826, Lima, Manning, *Correspondence* 3:1797.

26. Ibid.

27. Ibid.

28. Tudor to Clay, August 24, 1826, Lima, Manning, *Correspondence* 3:1809.

29. Tudor to Clay, April 26, 1826, Lima, Manning, *Correspondence* 3:1790.

30. Ibid.

31. Tudor to Clay, August 1, 1826, Lima, Manning, *Correspondence* 3:1804–5.

32. Tudor to Clay, August 24, 1826, Lima, Manning, *Correspondence* 3:1809–10.

33. Tudor to Clay, May 23, 1827, Lima, Manning, *Correspondence* 3:1830.

34. Tudor to Clay, February 23, 1826, Lima, *Correspondence* 3:1785.

35. Ibid.

36. Tudor to Clay, July 5, 1826, Lima, Manning, *Correspondence* 3:1799–1800.

37. Ibid.

38. Basadre, *Historia* 1:275.

39. Tudor to Clay, February 3, 1827, Lima, Manning, *Correspondence* 3:1820–21.

40. Ibid.

41. Tudor to Clay, November 25, 1826, Lima, Manning, *Correspondence* 3:1813.

42. Ibid.

43. Ibid.

44. Johnson, *Thence Round Cape Horn*, p. 35.

45. Tudor to Adams, October 17, 1824, Lima, Manning, *Correspondence* 3:1770.

46. Tudor to Adams, February 25, 1825, Lima, Manning, *Correspondence* 3:1778.

47. J. B. Prevost to Adams, January 10, 1825, Lima, Manning, *Correspondence* 3:1777–78.

48. Tudor to Adams, January 10, 1825, Lima, Manning, *Correspondence* 3:1777–78.

49. Tudor to Clay, August 1, 1826, Lima, Manning, *Correspondence* 3:1805.

50. Tudor to Adams, February 25, 1825, Lima, Manning, *Correspondence* 3:1778.

51. Tudor to Clay, February 23, 1826, Lima, Manning, *Correspondence* 3:1783.

52. Louis Clinton Nolan, "The Diplomatic and Commercial Relations of the United States and Peru, 1826–1875" (Ph.D. diss., Duke University, 1935), p. 82.

53. Clay to Cooley, November 2, 1826, Washington, Manning, *Correspondence* 1:277.

54. Tudor to Clay, August 24, 1826, Lima, Manning, *Correspondence* 3:1808.

55. Pickett to Calhoun, March 3, 1845, Lima, Manning, *Correspondence* 10:537.

56. Reasons for the war are composed from Basadre, *Historia* 1:295–96, and Arturo García Salazar, *Resúmen de la historia diplomática del Perú* (Lima: J. Rivas Berrio, 1930), pp. 47–70.

57. Tudor to Van Buren, August 1, 1829, Rio de Janeiro, Manning, *Correspondence* 3:1845.

58. Ibid.

59. Tudor to Clay, November 27, 1827, Lima, Manning, *Correspondence* 3:1843; Basadre, *Historia* 1:311, mentions this effort made by the English and the Americans.

60. Clay to Mariategui, December 30, 1828, Washington, Manning, *Correspondence* 1:300–302; Clay to Larned, January 1, 1829, Washington, Manning, *Correspondence* 1:300–302.

61. Basadre, *Historia* 1:339–40.

62. Larned to Van Buren, September 2, 1832, Lima, Manning, *Correspondence* 10:303.

63. Larned to Forsyth, October 24, 1836, Lima, Manning, *Correspondence* 10:428; Harold Eugene Davis, "Relations during the Time of Troubles, 1825–1860," in *Latin American Diplomatic History: An Introduction*, ed. Harold Eugene Davis, John J. Finan, and F. Taylor Peck (Baton Rouge: Louisiana State University Press, 1977), pp. 91–92; García Salazar, *Resúmen*, pp. 93–94.

64. Basadre, *Historia* 2:144.

65. Ibid., p. 146; García Salazar, *Resúmen*, pp. 97–98.

66. Larned to Forsyth, September 3, 1836, Lima, Manning, *Correspondence* 10:418.

67. Larned to Forsyth, August 20, 1836, Lima, Manning, *Correspondence* 10:416.

68. Larned to Forsyth, September 3, 1836, Lima, Manning, *Correspondence* 10:417–18.

69. Larned to Forsyth, October 24, 1836, Lima, Manning, *Correspondence* 10:428.

70. Larned to Forsyth, February 13, 1836, Lima, Manning, *Correspondence* 10:388.

71. Larned to Livingston, September 30, 1832, Lima, Manning, *Correspondence* 10:315–16.

72. Larned to Sierra, May 19, 1836, Lima, Manning, *Correspondence* 3:397.

73. Larned to Forsyth, January 14, 1837, Lima, Manning, *Correspondence* 10:450.

74. On the 1851 treaty, see Nolan, "Diplomatic and Commercial Relations," p. 52.

75. Crallé to Bryan, October 30, 1844, Washington, Manning, *Correspondence* 10:232–33.

76. Ibid.

77. Nolan, "Diplomatic and Commercial Relations," p. 51.

78. Larned to Forsyth, August 13, 1835, Lima, Manning, *Correspondence* 10:353.

79. Ibid.

80. Bartlett to Forsyth, October 4, 1838, Lima, Manning, *Correspondence* 10:471.

81. Bartlett to Forsyth, January 20, 1839, Lima, Manning, *Correspondence* 10:477.

82. Buchanan to Jewett, March 17, 1847, Washington, Manning, *Correspondence* 10:237; see also Basadre, *Historia* 3:132–33.

83. Buchanan to Jewett, June 1, 1846, Washington, Manning, *Correspondence* 10:233.

84. Larned to Forsyth, March 26, 1835, Lima, Manning, *Correspondence* 10:331.

85. Larned to Forsyth, January 20, 1836, Lima, Manning, *Correspondence* 10:384.

86. Larned to Forsyth, September 7, 1835, Lima, Manning, *Correspondence* 10:1835.

87. Pickett to Upshur, July 3, 1844, Lima, Manning, *Correspondence* 10:1844.

88. Ibid.

89. Pickett to Calhoun, December 23, 1844, Lima, Manning, *Correspondence* 10:535.

90. Ibid.

91. Ibid.

92. Bartlett to Forsyth, March 14, 1839, Lima, Manning, *Correspondence* 10:479–80.

93. Pickett to Forsyth, September 16, 1840, Lima, Manning, *Correspondence* 10:508–9.

94. Ibid.

95. Pickett to Webster, April 23, 1842, Lima, Manning, *Correspondence* 10:520.

96. Larned to Forsyth, July 25, 1835, Lima, Manning, *Correspondence* 10:349.

97. Larned to Livingston, January 13, 1832, Lima, Manning, *Correspondence* 10:307–8.

98. Forsyth to Larned, August 26, 1835, Washington, Manning, *Correspondence* 10:225.

99. Ibid.

100. Basadre, *Historia* 3:116.

101. Manning, *Correspondence* 6:vii.

102. Ibid.

103. S. B. Prevost to Buchanan, December 9, 1846, Lima, Manning, *Correspondence* 10:547–49.

104. S. B. Prevost to Buchanan, February 1, 1847, Lima, Manning, *Correspondence* 10:551.

105. Thomas J. Dodd, "Peru" in *Latin American Foreign Policies: An Analysis*, ed. Harold Eugene Davis and Larman C. Wilson (Baltimore: Johns Hopkins University Press, 1975), p. 362.

106. Basadre, *Historia* 3:118.

107. Clay to Buchanan, January 12, 1848, Lima, Manning, *Correspondence* 10:561–62.

108. Manning, *Correspondence* 10:241.

Chapter 4
Impossible Job! Impossible Man! Thomas Sumter, Jr., and Diplomatic Relations between the United States and the Portuguese Court in Brazil, 1809–1821

1. Secretary of State Robert Smith to Sumter, August 1, 1809, Diplomatic and Consular Instructions, All Countries, vol. 7, National Archives. The Department of State General Records cited herein are housed in the National Archives, Washington, D.C., and are available on microfilm: Notes from the Portuguese Legation; Notes to Foreign Legations; Diplomatic Instructions, All Countries; Dispatches from United States Ministers to Brazil; and Instructions to Consuls. Dispatches from United States Consuls in Rio de Janeiro, unavailable on microfilm, was consulted at the National Archives.

2. Robert Livingston to Thomas Jefferson, October 28, 1802, Jefferson Papers, vol. 127, fols. 21900–902, Library of Congress; see also Anne King Gregorie, *Thomas Sumter* (Columbia, S.C.: R. L. Bryan, 1931), p. 248.

3. Sumter to Smith, September 3, 1810, January 11, 1811, and Sumter to Secretary of State James Monroe, September 24, 1812, Dispatches from United States Ministers to Brazil, vol. 1.

4. Monroe to Sumter, June 10, 1816, Diplomatic Instructions, All Countries, vol. 8.

5. Secretary of State John Quincy Adams to John Graham, April 24, 1819, Diplomatic Instructions, All Countries.

6. Antonia Fernanda Pacca de Almeida Wright, *Desafio Americano à preponderância Britânica no Brasil, 1808–1850* (Rio de Janeiro: Departamento de Imprensa Nacional, 1972), chap. 5. See also Alan K. Manchester, *British Preeminence in Brazil* (n.p.: Hippocrene Books, 1964).

7. William Spence Robertson, *France and Latin American Independence* (Baltimore: Johns Hopkins University Press, 1939), p. 22; see also Sumter to Monroe, October 1, 1812, Dispatches from United States Ministers to Brazil, vol. 1.

8. Great Britain, Foreign Office, *British and Foreign State Papers* (London: James Ridgway and Sons, 1841), 1:543–57.

9. Sumter to Monroe, October 1, 1812, Dispatches from United States Ministers to Brazil, vol. 1. These note an intercepted letter from Lord Strangford to Lord Castlereagh, September 30, 1812.

10. Sumter to the Conde de Linhares, January 3, 1812, Sumter to the Conde de Galves, May 17 and 13, 1813, the Conde de Galves to Sumter, May 22, 1813, all in Brazil, Ministerio das Relações Exteriores, Arquivo Histórico do Itamaratí (hereafter cited as MRE/AHdI), Coleções Especiais (3), Casos com Estrangeiros, Estados Unidos—1812–13, Group 10, Lot 186, Bundle 1. See also Sumter to Monroe, May 9 and February 22, 1813, Dispatches from United States Ministers to Brazil, vol. 1.

11. Sumter to the Conde de Aguiar, January 15, 1813, Dispatches from United States Ministers to Brazil, vol. 1.

12. James Barnes, *Naval Actions of the War of 1812* (New York: Harper and Brothers, 1896), pp. 239–40.

13. Ibid., p. 113. See also Albert Gleaves, *James Gleaves, Commander of the "Chesapeake"* (New York: G. P. Putnam's Sons, 1904), pp. 115–16, and H. A. S. Dearborn, *The Life of William Bainbridge, Esq., of the United States Navy*, ed. James Barnes (Princeton, N.J.: Princeton University Press, 1931), p. 98.

14. Joseph Rademaker to Monroe, March 27, 1813, Notes from the Portuguese Legation, vol. 1.

15. Sumter to Monroe, February 22, 1813, Dispatches from United States Ministers to Brazil, vol. 1.

16. Rademaker to Monroe, March 27, 1813, Notes from the Portuguese Legation, vol. 1.

17. See Lawrence Hill, *Diplomatic Relations between the United States and Brazil* (Durham, N.C.: Duke University Press, 1932), pp. 16–19; John F. Cady, *Foreign Intervention in the Rio de la Plata, 1838–1850* (Philadelphia: University of

Pennsylvania Press, 1929), pp. 2–9; William R. Manning, "An Early Diplomatic Controversy between the United States and Brazil," *Hispanic American Historical Review* 1 (May 1918): 126–28; and John Street, "Lord Strangford and the Río de la Plata, 1808–1815," *Hispanic American Historical Review* 33 (November 1953): 477–510.

18. Antonio Correa da Serra to Adams, March 8, October 15, and December 11, 1818, and March 17 and December 23, 1819, Notes from the Portuguese Legation, vol. 1.

19. Hill, *Diplomatic Relations*, p. 17; Monroe to Correa da Serra, December 27, 1816, March 14 and October 23, 1817, and April 22, 1819, Notes to Foreign Legations, vol. 2.

20. Hill, *Diplomatic Relations*, p. 25.

21. Instructions of the Provisional Government of Pernambuco to Antonio Gonçalves da Cruz, March 27, 1817, and Gonçalves da Cruz to the Provisional Government of Pernambuco, no date, both in MRE/AHdI, 3 Coleções Especias (30), Documentação Anterior a 1822, Capitania de Pernambuco (Revolução de Pernambuco), Group 5, Lot 195, Bundle 5; see also Correa da Serra to Richard Rush and Adams, May 13, 1817, and October 13, 1818, Notes from the Portuguese Legation, vol. 1; Rush to Correa da Serra, May 22, 24, and 28, 1817, Notes to Foreign Legations, vol. 2; Rush to Sumter, July 18, 1817, and August 27, 1818, Diplomatic Instructions, All Countries, vol. 8; see also the excellent study of Mary Ellis Kahler, "Relations between Brazil and the United States, 1815–1825, with Special Reference to the Revolutions of 1817 and 1824" (Ph.D. diss., American University, 1968). It is interesting to note that Ray also participated in the revolution of 1824 and for this offense was banished from Brazil. But he was permitted to return to Pernambuco in 1837 as consul.

22. *Memoirs of John Quincy Adams, Comprising Portions of His Diary from 1795 to 1848*, ed. Charles Francis Adams (Philadelphia: J. B. Lippincott, 1874–77), 4:340.

23. Accounts of this incident may be found in Sumter to Monroe, September 29, 1815, Dispatches from United States Ministers to Brazil, vol. 1; see also Hill, *Diplomatic Relations*, pp. 7–8.

24. Sumter to Henry Hill, November 4, 1818, Dispatches from United States Consuls in Rio de Janeiro, pt. 1, vol. 1.

25. Adams to Graham, April 24, 1819, Diplomatic Instructions, All Countries, vol. 8.

26. Sumter to Hill, November 4, 1818, Dispatches from United States Consuls in Rio de Janeiro, pt. 1, vol. 1.

27. *Memoirs of John Quincy Adams* 4:339; see also Joseph Agan, *The Diplomatic Relations of the United States and Brazil* (Paris: Jouve et Cie, 1926), p. 119.

28. Agan, *Diplomatic Relations*, pp. 120–22.

Chapter 5
Initiating United States
Relations with Argentina

1. Forbes to Adams, January 24, 1824, Dispatches from U.S. Ministers to Argentina, 1817–1906, vol. 2 (Microcopy M-69), Department of State General Records, National Archives, Washington, D.C. Cited hereafter as Dispatches.

2. Harold F. Peterson, *Argentina and the United States, 1810–1960* (Albany: State University of New York, 1964), p. 81; Juan Estevan Guastavino, *San Martín y Simón Bolívar: Glorifobia y cochranismo póstumos* (Buenos Aires: J. L. Dasso, 1913), pp. 429–37. The government of Buenos Aires was responsible for the conduct of the foreign policy of the United Provinces of the Río de la Plata.

3. Peterson, *Argentina and the United States*, p. 82.

4. Rodney to President Monroe, February 10, 1824, *The Writings of James Monroe, including a Collection of His Public and Private Papers and Correspondence Now for the First Time Printed*, ed. Stanislaus Murray Hamilton, (New York: G. P. Putnam's Sons, 1898–1903), 6:430.

5. Norberto Piñero, *La política internacional argentina* (Buenos Aires: J. Ménendez y Hijo, 1924), p. 69.

6. William S. Robertson, "South America and the Monroe Doctrine," *Political Science Quarterly* 30 (March 1915): 98.

7. Ibid., p. 99.

8. Tomás de Iriarte, *Memorias: Estudio preliminar de Enrique de Gandia* (Buenos Aires: Ediciones Argentinas, "S.I.A.," 1946), 3:142–43.

9. Thomas Brabson Davis, *Carlos de Alvear, Man of Revolution* (Durham, N.C.: Duke University Press, 1955), p. 36.

10. Alvear to Rivadavia, October 18, 1824, in ibid., p. 169 n. 25.

11. Alvear to Rivadavia, October 12, 1824, Gregorio F. Rodríguez, *Contribución histórica y documental* (Buenos Aires: Casa Jacobo Peuser, 1921–22), 2:59–60.

12. Quoted in Joseph Byrne Lockey, *Pan-Americanism: Its Beginnings* (New York: Macmillan, 1920), p. 255 and n. 61.

13. Dexter Perkins, *The Monroe Doctrine, 1823–1826* (Cambridge: Harvard University Press, 1927), pp. 150–54, 159.

14. Forbes to Monroe, March 22, 1824, Arthur P. Whitaker, *The United States and the Independence of Latin America, 1800–1830* (New York: Russell and Russell, 1962), p. 537. See also Rodney to Adams, May 22, 1824, Dispatches 2.

15. Forbes to Adams, August 13, 1824, Dispatches 2. Forbes frequently complained of the strong British presence; see, for example, Forbes to Adams, December 4, 1820, Dispatches 1, pt. 2, and Forbes to Adams, April 1, 1821, Dispatches 1, pt. 2.

16. Forbes to Adams, November 11, 1824, Dispatches 2.

17. Ibid. See also E. J. Pratt, "Anglo-American Commercial and Political Rivalry on the Plata, 1820–1830," *Hispanic American Historical Review* 11 (August 1931): 316–17, and, for later in the century, Joseph Smith, *Illusions of Conflict: Anglo-American Diplomacy toward Latin America, 1865–1896* (Pittsburgh: University of Pittsburgh Press, 1979), pt. 1.

18. For the original Spanish version see *Mensage del gobierno a la cuarta legislatura*, enclosed with Forbes to Adams, March 31, 1824, Dispatches 2.

19. Piñero, *Política internacional*, p. 69; Isidoro Ruiz Moreno, *Historia de las relaciones exteriores argentinas, 1810–1955* (Buenos Aires: Editorial Perrot, 1961), pp. 300–301.

20. Davis, *Carlos de Alvear*, p. 48; Ruiz Moreno, *Historia*, p. 301.

21. De la Cruz to Forbes, August 24, 1826, enclosed in Forbes to Secretary of State Henry Clay, September 5, 1826, Dispatches 3.

22. Minutes of a conference between Forbes and Rivadavia, August 17, 1826, Dispatches 3.

23. Clay to Forbes, January 3, 1828, in William R. Manning, ed., *Diplomatic Correspondence of the United States concerning the Independence of Latin American Nations* (New York: Oxford University Press, 1925), 1:292–93. See also U.S. Congress, *Register of Debates in Congress*, 19th Cong., 1st sess., vol. 2, pt. 2, col. 2269, for Daniel Webster's comments, and Peterson, *Argentina and the United States*, p. 83.

24. Clay to Forbes, January 3, 1828, Manning, *Diplomatic Correspondence* 1:292.

25. Watt Stewart, "Argentina and the Monroe Doctrine, 1824–1828," *Hispanic American Historical Review* 10 (February 1930): 32; Ruiz Moreno, *Historia*, p. 301. For the South American and British perspectives, see Ron L. Seckinger, "South American Power Politics during the 1820s," *Hispanic American Historical Review* 56 (May 1976): 241–67.

26. For a detailed presentation of the issues, see Julius Goebel, Jr., *The Struggle for the Falkland Islands: A Study in Legal and Diplomatic History* (New Haven: Yale University Press, 1927); Paul Groussac, *Les Iles Malouines: Nouvel Exposé d'un vieux litige . . .* , Biblioteca Nacional, Yearbook 6 (Buenos Aires: Biblioteca Nacional, 1910); José Luís Muñoz Azpiri, *Historia completa de las Malvinas*, 3 vols. (Buenos Aires: Oriente, 1966).

27. Paul D. Dickens, "The Falkland Islands Dispute between the United States and Argentina," *Hispanic American Historical Review* 9 (August 1929): 472.

28. Dexter Perkins, *The Monroe Doctrine, 1826–1867* (Baltimore: Johns Hopkins University Press, 1933), p. 7.

29. Van Buren to Forbes, February 10, 1831, Dispatches 4.

30. Dickens, "Falkland Islands Dispute," p. 474.

31. Goebel, *Struggle for the Falkland Islands*, p. 439.

32. Slacum to Secretary of State Edward Livingston, dispatches from August 1831 to March 1832, Dispatches 4.

33. Anchorena to Slacum, December 3, 9, 1831, Dispatches 4.

34. Goebel, *Struggle for the Falkland Islands*, p. 441; Dickens, "Falkland Islands Dispute," p. 476; William B. Hatcher, *Edward Livingston: Jeffersonian Republican and Jacksonian Democrat* (Baton Rouge: Louisiana State University Press, 1940), p. 409.

35. Henry Stanley Ferns, *Britain and Argentina in the Nineteenth Century* (Oxford: Oxford University Press, 1960), p. 229.

36. Goebel, *Struggle for the Falkland Islands*, p. 445.

37. Gordon Ireland, *Boundaries, Possessions, and Conflicts in South America* (Cambridge: Harvard University Press, 1938), pp. 257–58.

38. Baylies to Livingston, May 18, 1832, Dispatches 4.

39. *Memoirs of John Quincy Adams, Comprising Portions of His Diary from 1795 to 1848*, ed. Charles Francis Adams (Philadelphia: J. B. Lippincott, 1874–77), 9:447.

40. Dexter Perkins, *John Quincy Adams*, vol. 4 of *The American Secretaries of State and Their Diplomacy*, ed. Samuel Flagg Bemis (New York: Cooper Square Publishers, 1928–80), p. 253.

41. Ferns, *Britain and Argentina*, p. 229; Great Britain, Foreign Office, *British and Foreign State Papers*, 20:364; Goebel, *Struggle for the Falkland Islands*, p. 452.

42. *Memoirs of John Quincy Adams* 9:446.

43. U.S. Congress, Senate, Executive Documents, 32d Cong., 1st sess., 1851–52, vol. 10, document 109, pt. 2, pp. 9–14.

44. Ibid., p. 15.

45. *Memoirs of John Quincy Adams* 9:447.

46. John F. Cady, *Foreign Intervention in the Río de la Plata* (Philadelphia: University of Pennsylvania Press, 1929), p. 20; Perkins, *Monroe Doctrine, 1826–1867*, p. 7.

47. Peterson, *Argentina and the United States*, p. 113.

48. Perkins, *Monroe Doctrine, 1826–1867*, p. 8; Goebel, *Struggle for the Falkland Islands*, p. 460.

49. John Arthur Logan, *No Transfer: An American Security Principle* (New Haven: Yale University Press, 1961), p. 207.

50. U.S. Congress, Senate, Executive Document 109, p. 15. See also Albert Bushnell Hart, *The Monroe Doctrine: An Interpretation* (Boston: Little, Brown, 1916), p. 105.

51. Robert Greenhow, "The Falkland Islands: A Memoir, Descriptive, Historical, and Political," *Merchant's Magazine and Commercial Review* 6 (February 1842): 143.

52. Ibid., pp. 149–50.

53. Perkins, *Monroe Doctrine, 1826–1867*, pp. 8–9.

54. *Times* (London), June 1, 1833, p. 3.

55. Cited in Peterson, *Argentina and the United States*, p. 115.

56. John Lynch, *Argentine Dictator: Juan Manuel de Rosas, 1829–1852* (Ox-

ford: Clarendon Press, 1981), p. 267; James R. Scobie, *Argentina: A City and a Nation* (New York: Oxford University Press, 1971), pp. 101–2.

57. Cady, *Foreign Intervention*, p. 57; Davis, *Carlos de Alvear*, pp. 127–28; Peterson, *Argentina and the United States*, pp. 115–16.

58. Quoted in Davis, *Carlos de Alvear*, p. 127.

59. U.S. Congress, Senate, 25th Cong., 3d sess., February 11, 1839, *Congressional Globe* 7:187.

60. Perkins, *Monroe Doctrine, 1826–1867*, pp. 55–56; Lynch, *Argentine Dictator*, pp. 267, 269–70; Andrés M. Carretero, ed., *El pensamiento político de Juan M. de Rosas* (Buenos Aires: Editorial Platero, 1970), pp. 117–19.

61. Cited in Goebel, *Struggle for the Falkland Islands*, pp. 461–62.

62. Perkins, *Monroe Doctrine, 1826–1867*, p. 83; Lynch, *Argentine Dictator*, pp. 269–94.

63. *Nile's Register* 68 (June 7, 1845), cited in Perkins, *Monroe Doctrine, 1826–1867*, p. 83.

64. "The South American Republics and the Monroe Doctrine," *National Quarterly Review* 13 (June 1866): 135–37.

65. José Luís Muñoz Azpiri, *Rosas frente al imperio inglés: Historia íntima de un triunfo argentino* (Buenos Aires: Ediciones Theoría, 1960), p. 36.

66. William Brent to William G. Ousely, September 23, 1845, William R. Manning, ed., *Diplomatic Correspondence of the United States: Inter-American Affairs, 1831–1860* (Washington, D.C.: Carnegie Endowment for International Peace, 1932–39), 1:293–94.

67. Harris to Secretary of State James Buchanan, July 14, 1846, Dispatches 6.

68. Buchanan to Harris, March 30, 1846, in Manning, *Diplomatic Correspondence: Inter-American Affairs* 1:31.

69. Harris to Buchanan, July 14, 1846, Dispatches 6.

70. Ibid. For Brent's fears about the British, see his notes to Buchanan, November 14, 1845, and February 2, 1846, Manning, *Diplomatic Correspondence: Inter-American Affairs* 1:312, 323–25.

71. Lynch, *Argentine Dictator*, p. 292.

72. Harris to Webster, September 20, 1850, Manning, *Diplomatic Correspondence: Inter-American Affairs* 1:502.

73. Harris to Buchanan, September 15, 1846, Dispatches 6.

74. Harris to Buchanan, June 16, 1847; see also Harris to Secretary of State John M. Clayton, October 10, 1849, Dispatches 6.

75. Quoted in Davis, *Carlos de Alvear*, p. 133.

76. Ibid.

77. Ibid., p. 161.

78. W. W. Pierson, "Alberdi's Views on Europe and the United States," *Hispanic American Historical Review* 3 (August 1920): 371–72.

79. Ibid., p. 370.

80. C. K. Webster, ed., *Britain and the Independence of Latin America,*

1812–1830: Select Documents from the Foreign Office Archives (Oxford: Oxford University Press, 1938), 1:40–41.

81. Baylies to Livingston, May 18, 1832, Dispatches 4.

Chapter 6
The United States and Mexico, 1810–1850

1. Private interests played important roles in other nations of Latin America, including Nicaragua, in the age of William Walker. Mexico was unique, however, in being subjected to mass movements by Anglo-Americans within her national territory.

2. Verner W. Crane, *The Southern Frontier, 1670–1732* (Durham, N.C.: Duke University Press, 1928); Herbert Bolton and Mary Ross, *The Debatable Land* (Berkeley: University of California Press, 1925); John Francis Bannon, ed., *Bolton and the Spanish Borderlands* (Norman: University of Oklahoma Press, 1964); John Tate Lanning, *The Spanish Missions of Georgia* (Chapel Hill: University of North Carolina Press, 1935); Woodbury Lowery, *The Spanish Settlements within the Present Limits of the United States, 1513–1561*, 2 vols. (1901; reprint, New York: Russell and Russell, 1959).

3. John Francis Bannon, *History of the Americas*, 2d ed. (New York: McGraw-Hill, 1963), 1:427–44; Jack D. L. Holmes, ed., *Documentos ineditos para la historia de la Luisiana, 1792–1810* (Madrid: Colección Chimalistac, 1963), vol. 15. For an extensive bibliography of works and documents on the Louisiana frontier, see Jack D. L. Holmes, *A Guide to Spanish Louisiana, 1762–1806* (New Orleans: A. F. Laborde, 1970).

4. Charles C. Griffin, "The Enlightenment and Latin American Independence," in *The Origins of the Latin American Revolutions, 1808–1826*, ed. R. A. Humphreys and John Lynch (New York: Knopf, 1965), pp. 38–51; Sir Charles Kingsley Webster, "British, French, and American Influences," in ibid., p. 76.

5. Ray Allen Billington, *Westward Expansion: A History of the American Frontier*, 2d ed. (New York: Macmillan, 1960), pp. 221–68, 323, 466–82; Bannon, *History of the Americas* 1:427–44; James Morton Callahan, *American Foreign Policy in Mexican Relations* (New York: Macmillan, 1932), p. 1.

6. Justo Sierra [Méndez], *The Political Evolution of the Mexican People*, trans. Charles Ramsdell (Austin: University of Texas Press, 1969), pp. 137–38; Justo Sierra blames most of the problems after the beginning of the reign of Charles IV on self-seeking officials in New Spain. See also Holmes, *Documentos ineditos*, vol. 15; Jack D. L. Holmes, *Gayoso: The Life of a Spanish Governor in the Mississippi Valley, 1789–1799* (Baton Rouge, 1965). It might be noted that Miró expressed the hope that General James Wilkinson might assist Spain by convincing the Anglo-Americans of the west to throw themselves into Spanish arms. In 1795, however, the Treaty of San Lorenzo fixed the thirty-first parallel

as the northern boundary of Spanish Florida, and the Anglo-American frontiersmen were granted the right to navigate the Mississippi and store their wares in New Orleans.

7. Arthur P. Whitaker, *The United States and the Independence of Latin America, 1800–1830* (New York: Russell and Russell, 1962). Although the measure was revoked in 1799, it was an important step in the establishment of United States contacts in Latin America: see Eduardo Arcila Farías, "Commercial Reform in New Spain," in *The Origins of the Latin American Revolutions, 1808–1826*, ed. R. A. Humphreys and John Lynch (New York: Knopf, 1965), pp. 151–68.

8. Bannon, *History of the Americas* 1:88, 427–44.

9. Callahan, *American Foreign Policy*, pp. 1–5; Vito Alessio Robles, *Coahuila y Texas en la época colonial* (Mexico City: Editorial Cultura, 1938), p. 617; Whitaker, *United States and the Independence of Latin America*; Charles Carroll Griffin, *The United States and the Disruption of the Spanish Empire, 1810–1822: A Study of the Relations of the United States with Spain and with the Rebel Spanish Colonies* (New York: Columbia University Press, 1937); Roy F. Nichols, "Trade Relations and the Establishment of the United States Consulates in Spanish America, 1779–1809," *Hispanic American Historical Review* 13 (August 1933): 289–313; Max L. Moorhead, *New Mexico's Royal Road: Trade and Travel on the Chihuahua Trail* (Norman: University of Oklahoma Press, 1958), pp. 55–60; Hubert Howe Bancroft, *History of Mexico* (San Francisco: History Company, 1886–88), 4:32–33.

10. *Denuncia de mercancías de contrabando expendidas en la feria del Saltillo* (1808), quoted in Alessio Robles, *Coahuila y Texas . . . colonial*, p. 623.

11. Bancroft, *History of Mexico* 4:33; Alessio Robles, *Coahuila y Texas . . . colonial*, pp. 617–53; report by Governor Salcedo, August 8, 1810, quoted in Mattie Austin Hatcher, *The Opening of Texas to Foreign Settlement, 1801–1821* (Austin: University of Texas Press, 1927), pp. 147–81; Santiago Roel, *Nuevo León: Apuntes históricos* (Monterrey: n.p., 1952), pp. 57–58; Justo Sierra, *Political Evolution*, pp. 144–46.

12. Harold A. Bierck, "Origins of Interamerican Trade to 1815," *Annals of the Southeastern Conference on Latin American Studies* 1 (March 1970): 5–15; Whitaker, *United States and the Independence of Latin America*; Farías, "Commercial Reform in New Spain," pp. 151–68; Nichols, "Trade Relations."

13. Bancroft, *History of Mexico* 4:19; writing in the 1880s, Bancroft saw the movement for independence in the United States as one of the "precedents of the successful uprising of peoples against the oppression of rulers." See also Webster, "British, French, and American Influences," p. 76, and Timothy E. Anna, *The Fall of the Royal Government in Mexico City* (Lincoln: University of Nebraska Press, 1978), pp. ix–xix; Anna plays down the U.S. and French ideals as a force in the Mexican movement for independence. For a more complete treatment of the events during this time, see Hugh M. Hamill, Jr., *The*

Hidalgo Revolt: Prelude to Mexican Independence (Gainesville: University of Florida Press, 1966).

14. Report by Governor Manuel Salcedo, August 8, 1810, quoted in Hatcher, *Opening of Texas*, pp. 147–81.

15. Bancroft, *History of Mexico* 4:237–41; Carlos E. Castañeda, *Our Catholic Heritage in Texas: 1519–1936* (New York: Arno Press, 1950), 6:1–15; Alessio Robles, *Coahuila y Texas . . . colonial*, pp. 627–35. The provisional government in San Antonio under Juan Bautista Casas was linked to Hidalgo.

16. Alessio Robles, *Coahuila y Texas . . . colonial*, pp. 635–52. Hidalgo resigned as head of the movement, and leadership passed to Allende with great celebration in Saltillo (Castañeda, *Our Catholic Heritage* 6:12–42). Hidalgo had appointed Pascasio Ortíz de Letona as envoy plenipotentiary to the United States to seek aid and treaties of alliance and commerce at the end of 1810, but Ortíz was apprehended before he left Mexico, and he poisoned himself rather than face execution (William H. Timmons, *Morelos: Priest Soldier Statesman of Mexico* [El Paso: Texas Western Press, 1963]).

17. Timmons, *Morelos*, pp. 44–55, 140–41, 153–60. Timmons discusses a number of U.S. citizens who served Morelos in his movement.

18. Ibid., p. 143; Bancroft, *History of Mexico* 4:540–44; Castañeda, *Our Catholic Heritage* 6:43–78; Callahan, *American Foreign Policy*, pp. 7–8; Harris Gaylord Warren, *The Sword Was Their Passport: A History of American Filibustering in the Mexican Revolution* (Baton Rouge: Louisiana State University Press, 1943), pp. 29–32; Alessio Robles, *Coahuila y Texas . . . colonial*, p. 655; Shaler to Secretary of State James Monroe, May 7 and 22, 1812, quoted in Castañeda, *Our Catholic Heritage* 6:69.

19. Castañeda, *Our Catholic Heritage* 6:53–120; Callahan, *American Foreign Policy*, pp. 8–9; Alessio Robles, *Coahuila y Texas . . . colonial*, pp. 567–659; Warren, *The Sword*, p. 35; Bancroft, *History of Mexico* 6:542–43. Each of these authors gives a different estimate of the size of the force involved in these movements. Alessio Robles praises Gutiérrez for his refusal to become a "dócil instrumento del incipiente imperialismo norteamericano" (p. 567); John H. Robinson to Secretary of State James Monroe, July 26, 1813, cited in Castañeda, *Our Catholic Heritage* 6:92.

20. Frederick B. Artz, *Reaction and Revolution, 1814–1832* (New York: Harper and Brothers, 1934), pp. 1–22, 110–48; Anna, *Fall of the Royal Government*, pp. 183–200.

21. Callahan, *American Foreign Policy*, pp. 1–29; Castañeda, *Our Catholic Heritage* 6:148–49, 160–71; Vito Alessio Robles, *Coahuila y Texas desde la consumación de la independencia hasta el tratado de paz de Guadalupe Hidalgo* (Mexico City: n.p., 1945–46), 1:61 (cites report of the governor of Texas, Antonio Martínez), 67–75; Alessio Robles, *Coahuila y Texas . . . colonial*, pp. 664–65; Arredondo, *Proclama, Monterrey*, March 13, 1821, quoted in Alessio Robles, *Coahuila y Texas* 1:69; Hatcher, *Opening of Texas*. Note: Where Alessio Robles, *Coahuila y Texas*, is cited, it refers to the two-volume work on the period after independence.

22. Castañeda, *Our Catholic Heritage* 6:136–40.

23. Ibid., pp. 140–47; Warren, *The Sword*, 148–49; Justo Sierra, *Political Evolution*, pp. 165–66. Justo Sierra had great praise for Mina's high motives but criticized him for collaborating with forces from the United States.

24. Billington, *Westward Expansion*, pp. 310–421, 483–508.

25. Alessio Robles, *Coahuila y Texas . . . colonial*, pp. 662–63. Alessio Robles, *Coahuila y Texas* 1:61; Callahan, *American Foreign Policy*, pp. 9–19; Castañeda, *Our Catholic Heritage*, 6:160–71.

26. Hatcher, *Opening of Texas*, pp. 278–86; Alessio Robles, *Coahuila y Texas* 1:61. Alessio Robles cites a report of Governor Martínez.

27. Alessio Robles, *Coahuila y Texas . . . colonial*, p. 663; Castañeda, *Our Catholic Heritage* 6:171.

28. Artz, *Reaction and Revolution*, pp. 63–81, 89–96, 110–48; Oakah L. Jones, Jr., *Santa Anna* (New York: Twayne, 1968), pp. 27–31; Justo Sierra, *Political Evolution*, pp. 167–71; Agustín de Iturbide, *Memorias de Agustín de Iturbide*, ed. Carlos Navarro y Rodrígo (Madrid: Biblioteca Ayacucho, 1919), pp. 1–207; Romeo Flores Caballero, *Counterrevolution: The Role of the Spaniards in the Independence of Mexico, 1804–1838*, trans. Jaime E. Rodríguez O. (Lincoln: University of Nebraska Press, 1974), pp. 62–66 (original Spanish edition published by El Colegio de México in 1969).

29. Wilcocks to Adams, October 25, 1821, William R. Manning, ed., *Diplomatic Correspondence of the United States: Inter-American Affairs, 1831–1860* (Washington, D.C.: Carnegie Endowment for International Peace, 1932) (hereafter cited as Manning, *Dip. Corr.*). Wilcocks brought with him a message from Foreign Minister José Manuel Herrera, expressing hopes for closer relations (Herrera to Adams, November 20, 1821, and September 24, 1822, Manning, *Dip. Corr.* See also William Spence Robertson, *Iturbide of Mexico* (Durham, N.C.: Duke University Press, 1952), pp. 159–60, 191–212. At the same time, James Wilkinson, who was also in Mexico, praised Iturbide in his correspondence to Monroe. After going into exile, Iturbide remained interested in the possibility of a tie with the United States as well as with Great Britain.

30. Bancroft, *History of Mexico* 4:734–88; Robertson, *Iturbide*, pp. 191–212; Flores Caballero, *Counterrevolution;* J. Fred Rippy, *Joel R. Poinsett, Versatile American* (Durham, N.C.: Duke University Press, 1935), pp. 90–106. Poinsett's view was shared by General Andrew Jackson, who had turned down the opportunity to be ambassador to Mexico. See also Alessio Robles, *Coahuila y Texas* 1:135–38; Iturbide, *Memorias*, pp. 211–357. Iturbide says that he accepted the crown to avoid chaos in his nation.

31. Callahan, *American Foreign Policy*, pp. 22–23; Alessio Robles, *Coahuila y Texas* 1:134–35; Stratford Canning (British minister to the United States) to Bagot, March 30, 1823, quoted in Manning, *Early Diplomatic Relations between the United States and Mexico* (1916; reprint, New York: Greenwood, 1968), p. 15; statement by "Secretaría de Relaciones Exteriores," quoted in Alessio Robles,

Coahuila y Texas 1:138 ("sin duda, otro objeto que el de miras ambiciosas sobre la Provincia de Texas").

32. Hubert Howe Bancroft, *History of Arizona and New Mexico, 1530–1888* (San Francisco: History Company, 1889; a facsimile of the 1889 edition, Albuquerque: Horn and Wallace, 1962), pp. 283–309.

33. Callahan, *American Foreign Policy*, pp. 22–23; Eligio Ancona, *Historia de Yucatán desda la época más remota hasta nuestros días* (Mérida: Imprenta de M. Heredia Argüelles, 1878) 3:178–208; Robertson, *Iturbide*; Lorenzo de Zavala, *Ensayo crítico de las revoluciones de México desde 1808 hasta 1830* (1831; reprint, Mexico: Editorial Porrúa, 1969), pp. 84–96.

34. Alessio Robles, *Coahuila y Texas . . . colonial*, pp. 664–65; Alessio Robles, *Coahuila y Texas* 1:62–78, 101–16; Hatcher, *Opening of Texas*; Carlos Pereyra, "La situación desfavorable de la población mexicana," in *Obras de Lorenzo de Zavala*, ed. Manuel González Ramírez (Mexico: Editorial Porrúa, 1976), p. 608; Moorhead, *New Mexico's Royal Road*, pp. 60–65; Flores Caballero, *Counterrevolution*, pp. 62–66; Bancroft, *History of Mexico* 4:734–88; Jones, *Santa Anna*, pp. 27–39.

35. Alessio Robles, *Coahuila y Texas* 1:98–100, 117–42; Bancroft, *History of Mexico* 5:1–19; Flores Caballero, *Counterrevolution*; Nettie Lee Benson, "Introduction," to Miguel Ramos de Arizpe, *Report to the August Congress on the Natural, Political, and Civic Conditions of the Provinces of Coahuila, Nuevo León, Nuevo Santander, and Texas of the Four Eastern Interior Provinces of the Kingdom of Mexico*, translated by Nettie Lee Benson (Austin: University of Texas Press, 1950), pp. vii–xiii; Nettie Lee Benson, *La diputación provincial y el federalismo mexicano* (Mexico: El Colegio de México, 1955); Ancona, *Historia de Yucatán* 2:513–23.

36. Lorenzo de Zavala, *Ensayo crítico*, pp. 187–89; Manning, *Early Diplomatic Relations*, pp. 24–29. Colonel José Anastasio Torrens, secretary of the Mexican legation who had been left in charge of affairs after the departure of Zozaya in 1823, maintained contact with Secretary of State Adams in late 1823 but received no pay from Mexico and could not even pay his board; Lucas Alaman, on November 8, 1823, pointed out that internal problems limited relations with all foreign powers but expressed positive feelings toward the United States (Manning, *Early Diplomatic Relations*, pp. 15–19, 23).

37. Artz, *Reaction and Revolution*, p. 171; "El General Victoria, al cerrarse las sesiones del congreso, en 21 de Mayo de 1825," *Un siglo de relaciones internacionales de México (A través de los mensajes presidenciales)*, Archivo Histórico Diplomatico Mexicano, vol. 39 (Mexico City: Publicaciones de la secretaría de relaciones exteriores, 1935), pp. 4–5; "El General Victoria, al abrirse las sesiones ordinarias del congreso general, en 1 de enero de 1826," (Ibid., pp. 5–9). Other documents (Ibid., pp. 10–26) further illustrate the preference given to England over the United States. See also Robert W. Randall, *Real del Monte: A British Mining Venture in Mexico* (Austin, Tex.: Institute of Latin American Studies, 1972).

38. José Fuentes Mares, *Poinsett: Historia de una gran intriga* (Mexico City, 1958); Alessio Robles, *Coahuila y Texas* 1:139–42; William R. Manning, *Texas and the Boundary Issue, 1822–1829*, (Austin, Texas: Reprinted from *Southwestern Historical Quarterly*, January 1914), pp. 231–54.

39. Manning, *Texas and the Boundary Issue*, pp. 231–54; Manning, *Early Diplomatic Relations*, pp. 23–178 (many reports of Obregón are included in these pages); Callahan, *American Foreign Policy*, pp. 19–53; Bancroft, *History of Arizona and New Mexico*, pp. 329–43 (especially table on p. 332 showing trade growth between 1822 and 1843).

40. Flores Caballero, *Counterrevolution*, pp. 81–111; Manning, *Early Diplomatic Relations*, especially Poinsett to Clay, May 10, 1827, p. 232.

41. Zavala, *Ensayo crítico*, pp. 233–39; Gene M. Brack, *Mexico Views Manifest Destiny, 1821–1846: An Essay on the Origins of the Mexican War* (Albuquerque: University of New Mexico Press, 1975), pp. 15–18; David M. Pletcher, *The Diplomacy of Annexation: Texas, Oregon, and the Mexican War* (Columbia: University of Missouri Press, 1973), pp. 31–63; Fuentes Mares, *Poinsett;* Curt Lamar, "Genesis of Mexican–United States Diplomacy: A Critical Analysis of the Alaman-Poinsett Confrontation, 1825," *Americas* 38, no. 1 (July 1981): 87–110.

42. Arthur M. Schlesinger, Jr., *The Age of Jackson* (Boston: Little, Brown, 1945).

43. Bancroft, *History of Mexico* 5:33–40; Zavala, *Ensayo crítico*, pp. 221, 383–415, 508–23.

44. Justo Sierra, *Political Evolution*, pp. 194–202; Jones, *Santa Anna*, pp. 40–59; Francisco de Paula de Arrongoiz, *México desde 1808 hasta 1867*, 2d ed. (Mexico City: Editorial Porrúa, 1968), pp. 346–71; Mariano Cuevas, *Historia de la nación mexicana*, 3d ed. (Mexico City: Editorial Porrúa, 1965), pp. 557–92.

45. Jones, *Santa Anna*, pp. 40–59; Justo Sierra, *Political Evolution*, pp. 202–4; Cuevas, *Historia*, pp. 593–601.

46. Cuevas, *Historia*, pp. 557–64, 588–92; Alessio Robles, *Coahuila y Texas* 1:315.

47. Van Buren to Poinsett, August 25, 1829, Manning, *Dip. Corr.* (this letter was delivered to Poinsett by his replacement, Anthony Butler); Van Buren to Butler, October 16, 1829, and April 1, 1830, Manning, *Dip. Corr.*

48. "El Generál Guerrero, al cerrar las sesiones en las cámaras de la unión, en 23 de mayo de 1829," in *Un Siglo de relaciones internacionales de México (A través de los mensajes presidenciales)*, Archivo Histórico Diplomático Mexicano, vol. 39 (Mexico City: Publicaciones de la secretaría de relaciones exteriores, 1935).

49. Castañeda, *Our Catholic Heritage* 6:199–235; Alessio Robles, *Coahuila y Texas* 1:282–301; Austin to Mier y Terán, June 30, 1828, quoted in Alessio Robles, *Coahuila y Texas* 1:296–97; Miguel A. Sánchez Lamego, *La vida militar del general de división D. Manuel de Mier y Terán*, quoted in Alessio Robles,

Coahuila y Texas 1:280–93; Piedras to Mier y Terán, December 8, 1829, Alessio Robles, *Coahuila y Texas* 1:350.

50. Castañeda, *Our Catholic Heritage* 6:241–44; Alessio Robles, *Coahuila y Texas* 1:352–63.

51. Margaret Swett Henson, *Juan Davis Bradburn: A Reappraisal of the Mexican Commander of Anáhuac* (College Station: Texas A and M University Press, 1982), pp. 47–118; Alessio Robles, *Coahuila y Texas* 1:368–75, 381–409; Castañeda, *Our Catholic Heritage* 6:245–56.

52. José María Tornel y Mendívil, "Relations between Texas, the United States of America, and the Mexican Republic" (Mexico City, 1837), translated with notes by Carlos E. Castañeda in *The Mexican Side of the Texas Revolution* (New York: Arno Press, 1976), pp. 284–378. In an earlier publication, Tornel indicated that even before he took up his official position he was approached by an agent of Thomas Hart Benton who proposed to purchase Texas: see José María Tornel, "Manifestación del Ciudadano José María Tornel al público," Mexico City, 1833, quoted in dispatch of Butler to Louis McLane, February 4, 1834, Manning, *Dip. Corr.*

53. Ramón Múzquiz, prefect of Béjar, quoted in Alessio Robles, *Coahuila y Texas* 1:457; Ramón Múzquiz to governor of Coahuila y Texas, March 11, 1833, quoted in ibid., p. 458; Vicente Filísola, *La guerra de Tejas*, various quotes in ibid., pp. 453–72.

54. Butler to Jackson, May 25, 1831, Manning, *Dip. Corr.*; Minutes of the first conversation of Anthony Butler with Lucas Alaman, minister of foreign affairs of Mexico, on the subject of Texas, Mexico, July 2, 1832, and second conversation, July 10, 1832, ibid.; Butler to Livingston, August 12, 1832, ibid. For further information on the anti-United States climate in Mexico, see Brack, *Mexico Views Manifest Destiny*, pp. 57–73.

55. Henson, *Juan Davis Bradburn*, pp. 87–118; Alessio Robles, *Coahuila y Texas* 1:399–409. The Texans accepted the Plan of Veracruz on June 13, 1832, at a meeting on Turtle Bay.

56. Alessio Robles, *Coahuila y Texas* 1:469–81; Castañeda, *Our Catholic Heritage* 6:256. Juan N. Almonte reported that secession was very likely, and Juan Cortina stated, "El Estado de Texas es perdido muy pronto, si no se toman medidas para salvarlo."

57. Butler to McLane, August 5, 1833, Butler to Carlos García, Mexican minister of foreign affairs, September 6, 1833, Butler to McLane, October 9, 1833, and February 4, 1834, all in Manning, *Dip. Corr.*

58. Butler to Francisco M. Lombardo, Mexican minister of foreign affairs, December 21, 1834, Manning, *Dip. Corr.*

59. Butler to Jackson, February 26, 1835, Manning, *Dip. Corr.*

60. Butler to Forsyth, June 17, 1835, Manning, *Dip. Corr.*

61. Van Buren to Butler, April 1, 1830, Edward Livingston to Butler, June 21, 1831, and February 27, 1832, McLane to Joaquín M. de Castillo y Lanzas,

December 31, 1833, Livingston to Montoya, April 18, 1832, and McLane to Butler, July 5, 1833, all in Manning, *Dip. Corr.*

62. Forsyth to Butler, July 2 and August 6, 1835, Manning, *Dip. Corr.*

63. Forsyth to Butler, November 9, 1835, Manning, *Dip. Corr.*

64. Juan N. Almonte, *Noticia estadística sobre Texas* (Mexico City, 1835).

65. Joaquín Moreno, *Diario de un escribiente de legación*, Archivo histórico diplomático mexicano, no. 16 (Mexico City: Publicaciones de la secretaria de relaciones exteriores, 1925).

66. Alessio Robles, *Coahuila y Texas* 1:489–538, 2:7–138. See especially Cos to Secretary of War and Marine, May 28, 1835, quoted in ibid., 2:22.

67. Ibid., 2:46, 47.

68. Castañeda, *Our Catholic Heritage* 6:265; Justo Sierra, *Political Evolution*, p. 214.

69. Colonel Domingo Ugartechea to General Cos, May 22, 1835, and Cos to Secretary of War and Marine, May 28, 1835, both in Alessio Robles, *Coahuila y Texas* 2:21–22.

70. Castañeda, *Our Catholic Heritage* 6:265–66; Alessio Robles, *Coahuila y Texas* 2:53.

71. Castañeda, *Our Catholic Heritage* 6:270; Richard G. Santos, ed., *Santa Anna's Campaign against Texas, 1835–1836* (Salisbury, N.C.: Texian Press, 1968), pp. 5–7.

72. Castañeda, *Our Catholic Heritage* 6:274.

73. Ortíz Monasterio to Forsyth, November 19, 1835, Manning, *Dip. Corr.*

74. Santos, *Santa Anna's Campaign*, pp. 7–17, 60–85.

75. Ibid., pp. 60–85.

76. Ibid., pp. 76–89; Alessio Robles, *Coahuila y Texas* 2:189.

77. Alessio Robles, *Coahuila y Texas* 2:89–138.

78. Ibid., pp. 157–76.

79. *El Anteojo*, November 4, 1835, quoted in Brack, *Mexico Views Manifest Destiny*, p. 70.

80. *Diario del Gobierno*, May 7, 1836, enclosed in Butler to Forsyth, May 8, 1836, Manning, *Dip. Corr.*

81. Ortíz Monasterio to Forsyth, November 19, 1835, Manning, *Dip. Corr.*

82. Tornel y Mendívil, "Relations between Texas and the United States" in Castañeda, *The Mexican Side of the Texas Revolution*, pp. 307, 358–59.

83. Ellis to Forsyth, May 19, 1836, Manning, *Dip. Corr.*

84. Document issued at San Felipe de Austin, June 22, 1835, quoted in Alessio Robles, *Coahuila y Texas* 2:30–31. "Vuestros hermanos los Estados Unidos del Norte os desean muy mucho la victoria. . . ."

85. Ibid., p. 46.

86. Ibid., p. 61.

87. Castañeda, *Our Catholic Heritage* 6:286–94.

88. Antonio López de Santa Anna, "Manifesto Which General Antonio López de Santa Anna Addresses to His Fellow Citizens" (May 1837), in Carlos

E. Castañeda, ed. and trans., *The Mexican Side of the Texas Revolution*, pp. 42–47.

89. Ellis to Forsyth, September 24, 1836 (in code), and Forsyth to Ortíz Monasterio, January 29, 1836, both in Manning, *Dip. Corr.*

90. Adams is quoted in Tornel, "Relations"; Castañeda, *Mexican Side of the Texas Revolution*, pp. 284–378.

91. Forsyth to Butler, November 9, 1835, Manning, *Dip. Corr.*

92. Joaquín M. de Castillo y Lanzas to Forsyth, Manning, *Dip. Corr.*

93. Forsyth to Ellis, January 29, 1836, Manning, *Dip. Corr.*

94. Ellis to Forsyth, June 25, 1836 (private), Manning, *Dip. Corr.*

95. Ellis to Forsyth, August 3, September 7, October 11 and 26, 1836, Manning, *Dip. Corr.*

96. Ellis to Ortíz Monasterio, September 26, 1836, Manning, *Dip. Corr.*

97. Ellis to Forsyth, September 24, 1836 (in code), Manning, *Dip. Corr.*

98. Manuel Eduardo de Gorostiza, *Don Manuel Eduardo de Gorostiza y la cuestión de Texas*, Archivo Histórico Diplomático Mexicano, no. 8, (Mexico City: Publicaciones de la Secretaría de Relaciones Exteriores, 1924); Dickins to Gorostiza, July 26 and August 1, 1836, Forsyth to Gorostiza, August 31 and September 16, 1836, Manning, *Dip. Corr.*

99. Memorandum of conference between Forsyth and Gorostiza, April 20, 1836, and Forsyth to Gorostiza, April 26, May 3, and May 10, 1836, Manning, *Dip. Corr.* In the letter of May 10, Forsyth did not admit that the force had been ordered to Nacogdoches but stated that it had been ordered "not to go beyond that point."

100. Gorostiza to Forsyth, April 28, May 4, and May 9, 1836, and note from Gorostiza to the United States Department of State, May 14, 1836, Gorostiza, *Don Manuel.*

101. Gorostiza to Forsyth, May 4, 1836, Manning, *Dip. Corr.*; report of Gorostiza to Mexican minister of foreign relations, June 24, 1836, Gorostiza, *Don Manuel.*

102. Gorostiza to Forsyth, May 9, 1836, Manning, *Dip. Corr.*; Gorostiza to Dickins, August 4 and 10, 1836, Gorostiza, *Don Manuel.*

103. Gorostiza to Mexican minister of foreign relations, July 12, 1836, Gorostiza, *Don Manuel.*

104. Gorostiza to Mexican minister of foreign relations, July 25, 1836, Gorostiza, *Don Manuel.*

105. Forsyth to Gorostiza, July 12, 1836, Manning, *Dip. Corr.*; in this note, Forsyth acknowledges Gorostiza's message that the Mexican congress had voided any agreement made by Santa Anna after his capture.

106. Gorostiza to Mexican minister of foreign relations July 6, 1836, Gorostiza, *Don Manuel.*

107. Forsyth to Gorostiza, September 16, 1836, Manning, *Dip. Corr.*

108. Gorostiza to Dickins, October 1, 1836, Gorostiza, *Don Manuel.*

109. Dickins to Gorostiza, October 13, 1836, Gorostiza, *Don Manuel.*

110. Gorostiza to minister of foreign relations, October 4, 1836, and Gorostiza to Dickins, October 15, 1836, Gorostiza, *Don Manuel*.

111. Gorostiza, *Don Manuel*, pp. i–xxvi; Manning, *Early Diplomatic Relations*, pp. 89–189.

112. Tornel, "Relations," p. 366; Ellis to Forsyth, May 19, 1836, and Ellis to Jackson, August 26, 1836, Manning, *Dip. Corr.*

113. Ellis to Ortíz Monasterio, September 26, October 21, November 4 and 10, and December 7, 22, 24, and 27, 1836, Ortiz to Ellis, November 15 and December 21, 1836, Ellis to Forsyth, November 20, December 14 and 27, 1836, Manning, *Dip. Corr.*

114. Morfit to Forsyth, August 13, 22, 23, and 27, September 6, 9, 10, and 14, 1836, and Forsyth to Morfit, June 23, 1836, Manning, *Dip. Corr.*

115. Santa Anna, "Manifesto," pp. 42–43; Jones, *Santa Anna*, pp. 7–75.

116. David Crockett, *The Life of Martin Van Buren, Heir-Apparent to the "Government" and the Appointed Successor of General Andrew Jackson* (Philadelphia: R. Wright, 1835), p. 13.

117. *The Autobiography of Martin Van Buren*, ed. John C. Fitzpatrick, annual report of the American Historical Association for the year 1918 (Washington, D.C.: U.S. Government Printing Office, 1920) (there is virtually no mention of Mexico or Texas in this work, which ends with the campaign of 1836); James C. Curtis, *The Fox at Bay: Martin Van Buren and the Presidency, 1837–1841* (Lexington: University Press of Kentucky, 1970), pp. 3–51, 166–67; Robert V. Remini, *Martin Van Buren and the Making of the Democratic Party* (New York: Columbia University Press, 1959); Holmes Alexander, *The American Talleyrand: The Career and Contemporaries of Martin Van Buren, Eighth President* (New York: Russell and Russell, 1935).

118. Alvin Laroy Duckett, *John Forsyth: Political Tactician* (Athens: University of Georgia Press, 1962), pp. 128–49, 192–93; Webster to Hiram Ketchum, January 28, 1837, *The Papers of Daniel Webster*, ed. Charles M. Wiltse and Harold D. Moser (Hanover, N.H.: University Press of New England, 1974–84), 4:182–85.

119. W. D. Jones to Forsyth, March 14, 1837, Manning, *Dip. Corr.*

120. Arrongoiz, *México*, pp. 371–76; Justo Sierra, *Political Evolution*, pp. 216–18; Alessio Robles, *Coahuila y Texas* 2:202–3.

121. *La primera guerra entre México y Francia*, Archivo Histórico diplomático Mexicano, vol. 23 (Mexico: Publicaciones de la Secretaría de Relaciones Exteriores, 1927), pp. vii–xxxv, Documents, pp. 3–343.

W. D. Jones, U.S. consul, reported that Gorostiza was very in seeking British support (Jones to Forsyth, January 5, 1839, Manning, *Dip. Corr.*). "La revista mexicana de derecho internacional," in Antonio de la Peña y Reyes, *La diplomacia mexicana: Pequeña revista histórica*, Publicaciones de la Secretaría de Relaciones Exteriores, no. 1 (Mexico: City, Archivo Histórico Diplomático Mexicano, 1923), p. 21.

122. Jones to Forsyth, June 22 and 27, 1839, and Ellis to Forsyth, July 13, 1839, Manning, *Dip. Corr.*

123. Charles A. Hale, *Mexican Liberalism in the Age of Mora, 1821–1853* (New Haven: Yale University Press, 1968), pp. 84, 145, 199. Among the other prominent liberals of the future who were in New Orleans at that time were Melchor Ocampo and Guillermo Prieto: see Cuevas, *Historia*, pp. 614–16, and C. Alan Hutchinson, "Valentín Gómez Farías and the 'Secret Pact of New Orleans,'" *Hispanic American Historical Review* 36 (November 1956): 471–89.

124. Moisés González Navarro, *Raza y Tierra: La guerra de castas y el henequén* (Mexico City: El Colegio de México, 1970), pp. 68–70; John L. Stephens, *Incidents of Travel in Central America, Chiapas, and Yucatán* (New York: Harper and Brothers, 1841), pp. 376–474; Nelson Reed, *The Caste War of Yucatán* (Stanford: Stanford University Press, 1964), pp. 27–29; Victor M. Suarez Molina, *La evolucion economica de Yucatán: A través del siglo XIX* (Mexico City: Ediciones de la Universidad de Yucatán, 1977), 1:27–28; Alessio Robles, *Coahuila y Texas* 2:270–74.

125. De Witt to Forsyth, October 14 and December 14, 1836, and January 26, 1837, Manning, *Dip. Corr.*

126. David J. Weber, *The Mexican Frontier, 1821–1846: The American Southwest under Mexico* (Albuquerque: University of New Mexico Press, 1982), pp. 109–14, 179–205, 241–85. For a case study in Mexican policy and efforts in California in this period, see C. Alan Hutchinson, *Frontier Settlement in Mexican California: The Híjar-Padrés Colony and Its Origins, 1769–1835* (New Haven: Yale University Press, 1969). The uprising of 1836–41 is covered in Irving Berdine Richman, *California under Spain and Mexico, 1535–1847* (Boston: Houghton Mifflin, 1911), pp. 257–66.

127. Ellis to Forsyth, June 9, August 20, and October 1, 1840, and Forsyth to Ellis, August 21, 1840, Manning, *Dip. Corr.*

128. Jones to Forsyth, April 26, 1837, Ellis to Forsyth, October 1 and 17, 1840, February 25, 1841, Manning, *Dip. Corr.*

129. Weber, *Mexican Frontier*, pp. 240–67.

130. Alessio Robles, *Coahuila y Texas* 2:202–4.

131. Ibid., pp. 204–22; LaBranche to Forsyth, October 25, 1839, and Barnard E. Bee (Texas chargé in the U.S.) to Forsyth, April 29, 1840, Manning, *Dip. Corr.*; Roel, *Nuevo León*, p. 137; Andrés Montemayor Hernández, *Historia de Monterrey* (Monterrey: Asociación de Editores y Libreros de Monterrey, 1971), pp. 119–22.

132. Alessio Robles, *Coahuila y Texas* 2:204–22; David M. Vigness, "Relations of the Republic of Texas and the Republic of the Rio Grande," *South-Western Historical Quarterly* 57 (January 1954): 312–21; David M. Vigness, "A Texas Expedition to Mexico, 1841," *Southwestern Historical Quarterly* 62 (July 1958): 18–28.

133. Ellis to Forsyth, October 17, 1840, and Juan de Diós Cañedo (Mexican foreign minister) to Ellis, August 6, 1840, Manning, *Dip. Corr.*; Gorostiza, *Don*

Manuel, pp. 196–206. Gorostiza denounced those in Mexico who denied that Texas could be retaken.

134. Brack, *Mexico Views Manifest Destiny*, p. 82.

135. Alessio Robles, *Coahuila y Texas* 2:187–90, 234–36; Gorostiza, *Don Manuel*, pp. 196–206; George H. Flood to Forsyth, June 22 and December 11, 1840, Manning, *Dip. Corr.*

136. Samuel Swartwout to William Wharton, December 21, 1836, quoted in Curtis, *Fox at Bay*, p. 155; Forsyth to Wharton and Hunt (appointed Texas ministers to the United States), March 13, 1837, Manning, *Dip. Corr.* At that time Forsyth stated that the United States recognized the Texas flag but did not accept the credentials of the two envoys (Forsyth to Hunt, August 25, 1837, Manning, *Dip. Corr.*).

137. Hunt to Forsyth, August 4, 1837, Manning, *Dip. Corr.*

138. Forsyth to Hunt, August 25, 1837, Manning, *Dip. Corr.*

139. La Branche to Forsyth, October 27, December 12, 1837, January 30, March 13, and April 16, 1838, Manning, *Dip. Corr.* La Branche, who arrived on October 24, 1837, was to remain in the post until April 2, 1840.

140. Curtis, *Fox at Bay*, pp. 158–59.

141. Speech by John Quincy Adams, text in *National Intelligencer*, December 12, 1837, quoted in ibid., p. 166.

142. Dunlap (Texas chargé to the United States) to Forsyth, and Barnard E. Bee (Texas chargé) to Forsyth, April 29, 1840, Manning, *Dip. Corr.*

143. Vail to Anson Jones, October 11, 1838, La Branche to Forsyth, December 12, 1838, and Jones to Vail, October 10, 1838, Manning, *Dip. Corr.*; Curtis, *Fox at Bay*, p. 166; Duckett, *John Forsyth*, pp. 199–211.

144. Forsyth to Dunlap, February 1840, and Dunalp to Forsyth, March 27, 1840, Manning, *Dip. Corr.*

145. Jones to Forsyth, December 31, 1838, and La Branche to Forsyth, October 25, 1839, Manning, *Dip. Corr.*

146. Bee to Forsyth, April 29, 1840, Manning, *Dip. Corr.*

147. Forsyth to Dunlap, July 17, 1839, and Forsyth to Bee, April 20 and May 4, 1840, Manning, *Dip. Corr.*

148. Forsyth to Castillo, March 1 and 17, 1837, Ortíz Monasterio to Forsyth, March 24, 1837, and Forsyth to Ortíz Monasterio, May 18, 1837, all in Manning, *Dip. Corr.*

149. Forsyth to Greenhow, May 27, 1837, and Forsyth to Ortíz Monasterio, May 22, 1837, Manning, *Dip. Corr.*

150. Jones to Forsyth, March 7 and April 2, 1837, and Greenhow to Forsyth, August 12, 1837, Manning, *Dip. Corr.*

151. Francisco Pizarro Martínez to Forsyth, November 18 and December 11, 1837, April 7 and 30, June 23, 1838, Manning, *Dip. Corr.*

152. Forsyth to Ellis, May 3, 18, 1839, Manning, *Dip. Corr.*

153. Tornel to Chamber of Deputies, June 18, 1839, translated and enclosed in Jones to Forsyth, June 22, 1839, Manning, *Dip. Corr.*

154. Ellis to Forsyth, July 13, November 14 and 16, 1839, and October 17, 1840, Manning, *Dip. Corr.*; Gorostiza, *Don Manuel*, pp. 196–206.

155. Forsyth to Dunlap, January 15, 1840, Manning, *Dip. Corr.*

156. Forsyth to Ellis, May 27, 1840, Manning, *Dip. Corr.*

157. Forsyth to minister of foreign affairs of Mexico, May 27, 1837, Manning, *Dip. Corr.*

158. Cuevas to Forsyth, July 29, 1837, Greenhow to Forsyth, August 12, 1837, Jones to Forsyth, January 3 and May 27, 1838, Pizarro to Forsyth, May 17 and September 3, 1838, and Forsyth to Pizarro, September 5, 13, and 22, 1838, all in Manning, *Dip. Corr.*

159. Forsyth to Pizarro, February 25, March 16, and May 8, 1839, and Forsyth to Ellis, May 3 and September 16, 1839, Manning, *Dip. Corr.*

160. Jones to Forsyth, June 22, 1839, and Ellis to Forsyth, July 13, September 21, and November 14 and 16, 1839, Manning, *Dip. Corr.*

161. Ellis to Forsyth, January 11, 1840, Manning, *Dip. Corr.*

162. Ellis to Forsyth, June 9, July 2 and 9, August 20, and October 1, 1840, Manning, *Dip. Corr.*

163. Forsyth to Ellis, August 21, 1840, Manning, *Dip. Corr.*

164. Curtis, *Fox at Bay*, pp. 191–97; Alexander, *American Talleyrand*, pp. 366 72.

165. Carl Schurz, *Henry Clay* (New York: Ungar, 1958), 2:172–98; Robert Gray Gunderson, *The Log-Cabin Campaign* (Lexington: University of Kentucky Press, 1957); Robert Seager II, *And Tyler Too: A Biography of John and Julia Tyler* (New York: McGraw-Hill, 1963).

166. Ephraim Douglass Adams, ed., *British Diplomatic Correspondence concerning the Republic of Texas, 1838–1846* (Austin: Texas State Historical Association, n.d., reprinted from the quarterly of the Texas State Historical Association, January 1912–October, 1917), pp. 1–2. Hereafter cited as Adams, *British Dip. Corr.*

167. Greenhow to Forsyth, August 12, 1837, Manning, *Dip. Corr.*

168. Daniel Webster to Edward Curtis, January 30, 1836, Webster to Edward Everett, May 7, 1836, Daniel Fletcher Webster (son) to Daniel Webster, July 19, 1836, Webster to Hiram Ketchum, January 28, 1837, and Webster to Nicholas Biddle, September 10, 1838, all in *Papers of Daniel Webster.*

169. Robert J. Morgan, *A Whig Embattled: The Presidency under John Tyler* (Lincoln: University of Nebraska, 1954), pp. 1–76. See also Schurz, *Henry Clay* 2:199–228.

170. Tyler to Webster, October 11, 1841, *Papers of Daniel Webster.* Although this collection contains many letters that are found in Manning's *Diplomatic Correspondence*, it also contains numerous additional letters and notes, especially those of a private nature.

171. Howard Jones, *To the Webster-Ashburton Treaty: A Study in Anglo-American Relations, 1783–1843* (Chapel Hill: University of North Carolina Press, 1977), pp. 60–180.

172. Webster to Samuel Jones Loyd, May 8, 1840, *Papers of Daniel Webster;* Webster to Joseph Eve, June 14, 1841, June 23, 1842, and March 17, 1843, Webster to Waddy Thompson, June 22 and July 13, 1842, January 31 and February 7, 1843, Manning, *Dip. Corr.*

173. Oliver Perry Chitwood, *John Tyler: Champion of the Old South* (New York: Russell and Russell, 1964), pp. 331–33; Morgan, *A Whig Embattled,* p. 74; William M. Meigs, *The Life of Thomas Hart Benton* (Philadelphia: J. B. Lippincott, 1924), pp. 321–62.

174. Madame Calderón de la Barca, *Life in Mexico during a Residence of Two Years in That Country* (London: J. M. Dent and Sons, 1843), pp. 342–84.

175. Ibid., pp. 410–15; Jones, *Santa Anna,* pp. 83–84; Alessio Robles, *Coahuila y Texas* 2:303–5; Jan Bazant, *Antonio Haro y Tamariz y sus aventuras políticas, 1811–1869* (Mexico City: El Colegio de México, 1985), pp. 29–40. When the *Bases organicas* first came into effect, General Nicolás Bravo was selected as president, but Santa Anna soon after returned to personal power.

176. Waddy Thompson to Webster, April 29 and June 20, 1842, *Papers of Daniel Webster.*

177. Alessio Robles, *Coahuila y Texas* 2:230; Arrongoiz, *México,* p. 381; Justo Sierra, *Political Evolution,* pp. 229–30; Cuevas, *Historia,* pp. 627–35; Calderón de la Barca, *Life in Mexico,* pp. 342–84.

178. John L. Stephens, *Incidents of Travel in Yucatán* (1843; reprint, New York: Dover, 1963), 1:7–45, 271–74; González Navarro, *Raza y Tierra,* pp. 70–72.

179. González Navarro, *Raza y Tierra.* See also Reed, *Caste War,* pp. 3–34.

180. The Mexican historian Cuevas asserts that the movement was influenced by Gómez Farías, who was supported "with money and troops from the United States, channeled through Texas" (*Historia,* p. 627).

181. Waddy Thompson to Webster, April 29 and June 20, 1842, *Papers of Daniel Webster.*

182. Webster to Waddy Thompson, January 30, 1843, *Papers of Daniel Webster.*

183. Charles Thompson to Secretary of State, March 17, May 30, September 5, and October 16, 1843, Dispatches from United States Consuls in Mérida, 1843–97, Microcopy N.T-29 (Roll 1), National Archives.

184. Alessio Robles, *Coahuila y Texas* 2:223–28; Calderón de la Barca, *Life in Mexico,* pp. 519–20.

185. Webster to Eve, March 30, 1842, Manning, *Dip. Corr.*

186. Joseph Milton Nance, *Attack and Counterattack: The Texas-Mexican Frontier, 1842* (Austin: University of Texas Press, 1964), p. ix.

187. Ibid., pp. 133–205; Eve to Webster, March 10 and 19, 1842, Manning, *Dip. Corr.*

188. Eve to Webster, July 25, August 22, September 22, 1842, and March 29, 1843, Eve to Fletcher Webster (acting secretary of state), April 21 and 28, 1843,

Samuel Houston to Eve, May 6, 1843, William S. Murphy to Hugh S. Legaré, June 5 and July 6, 1843, all in Manning, *Dip. Corr.*

189. Eve to Webster, February 10, 1843, Manning, *Dip. Corr.*

190. Nance, *Attack and Counterattack*, pp. 427–578; Eve to Webster, February 10, 1843, Manning, *Dip. Corr.*

191. Eve to Webster, January 6, 1842, Manning, *Dip. Corr.*

192. James Reily to Webster, June 11, 1842, and George Whitfield Terrell to Eve, October 15, 1842, in *Papers of Daniel Webster*; G. W. Terrell, acting secretary of state of Texas, to Eve, October 15, 1842, Eve to Joseph Waples, November 1, 1842, and Van Zandt to Webster, December 14, 1842, Manning, *Dip. Corr.*

193. Eve to Webster, December 18, 1842, Manning, *Dip. Corr.*; Webster to Thompson, January 31 and February 7, 1843, *Papers of Daniel Webster*.

194. Nicholas Biddle to Webster, January 12, 1843, *Papers of Daniel Webster*; Edward Everett, United States minister to England, to Webster, May 6 and June 17, 1842, Manning, *Dip. Corr.*

195. Webster to Bernard E. Bee (Texas chargé), April 13, 1841, Nathaniel Amory (Texas chargé ad interim) to Webster, May 19, 1841, Manning, *Dip. Corr.*

196. Webster to Eve, March 17, 1843, Manning, *Dip. Corr.*; Webster to Thompson, February 7, 1843, *Papers of Daniel Webster*. Webster wanted to assure Foreign Minister Bocanegra that the United States wanted to be fair and impartial in these matters.

197. Henry Blumenthal, *A Reappraisal of Franco-American Relations, 1830–1871* (Chapel Hill: University of North Carolina Press, 1959), pp. 38–39.

198. William Kennedy to Lord Aberdeen, October 20 and November 6, 1841, and January 10 and 28, 1842, Aberdeen to Charles Elliot, July 1, 1842, Adams, *British Dip. Corr.*

199. Elliot to Pakenham, April 14, 1843, Adams, *British Dip. Corr.*

200. Aberdeen to Elliot, June 3, July 1, and November 3, 1842, in Adams, *British Dip. Corr.*

201. Houston to Elliot, November 5, 1842, January 24 and May 13, 1843, Elliot to Aberdeen, August 29, 1842, and October 31, 1843, Adams, *British Dip. Corr.* See also Ephraim Douglass Adams, *British Interests and Activities in Texas, 1838–1846* (1910; reprint, Gloucester, Mass.: Peter Smith, 1963), pp. 97–122.

202. Llerena Friend, *Sam Houston: The Great Designer* (Austin: University of Texas Press, 1954), pp. 115–61. This treatment shows the complexities of Houston and his statements at the time and in later years. Friend agrees with Justin Smith that Houston was basically a pragmatist. See also Herbert Gambrell, *Anson Jones: The Last President of Texas* (Austin: University of Texas Press, 1947), pp. 275–99.

203. Eve to Webster, March 10, 1842, Manning, *Dip. Corr.*

204. William S. Murphy, U.S. chargé, to Hugh S. Legaré, acting secretary of state, June 5 and 16 and July 6, 1843, Manning, *Dip. Corr.*

205. Duff Green to President Tyler, July 3, 1843, quoted in Chitwood, *John Tyler*, p. 347; Duff Green to Abel P. Upshur, August 3, 1843, Manning, *Dip. Corr.*

206. Morgan, *A Whig Embattled*, especially quote by Tyler on p. 138.

207. Elliot to Percy Doyle, British chargé in Mexico, June 21, 1843, Adams, *British Dip. Corr.;* Murphy to Legaré (acting secretary of state), June 6 and July 8, 1843, Murphy to Upshur, September 23 and 24, December 5, Manning, *Dip. Corr.*

208. Upshur to Murphy, August 8, September 22, October 20, November 21, 1843, and January 23, 1844, Upshur to Van Zandt, October 16, 1843, Upshur to Edward Everett, U.S. minister to Great Britain (confidential), September 28, 1843, Everett to Upshur, November 3, 1843, Manning, *Dip. Corr.* See also Lord Aberdeen, British secretary of state for foreign affairs, to Richard Pakenham, British minister to the United States, December 26, 1843, Manning, *Dip. Corr.*: here it is stated that the British were attempting to persuade Mexico to recognize Texas independence but were in no way attempting to subvert affairs relating to slavery. Aberdeen asked that this be shared with the secretary of state.

209. Webster to Lewis F. Allen, November 25, 1843, and Webster to Charles Allen, December 9, 1843, *Papers of Daniel Webster*.

210. Murphy to Upshur, December 25, 1843, Manning, *Dip. Corr.*

211. Friend, *Sam Houston*, pp. 126–30.

212. Ibid., p. 130.

213. Nelson to Murphy, March 11, 1844, Manning, *Dip. Corr.*

214. Calhoun to Van Zandt and J. Pinckney Henderson, April 11, 1844, Calhoun to Murphy, April 13, 1844, and Calhoun to Benjamin E. Green (U.S. chargé in Mexico), April 19, 1844, Manning, *Dip. Corr.*

215. Calhoun to Almonte, April 22, 1844, Manning, *Dip. Corr.*

216. Quoted in Meigs, *Life of Thomas Hart Benton*, p. 347.

217. Calhoun to Tilghman A. Howard (chargé to Texas), June 18 and September 10, 1844, Calhoun to Van Zandt, August 14, 1844, Manning, *Dip. Corr.*

218. Morgan, *A Whig Embattled*, p. 146; Oscar Doane Lambert, *Presidential Politics in the United States, 1841–1844* (Durham, N.C.: Duke University Press, 1936), pp. 1–142.

219. Alexander, *American Talleyrand*, pp. 396–97; Schurz, *Henry Clay* 2:238–68.

220. Schurz, *Henry Clay* 2:238–68. Schurz points out that 15,812 votes cast in New York for James G. Birney gave Polk a victory over Clay by 5,080 votes, thus costing Clay the electoral votes that would have given him the presidency.

221. Ibid., pp. 269–315; Lambert, *Presidential Politics*, p. 134.

222. New York *Tribune*, March 1, 1845, quoted in Chitwood, *John Tyler*, p. 366.

223. Calhoun to Donelson, September 17, 1844, and March 3, 1845, Calhoun to Charles H. Raymond (Texas chargé), September 18, 1844, Manning, *Dip. Corr.*

224. Gambrell, *Anson Jones*, p. 357.

225. Tomás Murphy (Mexican minister in London) to Luís G. Cuevas (minister of foreign relations), December 1, 1844, and January 1, 1845, quoted in *Lord Aberdeen, Texas y California*, Archivo Histórico Diplomático Mexicano, no. 15 (Mexico City: Publicaciones de la Secretaria de Relaciones Exteriores, 1925). See also Aberdeen to Elliot, June 3, 1843, in Adams, *British Dip. Corr.*

226. Murphy to Cuevas, January 18, February 28, and April 1, 1845, in *Lord Aberdeen, Texas y California*. See also Aberdeen to Elliot, May 3, 1845, Adams, *British Dip. Corr.*, where Aberdeen says that if Mexico would recognize Texas independence, then both England and France would offer to mediate the boundary. See also Everett to Calhoun, February 26, 1845, Manning, *Dip. Corr.*

227. Gambrell, *Anson Jones*, pp. 362–404; Cuevas to Murphy, April 29, 1845, in *Lord Aberdeen, Texas y California*. See also Aberdeen to Elliot, January 23, 1845, and Charles Bankhead to Elliot, May 20, 1845, Adams, *British Dip. Corr.*

228. Houston to Elliot, May 13, 1843, in Adams, *British Dip. Corr.*; Speech of Sam Houston, January 20, 1844, and Houston to Jones, April 14, 1844, both in Gambrell, *Anson Jones*, pp. 309, 329. See also Friend, *Sam Houston*, pp. 140–41.

229. Jones to Postmaster Norton, February 17, 1844, Gambrell, *Anson Jones*, p. 327; see also pp. 133–48, 275–76, 285–304, 327–30.

230. Ibid., pp. 309–10, 338–52.

231. Donelson to Calhoun, November 24, December 5, 1844, Manning, *Dip. Corr.*; Donelson was convinced that Houston was strongly in favor of annexation but was afraid of English mediation with Mexico and other elements that might push for independence. See also Donelson to Jones, December 6, 1844, and Jones to Donelson, December 7, 1844, Manning, *Dip. Corr.*

232. Gambrell, *Anson Jones*, p. 387; Donelson to Calhoun, November 23, 1844, and Donelson to James Buchanan, March 28, 1845, Manning, *Dip. Corr.*; Elliot to Aberdeen (secret), April 2, 1845, Adams, *British Dip. Corr.*

233. Donelson to Buchanan, April 1, 3, and 12, May 6, 22, and 24, 1845, Donelson to Allen, August 14, 1845, Manning, *Dip. Corr.*; see also Charles M. Wiltse, *John C. Calhoun* (New York: Russell and Russell, 1968), 3:199–201.

234. Jones to Elliot, June 6, 1845, Adams, *British Dip. Corr.*; Ebenezer Allen (acting secretary of state of Texas) to Donelson, June 23, 1845, Manning, *Dip. Corr.*

235. Gambrell, *Anson Jones*, pp. 386–425; Kennedy to Aberdeen, December 5 and 16, 1844, Adams, *British Dip. Corr.* (Kennedy reported the pressures

being exerted by both Duff Green and Donelson); Donelson to Calhoun, May 22, 1845, and Donelson to Allen, May 24, 1845, Manning, *Dip. Corr.*

236. Charles Wickliffe to Buchanan, May 30, 1845, Manning, *Dip. Corr.*

237. Donelson to Buchanan, June 2 and 4, 1845, Manning, *Dip. Corr.*

238. Webster to Thompson, June 22, 1842, January 31 and February 7, 1843, Manning, *Dip. Corr.;* Webster to Thompson, January 30, 1843, *Papers of Daniel Webster.*

239. Considered by most Mexican historians to be an avid expansionist, Waddy Thompson was faithful to Webster's instructions, but he occasionally communicated directly with Tyler and became disillusioned.

240. Thompson to Webster, April 29, 1842, and Webster to Thompson, April 5, September 5, and October 13, 1842, Manning, *Dip. Corr.*

241. Bocanegra to Webster, May 12 and 31, 1842, Thompson to Webster, March 14, 1843, Bocanegra to Thompson, August 8, 1843, and Bocanegra to the Foreign Diplomatic Corps in Mexico, July 6, 1842, Manning, *Dip. Corr.*

242. Thompson to Webster, June 2 and 20, 1842, and January 5, 1843, Manning, *Dip. Corr.* (Tornel was especially hostile in his statements about Andrew Jackson); Brack, *Mexico Views Manifest Destiny*, pp. 98–125.

243. Thompson to Webster, September 10, 1842, Manning, *Dip. Corr.* Thompson referred to Almonte as the head of the liberal party.

244. Almonte, *Noticia estadística.*

245. Almonte to Webster, January 24 and March 14, 1843, and Almonte to Upshur, November 11, 1843, Manning, *Dip. Corr.*

246. Webster to Thompson, June 22, July 8 and 13, 1842, Manning, *Dip. Corr.*

247. Thompson to Webster, June 20, July 30, and August 16, 1842, Manning, *Dip. Corr.*

248. Webster to Thompson, July 8, December 14 and 30, 1842, and Fletcher Webster to Thompson, October 13, 1842, Manning, *Dip. Corr.*

249. Thompson to Webster, April 29, 1842, *Papers of Daniel Webster.* Thompson stated: "I believe that the Government would cede to us Texas and the Californias, and I am thoroughly satisfied that it is all we shall ever get for the claims of our Merchants on this country"; Thompson to Webster, June 20, 1842, Manning, *Dip. Corr.*

250. Thompson to Bocanegra, September 5 and October 11, 1842, Thompson to Webster, August 16, September 10, November 8, 12, and 30, and December 29, 1842, Manning, *Dip. Corr.*

251. Thompson to Webster, November 30, 1842, Manning, *Dip. Corr.;* Thompson indignantly asked of Webster, "Now am I with a drawn sword to demand the payment of this claim?"

252. Thompson to Webster, May 16, 1843, Thompson to Secretary of State, August 5, 1843, and Thompson to Upshur, October 3 and 14, 1843, Manning, *Dip. Corr.;* Alessio Robles, *Coahuila y Texas* 2:306.

253. Ellis to Webster, December 16, 1841, Manning, *Dip. Corr.;* Calderón de la Barca, *Life in Mexico.*

254. Webster to Ellis, January 3, 1842, Manning, *Dip. Corr.;* Buchanan and others to Webster, June 16, 1842, *Papers of Daniel Webster.*

255. Webster to Ellis, January 3 and February 26, 1842, Manning, *Dip. Corr.;* Webster to Edward Everett, March 30, 1842, *Papers of Daniel Webster.* In this last document, Webster expresses fear that the hostility generated by the incident might disrupt his efforts to establish peaceful relations with Mexico.

256. Webster to Thompson, April 5, 1842, Manning, *Dip. Corr.*

257. Thompson to Webster, April 29 and June 20, 1842, *Papers of Daniel Webster.*

258. Thompson to Webster, March 14 and April 11, 1843, and Thompson to Bocanegra, August 9, 1843, Manning, *Dip. Corr.* Thompson informed Webster that the prisoners he interviewed had indicated that they were well treated before the attempted escape (Thompson to Webster, May 24 and August 24, 1843, *Papers of Daniel Webster*).

259. Webster to Almonte, April 26 and 29, 1843, and Almonte to Webster, April 27, 1843, Manning, *Dip. Corr.*

260. Bocanegra to Thompson, July 21, August 8, and September (n.d.), 1843, Thompson to Secretary of State, August 5, 1043, and Thompson to Bocanegra, July 22, 1843, and August 9, 1843, Manning, *Dip. Corr.; Diario del Gobierno,* August 13, 1843, quoted in Thompson to Bocanegra, August 14, 1843, Manning, *Dip. Corr.*

261. Cuevas, *Historia,* p. 627; Richman, *California,* pp. 266–75.

262. Thompson to Webster, April 29, 1842, *Papers of Daniel Webster;* Thompson to the President of the United States, May 9, 1842, Manning, *Dip. Corr.*

263. Webster to Thompson (private), June 27, 1842, *Papers of Daniel Webster.* On January 30, 1843, in the midst of the problems over the Jones raid, the secretary of state sent a ciphered note in which he expressed deep interest in the territory and stated that it would be up to Thompson to "break the ice" on the subject (Webster to Thompson, January 30, 1843, *Papers of Daniel Webster;* Jones, *To the Webster-Ashburton Treaty,* p. 138).

264. James C. Pickett to Webster, September 6, 1842, *Papers of Daniel Webster;* Jones to Thompson, October 22, 1842, Manning, *Dip. Corr.* (Jones informed Thompson that while in Callao, Peru, he had received a letter from the U.S. consul in Mazatlán, John Parrott, with an article from the official Mexican paper which was highly offensive and belligerent, and had therefore assumed that war had begun. Pickett's letter from Lima, Peru, supported that claim).

265. Bocanegra to Thompson, December 19, 1842, Manning, *Dip. Corr.;* Thompson to Bocanegra, December 27, 1842, and Thompson to Webster, December 28, 1842, *Papers of Daniel Webster.*

266. Webster to Thompson, January 17, 1843, Manning, *Dip. Corr.*

267. Almonte to Webster, January 24 and February 7, 1843, and Webster to Almonte, January 21 and 30, 1843, Manning, *Dip. Corr.*

268. Tyler to Webster, February 9, 1843, *Papers of Daniel Webster*.

269. Webster to Almonte, March 3, 1843, Manning, *Dip. Corr.*

270. Bocanegra to Foreign Diplomatic Corps in Mexico, July 6, 1842, and Thompson to Webster, June 20, July 30, and August 16, 1842, Manning, *Dip. Corr.* In 1843 Thompson stated: "The Mexicans hate us with the hatred of a Spaniard—bitter and unchanging" (Thompson to Webster, January 30, 1843, *Papers of Daniel Webster*; here Thompson lashed out at Webster for not listening to information he sends and says that, if Webster has lost confidence in him, then he should be recalled).

271. Thompson to Upshur, October 3 and 14 and November 20, 1843, and March 25, 1844, and Green to Secretary of State, April 8, 1844, Manning, *Dip. Corr.*

272. Bocanegra to Thompson, September 1843, Upshur to Thompson, November 18, 1843, and Thompson to Upshur, March 25, 1844, Manning, *Dip. Corr.;* Moorhead, *New Mexico's Royal Road*, pp. 70–75; Arrongoiz, *México*, p. 379.

273. Richman, *California*, pp. 275–81; Weber, *Mexican Frontier*, pp. 202–41; Thompson to Upshur, October 3, 1843, and Green to Secretary of State, April 8, 1844, Manning, *Dip. Corr.*

274. González Navarro, *Raza y Tierra*, p. 72; Thompson to Bocanegra, August 9, 1843, and Thompson to Upshur, September 30, 1843, Manning, *Dip. Corr.*

275. Upshur to Thompson, July 12 and 27, and October, 20, 1843, Manning, *Dip. Corr.*

276. Thompson to Bocanegra, August 14, 1843, Thompson to Upshur, August 25, 1843, and Bocanegra to Thompson, August 23, 1843, Manning, *Dip. Corr.*

277. Upshur to Almonte, November 8, 1843, Manning, *Dip. Corr.*

278. Almonte to Upshur, November 3 and 11, December 11, 1843, Manning, *Dip. Corr.*

279. Thompson to Upshur, March 25, 1844, Thompson to Bocanegra, March 9, 1844, Bocanegra to Thompson, March 9, 1844, and Green to Secretary of State, April 8, 1844, Manning, *Dip. Corr.* Benjamin E. Green, who was left as chargé d'affaires ad interim, was much less optimistic, feeling that Santa Anna might involve Mexico in a foreign war to remain in power: see Green to Secretary of State, April 8, 1844, Manning, *Dip. Corr.*

280. Thompson to Upshur, February 2, 1844, and report of a conversation between Upshur and Almonte, February 16, 1844, Manning, *Dip. Corr.*

281. Calhoun to Green, April 19, 1844, Calhoun to Almonte, April 22, 1844, Calhoun to Shannon, June 20, 1844, and Green to Bocanegra, May 23, 1844, Manning, *Dip. Corr.*

282. Almonte to Calhoun, April 22, 1844, Green to Calhoun, April 25, May

16 and 30, 1844, Green to Bocanegra, May 31 and June 10, 1844, Bocanegra to Green, May 30, June 6, 12, 23, 25, July 2, 1844, Green to Calhoun, June 7, 15, 17, 21, 25, 28, July 14, and August 20, 1844, Thompson to Green, March 27, 1844, Green to Bocanegra, July 4 and 12, 1844, and Thomas O. Larkin (U.S. consul at Monterey, California) to Calhoun, August 18 and September 16, 1844, all in Manning, *Dip. Corr.*

283. Shannon to Calhoun, September 21, 1844, Shannon to Rejón, October 10, 1844, Rejón to Shannon, October 31, November 6 and 21, 1844, Manning, *Dip. Corr.*; Carlos A. Echánove Trujillo, "Manuel Crecencio Rejón," in *Enciclopedia Yucatanense* (Mexico City: La Comisión Reeditora de la Enciclopedia Yucatanense, 1977), 7:105–40. See also Alessio Robles, *Coahuila y Texas* 2:310–11.

284. Shannon to Calhoun, October 28 and November 12, 1844, and Shannon to Rejón, November 4 and 8, 1844, Manning, *Dip. Corr.*

285. Calhoun to Shannon, September 10, 1844, Richard K. Cralle (acting Secretary of State) to Shannon, October 1, 1844, Shannon to Calhoun, October 28, November 12 and 30, and December 9, 1844, Manning, *Dip. Corr.*

286. Shannon to Calhoun, January 9, 1845, Manning, *Dip. Corr.*

287. Shannon to Calhoun, January 16, 1845, and Larkin to Calhoun, January 25, 1845, Manning, *Dip. Corr.*

288. Almonte to Calhoun, March 6, 1845, Shannon to Secretary of State, March 27, 1845, Cuevas to Shannon, March 28, 1845, and Shannon to Cuevas, March 31, 1845, Manning, *Dip. Corr.*

289. Brack, *Mexico Views Manifest Destiny*, pp. 135–68; Joaquín M. de Castillo y Lanzas to Slidell, March 12, 1846, Manning, *Dip. Corr.*

290. Charles Sumner, for instance, denounced the move of the army into Texas as an act of aggression. Joshua Giddings accused Polk of fabricating deceptions and lies to bring on the conflict.

291. This is reflected in public school texts, television and radio programs, and in comic books throughout Mexico.

292. Buchanan to Slidell, November 10, December 17, 1845, and January 20, 1846, Manning, *Dip. Corr.*

293. *The Diary of James K. Polk during his Presidency, 1845 to 1849*, ed. Milo Milton Quaife, 4 vols. (Chicago: A. C. McClurg, 1910), especially entries for March 28 and 29 and April 3, 1846; see also Buchanan to Slidell, March 12, 1846, Manning, *Dip. Corr.*

294. Slidell to Buchanan, November 30, 1845, February 17, March 1, and April 2, 1846, Manning, *Dip. Corr.* See also Black to Peña y Peña, October 13 and November 3, 1845, Manning, *Dip. Corr.*

295. Parrott to Buchanan, July 26, 1845, Manning, *Dip. Corr.*

296. Peña y Peña to Murphy, November 28 and December 27, 1845, Murphy to Peña y Peña, November 1 and December 1, 1845, January 1, February 1, April 1, and June 1, 1846, all in *Lord Aberdeen, Texas y California.*

297. Buchanan to Slidell, January 20 and March 12, 1846, and Slidell to Buchanan, February 6, 1846, Manning, *Dip. Corr.*

298. Ward McAfee and J. Cordell Robinson, eds., *Origins of the Mexican War: A Documentary Source Book* (Salisbury, N.C.: Documentary Publications, 1982), 1:iii–xiv. This work points out that there is conflicting evidence relating to the exact motivation of Polk in his western policy. See also Mary Lee Spence and Donald Jackson, eds., *The Expeditions of John Charles Fremont*, 2 vols. (Urbana: University of Illinois, 1970), and Glenn W. Price, *Origins of the War with Mexico: The Polk-Stockton Intrigue* (Austin: University of Texas Press, 1967).

299. McAfee and Robinson, *Origins of the Mexican War* 1:87–131; *Diary of James K. Polk*, February 13, 16, and 17, 1846.

300. *Diary of James K. Polk*, April 28, 1846.

301. Ibid., May 13, 1846.

302. Justin H. Smith, *The War With Mexico*, 2 vols. (New York: Macmillan, 1919).

303. Bancroft, *History of Arizona and New Mexico*, pp. 337–473; Moorhead, *New Mexico's Royal Road*, pp. 123–51.

304. Larkin to Buchanan, March 27, April 2 and 17, June 1, July 18 and 20, and August 27, 1846, Manning, *Dip. Corr.*; Sloat to the Inhabitants of California, July 7, 1846, quoted in Manning, *Dip. Corr.* Sloat promised not only that property rights would be respected but also that the Catholic church would retain its property and function.

305. Shannon to Buchanan, April 6, 1845, Manning, *Dip. Corr.*

306. Thomas Ewing Cotner, *The Military and Political Career of José Joaquín de Herrera, 1792–1854* (Austin: University of Texas Press, 1949), pp. 110–51; Adams, *British Dip. Corr.*, pp. 477–509; Parrott to Buchanan, April 29, July 12 and 30, August 26, and September 25 and 29, 1845, Manning, *Dip. Corr.*

307. Slidell to Buchanan, December 17, 1845, and January 14, 1846, Black to Buchanan, December 20 and 30, 1845, and Peña y Peña to Slidell, December 20, 1845, Manning, *Dip. Corr.*

308. Slidell to Buchanan, March 18, 1846, and Black to Buchanan, March 19, May 23 and 26, and June 1, 1846, Manning, *Dip. Corr.*; Hale, *Mexican Liberalism*, pp. 145–47.

309. Black to Buchanan, August 6, September 17, and December 26, 1846, Manning, *Dip. Corr.* For a glimpse of the confused and confusing political alliances of convenience, see Bazant, *Antonio Haro y Tamariz*, pp. 41–45.

310. Black to Buchanan, February 24 and March 6, 1847, Manning, *Dip. Corr.*; José Maria Roa Barcena, *Recuerdos de la invasión norteamericana, 1846–1848*, 3 vols. (Mexico: Editorial Porrua, 1947); José Fernando Ramírez, *Mexico during the War with the United States*, trans. Elliott B. Scherr and ed. Walter V. Scholes (Columbia: University of Missouri Press, 1950).

311. Beach to Buchanan, June 4, 1847, Manning, *Dip. Corr.*

312. Edward H. Moseley, "The Religious Impact of the American Occupation of Mexico City, 1847–1848," in *Militarists, Merchants, and Missionaries:*

United States Expansion in Middle America, ed. Eugene R. Huck and Edward H. Moseley (Tuscaloosa: University of Alabama Press, 1970), pp. 39–52.

313. Nicholas Trist to Buchanan, October 25, 1847, Nathan Clifford to Buchanan, June 26, 1848, Manning, *Dip. Corr.;* Hale, *Mexican Liberalism,* pp. 188–214.

314. Parrott to Buchanan, July 26 and September 2, 1845, Slidell to Buchanan, January 14 and February 6 and 17, 1846, Manning, *Dip. Corr.;* Alessio Robles, *Coahuila y Texas* 2:303–70; Edward D. Fitchen, "Self-Determination or Self-Preservation?: The Relations of Independent Yucatán with the Republic of Texas and the United States, 1847–1849," *Journal of the West* 18, no. 1 (January 1979): 33–40.

315. Bancroft, *History of Arizona and New Mexico,* pp. 337–42; Moorhead, *New Mexico's Royal Road,* pp. 70–75, 123–51; Arrongoiz, *México,* p. 379.

316. Shannon to Buchanan, April 6, 1845, Parrott to Buchanan, August 26, 1845, and Larkin to Buchanan, July 10, September 29, and November 4, 1845, March 27, April 2, and 17, 1846, Manning, *Dip. Corr.;* Spence and Jackson, *Expeditions of John Charles Fremont.*

317. Leland Hargrave Creer, *The Founding of an Empire: The Exploration and Colonization of Utah, 1776–1856* (Salt Lake City, Utah: Bookcraft, 1947), pp. 42–188, 222–37; James H. McClintock, *Mormon Settlement in Arizona* (Tucson: University of Arizona Press, 1985), pp. 38–47; *Diary of James K. Polk,* May 13, 1846; Juanita Brooks, ed., *On the Mormon Frontier: The Diary of Hosea Stout, 1844–1861* (Salt Lake City: University of Utah Press, 1964), pp. 163–64.

318. McClintock, *Mormon Settlement,* pp. 48–52.

319. Creer, *Founding of an Empire,* pp. 339–89.

320. Bancroft, *History of Arizona and New Mexico,* pp. 474–90.

321. Jack Northrup, "The Trist Mission," *Journal of Mexican American History* 3 (1973): 13–31. Both Scott and Trist were concerned about the consequences of occupying Mexico City and losing contact with formal Mexican government. Many officers and men of Scott's army were critical of the decision, seeing an undue British influence in it.

322. Trist to Buchanan, February 2, 1848, Manning, *Dip. Corr.* See also Cotner, *Herrera,* pp. 152–71.

323. Trist to Buchanan, October 25, November 7, and December 6, 1847, Manning, *Dip. Corr.* This was true, according to Trist, especially of large property holders and members of the clergy. There was evidence that some of the liberals also favored annexation.

324. Schurz, *Henry Clay* 2:286.

325. Quotations from speeches of Cass and Calhoun in Alvin R. Sunseri, "Anglo Attitudes toward Hispanos, 1846–1861," *Journal of Mexican American History* 3 (1973): 76–88.

326. Quotes from Scott and Trist in Northrup, "Trist Mission," p. 25.

327. Cotner, *Herrera,* pp. 152–71.

328. Earl W. Fornell, "Texas and Filibusters in the 1850s," *Southwestern His-*

torical Quarterly 59 (April 1956): 411–28; Thomas W. Hemons (United States consul in Matamoros) to John Clayton, June 18, 1849, Dispatches from United States Consuls in Matamoros, Mexico, 1826–1906, (Microcopy), National Archives; Ernest C. Shearer, "The Carvajal Disturbances," *Southwestern Historical Quarterly* 55 (October 1951): 201–30; Ernest C. Shearer, "The Callahan Expedition, 1855," *Southwestern Historical Quarterly* 54 (April 1951): 430–51; Ronnie C. Tyler, "The Callahan Expedition of 1855: Indians or Negroes," *Southwestern Historical Quarterly* 70 (April 1967): 574–85.

329. William O. Scroggs, *Filibusters and Financiers: The Story of William Walker and His Associates* (New York: Macmillan, 1916).

330. The most sweeping concessions were made by the liberal government of Benito Juárez in the McLane-Ocampo treaty of 1859. This measure would have given the United States dominance in the Isthmus of Tehuantepec and virtual control over much of northern Mexico through railroad concessions. By the time the bill reached the United States Senate, however, sectional divisions ensured its doom.

331. Reed, *Caste War*, pp. 53–74; González Navarro, *Raza y Tierra*, pp. 76–85; Fitchen, "Self-Determination or Self-Preservation?" pp. 33–40.

332. Justo Sierra O'Reilly, *Diario de Nuestro Viaje a Los Estados Unidos* (Mexico City: José Porrua é Hijos, 1938); Justo Sierra to Buchanan, November 24, December 15 and 27, 1847, Manning, *Dip. Corr.*

333. Justo Sierra, *Diario*; Justo Sierra to Buchanan, February 13 and 24, March 3, 7, and 25, 1848, Manning, *Dip. Corr.*

334. Justo Sierra, *Diario*; Justo Sierra to Buchanan, April 3 and 21, 1848, Manning, *Dip. Corr.*

335. Justo Sierra, entry for April 29, 1848, and Document no. 32, "Message of the President of the United States," in *Diario*, pp. 36, 106–9.

336. Justo Sierra to Buchanan, May 23 and June 16, 1848, and documents quoted in Justo Sierra, *Diario*, pp. 116–18.

337. Cotner, *Herrera*, p. 228; Buchanan to Nathan Clifford, August 7, 1848, Manning, *Dip. Corr.*

Chapter 7
Early United States Recognition of Colombian Independence and Subsequent Relations to 1830

1. Although there are a great many published works on Bolívar, one of the best may still be *Simón Bolívar*, by Gerhard Masur (Albuquerque: University of New Mexico Press, 1948). An excellent work in Spanish is Indalecio Lievano Aguirre, *Bolívar* (Mexico: EDIAPSA, 1956). Robert F. McNerney, Jr., has published his translation of the account by Bolívar's favorite aide, *Bolívar and the*

War of Independence: "Memorias del General Daniel Florencio O'Leary" (Austin: University of Texas Press, 1970). Donald E. Worcester's *Bolívar* (Boston: Little, Brown, 1977) is short and readable, and Salvador de Madariaga's *Bolívar* (Gainesville: University of Florida Press, 1952) is more detailed.

2. For excellent coverage of this topic, see Robert L. Gilmore, "Federalism in Colombia, 1810–1858" (Ph.D. diss., University of California, 1949), and David Bushnell, *The Santander Regime in Gran Colombia* (Newark: University of Delaware Press, 1954).

3. Pedro de la Lastra to James Madison, December 1812 or January 1813, Records of the Department of State, Notes from Foreign Legations, Colombia, vol. 1, pt. 1, National Archives. All letters cited hereafter, unless otherwise noted, are from the same repository. Since they could be in various files within that department, the citation will list whether it is a diplomatic instruction, a United States consular dispatch, or a note to or from a foreign legation.

4. Until 1832 Colombia was one of three divisions of Gran Colombia, which also included Venezuela and Ecuador. Colombia was called New Granada until 1857, when it took its current name.

5. Thomas Blossom, "Antonio Nariño, Precursor of Colombian Independence" (Ph.D. diss., Duke University, 1956), p. 195. Blossom is quoting Eduardo Posada and Pedro M. Ibáñez, comps., *El precursor: Documentos sobre la vida pública y privada del General Antonio Nariño* (Bogotá: Biblioteca de Historia Nacional, 1903), 2:399–412.

6. Jesús María Henao and Geraldo Arrubla, *History of Colombia* (Durham, N.C.: Duke University Press, 1938), p. 26.

7. Miranda's speech of December 22, 1797, is quoted in W. H. Koebel, *British Exploits in South America* (New York: Century, 1917), p. 165.

8. Mary W. Williams, *Anglo-American Isthmian Diplomacy, 1815–1915* (Gloucester, Mass.: P. Smith, 1965), p. 26.

9. Richard Rush, minister to Great Britain, to John Quincy Adams, Secretary of State, May 27, 1818, Dispatches 20.

10. Castlereagh to Rush for transmittal to Adams, August 26, 1819, Dispatches 20.

11. John Quincy Adams, minister to Great Britain, to United States Secretary of State, January 22, 1816, Dispatches 20.

12. Ibid.

13. The official British position on the recognition of the independence was stated by George Canning on August 20, 1823, in correspondence with Richard Rush, United States minister to Great Britain. Canning proposed that his country and the United States issue a joint statement, the second point of which was, "We conceive the question of recognition of them [Spain's colonies] as Independent States, to be one of time and circumstances." Although he gave no specific reason for not agreeing to recognition, the expression "of time and circumstances" was broad enough to cover any conceivable cause for inaction. See Canning to Rush, Private and Confidential, Foreign Office, Au-

gust 20, 1823. Printed by W. C. Ford, "Some Original Documents on the Genesis of the Monroe Doctrine," *Proceedings of the Massachusetts Historical Society*, 2d ser., 15 (January 1902): 415–16, reprinted separately, Cambridge, 1902, and in *American Historical Review* 7 (July 1920): 676–96; this quote comes from Samuel Flagg Bemis, *The Latin American Policy of the United States* (New York: Harcourt, Brace, and World, 1943), p. 398 n. 12.

14. Samuel Eliot Morison, in *The Maritime History of Massachusetts* (Boston: Houghton Mifflin, 1941), p. 182, tells of several men who served with distinction, including William P. White, who had established a mercantile agency in Argentina and who gave so much aid that he was called "the Father of the Argentine Navy."

15. Count Fernán Núñez, Spanish ambassador to Great Britain, said that he considered the filibustering expedition from Kentucky and Tennessee to the Spanish New World as "offensive," according to John Q. Adams's dispatch to the Secretary of State, March 30, 1816.

16. Much of the U.S.-Colombian diplomatic action for 1825–40 was from the claims of United States seamen serving as privateers.

17. Rush to Secretary of State, August 3, 1818, Dispatches.

18. Manuel Torres, Colombian representative to the United States, to the President of the United States, March 22, 1820, Notes, vol. 1, pt. 1.

19. Clay's participation and the story of U.S. relations in obtaining recognition of Latin American independence are amply discussed in such well-known works as Arthur P. Whitaker, *The United States and the Independence of Latin America 1800–1830* (New York: Russell and Russell, 1962); Samuel Flagg Bemis, *Latin American Policy*, and his *John Quincy Adams and the Foundations of American Foreign Policy* (New York: Knopf, 1956); Dexter Perkins, *A History of the Monroe Doctrine* (Boston: Little, Brown, 1963).

20. *Autobiography of Martin Van Buren*, ed. J. C. Fitzpatrick (Washington, D.C.: U.S. Government Printing Office, 1918), p. 306.

21. *Gaceta de Colombia*, October 7, 1821, p. 4. This is the official newspaper and later is called such under the new title *Gaceta Oficial*.

22. Abbe de Pradt (archbishop of Malinas), *Congresos de Carlsbad* (Madrid: Imprenta de José del Collado, 1820), p. 85.

23. Rush to Secretary of State, April 22, 1822, Dispatches.

24. Ibid.

25. Ibid.

26. Lafayette to Clay, November 5, 1822, *The Private Correspondence of Henry Clay*, ed. Calvin Colton (New York: A. S. Barnes, 1856), pp. 67–68.

27. Rush to Secretary of State, May 6, 1822, Dispatches 1, no. 244. Italics Rush's.

28. Rush to Secretary of State, November 20, 1818, *Dispatches*.

29. *Gaceta de Colombia*, May 2, 1824, p. 2.

30. Henderson to Canning, March 4, 1825, British Foreign Office 18/16,

C. K. Webster, *Britain and the Independence of Latin America, 1812–1830* (New York: Octagon Books, 1970), 1:383–84.

31. Paul Knapland, *The British Empire, 1815–1939* (New York: Harper and Brothers, 1941), p. 89.

32. Ibid., p. 99.

33. Leland H. Jenks, *The Migration of British Capital to 1875* (New York: Knopf, 1938), p. 52.

34. José María Salazar to Secretary of State, December 1825, Notes, vol. 1, pt. 2.

35. James D. Richardson, ed., *Messages and Papers of the Presidents, 1789–1919* (Washington, D.C.: U.S. Government Printing Office, 1901), 2:326.

36. Dawkins to Canning, July 7, 1826, British Foreign Office 97/115, Webster, *Britain and the Independence* 1:414.

37. William R. Manning, ed., *Diplomatic Correspondence of the United States: Inter-American Affairs, 1831–1860* (Washington: Carnegie Endowment for International Peace, 1938), 5:2069.

38. Dawkins to Canning, July 7, 1826, Webster, *Britain and the Independence* 1:414–15.

39. Bolívar to Santander, June 10, 1825, in Archivo Santander, 13:73–77.

40. Colonel P. Campbell to George Canning, November 27, 1826, Webster, *Britain and the Independence* 1:425–26.

41. Ibid.

42. *Gaceta de Colombia*, May 5, 1825, p. 4.

43. Hamilton to Joseph Planta (private), March 8, 1825, Webster, *Britain and the Independence* 1:385.

44. Koebel, *British Exploits*, p. 175.

45. Torres to James Monroe, August 11, 1820, Notes 1, pt. 1.

46. Torres to Adams, February 20, 1821, William R. Manning, ed., *Diplomatic Correspondence of the United States concerning the Independence of the Latin American Republics* (New York: Oxford University Press, 1925), vol. 2, document 604. See also Rob Roy MacGregor, "The Treaty of 1846" (Ph.D. diss., Clark University, 1929), p. 43.

47. John Quincy Adams, *Memoirs*, as cited in Bemis, *Adams and the Foundations of American Foreign Policy*, p. 354.

48. Adams to Anderson, May 27, 1823, Bemis, *Adams and the Foundations of American Foreign Policy*, p. 466.

49. Louis Ospina Vásquez, *Industria y protección en Colombia, 1810–1930* (Medellín: Editorial Santa Fé, 1955), pp. 91–92.

50. Adams, *Writings*, as cited in Whitaker, *United States and the Independence of Latin America*, p. 596. The passage occurred in the draft of Adams's instructions to Anderson of May 27, 1823, but was deleted.

51. Adams to Anderson, May 27, 1823, Instructions 9, and Hunter Miller, comp., *Treaties and Other International Acts of the United States of America,*

1776–1863 (Washington, D.C.: U.S. Government Printing Office, 1931–48), 3:188.

52. Estados Unidos de Colombia, *Colección de tratados públicos* (Bogotá: 1866), commercial treaty between the United States and Colombia, 1825, art. 12, p. 29. See also MacGregor, "Treaty of 1846," p. 50. There is a six-page discussion of the principle of "free flag makes free goods" in the published minutes of the presidential cabinet, *Acuerdos del consejo de gobierno de la república de Colombia* (Bogotá: Imprenta Municipál, 1940), June 10, 1824, 1:211–17.

53. José María Salazar to Henry Clay, March 23, 1825, Notes 1, pt. 2.

54. Miller, *Treaties* 1:190. The *Gaceta de Colombia*, November 13, 1825, p. 2, stated that it was confirmed on May 6, 1825.

55. Raimundo Rivas, *Relaciones internacionales entre Colombia y los Estados Unidos, 1810–1850* (Bogotá: Imprenta Nacional, 1915), p. 76.

56. Bushnel, *Santander Regime*, pp. 157–58.

57. Anderson to Clay, January 26, 1826, and February 1, 1826, Dispatches 3, as cited in E. Taylor Parks, *Colombia and the United States, 1765–1934* (New York: Greenwood Press, 1968), p. 169.

58. Miller, *Treaties* 3:191.

59. These difficulties included the revolt of Páez in Venezuela, the extension of the Bolívar-Santander feud, Bolívar's abortive dictatorship, and the attempted assassination of Bolívar on September 25, 1828.

60. MacPherson to Adams, May 8, 1823, Dispatches 1.

61. MacPherson to Adams, July 21, 1824, Dispatches 1.

62. MacPherson to Clay, May 6, 1826, Dispatches 1.

63. *Acuerdos*, January 23, 1826, 2:117.

64. Richardson, *Messages and Papers* 2:341–42. This special message, which was delivered to the Senate and the House of Representatives of the United States on March 30, 1826, explained clearly the interchange over the treaties in question.

65. Salazar to Adams, Philadelphia, August 18, 1823, Notes 1, pt. 2. Appointments were made for consular posts in Savannah, Baltimore, New Orleans, Charleston, New York, and Boston and one post for Pennsylvania, Delaware, and western New Jersey.

66. MacPherson to Clay, May 6, 1826, Dispatches 1.

67. MacPherson to Martin Van Buren, September 1, 1829, Dispatches 1.

68. Ibid.

69. *Acuerdos*, April 1, 1826, 2:136.

70. MacPherson to Clay, May 6, 1826, Dispatches 1.

71. *Gaceta de Colombia*, March 5, 1826, p. 4.

72. Whitaker, *United States and the Independence of Latin America*, p. 598.

73. See Bushnell, *Santander Regime*, p. 164, for his comments and statistics to support this observation.

74. MacPherson to Clay, May 6, 1826, Dispatches 1.

75. José Manuel Restrepo, *Autobiografia*, vol. 30 of *Biblioteca de la presidencia de colombia* (Bogotá: Imprenta Nacional, 1957), pp. 26–27.

76. Ibid., p. 28.

77. Ibid., pp. 35–36.

78. Ibid., p. 42.

79. José Manuel Restrepo, "Memoria de la secretaría del interiór," presented to Congress, 1823, and found in an enclosure of Salazar to Adams, August 18, 1823, Notes 1, pt. 2.

80. Gilmore, "Federalism in Colombia," pp. 64–65.

81. Decree of Bolívar issued over the signature of José María del Castillo de Rada, secretary of the treasury, November 23, 1826, in Letras, Archivo Nacional de Colombia, Bogotá, Colombia, 1:79.

82. Decree of Bolívar issued over the signature of Nicholas M. Tanco, secretary of the treasury, December 23, 1828, Letras, 1:74A.

83. Rivas, *Relaciones internacionales*, p. 76; Parks, *Colombia and the United States*, p. 170.

84. *Gaceta de Colombia*, July 24, 1828, p. 4.

85. *Gaceta de Colombia*, October 19, 1828, p. 4. The *Gaceta* quoted the *Investigator* of Maine through a French periodical, the *Journal de Commerce*. In keeping with the Spanish system of surnames, the *Gaceta de Colombia* often refers to John Quincy Adams as "Mr. Quincy."

86. Thomas P. Moore, United States chargé d'affaires to Colombia, to Dr. Felix Restrepo, July 18, 1831, Letras, 1:580–84.

87. The decree was included as "Note II" in a communication by Moore dated November 21, 1831, and is reproduced in Miller, *Treaties* 3:192.

88. Miller, *Treaties* 3:193. The commercial arrangement by the U.S. government can be found in *Statutes at Large* 4, pp. 515–16.

89. Minister of Foreign Relations to Consejo de Estado, February 5, 1831, Letras, 1:351.

90. Minister of Foreign Relations to Consejo de Estado, February 13, 1831, Letras, 1:355–56.

91. Todd to Clay, May 8, 1823, *Private Correspondence of Henry Clay*, p. 78. Colonel William Duane of Philadelphia was editor of the pro-Latin American newspaper *Aurora*. He visited Colombia with his daughter during the early 1820s.

92. Adams to Anderson, May 27, 1823, MacGregor, "Treaty of 1846," p. 42. According to MacGregor, the full document is given in W. C. Ford's *The Writings of John Quincy Adams* (Cambridge, Mass.: J. Wilson and Son, 1902), 3:441–87.

93. Santander to Bolívar, September 9, 1823, *Cartas de Santander*, ed. Vicente Lecuna (Caracas: Lit. y Tip. del Comercio, 1942), 1:238. Anderson was selected to be the U.S. representative to the ill-fated congress of Panama in 1826, but he was destined never to carry out the assignment. While on his way to the meeting he was stricken at Cartagena and died on July 24, 1826, of

"fever and ague." A week earlier than the letter that bore the news about the minister, MacPherson, at Cartagena, informed the State Department of the death of another U.S. official. A Mr. Fudger, consul at Santa Marta, was murdered on July 13, 1826, "while asleep in his lodgings. He was stabbed to the heart, his throat cut, and his trunks pillaged of their contents. No trace of evidence has yet been discovered" (MacPherson to Clay, July 19, 1826, Dispatches 1).

94. Parks, *Colombia and the United States*, pp. 151–52. See also Manning, *Diplomatic Correspondence of the United States* 2:1310.

95. These citations were used on April 21, 1827, by José R. Ravenga, foreign minister of Caracas, in an effort to explain to the U.S. government why Watts's letter was published. Ravenga, in a letter to Clay (September 15, 1827, Notes 1, pt. 2) and in reference to Watts's letter, said, "Strange as its publications may have appeared to some persons, as it was calculated to produce some good, the Liberator thought that to refrain from giving it publicity, merely because it is not customary to do so, would have argued a misconception of the Government of your Excellency."

96. Restrepo to Watts, June 12, 1827, Manning, *Diplomatic Correspondence of the United States* 2:1314–15.

97. Parks, *Colombia and the United States*, pp. 153–58; Parks provides an excellent survey of the difficult position into which Harrison placed the United States. Rivas, *Relaciones internacionales*, p. 71, states that Harrison was working with the Masonic Lodges there.

98. Parks, *Colombia and the United States*, p. 155. See also Van Buren to Moore, April 2, 1829, Instructions 14, no. 1.

99. Jackson to Van Buren, March 27, 1829, as quoted in *Autobiography of Martin Van Buren*, p. 248.

100. Rivas, *Relaciones internacionales*, p. 72.

101. Moore to Señor Vicente Borrerro, minister of foreign relations of Colombia, January 11, 1831, as quoted by the *Gaceta de Colombia*, January 23, 1831, p. 3.

102. The invitation was tendered on October 27, 1831, by F. Francisco Pereira, secretary of the national convention, on behalf of the vice-president, Domingo Caicedo. Its notice was carried in the *Gaceta de Colombia*, November 13, 1831, p. 2.

103. Of the sixty-nine donors who contributed over five hundred pesos, Moore was listed as having given forty. Vice-President Caicedo gave seventy, General Obando fifty, and the others about five pesos each. William Turner, minister of Great Britain, and A. LeMoine, minister of France, were not listed as contributors (*Gaceta de la Nueva Granada*, December 8, 1831, p. 4).

104. *Gaceta de la Nueva Granada*, April 22, 1832, p. 5.

105. *Gaceta de la Nueva Granada*, July 8, 1832, p. 3.

106. Moore to Van Buren, May 21, 1831, Manning, *Diplomatic Correspondence of the United States* 2:1362–64, and Parks, *Colombia and the United States*,

p. 159. The circular letter dated May 3, 1831, which was sent to the various legations, was acknowledged by Moore on May 5, 1831, according to the *Gaceta de la Nueva Granada*, May 8, 1831, p. 2. In the issue of the *Gaceta* for December 8, 1831, which showed the changeover from the government of Domingo Caicedo, the U.S. response was the first one issued. That the U.S. response was thus treated was apparently a standard practice regardless of the acceptance data.

107. Request for that service was made from Washington by the secretary of state (McLane to McAfee, March 14, 1834, Instructions 15, no. 7). J. C. A. Williamson was assigned to La Guaira, Venezuela, on May 1, 1835, in order to conclude a commercial treaty with that country. The best account of U.S. diplomatic representatives in Colombia is, surprisingly, Francisco José Urrutia, *Paginas de historica diplomática: Los Estados Unidos de América y las repúblicas hispanoamerica de 1810 a 1830*, Biblioteca de Historia Nacional, vol. 20 (Bogotá: Imprenta Nacional, 1917). Urrutia devotes 15 pages to Todd, 31 to Anderson, 5 to Watts, 46 to Harrison, and 32 to Moore, most of which contain letters from the ministers to their U.S. secretaries of state.

108. J. Steuart, *Bogotá in 1836–1837, Being a Narrative of an Expedition to the Capital of New Granada and a Residence There of Eleven Months* (New York: Harper and Brothers, 1898), p. 20.

Chapter 8
Personnel Diplomacy: The United States and Chile, 1812–1850

1. Heman Allen to John Q. Adams, April 29, 1824, Dispatches from U.S. Ministers to Chile, 1823–1906, 1, Department of State General Records, National Archives, Washington, D.C. (cited hereafter as Dispatches). Allen received a nineteen-gun salute when he reached Valparaíso, a twenty-two-gun salute in Santiago, and Supreme Director Ramón Freire offered him a personal honor guard and residence at Chilean expense.

2. Allen to Henry Clay, November 5, 1825, Dispatches 1. Clay had served as secretary of state for over half a year before Allen found out.

3. Samuel Larned to Clay, June 9, 1829, Dispatches 3.

4. John Hamm to Martin Van Buren, July 20, 1831, Dispatches 3.

5. Hamm to "My Dear Friend," May 31, 1832, Dispatches 3.

6. Richard Pollard to John Forsyth, July 12, 1837, Dispatches 5.

7. John Pendleton to Abel P. Upshur, October 30, 1843, Dispatches 6.

8. William Crump to James Buchanan, March 18, 1846, Dispatches 6.

9. Seth Barton to Buchanan, April 25, 1848, Dispatches 7.

10. Arthur P. Whitaker, *The United States and the Independence of Latin America, 1800–1830* (New York: W. W. Norton, 1964), pp. 10–13. Colonial officials

in Chile were hard-pressed to know exactly what Madrid's trade policies were during this time. But, in reality, the Spanish Philippine Company maintained monopoly trade privileges to all ports on the west coast of South America.

11. William Spence Robertson, *Hispanic-American Relations with the United States* (New York: Oxford University Press, 1923), p. 188.

12. Roy F. Nichols, "William Shaler, New England Apostle of Rational Liberty," *New England Quarterly* 9 (1936): 72–74.

13. Whitaker, *United States and the Independencé*, p. 65.

14. J. Fred Rippy, *Joel R. Poinsett, Versatile American* (New York: Greenwood Press, 1968), p. 44. Mathew Arnold Hoevel, whom Poinsett had recently appointed as U.S. consul for Valparaíso, apparently got so drunk that he insulted Poinsett and lost his new post.

15. Ibid., pp. 46–47. Poinsett's reputation with Camilo Henríquez and others was substantial enough for them to have sought his advice on the drafting of a Chilean constitution, a protective tariff, and a tax code.

16. Ibid., p. 48.

17. Ibid., p. 49.

18. Whitaker, *United States and the Independence*, pp. 162–63. Brackenridge was assigned as secretary to special commissioners Theodorick Bland (his father-in-law), John Graham, and Caesar A. Rodney in late 1817, when they were sent as U.S. observers to the La Plata region and Chile (Edward Baxter Billingsley, *In Defense of Neutral Rights: The United States Navy and the Wars of Independence in Chile and Peru* [Chapel Hill: University of North Carolina Press, 1967], p. 11). Skinner was serving as postmaster of Baltimore when writing the "Lautaro" letters, and, like Porter, he was an ardent supporter of the Carrera faction against the more conservative O'Higgins wing of the Santiago patriots. Skinner loaned Carrera four thousand dollars in 1817, and in 1818 Commissioner Bland paid him a brief visit in Santiago (Whitaker, *United States and the Independence*, pp. 162–63).

19. Billingsley, *In Defense of Neutral Rights*, p. 20. Captain Biddle's brother, Nicholas, a Philadelphia banking tycoon, had taken an active interest in Latin America. As a friend and confidant of President Monroe, he urged a strong U.S. involvement there, believing that the future of those emerging nations was inextricably entwined with U.S. interests (ibid., p. 15). Prevost was the stepson of Aaron Burr and had served as Monroe's secretary when Monroe was U.S. minister to Spain (ibid., p. 19).

20. Ibid., pp. 29–30. When Biddle reached Callao, he did indeed successfully negotiate the release of the *Beaver* and the *Canton*, along with their cargoes. Similar success concerning the release of the merchantmen the *Lion*, the *Indus*, the *America*, and the *Levant* brought great praise and gratitude to Biddle. The Niles *Register* conservatively estimated that the captain's good services had resulted in the restoration of over $1 million in goods (Whitaker, *United States and the Independence*, pp. 283–85).

21. Billingsley, *In Defense of Neutral Rights*, p. 15.

22. Ibid., pp. 22–37, passim. Captain Charles Carey of the *Levant* had lost nearly half of his crew to the *Lautaro*.

23. Ibid. Consul Hill was a partner in the mercantile house of Lynch, Hill, and Zimmerman in Valparaíso; he no doubt speculated that his open friendship with and aid to the patriots would result in high profits later on (ibid., p. 153).

24. Henry Clay Evans, *Chile and Its Relations with the United States* (Durham, N.C.: Duke University Press, 1927), p. 25.

25. Prevost incorrectly felt that Biddle and Captain Charles Stewart of the USS *Franklin* favored the royalists, while he, of course, was a staunch patriot partisan (Billingsley, *In Defense of Neutral Rights*, pp. 166–68).

26. Billingsley, *In Defense of Neutral Rights*, p. 38. Nicholas Biddle forwarded this letter to President Monroe.

27. Whitaker, *United States and the Independence*, p. 135.

28. Ibid., pp. 135–36. One explanation for British trade's growing so rapidly was that Admiral Thomas Cochrane's blockades discriminated in favor of his homeland's merchants and against U.S. trade.

29. Allen to Adams, April 29, 1824, Dispatches 1. Egaña referred to the United States as Chile's "best and most powerful friend."

30. Francisco de Vicaña to Allen, April 1, 1825, Dispatches 1.

31. Allen to Clay, May 4, 1825, Dispatches 1.

32. Chargé Allen, nephew of Ethan Allen, was forty-four years old when he received his appointment to Santiago. He was a graduate of Dartmouth (1795, in law), had served in the Vermont state legislature, had been chief justice of the Chittenden county court, and was serving as U.S. marshal for the district of Vermont when he accepted President Monroe's appointment to the Chilean post (*National Encyclopedia of American Biography* 11:158).

33. Allen to Adams, April 29, 1824, Dispatches 1.

34. Allen to Adams, February 9, 1825, Dispatches 1.

35. Allen to Adams, April 29, 1824, Dispatches 1.

36. Allen to Adams, May 26, 1824, Dispatches 1. The Roman Catholic church would be maintained as the state religion of Chile under the 1833 constitution and would remain as such until disestablished by the 1925 constitution (Brian Loveman, *Chile: The Legacy of Hispanic Capitalism* [New York: Oxford University Press, 1969], pp. 136–37).

37. Allen to Adams, October 23, 1824, Dispatches 1. During the nuncio's brief stay in Santiago, Allen had refused to have any intercourse with him. After all, Allen emphasized, the papal court had not yet granted to Chile official recognition (Allen to Adams, April 29, 1824, Dispatches 1).

38. Allen to Adams, August 9, 1824, Dispatches 1.

39. Ibid. Allen was especially pleased over the banishment of the bishop of Santiago, for he had been the leading ultraconservative cleric in Chile, one whose "interventions in the affairs of government" had been injurious to the young republic's development. Allen did admit, however, that the bishop's

banishment had created "some disturbance" in the capital (Allen to Clay, January 24, 1826, Dispatches 1).

40. Antonio Pinto to Allen (translation), February 9, 1825, Dispatches 1.

41. Billingsley, *In Defense of Neutral Rights*, pp. 135–39.

42. Allen to Clay, May 4, 1825, Dispatches 1.

43. Allen to Clay, January 24, 1825, Dispatches 1. The patriots' hatred for the *General Brown* dated back to 1821, when this ship had given sanctuary and escape to Viceroy Joaquín de la Pezuela (Billingsley, *In Defense of Neutral Rights*, pp. 130–35).

44. Larned to Clay, October 12, 1825, Dispatches 1.

45. Ibid.

46. Larned to Clay, November 5, 1825, Dispatches 1. Larned explained to Clay that he felt obligated to respond to Egaña's articles, especially since "no one [else] ventured or thought proper to come out in our defense." This statement was an obvious slight against Chargé Allen, whose job Larned was actively seeking.

47. Larned to Clay, March 16, 1826, Dispatches 1.

48. Allen to Clay, April 4, 1826, Dispatches 1.

49. Larned to Clay, August 25, 1826, Dispatches 2.

50. José Ignácio Cienfuegos to Larned, July 12, 1826, Dispatches 2.

51. Francisco Pinto to Larned, September 17, 1826, Dispatches 2. Pinto referred to Larned as "mi guerido amigo" (Larned to Clay, November 10, 1826, Dispatches 2).

52. Larned to Clay, April 11, 1828, Dispatches 3.

53. Larned to Clay, November 1, 1827, Dispatches 2.

54. Allen to Clay, September 19, 1827, Dispatches 2. Confirmation of Larned's promotion did not reach him until April 14, 1827 (Larned to Clay, April 19, 1827, Dispatches 2). His official credentials did not arrive in Santiago until October 1828 (Larned to Clay, November 9, 1828, Dispatches 4).

55. Larned to Clay, November 1, 1827, Dispatches 4.

56. Larned to Clay, May 10, 1828, Dispatches 3. Larned's treaty proposal was based on the U.S. commercial treaty with Colombia (William R. Manning, ed., *Diplomatic Correspondence of the United States concerning the Independence of Latin America* [New York: Oxford University Press, 1925], 3:33–34).

57. Larned to Clay, January 23, 1829, Dispatches 3.

58. Ibid. Unfortunately, it was England, not the United States, that aggressively expanded its exports to Chile. By 1836, British exports amounted to over $4 million, while total U.S. exports to all of South America for that year were valued at only $2.5 million (Evans, *Chile and Its Relations*, p. 56).

59. Larned to Van Buren, July 8, 1829, Dispatches 3.

60. Larned to Van Buren, October 20, 1829, Dispatches 3.

61. Larned to Carlos Rodríquez, October 10, 1829, Dispatches 3.

62. Hamm to Van Buren, June 9, 1830, Dispatches 3.

63. Hamm to Van Buren, December 17, 1830, Dispatches 3.

64. Hamm to Van Buren, June 20, 1831, Dispatches 3.

65. Ibid.

66. William R. Sherman, *The Diplomatic and Commercial Relations of the United States and Chile, 1820–1914* (Boston: Gorman Press, 1926), p. 26.

67. Hamm to Edward Livingston, May 20, 1832, Dispatches 3.

68. Hamm to Livingston, October 5, 1832, Dispatches 3.

69. Loveman, *Chile*, p. 136. Protestants were allowed to own their own burial grounds in Chile (Evans, *Chile and Its Relations*, p. 51).

70. Hamm to Livingston, July 28, 1833, Dispatches 3.

71. Hamm to Livingston, July 29, 1833, Dispatches 3.

72. Luis Galdames, *A History of Chile*, trans. Isaac Joslin Coy (Chapel Hill: University of North Carolina Press, 1941), pp. 274–76. Bilbao's articles in *El Crepúsculo*, especially "Socialidad chilena," soon made him a constant source of irritation for most *pelucones*. Also, his writings were responsible for his expulsion from the University of Chile and his being fined for being "blasphemous and immoral" (ibid., p. 279).

73. Hamm to Livingston, November 23, 1833, Dispatches 3.

74. Sherman, *Diplomatic and Commercial Relations*, p. 29.

75. Ibid., pp. 31–32. Pollard was not even appointed until June 1834.

76. Pollard to Forsyth, March 18, 1835, Dispatches 4. While Pollard donated one hundred dollars to the earthquake relief fund, the consuls from England and France gave two hundred dollars each.

77. Pollard to Joaquín Tocornal, April 15, 1835, Dispatches 4. This treaty would also cut into U.S. flour exports to Peru, since Chilean flour exports would be cheaper.

78. Manuel Carvallo to Forsyth, November 15, 1834, Notes from the Chilean Legation, 1811–1906, 1, Department of State General Records, National Archives, Washington, D.C. (hereafter cited as Notes).

79. Pollard to Tocornal, April 15, 1835, Dispatches 4.

80. Ibid.

81. Pollard to Forsyth, March 18, 1836, Dispatches 4.

82. Pollard to Forsyth, June 11, 1836, Dispatches 4.

83. Pollard to Forsyth, August 17, 1836, Dispatches 4.

84. Pollard to Forsyth, December 12, 1838, Dispatches 5.

85. Pollard to Forsyth, February 12, 1837, Dispatches 5.

86. Pollard to Forsyth, April 15, 1837, Dispatches 5.

87. Pollard to Forsyth, July 12, 1837, Dispatches 5. Portales was known to be a dedicated Anglophile.

88. Pollard to Forsyth, January 1, 1838, Dispatches 5.

89. Pollard to Forsyth, November 13, 1838, Dispatches 5.

90. Pollard to Forsyth, April 10, 1839, Dispatches 5.

91. Pollard to Forsyth, September 29, 1839, Dispatches 5.

92. Ramón Renjifo to Pollard, September 30, 1839, Dispatches 5. Pollard

had already asked to be replaced (Pollard to Forsyth, June 11, 1839, Dispatches 5).

93. Pollard to Daniel Webster, October 1, 1841, Dispatches 5.

94. Pollard to Webster, June 25, 1842, Dispatches 5. News of Pollard's replacement had reached Santiago in November 1841, thus negating any real hopes he might have had in settling the *Good Return* and *Franklin* claims cases (Pollard to Webster, December 13, 1841, Dispatches 5).

95. Pollard to Forsyth, July 9, 1840, Dispatches 5. For full details concerning the intricate *Macedonian* case, see Thomas Ray Shurbutt, "United States Chargés d'Affaires to Chile, 1835–1848" (Ph.D. diss., University of Georgia, 1971), pp. 51–81.

96. Diego Barros Arana, *Un decenio de la historia de Chile (1841–1851)* (Santiago: Imprenta de S.A. García Valenquela, 1906), 2:161–62.

97. Pollard to Webster, July 7, 1841, Dispatches 5.

98. Pollard to Renjifo, January 19, 1842, Dispatches 5. Pollard may have supplied the basis for his own replacement through a "private" letter to Van Buren in September 1839. This letter, which should not have been filed with Pollard's dispatches, states that Pollard approved of Van Buren's solution to the U.S. bank crisis and that he hoped Van Buren would be reelected (Pollard to Van Buren, September 23, 1839, Dispatches 5).

99. Pendleton to Webster, June 19, 1842, Dispatches 5.

100. Pendleton to Webster, August 30, 1842, Dispatches 5.

101. Pendleton to Webster, February 15, 1843, Dispatches 4.

102. Pendleton to Webster, April 26, 1843, Dispatches 4.

103. Pendleton to Abel P. Upshur, June 20, 1843, Dispatches 4.

104. Pendleton to Yrarrazaval, January 9, 1844, Dispatches 4. In the *New Standard Dictionary of the English Language*, "Prescription" is defined as "1, the establishment of a claim of title to something under common law usually by use and enjoyment for a period fixed by statute; 2, the process of making claim to something by long use and enjoyment."

105. Yrarrazaval to Pendleton, February 2, 1844, Dispatches 4.

106. Pendleton to Yrarrazaval, February 5, 1844, Dispatches 4.

107. Yrarrazaval to Upshur, June 12, 1844, Notes 1.

108. Sherman, *Diplomatic and Commercial Relations*, pp. 45–46. Pendleton was appointed as U.S. chargé d'affaires to Buenos Aires in 1851 (*Dictionary of American Biography*, S. V. "Pendleton, John Strother").

109. William Crump to Manuel Montt, June 4, 1845, Dispatches 6.

110. *Biographical Directory of the American Congress, 1774–1961* (Washington, D.C.: U.S. Government Printing Office, 1961), p. 760. This was the only biographical source found concerning Crump, and it neglected to mention his mission to Chile.

111. Crump to Calhoun, June 3, 1845, Dispatches 6.

112. Crump to Buchanan, January 8, 1846, Dispatches 6.

113. Crump to Buchanan, May 25, 1847, Dispatches 6. Tocornal was the defense lawyer.

114. Crump to Buchanan, August 21, 1847, Dispatches 6. Crump considered these reparations claims totally unjustified.

115. Crump to Montt, September 10, 1847, Dispatches 6.

116. Crump to Buchanan, October 18, 1847, Dispatches 6.

117. Vial to Buchanan, October 28, 1847, Notes 1.

118. Barros Arana, *Un decenio*, pp. 553–54. Even though several sources mention Polk's close friendship with Barton, neither Polk's diary nor his biographies make any reference to Barton.

119. Ibid., p. 554.

120. Barton to Buchanan, December 30, 1847, Dispatches 6.

121. Barton to Buchanan, April 25, 1848, Dispatches 7.

122. John Bassett Moore, *History and Digest of the International Arbitrations.* . . . (Washington, D.C.: U.S. Government Printing Office, 1898), 8:347.

123. Evans, *Chile and Its Relations*, p. 74.

124. Barros Arana, *Un decenio*, pp. 270–71.

125. Oscar Lewis, *Sea Routes to the Gold Fields: The Migration by Water to California in 1849–1852* (New York: Knopf, 1949), pp. 148–49.

126. Barton to Buchanan, April 15, 1848, Dispatches 7.

127. Barton to Vial, April 22, 1849, Dispatches 7.

128. Barton to Clayton, November 30, 1849, Dispatches 7.

129. Barton to Vial, April 22, 1849, Dispatches 7.

130. Barton to Buchanan, July 29, 1848, Dispatches 7.

131. Barton to Clayton, November 30, 1849, Dispatches 7.

132. Clayton to Carvallo, August 11, 1849, Notes.

133. Barros Arana, *Un decenio*, p. 567.

134. Webster to Carvallo, August 8, 1850, Notes.

135. Galdames, *History of Chile*, pp. 528–29. *La Revista Católica* became the church's official organ for news and propaganda; at times it voiced opposing views from *El Mercurio*, the government's newspaper (ibid., p. 284).

136. Antonio Iñíquez Vicuna, *Historia del período revolucionario en Chile, 1848–1851* (Santiago: Imprenta del Comercio, 1905), pp. 238–41.

137. Barros Arana, *Un decenio*, p. 557. Barros Arana states that Barton had been divorced for twelve years and that the former Mrs. Barton had remarried.

138. Ibid.

139. Barton to Vial, April 18, 1849, Dispatches 7.

140. Ibid. Later, both Andrés Bello and Camilo Vial sent congratulatory notes—unofficial, of course—to Barton and Isabella.

141. Ibid. Barton became so fearful for his own safety that he ordered the *Independence* to remain in Valparaíso for his protection (Barton to Commodore Bradford Shubrick, March 8, 1949, Dispatches 7).

142. Barton to Clayton, April 19, 1849, Dispatches 7.

143. Barton to Clayton, May 26, 1849, Dispatches 7. This was the only time any mention was made concerning the pregnancy, and no records have been found to indicate what happened to the child, assuming there really was one (Barton to Shubrick, March 4, 1849, Dispatches 7).

144. Barros Arana, *Un decenio*, p. 562.

Select Bibliography

Books, Dissertations, and Monographs

Adams, Ephraim Douglass, ed. *British Diplomatic Correspondence concerning the Republic of Texas, 1838–1846*. Austin: Texas State Historical Association, 1918.

Agan, Joseph. *The Diplomatic Relations of the United States and Brazil*. Paris: Jouve et Cie, 1926.

Alessio Robles, Vito. *Coahuila y Texas desde la consumación de la independencia hasta el tratado de paz de Guadalupe Hidalgo*. 2 vols. Mexico: n.p., 1945.

Almonte, Juan N. *Noticia estadística sobre Texas*. Mexico City: n.p., 1935.

Anna, Timothy, E. *The Fall of the Royal Government in Peru*. Lincoln: University of Nebraska Press, 1979.

Arboleda, Gustavo. *Historia contemporánea de Colombia*. 6 vols. Bogotá: Lib. Camacho Roldán, 1919.

Arrongoiz, Francisco de Paula. *México desde 1808 hasta 1867*. 2d ed. Mexico: Editorial Porrúa, 1968.

Bancroft, Hubert Howe. *History of Arizona and New Mexico, 1530–1888*. San Francisco: History Company, 1889.

Bannon, John Francis. *Bolton and the Spanish Borderlands*. Norman: University of Oklahoma Press, 1964.

Barros Arana, Diego. *Un decenio de la historia de Chile (1841–1851)*. Santiago: Imprenta de S.A., García Valenquela, 1906.

Basadre, Jorge. *Historia de la República del Peru*. 7 vols. 6th ed. Lima: Editorial Universitaria, 1968.

Bemis, Samuel Flagg. *A Diplomatic History of the United States*. 5th ed. New York: Holt, Rinehart, and Winston, 1965.

———. *The Latin American Policy of the United States*. New York: Harcourt, Brace, and World, 1943.

Bernstein, Harry. *Origins of Inter-American Interest, 1700–1812*. Philadelphia: University of Pennsylvania Press, 1945.

Biblioteca de historia nacional. Bogotá: Lib. Academia de Historia, 1902.

Billingsley, Edward Baxter. *In Defense of Neutral Rights: The United States Navy and the Wars of Independence in Chile and Peru.* Chapel Hill: University of North Carolina Press, 1967.

Blossom, Thomas. "Antonio Nariño, Precursor of Colombian Independence." Ph.D. diss., Duke University, 1956.

Boletín de historia y antiguedades. Bogotá: Lib. Academia de Historia, 1902.

Bolton, Herbert, and Mary Ross. *The Debatable Land.* Berkeley: University of California Press, 1925.

Brack, Gene M. *Mexico Views Manifest Destiny, 1821–1846: An Essay on the Origins of the Mexican War.* Albuquerque: University of New Mexico Press, 1975.

Bushnell, David. *The Santander Regime in Gran Colombia.* Newark: University of Delaware Press, 1954.

Cady, John F. *Foreign Intervention in the Río de la Plata, 1838–1850.* Philadelphia: University of Pennsylvania Press, 1929.

Calderón de la Barca, Madame. *Life in Mexico during a Residence of Two Years in That Country.* London: J. M. Dent and Sons, 1843.

Carretero, Andres. *El pensamiento político de Juan M. de Rosas.* Buenos Aires: Editorial Platero, 1970.

Callahan, James Morton, *American Foreign Policy in Mexican Relations.* New York: Macmillan, 1932.

Crane, Verner. *The Southern Frontier, 1670–1732.* Durham, N.C.: Duke University Press, 1928.

Creer, Leland Hargrave. *The Founding of an Empire: The Exploration and Colonization of Utah, 1776–1856.* Salt Lake City: Bookcraft, 1947.

Cuevas, Mariano. *Historia de la nación mexicana.* Mexico: Editorial Porrúa, 1965.

Davis, Harold Eugene. "Relations during the Time of Troubles, 1825–1860." In *Latin American Diplomatic History: An Introduction,* edited by Harold Eugene Davis, John J. Finan, and F. Taylor Peck. Baton Rouge: Louisiana State University Press, 1977.

Davis, Harold Eugene, John J. Finan, and F. Taylor Peck. "The Origins and Nature of Latin American Foreign Policies." In *Latin American Diplomatic History: An Introduction,* edited by the authors. Baton Rouge: Louisiana State University Press, 1977.

Davis, Thomas Brabson. *Carlos de Alvear, Man of Revolution.* Durham, N.C.: Duke University Press, 1955.

Dolores Gámez, José. *Historia de la Costa de Mosquitos hasta 1894.* Managua: Talleres Nacionales, 1939.

Duckett, Alvin Laroy. *John Forsyth, Political Tactician.* Athens: University of Georgia Press, 1962.

Espinosa, J. Manuel. *Inter-American Beginnings of U.S. Cultural Diplomacy, 1936–1948.* Washington, D.C.: U.S. Government Printing Office, 1976.

Evans, Henry Clay. *Chile and Its Relations with the United States.* Durham, N.C.: Duke University Press, 1927.

Ferns, Henry Stanley. *Britain and Argentina in the Nineteenth Century*. Oxford: Oxford University Press, 1960.

Folkman, David I., Jr. *La vita de Nicaragua: El tránsito a través de Nicaragua*. Salt Lake City: University of Utah Press, 1972.

Friend, Llerena. *Sam Houston: The Great Designer*. Austin: University of Texas Press, 1954.

Fuentes Mares, José. *Poinsett: Historia de una gran intriga*. Mexico: n.p., 1958.

Gambrell, Herbert. *Anson Jones, The Last President of Texas*. Austin: University of Texas Press, 1947.

García Bauer, Carlos. *Antonio José de Irisarri, diplomático de América*. Guatemala: Editorial Universitaria, 1970.

Goebel, Julius, Jr. *The Struggle for the Falkland Islands: A Study in Legal and Diplomatic History*. New Haven: Yale University Press, 1927.

Griffith, William J. *Empires in the Wilderness: Foreign Colonization and Development in Guatemala, 1834–1844*. Chapel Hill: University of North Carolina Press, 1965.

Hamill, Hugh M., Jr. *The Hidalgo Revolt: Prelude to Mexican Independence*. Gainesville: University of Florida Press, 1966.

Henao, Jesús, and Gerardo Arrubla. *A History of Colombia*. Translated by J. Fred Rippy. New York: Greenwood Press, 1969.

Iñíquez Vicuna, Antonio. *Historia del período revolucionario en Chile, 1848–1851*. Santiago: Imprenta del Commercio, 1905.

Ireland, Gordon. *Boundaries, Possessions, and Conflicts in South America*. Cambridge: Harvard University Press, 1938.

Johnson, Robert Erwin. *Thence Round Cape Horn: The Story of United States Naval Forces on Pacific Station, 1818–1923*. Annapolis, Md.: United States Naval Institute, 1963.

Jones, Howard. *To the Webster-Ashburton Treaty: A Study in Anglo-American Relations, 1783–1843*. Chapel Hill: University of North Carolina Press, 1977.

Kahler, Mary Ellis. "Relations between Brazil and the United States, 1815–1825, with Special Reference to the Revolutions of 1817 and 1824." Ph.D. diss., American University, 1968.

Kemble, John H. *The Panama Route, 1848–1869*. Berkeley: University of California Press, 1943.

Kinsbruner, Jay. *The Spanish American Independence Movements*. Hinsdale, Ill.: Dreyden Press, 1973.

Kuethe, Allan J., ed. *The North American Role in the Spanish Imperial Economy*. Manchester, Engl.: Manchester University Press, 1984.

Lanning, John Tate. *The Spanish Missions of Georgia*. Chapel Hill: University of North Carolina Press, 1935.

Lynch, John. *Argentine Dictator: Juan Manuel de Rosas, 1829–1852*. Oxford: Clarendon Press, 1981.

———. *The Spanish American Revolution, 1808–1826*. New York: W. W. Norton, 1973.

McAfee, Ward, and J. Cordell Robinson. *Origins of the Mexican War: A Documentary Source Book.* 2 vols. Salisbury, N.C.: Documentary Publications, 1982.

McClintock, James H. *Mormon Settlement in Arizona.* Tucson: University of Arizona Press, 1985.

Manning, William R., ed. *Diplomatic Correspondence of the United States concerning the Independence of the Latin American Republics.* 3 vols. New York: Harper Brothers, 1925.

―――, ed. *Diplomatic Correspondence of the United States: Inter-American Affairs, 1831–1860.* 8 vols. Washington, D.C.: Carnegie Endowment for International Peace, 1938.

Markham, Clements R. *A History of Peru.* New York: Greenwood Press, 1968.

Mecham, J. Lloyd. *A Survey of United States–Latin American Relations.* New York: Houghton Mifflin, 1965.

Miller, Hunter, ed. *Treaties and Other International Acts of the United States of America, 1776–1863.* 8 vols. Washington, D.C.: U.S. Government Printing Office, 1931–48.

Monaghan, Jay. *Chile, Peru, and the California Gold Rush of 1849.* Berkeley: University of California Press, 1973.

Moorhead, Max L. *New Mexico's Royal Road: Trade and Travel on the Chihuahua Trail.* Norman: University of Oklahoma Press, 1958.

Morgan, Robert J. *A Whig Embattled: The Presidency under John Tyler.* Lincoln: University of Nebraska Press, 1954.

Muñoz Azpiri, José Luis. *Historia completa de las Malvinas.* 3 vols. Buenos Aires: Oriente, 1966.

―――. *Rosas frente al imperio inglés: Historia íntima de un triunfo argentino.* Buenos Aires: Ediciones Theoría, 1960.

Nance, Joseph. *Attack and Counterattack: The Texas-Mexican Frontier, 1842.* Austin: University of Texas Press, 1964.

Nolan, Louis Clinton. "The Diplomatic and Commercial Relations of the United States and Peru, 1826–1875." Ph.D. diss., Duke University, 1935.

Onís, José de. *The United States as Seen by Latin American Writers.* New York: Hispanic Institute in the United States, 1952.

Ospina Vásquez, Luis. *Industria y protección en Colombia, 1810–1930.* Medellín: Editorial Santa Fé, 1955.

Pacca de Almeida Wright, Antonia. *Desafio americano à preponderância britânica do Brasil, 1808–1850.* Rio de Janeiro: Departamento de Imprensa Nacional.

Parks, E. Taylor. *Colombia and the United States, 1765–1934.* New York: Greenwood Press, 1968.

Perkins, Dexter, *The Monroe Doctrine, 1823–1826.* Cambridge: Harvard University Press, 1927.

Peterson, Harold F. *Argentina and the United States, 1810–1960.* Albany: State University of New York, 1964.

Pinero, Norberto. *La política internacional Argentina.* Buenos Aires: J. Menéndez y Hijo, 1924.

Pletcher, David M. *The Diplomacy of Annexation: Texas, Oregon, and the Mexican War.* Columbia: University of Missouri Press, 1973.

Polk, James K. *The Diary of James K. Polk during His Presidency, 1845 to 1849.* Edited by Milo Milton Quaife. 4 vols. Chicago: A. C. McClurg, 1910.

Price, Glenn W. *Origins of the War with Mexico: The Polk-Stockton Intrigue.* Austin, Tex.: n.p., 1967.

Ramírez, José Fernando. *Mexico during the War with the United States.* Translated by Elliot B. Scherr; edited by Walter V. Scholes. Columbia: University of Missouri Press, 1950.

Restrepo, José Manuel. *Autobiografia.* Vol. 3 of *Biblioteca de la presidencia de Colombia.* Bogotá: Imprenta Nacional, 1957.

Rippy, J. Fred. *Historical Evolution of Hispanic America.* New York: F. S. Crofts, 1923.

———. *Joel R. Poinsett, Versatile American.* New York: Greenwood Press, 1968.

Rivas, Raimundo. *Relaciones internacionales entre Colombia y los Estados Unidos, 1810–1850.* Bogotá: Imprenta Nacional, 1915.

Roa Barcena, José María. *Recuerdos de la invasión norteamericana, 1846–1848.* 3 vols. Colección de Escritores Mexicanos. Mexico: Editorial Porrúa, 1947.

Robertson, William Spence. *France and Latin American Independence.* Baltimore: Johns Hopkins University Press, 1939.

———. *Hispanic-American Relations with the United States.* New York: Oxford University Press, 1923.

Robles, Vito Alessio. *Coahuila y Texas en la época colonial.* Mexico: D. F. Editorial Cultural, 1938.

Rodríguez, Mario. *The Cádiz Experiment in Central America, 1808–1826.* Berkeley: University of California Press, 1977.

———. *A Palmerstonian Diplomat in Central America: Frederick Chatfield, Esq.* Tucson: University of Arizona Press, 1964.

Rodríguez Beteta, Virgilio. *Ideologías de la independencia.* 4th ed. Guatemala: Secretaría de Información, 1965.

———. *La política inglesa en Centro América durante el siglo XIX.* Guatemala: Ministerio de Educacíon Pública, 1963.

Ruiz Moreno, Isidoro. *Historia de las relaciones exteriores Argentinas, 1810–1955.* Buenos Aires: Editorial Perrot, 1961.

Ryjord, John. *Foreign Interest in the Independence of New Spain.* Durham, N.C.: Duke University Press, 1935.

Salazar, Arturo García. *Historia diplomática del Peru.* Lima: J. Rivas Berrio, 1930.

Santos, Richard G. *Santa Anna's Campaign against Texas, 1835–1836.* Salisbury, N.C.: Texian Press, 1968.

Scobie, James R. *Argentina: A City and a Nation.* New York: Oxford University Press, 1971.

Sherman, William Roderick. *The Diplomatic and Commercial Relations of the United States and Chile, 1820–1914*. Boston: Gorham Press, 1926.

Smith, Joseph. *Illusions of Conflict: Anglo-American Diplomacy toward Latin America, 1865–1896*. Pittsburgh: University of Pittsburgh Press, 1979.

Stansifer, Charles L. *Ephraim George Squier: Diversos aspectos de su carrera centroamericana*. Managua: Revista Conservadora del Pensamiento Centroamericano, 1968.

Stuart, Graham H. *Latin America and the United States*. New York: Appleton-Century-Crofts, 1922.

Timmons, William H. *Morelos: Priest Soldier Statesman of Mexico*. El Paso: Texas Western Press, 1963.

Van Buren, Martin. *Autobiography of Martin Van Buren*. Edited by John C. Fitzpatrick. Washington, D.C.: U.S. Government Printing Office, 1918.

Warren, Harris Gaylord. *The Sword Was Their Passport: A History of American Filibustering in the Mexican Revolution*. Baton Route: Louisiana State University Press, 1943.

Weber, David J. *The Mexican Frontier, 1821–1846: The American Southwest under Mexico*. Albuquerque: University of New Mexico Press, 1982.

Webster, C. K. *Britain and the Independence of Latin America, 1812–1830: Select Documents from the Foreign Office Archives*. 2 vols. London: Oxford University Press, 1938.

Webster, Daniel. *The Papers of Daniel Webster: Correspondence, 1835–1839*. Edited by Charles M. Wiltse and Harold D. Moser. Hanover, N.H.: University Press of New England, 1980.

Whitaker, Arthur P. *The United States and the Independence of Latin America, 1800–1830*. New York: Russell and Russell, 1962.

Williams, Mary Wilhemine. *Anglo-American Isthmian Diplomacy, 1815–1915*. Gloucester, Mass.: P. Smith, 1965.

Woodward, Ralph Lee. *Central America: A Nation Divided*. New York: Oxford University Press, 1976.

Zavala, Lorenzo de. *Ensayo crítico de las revoluciones de México desde 1808 hasta 1830*. Mexico: Editorial Porrúa, 1969.

Articles

Dickens, Paul D. "The Falkland Islands Dispute between the United States and Argentina." *Hispanic American Historical Review* 9 (August 1929): 471–87.

Hutchison, C. Alan. "Valentín Gómez Farías and the 'Secret Pact of New Orleans.'" *Hispanic American Historical Review* 36 (November 1956): 471–89.

Lockey, Joseph B. "Diplomatic Futility." *Hispanic American Historical Review* 30 (August 1930): 265–94.

Manning, William R. "An Early Diplomatic Controversy between the United States and Brazil." *Hispanic American Historical Review* 1 (May 1918): 123–45.

Naylor, Robert A. "The British Role in Central America prior to the Clayton-Bulwer Treaty of 1850." *Hispanic American Historical Review* 40 (August 1960): 361–82.

Northrup, Jack. "The Trist Mission." *Journal of Mexican History* 3 (1973): 13–31.

Pratt. E. J. "Anglo-American Commercial and Political Rivalry on the Plata, 1820–1830." *Hispanic American Historical Review* 11 (August 1931): 302–35.

Seckinger, Ron L. "South American Power Politics during the 1820s." *Hispanic American Historical Review* 56 (May 1976): 241–67.

Stewart, Watt. "Argentina and the Monroe Doctrine, 1824–1828." *Hispanic American Historical Review* 10 (February 1930): 26–32.

Street, John. "Lord Strangford and the Río de la Plata, 1808–1815." *Hispanic American Historical Review* 33 (November 1953): 477–510.

Sunseri, Alvin R. "Anglo Attitudes toward Hispanos, 1846–1861." *Journal of Mexican American History* 3 (1973): 76–88.

Tornel y Mendínil, José María. "Relations between Texas, the United States of America, and the Mexican Republic." In *The Mexican Side of the Texas Revolution*, translated by Carlos E. Castañeda. New York: Arno Press, 1976.

Vigness, David M. "Relations of the Republic of Texas and the Republic of the Rio Grande." *Southwestern Historical Quarterly* 57 (January 1954). 312–21.

———. "A Texas Expedition to Mexico, 1841." *Southwestern Historical Quarterly* 61 (July 1958): 18–28.

Waddell, David. "Great Britain and the Bay Islands, 1821–1861." *Historical Journal* 2 (March 1959): 59–77.

Government Documents

For anyone researching U.S.–Latin American relations, the microfilm publications of the Department of State General Records, National Archives, Washington, D.C., are the primary reference source. These invaluable documents, for each Latin American country, are divided into three main categories: Diplomatic and Consular Instructions to U.S. representatives assigned to Latin American posts; Diplomatic Dispatches to the State Department from U.S. agents in Latin America; and Notes from Foreign Legations in the United States. Commonly referred to as Instructions, Dispatches, and Notes, these tens of thousands of pages of documents constitute a cornucopia of information. Included with official correspondence are copies of private letters, newspaper clippings, drafts of trade agreements and local ordinances and laws, economic statistics, and a huge variety of miscellaneous enclosures too numerous to mention here.

Gorostiza, Manuel Eduardo de. *Don Manuel Eduardo de Gorostiza y la cuestión de Texas*. Documentos Históricos Precedidos de una noticia biografia por

Antonie de la Peña y Reyes. Archivo Histórico Diplomático Mexicano, no. B. Mexico City: Publicaciones de la Secretaría de Relaciones Exteriores, 1924.

Great Britain, Foreign Office. *British and Foreign State Papers*. London: James Ridgway and Sons, 1841–1956.

La primera guerra entre México y Francia. Archivo Histórico Diplomático Mexicano, no. 23. Mexico City: Publicaciones de la Secretaría de Relaciones Exteriores, 1927.

Libros de Acuerdos: Official Minutes of the Consejo de Estado. Bogotá: Imprenta Nacional, n.d.

Ministerio de Relações Exteriores. Brasil: Arquivo Histórico do Itamaratí Coleções Especiais. 3 Casos com Estrangeiros, Estados Unidos 1812–1813, Pasta 10, Lata 186, Maçol.

Moreno, Joaquín. *Diario de un escribiente de legacíon*. Oficial de las lagaciones de México en París y Roma (1833–1836), Archivo Histórico Diplomático Mexicano, no. 16. Mexico City: Publicaciones de la Secretaría de Relaciones Exteriores, 1925.

Contributors

Lawrence A. Clayton, Professor of History at the University of Alabama, received his Ph.D. from Tulane University and has served as the Director of the Latin American Studies Program in Tuscaloosa since 1980. He has published numerous articles on Peruvian and Ecuadorean history and has written four books, including *Los astilleros de Guayaquil colonial* and *Grace, W. R. Grace and Company: The Formative Years, 1850–1930.* As the recipient of two Senior Fulbright Lecturing Awards, he has been a guest professor in Costa Rica and Peru.

Paul B. Goodwin, Jr., received his Ph.D. from the University of Massachusetts and is a professor of Latin American history at the University of Connecticut. He is the author of *Los ferrocarriles Britanicos y la U.C.R., 1916–1930* and *Global Studies: Latin America and the Caribbean,* and he has contributed articles to the *Hispanic American Historical Review* and the *Journal of Latin American Studies,* among others.

Eugene R. Huck, who received his doctorate from the University of Alabama, is Professor of History at Kennesaw State College, where he served as academic dean for ten years before returning to the classroom. He spent a year, 1958–1959, on a Fulbright Scholarship in Bogotá researching economic interaction between the United States and Colombia from 1820 to 1850. Professor Huck coedited *Militarists, Merchants, and Missionaries: United States Expansion in Middle America,* and he has written several articles on nineteenth-century Colombia.

The late Phil Brian Johnson (1941–1990) received his Ph.D. from Tulane University. He wrote articles and a *livrinho* on Ruy Barbosa, the Brazilian statesman, education reformer, and presidential hopeful. Professor Johnson was the founder and coeditor of *Revista Occidental* and *New World: A Journal of Latin American Studies* and was Professor of History at San Francisco State University at the time of his death.

325

EDWARD H. MOSELEY, who earned his doctorate at the University of Alabama, is Professor of History and Director of the Capstone International Program Center at the University of Alabama. The author of various publications, including *Yucatán: A World Apart*, Moseley devotes a great portion of his energies toward developing international exchange programs, symposia, and study-abroad opportunities for graduates and undergraduates.

WESLEY P. NEWTON, Professor Emeritus at Auburn University, now resides in Montgomery, Alabama, and currently is researching various topics in the history of air power. He is the author of *The Perilous Sky: United States Aviation Diplomacy and Latin America, 1919–1931*, and coauthor of *Delta: The History of an Airline*. Like professors Huck and Moseley, he is a former student of A. B. Thomas at the University of Alabama, where he received his Ph.D.

Editor T. RAY SHURBUTT earned his doctorate at the University of Georgia and is Professor of History and Coordinator of Latin American Studies at Georgia Southern University. Along with his numerous publications on nineteenth-century Chile and its relations with the United States, Shurbutt's other publications and research focus on the Spanish southeastern borderlands and Georgia history. Since 1983 he has served as editor of *Annals,* the yearly journal of the Southeastern Council on Latin American Studies.

CHARLES L. STANSIFER received his Ph.D. in Latin American history from Tulane University. As Professor of History and Director of the Center of Latin American Studies at the University of Kansas, Stansifer has published dozens of articles and essays on various Central American topics and has served as a guest lecturer in Costa Rica, Nicaragua, Guatemala, and Honduras.

ROBERT KIM STEVENS received his M.A. in Latin American history from Tulane University. He has been with the U.S. Department of State since 1966, serving tours in Bolivia, Brazil, and several European countries. The author of several studies on genealogical history, he lives in Washington, D.C.

Index